RETHINKING FEMINIST HISTORY AND THEORY

Essays on Gender, Class, and Labour

Edited by Lisa Pasolli and Julia Smith

Rethinking Feminist History and Theory considers the past, present, and future of feminist history and theory, emphasizing how feminism has influenced the histories of gender, class, and labour, and their intersections. This vibrant collection, inspired by the work of historian and women's studies scholar Joan Sangster, features essays from academics across multiple disciplines, highlighting the dynamism of feminist historical scholarship in Canada.

The book explores questions such as the following: How have women's resistance and radicalism been expressed, lived, represented, and repressed over the past century? How do we research these phenomena? How do we situate feminism in relation to other movements for egalitarian social change? Contributors explicitly address these recurring themes, aiming to chart new directions for future research and teaching.

While primarily Canadian focused, the collection includes global perspectives, with contributions from scholars in Chile, Finland, Sweden, and the UK. The essays emphasize the importance of cross-disciplinary collaboration, incorporating insights from labour studies, political economy, anthropology, legal studies, and feminist theory. Ultimately, *Rethinking Feminist History and Theory* engages deeply with Sangster's rich and wide-ranging work to understand and interpret women's experiences. It seeks to inspire future scholarship and teaching in feminist history and theory, showcasing the ongoing relevance and adaptability of feminist perspectives.

LISA PASOLLI is an associate professor of history at Queen's University.

JULIA SMITH is an assistant professor of labour studies at the University of Manitoba.

Rethinking Feminist History and Theory

Essays on Gender, Class, and Labour

EDITED BY LISA PASOLLI AND JULIA SMITH

UNIVERSITY OF TORONTO PRESS
Toronto Buffalo London

© University of Toronto Press 2025
Toronto Buffalo London
utorontopress.com

ISBN 978-1-4875-0846-3 (cloth)   ISBN 978-1-4875-3831-6 (EPUB)
ISBN 978-1-4875-2589-7 (paper)   ISBN 978-1-4875-3830-9 (PDF)

Library and Archives Canada Cataloguing in Publication

Title: Rethinking feminist history and theory : essays on gender, class, and labour / edited by Lisa Pasolli and Julia Smith.
Names: Pasolli, Lisa, editor | Smith, Julia, 1982– editor
Description: Includes bibliographical references.
Identifiers: Canadiana (print) 20240475550 | Canadiana (ebook) 20240475577 | ISBN 9781487508463 (cloth) | ISBN 9781487525897 (paper) | ISBN 9781487538309 (PDF) | ISBN 9781487538316 (EPUB)
Subjects: LCSH: Feminism – Canada – History. | LCSH: Feminist theory – Canada – History. | LCSH: Women – Political activity. | LCSH: Women – Social conditions. | LCSH: Women – Legal status, laws, etc.
Classification: LCC HQ1453 .R48 2025 | DDC 305.40971 – dc23

Cover design: Rebecca Lown
Cover image: Hamilton feminists at Toronto International Women's Day march, circa 1979. In forefront, Gail Moran, Joan Sangster, and Padma Manion. Photo courtesy of Joan Sangster.

We wish to acknowledge the land on which the University of Toronto Press operates. This land is the traditional territory of the Wendat, the Anishnaabeg, the Haudenosaunee, the Métis, and the Mississaugas of the Credit First Nation.

This book has been published with the help of a grant from the Federation for the Humanities and Social Sciences, through the Awards to Scholarly Publications Program, using funds provided by the Social Sciences and Humanities Research Council of Canada.

University of Toronto Press acknowledges the financial support of the Government of Canada, the Canada Council for the Arts, and the Ontario Arts Council, an agency of the Government of Ontario, for its publishing activities.

Contents

Preface ix

Acknowledgments xiii

Introduction 3
JUDY FUDGE

Part One: Women, Labour, and the Left

1 "Don't Dare": Labour, Feminism, and the Left on Strike at Dare Foods, 1972–1973 19
   MASON GODDEN

2 The Poet and the Nun: Class-Struggle Feminism in Windsor, Ontario, during the 1970s 40
   SEAN ANTAYA

3 "Most Women Would Prefer to Keep Their Mouths Shut": Challenging Sexual Harassment within the Canadian Broadcasting Corporation, 1981–1986 61
   BARBARA M. FREEMAN

4 The 1995 Calgary Laundry Workers' Strike: A Case Study on the Power and Limits of Racialized Women's Class Struggle 80
   ANDREA SAMOIL

Part Two: Gender and Politics

5 "Giving Women a Voice": Annie Townley, the Labour Party, and Women's Politicization in South-West England in the Interwar Years   103
   JUNE HANNAM

6 *Centros de Madres*: From Their Origins to Their Radicalization under Salvador Allende's Government   124
   GABRIELA CASTILLO

7 A Global Turning Point for Equal Pay Struggles: International Women's Year, 1975   144
   SILKE NEUNSINGER AND RAGNHEIÐUR KRISTJÁNSDÓTTIR

8 The Impact of Communism and Socialism on Women's Struggles and Social Entitlements in the Twentieth Century: A Global Overview   163
   ALVIN FINKEL

Part Three: Violence and the Law

9 The Seduction of Vivian MacMillan: Scandal, Politics, and Perception in Depression-Era Alberta   187
   P.E. BRYDEN

10 Rehabilitating "the Girls": Women's Employment and Expertise in the Prison for Women, 1949–1965   206
   KATIE-MARIE McNEILL

11 Battered Women and Self-Defence before *R. v. Lavallee*: The Forgotten Case of *R. v. Whynot (Stafford)*   229
   NADIA VERRELLI AND LORI CHAMBERS

Part Four: Theory and Method

12 From Dreams of Equality to One Hundred Years of Struggle: Radical Women's Biographies in the History of Canadian Politics   253
   LINDA KEALEY

13 Revisiting *Many Tender Ties*: A Materialist Reading of Sylvia Van Kirk's Text 270
    D.Y. TURNER

14 Gender, Migration, and the Temporalities of Late Capitalism: Social Reproduction in the Economies of Affect 290
    WINNIE LEM

15 Joan Sangster's Socialist-Feminist History 309
    TED McCOY

Contributors 327

Preface

In June 2019, scholars from across Canada and the United States, and from as far away as the UK, Sweden, and Iceland, gathered at Trent University. The occasion was a conference on feminism, history, and theory. Over two invigorating days, we explored the connected histories of gender, class, race, and colonialism in Canada and internationally. Since the first conference on Canadian women's history was held at Trent in 1993, this conference had special significance. It brought together many of the same feminist historians who had gathered just over twenty-five years prior and, in conversations across disciplines and generations, allowed for reflection on how the field has changed and where it is headed in the future.

This gathering of feminist scholars had another impetus, too: to celebrate the work of Joan Sangster, who retired in 2019 after a thirty-five-year career at Trent. There was no better way to mark Joan's retirement than to invite reflection on the fields she had such an important role in shaping. And to say that she has shaped our histories of women, gender, class, labour, feminism, and colonialism is no mere retirement platitude. Her list of publications includes nine monographs, eight co-edited collections, fifty-seven peer-reviewed articles, and dozens of other book chapters, review essays, and conference papers, and even a play. She served as the president of the Canadian Historical Association from 2015 to 2017 and has devoted years of service to Canadian and international professional associations. Joan served as co-editor of *Labour/Le Travail*, and journals like *Labor: Studies in Working Class History of the Americas* and the *Journal of the Canadian Historical Association* have also benefited from her editorial oversight. The colleagues, collaborators, and students who gathered to mark her retirement also attested to the fact that her influence extends beyond the borders of academic history to include women's studies, legal studies, sociology, labour studies, and more. As well, the list of conference attendees reflects Joan's transnational connections, demonstrating that her commitment to histories of women's lives and work has always been enhanced by connections with scholars and scholarship outside of Canada.

This collection grew out of that conference. It offers a sampling of papers presented, chosen to highlight how Joan's body of work has been taken up by scholars in many historical fields, disciplines, and career stages. Because of her extensive knowledge of Joan's work and the many fields to which Joan has contributed, we invited Judy Fudge to write the introduction that opens the collection. In her expansive piece, Fudge dives deep into Joan's scholarship and offers her reflections on how it has pushed feminist history and theory in new directions. We won't retread the same ground here, but as co-organizers of the conference and Joan's former PhD (Julia) and postdoc (Lisa) supervisees, we want to include a short note in this preface to comment on Joan's influence as a mentor and colleague.

Personally, we have learned much from Joan's scholarship, from her early work on organizing women telephone workers to her recent work on the history of feminism in Canada. Now that we are both in academic positions, we have the pleasure of teaching Joan's work and experiencing it again through the eyes of students. This has given us a new level of appreciation for her scope and rigour, and especially the way she navigates so clearly through complex theoretical waters. As we prepared for the conference, we gathered notes from Joan's former students over the years. What stood out was not only how generous Joan had always been with her knowledge, but how many people carried Joan's feminist training with them into worlds beyond academia, into government, NGOs, and activism.

We have also learned much from Joan about how to be a scholar. The lessons are still sinking in, but Joan modelled constant curiosity, productive collaborations, and prioritizing frequent archive trips even amid heavy administrative loads. Watching Joan work gave us a greater appreciation for how to navigate institutional politics, especially in advocating for students. We learned how rewarding it can be to organize conferences, to create opportunities for scholars with common interests to gather and think together. We learned about combining scholarship with activism, and to always be aware of the political positions from which we work and write. We learned about the pleasures of a barbeque, a good television show or mystery novel, and the company of cats. We hope that we can pass some of these lessons along to our own students.

At the conference, long-time childcare worker and advocate Susan Scoffin announced the creation of the Joan Sangster Fund for Child Care Advocacy. This fund is a reminder that Joan's feminist scholarship always linked to her feminist activism, and that for Joan telling stories about women's lives in the past is part of a project of valuing and improving women's lives in the present and future. The royalties for this collection will be donated to the fund.

Lisa Pasolli and Julia Smith

Acknowledgments

Our first thanks are to the authors in this volume, who remained patient and supportive through its long publication process. Thank you also to the anonymous reviewers for their comments and suggestions, and to the team at University of Toronto Press: Antonia Pop, Suzanne Rancourt, Janice Evans, Rebecca Russell, Rebecca Lown, and Len Husband. We would like to thank Dimitry Anastakis for his advice and guidance, as well as Jonathon Zimmer, who provided timely bibliographic assistance. This collection grew out of a conference held at Trent University in Peterborough, Ontario, in 2019, and we thank the presenters for their scholarship, the attendees for their engagement, and our fellow organizers, particularly Sarah Jessup, for their work to bring people together to reflect on feminist history and theory. We first met while completing our doctoral (Julia) and postdoctoral (Lisa) studies at the Frost Centre for Canadian Studies and Indigenous Studies, and we are grateful to the many people who made it such a vibrant and intellectually stimulating place to be. Finally, we thank Joan Sangster for her scholarship, mentorship, and friendship.

RETHINKING FEMINIST HISTORY AND THEORY

Essays on Gender, Class, and Labour

Introduction

JUDY FUDGE

Women's history, the essential tool in creating feminist consciousness in women, is providing the body of experience against which new theory can be tested and the ground on which a feminist vision can be built.
– Gerda Lerner, *Why History Matters*[1]

Joan Sangster's scholarship has shaped the terrain of Canadian women's and labour history, and she has made signal contributions to feminist theory, historiography, legal history, the history of the left, Indigenous studies, and the cultural history of the Canadian north. Women and labour have been the central subjects of her readable and rigorous research; power, inequality, coercion, culture, and representation are recurring motifs. While her empirical work focuses on Canada, adding layers of analysis and incorporating ever more dimensions to the stories she recounts, Sangster has been an indispensable interlocutor in international conversations about women's history and feminist theory and historiography. She approaches the past with a combination of capacious curiosity and analytic acuity, which she expresses with verve.[2] Her curiosity is purposeful; as a feminist historian, the "woman question" – women's emancipation, how to achieve it, and what it means – has been her enduring interest. It shapes the way she views history, the topics she explores, and the concepts she deploys. Sangster believes, for the same reasons that Gerda Lerner expresses above, that women's history matters, and it matters not only for women, since the woman question is "one of the organization of society as a whole."[3]

Feminism, history, and theory are the three recurring themes that characterize Sangster's engaging, wide-ranging, and beautifully written scholarship. They are difficult to disentangle because they are so tightly interwoven. Inspired by the intellectual vitality and political possibilities of socialist feminism in Canada in the late 1970s and early 1980s, Sangster's first book, *Dreams of Equality*, explores women in left parties between 1920 and 1950 and how they both framed and addressed the woman question. In it she wanted to retrieve the history of women socialists in Canada "to understand what historical conditions encourage, or stifle, women's radicalism."[4] Her goal was not only to historicize feminism, to understand the movements and events that shaped it as a political project, but also to excavate and recover the different varieties. Sangster's early research charted some of the different "streams of feminism," which she proposed was a more accurate metaphor than waves for capturing feminist thought and organizing in Canada.[5] It demonstrated the need for what Joan Kelly dubbed a "doubled vision," simultaneous attention to productive and reproductive relations.[6]

This doubled vision is exemplified in *Earning Respect*, which focuses on a small town in Ontario from 1920 to 1960 and analyses the "social, familial, and psychic structures that shape male dominance" in "the historical context of class relations."[7] It is what Sangster means by seeing the past "through feminist eyes," the title of a collection of her previously published essays on Canadian women's history, in which she reflects on the broader intellectual, political, and theoretical themes of her work in several scene-setting new essays.[8] As a *materialist*, she is committed to understanding how broader dynamics around accumulation, expropriation, and colonialism shape the circumstances under which people act; as a *feminist*, she is interested in investigating how women, their roles, and their labour are experienced, represented, valued, organized, resisted, and transformed.

The term "women" continues to figure more prominently in Sangster's writing than the term "gender." This preference is both political (since Sangster is a feminist committed to women's emancipation) and theoretical (since it emphasizes her commitment to materialism). However, for Sangster, "women" does not suggest a unitary ontological category that refers to either biology or shared experience; instead, she views gender, like class and race, as a socially constructed process influenced by the other social processes with which it is entwined and within which human beings try to fashion lives they have reason to value.[9] Because she is interested in the relationship between experience and consciousness, and how people come to either accept, challenge, or resist exploitative and unequal relations, from the outset she has been attentive to how women were positioned in relation to one another on the basis of class, immigration, ethnicity, language, and race. In her early work on women in left parties, for example, she discovered ethnicity was critical to understanding the Communist Party and women's role within it.[10]

Sangster also recounts how women came to negotiate their social location and how some (like the Polish displaced persons who were recruited as bonded labour by Liberal member of Parliament Ludger Dionne to work in his textile mill after the Second World War) resisted their social positioning as "helpless and dependent immigrant[s]."[11] It is this attention to women's voices and their accounts of their experience that makes her work so vibrant. In *Transforming Labour*, she uses a short autobiographical account by Edna Manitowabi, a young Anishinaabe woman, to complicate the prevailing narrative of Indigenous women workers. Depicted as morally and culturally unable to adapt to wage labour, Indigenous women working in Prairie communities after the Second World War were subjected to gendered and racialized processes of segregation that made them especially vulnerable to material disadvantage, racist denigration, and state-sanctioned "hostility and violence."[12]

This commitment to having women voice their own experience is not simply a retreat to positivism. Nor does it come at the expense of an appreciation of how dominant discourses and ideologies are linked to institutions such as courts and reformatories that can use coercive forms of power to stifle alternative ways of being and living. Sangster's shift in focus from women's political activism and the interaction of paid and unpaid work to how women's and girls' sexuality and family relations were regulated by the "complex of [legal] institutions, codes, practices, and personnel designed to govern, control, and aid women" reflects both a broadening of working-class history to include the "so-called 'under-class' that often fell through the cracks of wage work and organized labour" and a deeper engagement with poststructuralist and deconstructivist theories best exemplified by Foucault.[13] Yet, even in documents such as court records and expert reports that are so distant from the girls caught up in the juvenile justice system, Sangster digs for the traces of their voices, the kernels of truth, that reveal these young women's social existence.[14]

Experience is critical to Sangster's materialist feminism and to why history matters. She draws on E.P. Thompson's idea of experience as a "junction concept" between social consciousness and social being, which she likens to the shift between the first- and third-person perspective.[15] It is our capacity as self-aware and (even if only occasionally) self-reflective beings to make this shift and to explore the critical dissonance between the two perspectives that opens up the possibility of new imaginaries and social transformation.[16] This dialectic is another form of doubled vision. Sangster stresses "the importance of human agency in meaning making."[17]

History, therefore, matters because it is an act of meaning making that, at its best, helps us to understand how present actions, events, ideas, and aspirations are the product of a range of converging forces, relations, actions, and imaginaries. In *Regulating Girls and Women*, Sangster explores the "perils of protection," especially the use of police and courts to save young women from sexual exploitation. She explains that "while history does not offer pat solutions to present dilemmas, it may stimulate some sobering second thoughts on current debates – by dissecting the changing definitions of criminality and the process by which law constituted gender, race, and class relations; by mounting a critique of past reform efforts; and, importantly, by suggesting how the law affected the lives of girls and women who came into conflict with it."[18] In *Girl Trouble*, Sangster cautions of the need "to ask hard questions about current protective practices in light of yesterday's experiences."[19] Feminists who advocate using the coercive and symbolic power of the law to protect women from sexual commodification and human trafficking would be well advised to heed this warning and consider how in the past such repressive technologies operated to stigmatize women, especially those who were racialized or Indigenous, and to further narrow, rather than expand, their ability to control their own lives in light of the already constrained options available to them.[20]

Another benefit of looking to the past to examine "the changing contexts framing women's conflicts with the law, and the strategies women employed to deal with these conflicts" is that it reveals "differences between women and the importance of class and race in women's criminalization."[21] This understanding of the interplay of social location, social consciousness, and historical change links to Sangster's conception of feminist history as undergoing a "constant process of reexamination" as "our society, political concerns, and theoretical assumptions change."[22] It is clear to Sangster that "the intellectual standpoint of historians, the sources they can access, the audience for whom they write, and why, matter a great deal."[23] One of the many reasons her work is so compelling is that she always reveals the political, historical, and theoretical stakes at play in her research and that shape her choices.

Like Lerner, Sangster engages in ongoing dialogue between history and theory, and it is this aspect of her scholarship that draws political economists and social theorists as well as historians to her work. Her work exemplifies an acute understanding of contemporary theoretical debates over epistemology and ontology, especially the frisson released when poststructuralist critiques of realism and associated concepts such as experience gained ascendancy in the English-speaking world in the late 1980s. Sangster's work exemplifies an approach to writing history that is articulate and explicit about the theoretical questions that inform its choice of topics and sources. Historians, however, approach theory differently than social and political theorists or sociologists, for they test and refine concepts through a dialogue with historical sources. Historians are attuned to the relationship between meaning and context. The contrasting approaches to theory by social theorists and historians are most evident in Sangster and Meg Luxton's response to Nancy Fraser's claim that there is an elective affinity between feminism and neoliberalism.[24] They argue that Fraser's social-theoretical inclination toward abstract schemas is at odds with her attempt to historicize feminism and, as a result, she provides an account of contemporary feminism that reduces it exclusively to liberal feminism in the United States. Thus, Fraser depicts feminism as following a unidirectional trajectory, one that ignores the countercurrents and more radical streams of feminism in Canada and elsewhere. By contrast, Sangster and Luxton's goal is to revive socialist-feminist strategizing and its anti-capitalist heritage for the twenty-first century.[25]

Critical to Sangster's significant theoretical contribution is her ability to maintain a doubled vision across a number of dimensions, such as social reproduction–production and social being–social consciousness, while simultaneously extending it to the dialectical relationship between culture and political economy. It is as if she is able to see both the duck and the rabbit at the same time in the image that Wittgenstein used to illustrate *aspect perception*, which is how an image can be seen in two ways – as *either* a duck or a rabbit – but rarely as both. Sangster's form of critical realism is sensitive to the symbiotic relationship between the mental and material, and she is adept at using Foucauldian conceptual tools such as discourse and discipline to deepen and expand a political economy analysis. Always interested in questions of representation, ideology, and discourse, in her 2016 book *The Iconic North*, Sangster explores the cultural representation of the North and northern indigeneity and how it helps us to understand the colonial project in postwar Canada. She frames her study of the cultural constructions of the North within the changing political economy and history of postwar Canada, and she explores how this interaction shaped persisting colonial relations. She emphasizes women both as cultural producers (here, Sangster studies white women visitors' writings about their encounters with the North) and as cultural products (in images fashioned by popular magazines and on television and in film). Her goal is to unearth the relationship between the cultural production of these images and social relations of power by tracing how representations of the North and northern indigeneity circulated in postwar Canada. Locating patterns and concentrations of power is a key feature of Sangster's research. She always asks "the classical political economy question – 'Who benefits the most'?"[26] As a good historian, she does not take the answer to this question for granted. But, as her influential body of work demonstrates, she knows where to look, and she has the conceptual tools to find answers across a range of different contexts.

It is fitting that in her most recent monographs Sangster has returned explicitly to the woman question. In *One Hundred Years of Struggle*, she reads the extension of suffrage to women against the grain, emphasizing other bases of exclusion by painting an overview of the rich diversity of suffrage histories, extending from editorials published by the Black newspaper editor Mary Ann Shadd Cary in the 1850s to the final extension of universal suffrage in 1960, when Status Indians were enfranchised. In *Demanding Equality*, she comes full circle to where she started with *Dream of Equality*, with feminism as a movement for social justice.[27] Concentrating on feminism as a collective project of resistance from the mid-nineteenth century to the 1980s, Sangster emphasizes the different ways that feminists approach equality and how these different approaches link to other struggles for social justice. It is, like all her work, animated by a belief in the possibility of emancipation grounded in the enduring capacity of human beings to give meaning and voice to their experience and to make their own history.

The editors of this volume, Lisa Pasolli and Julia Smith, have curated a fascinating collection of essays inspired by the questions that motivated Sangster's work: How have women's resistance and radicalism been expressed, lived, represented, and repressed over the past century? How do we research them? How do we situate feminism in relation to other movements for egalitarian social change? The contributors also explicitly address central topics and recurring themes in Sangster's work, which are grouped into four parts: "Women, Labour, and the Left"; "Gender and Politics"; "Violence and the Law"; and "Theory and Method." While most of the chapters have a Canadian focus, one looks at the South West of England, another at Chile, and three operate at different scales or spacialities – the global, international, and transnational.

The four chapters in part 1, "Women, Labour, and the Left," explore how women's experience in paid work can lead to resistance and the kinds of activists and organizations that support it. The first two chapters contribute to Sangster's goal of revitalizing the history of socialist feminism in Canada by highlighting working women's radicalism and the close relationship between certain streams of feminism and radical left politics. In "'Don't Dare': Labour, Feminism, and the Left on Strike at Dare Foods, 1972–1973," Mason Godden recounts how a strike that began over unequal pay in a plant in Kitchener was supported by a strong alliance between organized labour, the feminist movement, and the New Left. Uncowed by Dare's use of a notorious strike-breaking firm, the striking workers and their allies picketed the plant and organized boycotts of the cookie manufacturer's wares, which led to violence, labour injunctions, and the involvement of the courts. Although the strike did not achieve equal pay for the women workers, Godden shows how it radicalized them and solidified an emerging progressive coalition.

The second chapter, "The Poet and the Nun: Class-Struggle Feminism in Windsor, Ontario, during the 1970s," Sean Antaya focuses on the trajectory of two activists, Bronwen Wallace and Pat Noonan, the poet and the nun, and unearths a radical stream of the women's movement that was active in Windsor and that, among its many activities, supported the Dare strikers. He shows how the biographies of these two activists downplayed their radical working-class politics, lending credence to the view that the second wave of feminism was a liberal project.

Barbara M. Freeman's chapter, "'Most Women Would Prefer to Keep Their Mouths Shut': Challenging Sexual Harassment within the Canadian Broadcasting Corporation, 1981–1986," moves into the 1980s and uses feminist oral history to reclaim the lived experience of women journalists who were sexually harassed when they worked at the CBC. Recounting how "most women would prefer to keep their mouths shut" at a time when the harm of sexual harassment was just beginning to be named, Freeman shows how the corporation was slow to act and that, when it did, it implemented a policy that left the majority of power in the mostly male managers' hands.

The silence of the women journalists was in contrast to an illegal strike by laundry workers, many of whom were immigrant and racialized women, in a Calgary hospital in 1995. They struck to protest the Alberta government's decision to contract out their jobs. In "The 1995 Calgary Laundry Workers' Strike: A Case Study on the Power and Limits of Racialized Women's Class Struggle," Andrea Samoil portrays how these essential but poorly paid and underappreciated workers challenged the occupational hierarchy and promised to kindle the broader solidarity needed to fuel a general strike. She also reveals how the labour leadership, even though it included women who supported feminism, such as the national president of the Canadian Union of Public Employees and the head of the Alberta Federation of Labour, reined in the growing militancy of public sector unions in the face of charges that the strike was contrary to industrial legality. The workers' jobs were ultimately contracted out, but the strike demonstrated the value of these women's work and their militancy, a lesson too often forgotten by the "legalized" labour movement, which tends to reflect, rather than subvert, racialized and gendered hierarchies.

Part 2, "Gender and Politics," composed of four chapters, moves from the workplace to politics more generally and away from Canada to consider the different ways feminists have engaged with politics. These chapters substantiate Sangster's call for a doubled vision by revealing how gendered and class-based inequalities are bound up with racialized, religious, and ethnic hierarchies and how women can simultaneously challenge and transform these unequal social relations. In "'Giving Women a Voice': Annie Townley, the Labour Party, and Women's Politicization in South-West England in the Interwar Years," June Hannam examines the political journey of one local activist, Annie Townley. This chapter demonstrates that women became active citizens and supported Labour politics not just for ideological reasons, but because this work established affective bonds and solidified personal relationships, reinforcing the importance of examining, rather than dismissing, women's emotional experience in the process of radicalization.

Shifting scales from the individual to the institutional, Gabriela Castillo's "*Centros de Madres*: From Their Origins to Their Radicalization under Salvador Allende's Government" explores one of the few public spaces available to women in Chile – the *centros de madres* – to reveal how these spaces were instrumentalized by a series of governments until their radicalization under Salvador Allende. Founded by the Chilean government in the late nineteenth century, these mothers' centres were non-profit private corporations designed to turn low-income women into what the state viewed to be "better" mothers and wives – roles that reflected the patriarchal influence of the Catholic Church. Castillo shows how the *centros de madres* reflected and amplified prevailing social and political understandings of women's role in society, as it shifted from the 1890s, when virtuous women remained in the home to be mothers, to the 1970s under Allende, when women were regarded both as mothers and waged workers.

The indignity of unequal pay has been a flashpoint for women's collective resistance, which has taken a variety of forms, from the Dare strike to the international campaign for equal pay. In their chapter, "A Global Turning Point for Equal Pay Struggles: International Women's Year, 1975," Silke Neunsinger and Ragnheiður Kristjánsdóttir treat 1975, which the United Nations declared as International Women's

Year, as creating a new political opportunity structure used by women's groups in Iceland, South Africa, and India to struggle for equal pay in their local and national contexts. Despite critical differences in the three countries (Iceland is small and homogeneous, whereas India and South Africa are large countries riven by hierarchies of race, religion, and caste), there were remarkable similarities in the struggle for equal remuneration. Neunsinger and Kristjánsdóttir use a microspatial approach to bring women activists back into view, and they trace multiscalar and geographical connections between transnational activists to reveal the role of women workers in global labour history.

Alvin Finkel's chapter, "The Impact of Communism and Socialism on Women's Struggles and Social Entitlements in the Twentieth Century: A Global Overview," rounds out this discussion by explicitly turning to the woman question as it was taken up by socialist and social democratic governments around the globe. He considers the extent to which leftist and generally male-dominated regimes have delivered greater equality and opportunity for everyone regardless of gender and focuses on broad social policies affecting women. Although communism and social democracy have proven friendlier to women's rights than conservatism and liberalism, independent feminist movements have generally been more active in liberal North America than in European states where social democrats are strongest and virtually nonexistent in one-party states. Despite the profoundly different degree of social inequality across political formations, narrowest in communist and most extreme in conservative states, women have continued to shoulder a disproportionate burden of unpaid household work and to receive lower wages than their male counterparts.

The chapters in part 3, "Violence and the Law," move from work and politics to violence, law, and regulation. They investigate women's experiences with the legal and carceral system – as victims, perpetrators, and reformers. They illustrate the different ways that women resist subordination and the capacity of the legal system to challenge and reinforce gendered and sexualized hierarchies of power. In "The Seduction of Vivian MacMillan: Scandal, Politics, and Perception in Depression-Era Alberta," Penny Bryden probes the sexual politics of Depression-era Alberta by digging beneath the surface of a highly publicized seduction case brought by Vivian MacMillan, a young woman groomed by the premier of Alberta, John Brownlee. This highly publicized trial, as Sangster argues elsewhere about other prominent court proceedings, "both reflected and constructed public thinking" about, in this case, sexual assault.[28] What was remarkable about this case was the profound disjunction between the views of the public, personified by the jury, and the court. The jury found that Brownlee had seduced MacMillan and awarded her and her father substantial compensation for the wrong; the trial judge overruled the jury and found in Brownlee's favour. Although the case eventually went to the Supreme Court of Canada, and the jury's award in MacMillan's favour was ultimately restored, as Bryden recounts, the original jury finding, unanimously indicting the coercive sexual relationship imposed by the premier on MacMillan as a condition of her employment, has largely been ignored in retellings of the case, normalizing the sexual predation of women by powerful men. Bryden's chapter reminds us of the importance of what Sangster calls "reading against the grain."

Moving from the courts to the prison, Katie-Marie McNeill's chapter, "Rehabilitating 'the Girls': Women's Employment and Expertise in the Prison for Women, 1949–1965," brings together two areas of Sangster's research, women's work and the regulation of criminalized women, by focusing on the middle-class women who, as employees and as volunteers, developed prison rehabilitation programs between 1949 and 1965. The first date marks the establishment of the first formal educational and vocational programs in the prison for women (P4W), while the second is the year that the first superintendent of that prison resigned. Despite the success of these programs in reducing recidivism, McNeill describes how the recommendations for reforming the Canadian prison system were routinely disregarded by the male-dominated Penitentiary Service. Rehabilitation services developed by women might be good for women, but the Penitentiary Service was not going to apply them to men. McNeill recounts how the Penitentiary Service preferred a more disciplinary approach to imprisonment, ultimately driving out the first woman superintendent, who favoured rehabilitation over punishment. Respectable, middle-class women reformers were constrained by the carceral approach favoured by the male-dominated Canadian prison system.

The final chapter in this part, "Battered Women and Self-Defence before *R. v. Lavallee*: The Forgotten Case of *R. v. Whynot (Stafford)*," by Nadia Verrelli and Lori Chambers, turns to a forgotten 1983 case, this time to centre the experience of Jane Hurshman, who killed her abusive common law partner and claimed self-defence. What made the case distinctive and attracted national media attention was that Hurshman did not act in the context of imminent threat of death; she shot her partner while he was sleeping in the context of a long history of his violent abuse of her and murderous threats against her, her family, and her neighbours. The jury sided with Hurshman and found her not guilty of murder. Unlike in the seduction trial involving MacMillan, the trial judge upheld the jury's determination. However, the Crown successfully appealed, and instead of enduring a new trial, Hurshman pled guilty to manslaughter and was sentenced to six months in prison. After her release, she became an activist against domestic violence, working with battered women and advocating for services for them. Verrelli and Chambers explain not only how influential this case was for subsequent jurisprudence – the Supreme Court of Canada later affirmed the availability of a self-defence in cases of intimate partner violence – they also recount the toll it inflicted on Hurshman.

Part 4, "Theory and Method," takes up questions of method and theory that have been central to Sangster's work. The first three chapters in this part expand the repertoire of approaches, methods, and techniques available to historians who are eager to investigate women's bodies, experiences, and voices in the past. In "From Dreams of Equality to One Hundred Years of Struggle: Radical Women's Biographies in the History of Canadian Politics," Linda Kealy uses the biographies of activist women on the left to illustrate the need to broaden how we conceive of what is "radical" about their activism. Drawing on the biographies of five Canadian women radicals, all white, Kealey shows that women in left politics ran the risk of being considered bourgeois if they were considered by male colleagues to be "too" interested in feminism and suffragism. Kealey argues that biography, despite its limits, especially for working-class and poor women who rarely left personal papers, is a rich source for understanding the ambivalent and transgressive place occupied by women who were active in left political spaces.

In "Revisiting *Many Tender Ties*: A Materialist Reading of Sylvia Van Kirk's Text," her new materialist or Deleuzian rereading of Sylvia Van Kirk's influential book on Indigenous women in the fur trade between 1670 and 1877, *Many Tender Ties*, D.Y. Turner addresses the thorny question of how the experiences of subalterns can be found in the colonial archive. Turner argues that Van Kirk's text reveals "the somatic realities, material presence and affective power of the women she sought to study" by articulating their relationships with the men with whom they were partnered, the industries in which they worked, and the nations within which they lived. In Turner's rereading, *Many Tender Ties* does not represent the lone, individual Indigenous, mixed, or Métis woman but, rather, the power of these women's bodies to affect and be affected, not only by the other bodies with whom they were immediately connected, such as their husbands and children, but also by the historian.

In "Gender, Migration, and the Temporalities of Late Capitalism: Social Reproduction in the Economies of Affect," Winnie Lem uses ethnography to move beyond conventional linear understandings of time to reveal different time scales that intersect and overlap; some are linear and aligned with industrial capitalism, while others are cyclical and follow the rhythms of the biophysical world and nature. Drawing on Henri Lefebrve's rhythmanalysis, Lem investigates how women who have relocated from China to France to provide care and sex as undocumented migrants in the affective economy navigate the challenges of the clashing temporalities of financialized capitalism and the reproduction of families. She argues that it is critical to understand how both spatiality and temporality shape migration and the experiences of women who are dislocated by capitalist expansion and caught up in its circuits of accumulation.

Ted McCoy's chapter, "Joan Sangster's Socialist-Feminist History," completes the section by delving into Sangster's socialist-feminist approach to history as revealed in her writing. He chronicles how the confluence of two vibrant and newly emerging springs of historical research in the 1970s, women's history and the new labour history, shaped Sangster's distinctive feminist materialist approach. This approach, as McCoy shows, was neither narrow nor doctrinaire, as Sangster's work evolved to incorporate some of the methodologies of postmodernism and to address questions of race, ethnicity, and representation in women's history.

The chapters in this collection engage with various aspects of Sangster's rich and wide-ranging work, and all are committed, despite differences in topic and approach, to excavating and understanding women's experiences and how meaning is made of them. Sangster's research demonstrates the need to come at the *women* question from new angles, to draw out different perspectives, and to use a range of sources and materials (from cases and newspaper reports to television shows and films) to depict and contextualize competing representations and understandings of women's place and value in the world. Her attention to differences in power and to the subtle interplay of its various forms makes her sensitive to the hierarchies that divide women without undermining her belief in the possibility for solidarity and transformation.

Sangster's work can also be a jumping-off point to explore new epistemological and methodological questions. What is the relationship between oral history and ethnography? How are they different, and what can they learn from each other? How do we retrieve the experiences and voices of women who either have not left or do not figure in written records? How do spatiality *and* temporality shape the experiences of women? Sangster's research on Indigenous women's labour and representations of the North gives rise to a range of questions about how to understand "'Canada as an evolving colonial entity' with layers of colonial relations that change over time and involve different groups."[29] It also directs us to question, and not just assume, the relationship between different social processes, such as Eurocentrism and colonialism, for example, and to regard their relationship as posing a historical question the answer to which depends on the colonial project under investigation. By seeing the past though feminist eyes, Sangster demonstrates that is it possible to keep theory and history, culture and political economy, and social identity and social location within the same field of vision, and it is this skill that makes her historical research so inspiring.

NOTES

1. Gerda Lerner, *Why History Matters: Life and Thought* (Oxford: Oxford University Press, 1997), 211.
2. Joan Sangster, *The Iconic North: Cultural Constructions of Aboriginal Life in Postwar Canada* (Vancouver: UBC Press, 2016), viii, quoting Zora Neale Hurston to the effect that research is simply "formalized curiosity. It is poking and prying with a purpose."
3. Eleanor Marx and Edward Aveling, "The Woman Question from a Socialist Point of View," *Westminster Review* 125 (January–April 1886): 21.
4. Joan Sangster, *Dreams of Equality: Women on the Canadian Left, 1920–50* (Oxford: Oxford University Press, 1989), 8–9.
5. Joan Sangster and Meg Luxton, "Feminism, Capitalism and the Problems of Amnesia: A Response to Nancy Fraser," *Socialist Register* 49 (2013): 288–309, 294.
6. Joan Kelly, "The Doubled Vision of Feminist Theory: A Postscript to the 'Women and Power' Conference," *Feminist Studies* 5, no. 1 (1979): 216–27; Joan Sangster, *Through Feminist Eyes: Essays on Canadian Women's History* (Edmonton: Athabasca University Press, 2011), 97.
7. Joan Sangster, *Earning Respect: The Lives of Working Women in Small-Town Ontario, 1920–1960* (Toronto: University of Toronto Press, 1995), 7.
8. Sangster, *Through Feminist Eyes.*
9. Sangster, *Through Feminist Eyes,* 128; Sangster, *The Iconic North,* 17.
10. Sangster, *Dreams of Equality,* 43, 46–7.
11. Joan Sangster, *Transforming Labour: Women and Work in Post-war Canada* (Toronto: University of Toronto Press, 2010), 75.
12. Sangster, *Transforming Labour,* 230–1.
13. Joan Sangster, *Regulating Girls and Women: Sexuality, Family, and the Law in Ontario, 1920–1960* (Toronto: Oxford University Press, 2001), 2; Joan

Sangster, *Girl Trouble: Female Delinquency in English Canada* (Toronto: Between the Lines, 2002).
14 Sangster, *Girl Trouble*, 4.
15 Sangster, *Through Feminist Eyes*, 357.
16 Sangster, *Through Feminist Eyes*, 357.
17 Joan Sangster, "Invoking Experience as Evidence," *Canadian Historical Review* 92, no. 1 (March 2011): 135–62, 161.
18 Sangster, *Regulating Girls and Women*, 1–2.
19 Sangster, *Girl Trouble*, 3.
20 Sangster, *Regulating Girls and Women*, chap. 4.
21 Sangster, *Regulating Girls and Women*, 3.
22 Joan Sangster, *One Hundred Years of Struggle: The History of Women and the Vote in Canada* (Vancouver: UBC Press, 2018), 270.
23 Sangster, *One Hundred Years of Struggle*, 270.
24 Sangster and Luxton, "Feminism, Capitalism and the Problems of Amnesia"; Nancy Fraser, "Feminism, Capitalism and the Cunning of History," *New Left Review* 56, no. 2 (March–April 2009): 97–117.
25 Sangster and Luxton, "Feminism, Capitalism and the Problems of Amnesia," 295.
26 Sangster, *Transforming Labour*, 232.
27 Joan Sangster, *Demanding Equality: One Hundred Years of Canadian Feminism* (Vancouver: UBC Press, 2021).
28 Joan Sangster, "The Meanings of Mercy: Wife Assault and Spousal Murder in Post–Second World War Canada," *Canadian Historical Review* 97, no. 4 (December 2016): 515.
29 Sangster, *The Iconic North*, 12, citing Joyce Green, "Towards a Détente with History: Confronting Canada's Colonial Legacy," *International Review of Canadian Studies* 12 (Fall 1995): 85.

PART ONE

Women, Labour, and the Left

1 "Don't Dare": Labour, Feminism, and the Left on Strike at Dare Foods, 1972–1973

MASON GODDEN

In 1972, 375 United Brewery Workers (UBW) went on strike at Dare Foods in Kitchener, Ontario, after the company offered an unequal wage increase to its workers: fifty-five cents for men and forty-five cents for women. Ninety per cent of the Dare workers were women whose jobs subjected them to long hours, unsafe working conditions, and abuse and neglect from management. The Dare strike became an important flashpoint for activists during the 1970s, and drew several allies to its cause, such as labour unions from across Ontario, feminist organizations, and student New Leftists from the universities of Waterloo, York, and Toronto. Though the strike began over unequal pay, it eventually addressed other key issues that women, unions, and leftists grappled with in the postwar period, such as violent picket lines, labour injunctions, and the industrial legality of secondary pickets and boycotts. The allies that the Dare women were able to marshal were invaluable to the success of the strike, as each ally mobilized around what they thought the key issues of the strike were. Though wage parity between male and female workers was not achieved by the strike, other important concessions from the company were won, and a palpable critique of postwar industrial legality was mounted.

Most significantly, the Dare strike ensured that the historical relationship between organized labour, the feminist movement, and the left coalesced into a strong alliance during the 1970s. Feminist organizing alongside labour and the left during the late nineteenth and early twentieth centuries was fraught with challenges, since women's participation in then-male-led trade unions and left-wing political parties was delimited along highly gendered lines.[1] In the labour movement, this began to change due to the influx of married women and mothers into unionized jobs after the Second World War, which in turn led to the emergence of a "working-class feminism" in both the labour movement and the women's movement.[2] Some working women sought to reform unions from within by advocating for pay equity, maternity leave, and sexual harassment awareness while also steering their unions toward more radical agendas such as LGBTQ and abortion rights.[3] Other working women formed independent unions using grassroots organizing principles in an attempt to build gender- and class-based activism in industries with high concentrations of female employment.[4] The British Columbia–based Service, Office, and Retail Workers' Union of Canada (SORWUC) saw success along such lines in the 1970s as it organized women in industries considered unorganizable by the mainstream labour movement such as "banks, day-care centres, offices, pubs, and restaurants."[5]

Likewise, the working-class theoretical accent brought to the women's movement by a renewed socialist feminism allowed working women to identify a common cause with the New Left and mount a "socialist feminist rebellion" during the period.[6] As Sean Antaya's chapter in this collection elaborates, feminists not only participated in but created and led New Left groups, demonstrating that a successful balance between working-class feminism and revolutionary leftist politics could be maintained. Working women in the 1970s thus came to recognize both unions and leftist groups as vehicles for progressive labour and gender reforms while remaining cognizant that such institutions could also reinforce gender inequalities within their membership.[7]

The alliance between labour, feminism, and the left was fraught with tension and contradiction during the decade. Not all working women were ready to accept the prominent role that lesbian women played in the women's movement, and some women's liberationists feared that working women would bring a narrow economism to women's issues.[8] Operating outside of the mainstream of organized labour led to the marginalization of feminist unions such as SORWUC, which was written off by some unions as a "women's liberation organization" rather than a trade union.[9] Recalling the initial encounters between the feminist movement and the New Left, Judy Rebick argues that the secondary position women held in leftist organizations in previous eras was reproduced in the New Left due to the high concentration of men involved in the early iterations of the movement.[10] Labour, feminism, and the left were thus complementary social movements, but cooperation between them was not always easy to achieve.

Focusing only on the challenges of this alliance, however, obscures the role that working-class feminism played in accentuating the broader women's movement and obfuscates the broader political arena to which the feminist movement introduced working women.[11] Depictions of the

New Left as a sexist movement similarly downplay the important contributions women made to leftism during the postwar period, and also overlook the critical role that women played in left-wing politics during the late nineteenth and early twentieth centuries despite the gendered constraints on their political involvement in those periods.[12] Instead, this chapter calls attention to the strong socialist-feminist current of the women's movement that, in the 1970s, mobilized working women in service of various social justice issues that were also pertinent to leftists.[13] Accordingly, this chapter emphasizes the positive outcomes of organized labour's alliance with the women's movement and the New Left by documenting the successful organizing efforts, campaigns, and concessions won in the Dare strike.

Rather than seeing the literatures on labour, feminism, and the left as disparate pieces of a "fragmented" history, this chapter treats such writings as deeply interconnected parts of a complex social history.[14] It aims to highlight working women's roles as militant actors with the collective agency to withhold their labour and fight for their rights when exploited.[15] Guided by a theoretical approach to historical materialism inspired by Joan Sangster, whose work has consistently questioned how "working people negotiate, accommodate, understand, and resist changes in social and material life," this chapter examines how working women relied on their unions, the women's movement, and the New Left to combat the inequities exacerbated by capitalism in the 1970s.[16] Understanding how the strike unfolded for the three movements in question can provide important insights into how social movements have worked together historically to achieve common goals. The successful campaigns undertaken in the Dare strike may also serve as useful roadmaps for a rejuvenated labour-feminist-left alliance today and suggest some ways in which future labour disputes might be aided by like-minded social justice movements.

Dare Foods had operated in Canada for eighty years by the time of the 1972 strike. The company began in 1892 as a family-owned grocery store managed by German-Canadian entrepreneur Charles H. Doerr in Kitchener (then named Berlin).[17] As the homemade cookies sold in his store became more popular, Doerr expanded into manufacturing, and by 1919 was selling various baked goods and hard candies to the wider Kitchener region. In 1956, Doerr's company – now named Dare, and run by his grandson Carl – started distributing its cookie and candy products in the United States.[18] Entry into the American market intensified the conditions of production for the 375 workers employed at Dare's headquarter plant in Kitchener, leading them to organize under the UBW in 1968. The company's wage increase offer to the UBW during bargaining negotiations for a second contract in 1972 exemplified the unequal working conditions on Dare's shop floor.[19] The ten-cent disparity between male and female wages contained in Dare's offer would ensure that female employees, who were categorized as packers despite the many additional tasks they often took on, remained in "the lowest paid job in the plant."[20]

Though unequal pay and job classification were important issues for the union, many other factors informed the decision to strike. The Dare plant was one of the few remaining workplaces after the 1950s that exceeded an eight-hour workday. The use of work speed-ups in the plant by "insensitive supervisors" abounded, and women workers faced some of the more difficult and dangerous working conditions.[21] Their positions required them to stand for the entirety of their shift and work in hot kitchens that reached up to 130 degrees with no fans or adequate ventilation. They received lunch and bathroom breaks only if they had reached production quota. Shouting and verbal abuse from plant supervisors were daily occurrences. Female employees were also frequently passed over for promotions. Company supervisors routinely approached favoured candidates in private and offered better-paying positions secretly without giving others the opportunity to apply. Many of the female packers thus felt discouraged from applying for any promotions that would pay better since the company had "[made] up their minds ahead of time who [was] going to get the job before the job [was] even posted."[22] Dare representatives were "exasperated" by such claims when they became public, and defended the company by explaining that women "[didn't] want the responsibility" of higher-paying jobs and that "there would be chaos" in the plant if women "just walked off" to the bathroom, leaving cookies to "pile up."[23]

Furthermore, an informational pamphlet distributed by key feminist allies in the strike, Madeleine Parent and the Ontario Committee on the Status of Women (OCSW), revealed that women were required to "wear [uncomfortable] dress type uniforms" that were not at all conducive to working in the hot kitchens.[24] Parent and the OCSW threatened to involve the Women's Bureau if the Dare women's conditions did not improve, and chastised mainstream labour unions for not accommodating women's issues, noting that the Dare women were like many other workers in Canada who were paid less despite equal work responsibilities to men.[25] Attracting the attention of Parent and the OCSW allowed the strike to occupy the attention of both the women's movement and the labour movement. As the militant co-founder of the Confederation of Canadian Unions (CCU), an alternative labour body established in 1969 to oppose American influence over the Canadian

Labour Congress, Parent had a vast network of labour locals to draw on for strike support.[26] The OCSW, formed by Toronto feminists in response to the findings of the 1970 Royal Commission on the Status of Women, drew on public and state support for the feminist principles championed by the commission and could therefore provide financial aid and public support to the Dare women. The OCSW proved to be a particularly important feminist ally in the Dare strike, as it played a critical role in "raising publicity, fundraising, [supporting] the boycott of Dare products, and [instigating] a short-lived attempt to mediate between the union and management during the strike."[27]

The strike officially began at midnight on 28 May 1972 after nearly a month of stalemated negotiations.[28] "Well-organized and extremely orderly" picket lines totalling 200 workers, feminists, and supporters formed outside the plant.[29] On 6 June 1972, however, "violence broke out ... after pickets tried to halt truckloads of goods being removed from the plant" by strikebreakers employed by Canadian Driver Pool (CDP).[30] A notorious strikebreaking firm known throughout Ontario in the 1970s for aiding strikebound employers, CDP was heavily criticized by former *Toronto Telegram* reporter Marc Zwelling, who in his report on the use of strikebreaking labour in Ontario for the Ontario Federation of Labour (OFL) concluded that although strikebreaking opposed the values of fair collective bargaining, it was ultimately a tactic endorsed by the state and enforced by police.[31] Zwelling's report would eventually be published by the OFL and serve as not only a detailed historical index of strikebreaking usage in Ontario, but a poignant criticism of the state's complicity in strikebreaking. Historically, Canadian industrial law had favoured employer prerogatives during strikes, resulting in "significant limitations" on "trade union activity" to help management continue business as usual.[32] Until significant restrictions were put on the use of injunctions and strikebreaking in the late 1970s, laws outlining the extent to which employers could use strikebreakers remained vague. In fact, the use of strikebreaking in the early twentieth-century metalworking industry often went unchallenged by workers.[33] By the 1970s, however, striking workers who contended with strikebreaking labour became outspoken of their rejection of its usage.

On the Dare picket line, this rejection played out violently. Strikers threw stones at CDP vans as they left the plant, slashed the tires of any vehicles in range, and allegedly threw Molotov cocktails and rocks through the plant windows, resulting in an estimated total of $40,000 worth of property damage.[34] In response to the violence, the Ontario Supreme Court passed an injunction on 12 June 1972 that placed strict limitations and regulations on subsequent UBW-led pickets.[35] The union promised to respect the injunction, and Dare promised the UBW that it would no longer employ CDP labour. But Dare proved its promise to be empty when management rescinded their proposed wage offer and continued to employ CDP, provoking further violence from the strikers. An unidentified group of strikers followed CDP delivery trucks carrying Dare products to Toronto and attempted to force the trucks off the road.[36] A handful of Dare employees, "who had tired of the [then]-seven-week strike" and were persuaded back to work by phone calls and letters sent by management, were barred from entry by a human chain made by the strikers.[37] "Shoving and shouting" resulted, drunkenness and tire-slashing proliferated, and Kitchener police were called to quell the disturbance, with the six officers initially monitoring the picket line soon numbering twenty-five.[38] The police had to use force in order to break apart the chain that had formed to block returning employees, and ultimately arrested three young picketers, David Rushton, Gilbert Bailey, and Paul Pugh.[39] Though he was not arrested, video footage taken by a Dare representative from inside the plant caught Louis Dautner, the international representative for the UBW, using force to try to break the police corridor.[40]

In total, eight men, including Rushton, Bailey, Pugh, and Dautner, and one woman, Pauline Breen, were issued summons to appear in court for their part in the altercation. The injunction forbid much of the activity that had taken place on the picket line, particularly "interference" or "coercion" that would prevent returning Dare employees or CDP strikebreakers from entering the plant.[41] Rushton, who had harboured a concealed weapon on the picket line, was ordered to report twice per week to Kitchener police, stay one thousand feet away from the plant at all times, and refrain from contacting fellow union members.[42] His behaviour on the picket line also received particularly negative attention in the local press.[43] He became the only indirect casualty of the strike after he took his own life, a decision that his friends attributed to "depression" caused by his inability to participate in union activity and the public condemnation he had received in the media during the trial.[44] Justice Donnelly, the judge presiding over the Dare strikers' violation of the injunction, ruled that Dautner, Pugh, and fellow strikers Andrew Diamond, Wayne Zettler, Reid Scott, and Jack Horne were all guilty of violating the injunction.[45] Jail sentences were given to all of the men except for Horne, who was exempted because his wife and daughter were both ill.[46] Dautner and Diamond received sixty-day jail sentences, Zettler and Pugh received thirty days, and Scott received ten.[47] Though Dautner, Daimond, and Zettler attempted to appeal their sentences, Donnelly dismissed their cases without reason.[48] Pugh and

Scott, who did not appeal their sentences, were "escorted by 15 sign-carrying friends" to the police station as they turned themselves in to face their sentences, hailed as heroes by the UBW for openly defying the court's injunction.[49]

The outbreak of violence on the Dare picket line was not at all uncomplicated. The trial of the strikers revealed that violence surrounded Dare, from its working conditions to the way it handled worker unrest. As recent scholarship on workplace violence reminds us, definitions of violence extend beyond what is "formally considered" to be violent.[50] The sweltering heat, uncomfortable uniforms, limited bathroom breaks, and verbal abuse that the Dare women faced on the job exemplified the informal violence that existed at Dare before the strike, given that they were physical and psychological detriments caused by the "profit motive" of industrial capitalism.[51] The formal violence committed by the police against striking workers was merely a continuation of the historical trend since the nineteenth century toward state-sanctioned violence in defence of management's right to operate unimpeded.[52] For the strikers, violence clearly manifested out of desperation, as they believed there were little or no alternative means of protesting management's use of injunctions and strikebreakers. During the court proceedings, it was revealed that Dautner had made a phone call to a strikebreaker and threatened to vandalize their home and car if they crossed the picket line.[53] Zettler committed what Justice Donnelly described as "a cowardly attack" against Dare employee Garry Moore, holding him to the ground and strangling him while threatening to kill his wife (who was also a Dare worker) if she returned to work.[54] Pugh shouted profanity, insults, and threats at female strikebreakers as they exited the plant one night, and Scott and Horne both "bumped" into and "shoved" strikebreakers on the picket line while Dautner and Diamond did little to contain the violence despite their roles as picket captains.[55] Like the Artistic Woodwork strike that occurred in Toronto one year later, the Dare strike made it clear that workers in the 1970s were prepared to upset the "public order" if their "livelihood" and legal rights were jeopardized.[56]

The ease and rapidity with which employers could obtain legal strikebreaking labour and injunctions in the 1970s brought the "repressive power of the state" to bear on the Dare workers, and their violent response attested to their staunch defiance of an industrial legality they considered unfair.[57] But not all of the strikers' allies were immediately convinced that violence was the ideal tool to combat management's manipulation of industrial law. The OCSW was initially hesitant to place its support behind the strikers, as it believed condemning the female strikebreakers brought in by CDP would antagonize women who were gaining employment out of necessity rather than malice. Madeleine Parent managed to simplify the situation for the OCSW by arguing that "the women on strike were fighting for justice, and that many more women, and all society, would benefit if [the Dare strikers] won," making the violent tactics of the UBW more palatable.[58]

Dare used the violence and property damage as a pretext to pursue legal prosecution of the strikers. In October of 1972, the company sought $1.6 million in damages from the Supreme Court of Ontario, $100,000 of which was proposed for punitive damages against each defendant found guilty of breaching the injunction.[59] Dare also urged the Supreme Court to grant a separate injunction against the growing boycott of Dare products in order "to protect the company's name."[60] Dare's attempt to portray the boycott as illegal was not a novel tactic used by management to break strikes. Industrial law in the 1970s clearly outlined that primary picketing (the picketing of the business where strikers were employed) could be regulated by injunctions, but the regulation of secondary pickets (demonstrations and boycotts against businesses and companies affiliated with the striking business) "was not always clear."[61] Common law mandated that the granting of secondary injunctions be left to the discretion of individual judges.[62] Legal ambiguities notwithstanding, the Canadian state had a historical record of anti-labour prejudices. As minister of labour in the early 1900s, William Lyon Mackenzie King called for the outlawing of boycotts and other strike tactics after a heated attempt at conciliation with striking miners in Rossland, British Columbia, in 1903.[63] Even the 1960s and 1970s – two decades that witnessed a series of successful boycotts such as Cesar Chavez's grape boycott in the United States in 1965 and the Kraft foods boycott in 1971 – saw companies win injunctions against secondary picketing, as was the case in *Hersees v. Goldstein* in 1963.[64] Boycotts were thus a common tactic for striking workers, and they were often fought by management, but with varying degrees of success. During the Dare strike, bumper stickers that read "Don't buy Dare products" and other pieces of merchandise that were distributed to raise awareness of the boycott were considered illegal by the company, but the courts did not agree, allowing the boycott to become one of the strike's most successful campaigns.[65]

The boycott had begun as early as the strike's third week, and expanded beyond Dare products, reaching "businesses which did any service" for Dare.[66] Its popularity encouraged some companies like Day and Ross (a freight company) and Riordan Rentals (a car-leasing firm) to end their business with Dare completely. Pickets formed outside of the companies that continued their business with Dare, such as "Newtex Cleaners, Hertz Rent-a-Car, Sanderson's Tire Service" and a taxi company that strikebreakers used to get themselves to and from the plant.[67] These pickets were a key point of entry for various allies to mobilize in solidarity with the Dare strikers. Joined by the OCSW, the Guelph Women's Centre aided the UBW in distributing pamphlets to local grocery stores that were informing consumers about the boycott and encouraging them not to buy Dare cookies. The OCSW also organized striking Dare women into pickets outside of stores that sold Dare products, such as "Loblaws, A&P, Miracle Mart, and Dominion."[68] The boycott was highly effective, evidenced not only by the several reports made to the UBW that there were "very few Dare cookies on [store] shelves," but also by its provincial scope.[69] One OCSW-led picket took place outside of the St. James Town Dominion store and Towne Mall in Toronto, where Dare women shared literature with shoppers about Dare's exploitative and abusive workplace culture. Sean Antaya's chapter in this collection reveals that the Windsor New Tendency's women's group, the Socialist Women's Caucus, carried on the boycott in Windsor and rallied Windsor-based supporters to the Kitchener picket line.

The boycott also attracted the support of youthful radicals aligned with the New Left, which in Kitchener was best represented by students at the University of Waterloo. Waterloo students used their campus newspaper, *The Chevron*, to inform the student body of the boycott and provide a strong leftist commentary on the strike. Student newspapers had become important venues for leftist engagement with social justice issues by the 1960s, and *The Chevron* was no exception to this pattern.[70] The paper was well known among leftists in the Kitchener community and was thus a reliable source of activist knowledge and engagement.

The Chevron's coverage of the strike began in June 1972, shortly after the demonstrations against strikebreaking began. Its inaugural issue on the strike on 9 June 1972 claimed that "coverage in the local media of the two-week strike at Dare ... [had] been extensive, yet incomplete" and that due to the "broad implications" of the strike for all unions in Canada, it had the obligation to "provide a more cogent representation" of the strike.[71] *The Chevron*'s first few issues on the strike echoed well-trod criticisms of CDP director Richard Grange, Dare CEO Clifford Dare, and the use of injunctions.[72] Later issues encouraged Waterloo students to participate in the boycott and buy anti-Dare merchandise.[73] When Dare sued the UBW and the OFL for property damage, *The Chevron* was quick to defend the strikers, reminding readers that "physically violent acts can erupt when workers must confront low wages, an unjust legal system, an arrogant management, an unthinking city government and a gang of strike-breakers."[74] *The Chevron*'s reportage of the strike eventually reached the Dare strikers, who made sure to voice their appreciation to their student allies. Pauline Breen wrote to *The Chevron* prior to her summons to appear in court, thanking the editorial board for writing about "the truth."[75] Another striker praised the paper for its research on the strike, which in their mind had surpassed that done by local newspapers.[76]

New Left interest in the Dare strike was not limited to the students at Waterloo. Student newspapers at York University and the University of Toronto were also tracking the strike's developments and injecting left politics into their reporting. York University's *Pro Tem* contained biting and sarcastic commentary on both CDP and Clifford Dare, calling the former "goons" and the latter a "self-made man," "motivated" by the fact that "he made it on his own, so the bastards in the union can bloody-well do the same without his help."[77] *Pro Tem*'s sardonic commentary irritated Dare management so strongly that it had its legal counsel forward a letter to a student reporter, warning him that his editorial violated the injunction.[78] At the same time, the *Varsity*, the University of Toronto's nearly one-hundred-year-old student newspaper, showed its support for the boycott by printing images of popular Dare cookies with the caption "This beautiful variety of baked goods should not be on your grocers' shelf."[79] Another image showed Dare's "pantry packs" (bulk packages of cookies at a discounted price) with the phrase "Don't Dare" superimposed over top of them.[80] One issue even published the words to an anonymous "striker's poem": "Oh Dare was a place, / That kept women in place, / By raising the pace, / On the belts. The women complained, / They were hot and they pained, They called Dare insane, / Because they felt angry."[81]

New Left solidarity transformed into formal strike participation in February 1973 when Waterloo, York, and University of Toronto students – joined by renowned Canadian political economist and Waffle co-founder Melville "Mel" Watkins – helped Dare strikers "bog down operations" at the Canadian National Express terminal (CN) in Toronto for over two hours.[82] Though CN representatives insisted that no Dare products were handled at the Toronto terminal, the demonstrators insisted on "embarrassing" CN for its complicity in shipping Dare cookies.[83] The strikers and their allies "stood in front of CN trucks leaving and entering the express yard and in some cases were pulled from the path by CN [employees] and York Regional Police."[84] Incoming CN trucks refused to enter the yard out of fear of crossing the picket line. This event gave New Leftists the opportunity to transcend their theoretical solidarity with the strikers by "putting theory into action" and building a palpable relationship with workers on the picket line.[85]

One month after the CN demonstration, the Dare women gained a valuable feminist ally, the Women's Place, a resource library for aspiring feminists and eventual headquarters for lesbian activism in Toronto.[86] The Women's Place invited the Dare women to participate in a demonstration at Toronto's Nathan Phillips Square on International Women's Day, where strikers "shook hands with curious passers-by, chanted 'heaven help the working girl in a world that's run by men' ... and put on a brief skit showing women rebelling against their male bosses" by pouring hot coffee over their heads.[87] A women's group known as the Beautyshop Quartet also joined the demonstrations and led the women in song and dance. Madeleine Parent and the Canadian Textile and Chemical Union (CTCU), an affiliate of the CCU, rallied CTCU-organized workplaces such as the Puretex Knitting Company, Harding Carpets, and Texpack to join in the Dare women's International Women's Day demonstration, and urged CTCU workers to support the Dare boycott and write to the Ontario labour minister.[88]

Additionally, unions from across Ontario lent crucial strike support to the UBW. On 21 March 1973, fifty "placard-carrying demonstrators" marched and sang outside of Queen's Park in Toronto, where OFL president David Archer called for all of Ontario's labour councils to stand in solidarity with the Dare strikers.[89] The demonstrators also tried to pressure the provincial government into imposing stricter labour laws surrounding injunctions and strikebreaking.[90] While delivering a speech that only mildly denounced the existing inadequacies of industrial law, provincial Liberal leader Robert Nixon was "booed and heckled" by demonstrators for not taking a firmer stance.[91] This rally was followed by a march from Kitchener's Victoria Park to the steps of city hall on 14 April 1973 that totalled over 1,100 supporters.[92] A third rally was planned, but there were fears that the strike was nearing an unfavourable end. By May of 1973, nearly one year after the strike began, 110 of the original 375 strikers had returned to work at Dare or found work elsewhere.[93] The UBW faced possible decertification from the Ontario Labour Relations Board (OLRB), who were mandated by Ontario labour law to hold union decertification votes if contract negotiations extended beyond one year.[94] Strikers and supporters alike were therefore concerned that the third rally would be sparsely attended as momentum and morale dwindled.[95]

The exemplary turnout of 3,500 demonstrators at the rally showed that while there were certainly troubles on the horizon, the strike had no shortage of supporters.[96] The rally, made up of leftists, feminists, strikers, and New Democratic Party MPPs, "moved peacefully through downtown Kitchener to a parking lot next to a police station" while chanting "Don't buy Dare," and eventually congregated in Mackenzie King Square to sing and hear "speeches from representatives of major unions" such as the Canadian Union of Public Employees.[97] A representative from the Spanish Workers' Association spoke to the crowd via interpreter, and a local Marxist group's banners could be seen in the crowd alongside the banners of Teamsters and Steelworkers.[98] Even Kitchener's United Church of Canada, "concerned over the animosity dividing workers and the community," aided the strike by "urging" the Ontario labour minister via telegram to "review the situation with the aim of a reconciliation in the dispute."[99]

Aware of their possible decertification by the OLRB, the UBW tried to remain positive during the rally but heard only "rhetoric and roars" from the crowd.[100] Their fears were realized on 1 February 1974 when the OLRB vote officially decertified the UBW with a resounding 232 members in favour of removing the union.[101] Two months passed before the Bakery, Confectionery and Tobacco Workers' International Union (BC&T) reorganized the Dare workers into BC&T Local 264.[102] The collective agreement between the BC&T and Dare in 1976 contained a clause that automatically unionized all workers in the plant via mandatory checkoff, a clause that Dare management had fought against while negotiating with the UBW despite its entrenchment in industrial law due to the Rand formula.[103] It also mandated that the company adjust oven temperatures and that workers be granted bathroom breaks when requested.[104] Overtime was limited to fifteen minutes, and wages for overtime work were greatly improved. A second fifteen-minute break was added to each worker's schedule, and in the event of overtime, workers were to be given another thirty-minute break for supper during their shift.[105] The work week was finally reduced to forty hours.[106] The new collective agreement outlined that job postings were to be made available to all workers in order to prevent the company from privately offering vacant positions to favoured job candidates.[107] Life insurance of $2,000 was provided to each worker regardless of position or seniority, with the option of $1,000 of extra coverage available to workers who opted to pay higher union dues, and health insurance was paid in full, something that previous agreements under the UBW had not achieved.[108]

The BC&T thus provided increased job security to the Dare workers and greatly improved their working conditions, though the new collective agreement failed to rectify the unequal pay between male and female employees. Packers received a pay raise amounting to $5 per hour, a sizeably better wage than what they made with the UBW, but they remained the lowest-paid position in the plant.[109] While unions were a key site of feminist transformation for working women in the 1970s, "entrenched masculinist ideas" still required contestation, particularly regarding the issue of pay equity.[110] According to Rosemary Warskett, three common justifications for rigidly stratified pay classifications were used by unions throughout the nineteenth and twentieth centuries: "Wages for skills" emerged out of craft union fears that women and immigrant workers would be used by management as "dilutees" to drive down the high wages associated with craft work; conversely, "wages for living" stressed that the wages of the lowest-paid workers needed to cover the minimum cost of living in the event that wage gains were eroded, whether by economic crisis or low-skilled dilution; relatedly, "wages for the family head" was premised on the assumption that women's paid employment was temporary and supplemental to the primary wage of male heads of household.[111] Despite the groundswell of feminist organizing around pay equity issues in the postwar period, unions were slow and sometimes resistant to meet the challenge. Even legislative approaches to rectifying pay inequity were uneven. Ontario's 1987 Pay Equity Act, which applied to both the public and private sector, was novel for its placement of onus on the employer to proactively address pay inequities.[112] Other jurisdictions, such as the United Kingdom, relied on "individual complaint-based mechanism[s]" to resolve pay equity concerns.[113] Still, the act proved itself a "piecemeal legal reform" due to its significant blind spots, as well as the limitations imposed on it by Mike Harris's Progressive Conservative government during the 1990s.[114] As one recent study indicates, the pay gap between men and women in Canada has diminished slightly since the 1960s, but still persists, as do middling attempts at legislative reform.[115]

Though equal pay was not achieved by the Dare strike, labour, feminism, and the left's alliance strengthened during the strike and had transformative outcomes for those involved. The Dare women learned much from their work with feminists and leftists, with one striker, Grace Litwiller, commenting that "the strike has done something for some women ... It's made them realize that they have rights. Now they speak up without being bossy. This is something wonderful to see and it's not just happening to young women, women are now just coming out of themselves."[116] Similarly, fellow striker Diane Proderer reflected, "[Before the strike] I was a union member because I had to be a union member ... I've wakened up a lot since then."[117] As Andrea Samoil's chapter in this collection affirms, women working for the lowest wages and on the lowest rungs of workplace seniority had no less potential than other workers to critically disrupt industrial operations and change common perceptions about unequal wages. The Dare women, like the Calgary laundry workers Samoil examines, had no prior strike experience, but were willing to wade into new and dangerous territory to fight for better working conditions and legal protections. The Dare women fought a repressive legal regime that served at nearly every turn to criminalize and punish them yet bound together in solidarity with their union and their allies to achieve success.

The boycott of Dare products was so influential that "even after the strike ended ... many women still refused to buy Dare cookies."[118] Dare's sales in Canada had dropped nearly $2 million over the course of the strike, but its foothold in the American market, where the boycott had no measurable effect, ensured that no serious financial loss was incurred by the company.[119] The strike campaign also proved that the male union hierarchy that typified the Canadian labour movement could successfully integrate feminist politics into strike mobilizations and achieve important victories for working women. The New Left demonstrated an equivalent receptiveness to feminist politics and opened its ranks to the young feminists and working women fighting for respect and equity at work. The Dare strike was thus a capstone in Canadian labour, feminist, and left-wing organizing during the 1970s and remains an important historical moment in the alliance between the three movements. More than anything, the strike proved that this historical partnership could effectively muster, in the words of Joan Sangster, "energetic militancy, a coherent commitment to a social(ist) transformation, and an optimistic political belief in the possibility of the working-class' ability" to challenge the injustices of capitalism and – more importantly – "change the world."[120]

NOTES

1 Linda Kealey, *Enlisting Women for the Cause: Women, Labour, and the Left in Canada, 1890–1920* (Toronto: University of Toronto Press, 1998), 11–12.
2 Heather Jon Maroney, "Feminism at Work," in *Feminism and Political Economy: Women's Work, Women's Struggles*, ed. Heather Jon Maroney and Meg Luxton (Toronto: Methuen Publications, 1987), 54.
3 Linda Briskin and Lynda Yanz, "Introduction," in *Union Sisters: Women in the Labour Movement*, ed. Linda Briskin and Lynda Yanz (Toronto: The Women's Press, 1983), 9.
4 Maroney, "Feminism at Work," 59.

5 Julia Smith, "An 'Entirely Different' Kind of Union: The Service, Office, and Retail Workers' Union of Canada (SORWUC), 1972–1986," *Labour/Le Travail* 73 (Spring 2014): 23.
6 Joan Sangster, "Radical Ruptures: Feminism, Labor, and the Left in the Long Sixties in Canada," *American Review of Canadian Studies* 40, no. 1 (2010): 7–8.
7 Linda Briskin, "Women's Challenge to Organized Labour," in Briskin and Yanz, *Union Sisters*, 260.
8 Carolyn Egan and Lynda Yanz, "Building Links: Labour and the Women's Movement," in Briskin and Yanz, *Union Sisters*, 367–8.
9 Smith, "An 'Entirely Different' Kind of Union," 24.
10 Judy Rebick, *Ten Thousand Roses: The Making of a Feminist Revolution* (Toronto: Penguin Group, 2005), 8.
11 Meg Luxton, "Feminism as a Class Act: Working-Class Feminism and the Women's Movement in Canada," *Labour/Le Travail* 48 (2001): 64–5.
12 For an overview of the relationship between labour, feminism, and the left in Canada during the postwar period, see Sangster, "Radical Ruptures"; a detailed account of women's involvement in the Canadian left at the turn of the twentieth century can be found in Kealey, *Enlisting Women for the Cause*.
13 Peter Graham and Ian McKay, *Radical Ambition: The New Left in Toronto* (Toronto: Between the Lines, 2019), 300.
14 Bettina Bradbury, "Women and the History of Their Work in Canada: Some Recent Books," *Journal of Canadian Studies* 28, no. 3 (Fall 1993): 160.
15 Bettina Bradbury, "Women's History and Working-Class History," *Labour/Le Travail* 19 (Spring 1987): 23.
16 Joan Sangster, *Transforming Labour: Women and Work in Post-war Canada* (Toronto: University of Toronto Press, 2010), 11.
17 "Carl Dare Built a Lasting Canadian Food Company," *Waterloo Region Record*, 11 April 2014, https://www.therecord.com/news/waterloo-region/2014/04/10/carl-dare-built-a-lasting-canadian-food-company.html.
18 "Carl Dare Built a Lasting Canadian Food Company."
19 "The Original Issues," *Pro Tem*, 18 October 1972, 4.
20 "Women's Group Backing Encourages Dare Strikers," *Kitchener-Waterloo Record*, 21 September 1972.
21 "Women's Group Backing Encourages Dare Strikers."
22 "Bargaining in Bad Faith," *Perspective on Dare*, n.d., 4, in University of Waterloo Special Collections & Archives, GA 282 Dare Foods Limited, file 4, Dare Strike Clippings – 1972–92.
23 "Bargaining in Bad Faith," 4.
24 "Women's Group Backing Encourages Dare Strikers."

25 "Status Group May Complain for Women," *Globe and Mail*, 9 November 1972, W6.
26 For detailed accounts of the CCU's origins, see Andrée Levesque, ed., *Madeleine Parent: Activist* (Toronto: Sumach Press, 2005); Rick Salutin, *Kent Rowley: The Organizer* (Toronto: Lorimer, 1980). The CCU's penchant for organizing immigrant women workers established Parent as a leading voice within the Canadian labour and women's movements.
27 Ian Milligan, *Rebel Youth: 1960s Labour Unrest, Young Workers, and New Leftists in English Canada* (Vancouver: UBC Press, 2014), 133–4.
28 "Dare Strike: A Brief History," *Perspective on Dare*, n.d., 1, in University of Waterloo Special Collections & Archives, GA 282 Dare Foods Limited, file 4, Dare Strike Clippings – 1972–92.
29 "Dare Strike: A Brief History," 1; see also "New Trouble on Picket Line at Dare Plant," *Globe and Mail*, 11 July 1972, 8.
30 "New Trouble on Picket Line at Dare Plant," 8.
31 Marc Zwelling, *The Strike Breakers: The Report of the Strike-Breaking Committee of the Ontario Federation of Labour and the Labour Council of Metropolitan Toronto* (Toronto: Ontario Federation of Labour, 1972), 12.
32 Judy Fudge and Eric Tucker, "Forging Responsible Unions: Metal Workers and the Rise of the Labour Injunction in Canada," *Labour/Le Travail* 37 (Spring 1996): 81.
33 Fudge and Tucker, "Forging Responsible Unions," 88.
34 One unmarked document in the Dare Foods collection at University of Waterloo Special Collections & Archives appears to be authored by a company representative and describes the use of Molotov cocktails by the strikers. See also "New Trouble on Picket Line at Dare Plant," 8, which notes that tire-slashing instruments were provided to the Dare strikers beforehand by unidentified allies.
35 "Dare Workers Vote to Dislodge Brewery Union," *Globe and Mail*, 1 February 1974, 2.
36 "To All Union Members within Dare Foods Group of Employees," *Kitchener-Waterloo Record*, 14 June 1972; see also "Man Asphyxiated: Picket Line Mourns Striker Found Dead," *Kitchener-Waterloo Record*, in University of Waterloo Special Collections & Archives, GA 282 Dare Foods Limited, file 4, Dare Strike Clippings – 1972–92.
37 "New Trouble on Picket Line at Dare Plant," 8.
38 Undated and unlabelled headlines in the Dare Foods collection at Waterloo Special Collections & Archives read "Three Dare pickets, drunk are convicted" and "Tire-slasher supplier at strike fined." Descriptions of the picket line violence can be found in "Andrew Diamond et al. and Dare Foods – Reasons for Judgement," 6, in Library and Archives Canada (hereafter LAC), Diamond v. Dare Foods, RG125, R927, vol. 1941, file 13288.

39 "New Trouble on the Picket Line at Dare Plant," *Globe and Mail*, 11 July 1972, 8.
40 "Andrew Diamond et al. and Dare Foods – Reasons for Judgement," 7, LAC, Diamond v. Dare Foods, RG125, R927, vol. 1941, file 13288.
41 "New Trouble on the Picket Line at Dare Plant," 8.
42 "Man Asphyxiated: Picket Line Mourns Striker Found Dead."
43 "Severity of the Law," *Perspective on Dare*, n.d., 1, in University of Waterloo Special Collections & Archives, GA 282 Dare Foods Limited, file 4, Dare Strike Clippings – 1972–92.
44 "Dare Pickets Mourn Asphyxiated Striker," *Globe and Mail*, 9 August 1972, 4; "Man Asphyxiated: Picket Line Mourns Striker Found Dead."
45 "6 Strikers Convicted of Contempt of Court," *Toronto Star*, 2 March 1973, 2.
46 "5 Jailed for Dare Picket Line Violence," *Toronto Star*, 8 March 1973, 67.
47 "5 Jailed for Dare Picket Line Violence," 67.
48 "Andrew Diamond et al. and Dare Foods – Affidavit," 2–3, LAC, Diamond v. Dare Foods, RG125, R927, vol. 1941, file 13288.
49 "Friends Escort Strikers to Jail," *Globe and Mail*, 23 March 1973, 9.
50 Jeremy Milloy, "Introduction: Accounting for Violence," in *The Violence of Work: New Essays in Canadian and US Labour History*, ed. Jeremy Milloy and Joan Sangster (Toronto: University of Toronto Press, 2021), 4.
51 Milloy, "Accounting for Violence," 4–5, 7.
52 Milloy, "Accounting for Violence," 4.
53 "Andrew Diamond et al. and Dare Foods – Reasons for Judgement," 8.
54 "Flouted Injunction in Strike at Dare, Six Men Sentenced," *Globe and Mail*, 8 March 1973, 5.
55 "Disobeyed Order, Injunction, 6 Are Guilty in Dare Incidents," *Globe and Mail*, 2 March 1973, 35.
56 Ian Milligan, "The Force of All Our Numbers: New Leftists, Labour, and the 1973 Artistic Woodwork Strike," *Labour/Le Travail* 66 (Fall 2010): 68.
57 Milligan, "The Force of All Our Numbers," 39.
58 Lynn McDonald, "The Challenge Accepted: The Founding of the Ontario Committee on the Status of Women," in *White Gloves Off: The Work of the Ontario Committee on the Status of Women*, ed. Beth Atcheson and Lorna Marsden (Toronto: Second Story Press, 2018), 50.
59 "Struck Firm Seeking $1.6 Million Damages," *Globe and Mail*, 7 October 1972, 2.
60 "Struck Firm Seeking $1.6 Million Damages," 2.
61 Charles W. Smith, "'We Didn't Want to Totally Break the Law': Industrial Legality, the Pepsi Strike, and Workers' Collective Rights in Canada," *Labour/Le Travail* 74 (2014): 94.
62 Smith, "We Didn't Want to Totally Break the Law," 94.

63 Gregory S. Kealey, *Workers and Canadian History* (Montreal: McGill-Queen's University Press, 1995), 431.
64 For Chavez's personal recollection of the US grape boycott, see Jacques E. Levy and Cesar Chavez, *Cesar Chavez: Autobiography of La Causa* (Minneapolis: University of Minnesota Press, 2007), particularly chap. 3, "National Spotlight." See also Marc Zwelling, "The Kraft Boycott," *Canadian Dimension* 8, no. 4–5 (1972): 8, 10, and 64 for an account of the Kraft boycott. The *Hersees v. Goldstein* injunction is discussed in detail in Smith, "We Didn't Want to Totally Break the Law."
65 "Struck Firm Seeking $1.6 Million Damages," 2.
66 "Boycott Dare Products," *Perspective on Dare*, n.d., 1, in University of Waterloo Special Collections & Archives, GA 282 Dare Foods Limited, file 4, Dare Strike Clippings – 1972–92.
67 "Dare Strikers Picket Hertz Truck Office," *Kitchener-Waterloo Record*, 23 February 1973. The Hertz picket in February 1973 was led by and mostly composed of women.
68 "Boycott Dare Products," 1.
69 "Women's Group Backing Encourages Dare Strikers."
70 See Benjamin Isitt, *Militant Minority: British Columbia Workers and the Rise of a New Left, 1948–1972* (Toronto: University of Toronto Press, 2011). Isitt argues that student newspapers were catalysts for New Left activism. He offers the University of British Columbia's student newspaper the *Ubyssey* and the Montreal-based paper *Our Generation against Nuclear War* as examples of popular publications that prompted student engagement with left-wing issues such as nuclear disarmament and decolonization.
71 "The Dare Strike: The Issues," *Chevron*, 9 June 1972, 1, https://issuu.com/uw_imprint/docs/1972-73_v13-n05_chevron.
72 "Scabbing: A Modern Industry," *Chevron*, 9 June 1972, 2, https://issuu.com/uw_imprint/docs/1972-73_v13-n05_chevron.
73 "Dare Boycott Bolstered by OFL," *Chevron*, 15 September 1972, 3, https://issuu.com/imprintuw/docs/1972-73_v13-n12_chevron_20100813_201611.
74 "Dare Sues OFL," *Chevron*, 13 October 1972, 3, https://issuu.com/imprintuw/docs/1972-73_v13-n19_chevron1.
75 "Response to Dare Coverage," *Chevron*, 7 July 1972, 7, https://issuu.com/uw_imprint/docs/1972-73_v13-n08_chevron.
76 "Response to Dare Coverage," 7.
77 "The Real Issue," *Pro Tem*, 18 October 1972, 4; "Dare Products Boycott," *Pro Tem*, 18 October 1972, 5.
78 "Glendon Student Defies Dare," *Chevron*, 17 November 1972, 1, https://issuu.com/uw_imprint/docs/1972-73_v13-n24_chevron. The "grounds" upon which Dare believed it could prosecute the York student in question, Bob Edwards, was circumstantial evidence linking his editorial to the

cancellation of many grocery stores' contracts with Dare in support of the boycott. It was quickly discovered, however, that the stores' contracts with Dare were cancelled well before Edwards's editorial was published.
79 "Dare to Struggle," *Varsity*, n.d.
80 "Strikers Want Equal Pay for Women: Major Food Chains Back Dare Boycott," *Varsity*, 11 October 1972, 6.
81 "Strikers Want Equal Pay for Women: Major Food Chains Back Dare Boycott," 6.
82 See "75 Block CN Express Terminal to Support Kitchener Strike," *Toronto Star*, 9 February 1973, 55; "Help Wanted in Winning Dare Strike," *Varsity*, 7 February 1973, 3. The total number of demonstrators at CN was disputed: the *Toronto Star* estimated 75, while the *Varsity* estimated 150.
83 "75 Block CN Express Terminal to Support Kitchener Strike," *Toronto Star*, 9 February 1973, 55.
84 "75 Block CN Express Terminal to Support Kitchener Strike," 55.
85 Milligan, "The Force of All Our Numbers," 71.
86 Nancy Adamson et al., eds., "The Women's Place (Toronto)," *Rise Up! A Digital Archive of Feminist Activism*, https://riseupfeministarchive.ca/activism/organizations/the-womens-place-toronto/.
87 "Dare Strikers Help Mark Women's Day," *Kitchener-Waterloo Record*, 9 March 1973.
88 "CTCU Supports Dare Strikers," *CTC Bulletin*, March 1973, LAC Microfilm Holdings.
89 "Dare Union Organizing Mass Protest," *Kitchener-Waterloo Record*, 14 February 1973, 3; "Plea for General Union Support Made at Dare Demonstration," *Globe and Mail*, 22 March 1973, 57.
90 "Dare Union Organizing Mass Protest," 3.
91 "Plea for General Union Support Made at Dare Demonstration," *Globe and Mail*, 22 March 1973, 57.
92 The march garnered plenty of media attention, likely because it opened with a free concert headlined by Canadian satirist Dave Broadfoot. "Don't Dare Miss This Parade," *Kitchener-Waterloo Record*, n.d., in University of Waterloo Special Collections & Archives, GA 282 Dare Foods Limited, file 4, Dare Strike Clippings – 1972–92; "Dare Union Plans March, Talks Go On," *Kitchener-Waterloo Record*, 30 April 1973; "Dare: A Day of Concern," *Kitchener-Waterloo Record*, n.d., in University of Waterloo Special Collections & Archives, GA 282 Dare Foods Limited, file 4, Dare Strike Clippings – 1972–92.
93 "3,500 Support Dare Strike in Kitchener," *Toronto Star*, 28 May 1973, 34.
94 "3,000 at Dare Rally: Union Near End, Fight Isn't," *Kitchener-Waterloo Record*, 28 May 1973.
95 "Unionist Says Dare Strikers 'Left in Cold,'" *Globe and Mail*, 9 April 1979, 2.

96 "5,000 Union Men March in Support of Dare Strikers," *Globe and Mail*, 28 May 1973, 4. A conflicting estimate claims that five thousand total demonstrators attended the rally.
97 "3,500 Support Dare Strike in Kitchener," 34; "5,000 Union Men March in Support of Dare Strikers," 4.
98 "5,000 Union Men March in Support of Dare Strikers," 4.
99 "No Sign of a Settlement at Dare: A Strike That's a Year and $250,000 Old," *Globe and Mail*, 26 May 1973, 1.
100 "3,000 at Dare Rally: Union Near End, Fight Isn't."
101 "Dare Employees Vote against Having Union," *Toronto Star*, 2 February 1974, D16.
102 "1972 Strike," in University of Waterloo Special Collections & Archives, GA 282 Dare Foods Limited, file 42, 1967 Surrey, BC Strike.
103 Judy Fudge and Eric Tucker, *Labour before the Law: The Regulation of Workers' Collective Action in Canada, 1900–1948* (Toronto: University of Toronto Press, 2001), 285. Coverage guarantees can be found in Article 3 of Dare Foods and Local 264 of the BC&T 1976, 2, in Archives of Ontario RG 7-33 – Company-Union Agreements: Dare Foods (Biscuit Division) Limited. The final agreement between Dare and the UBW before its decertification in 1974 can be found in the same collection as the BC&T agreement in the Archives of Ontario.
104 Dare Foods and Local 264 of the BC&T 1976, Article 3, 6. Whether women's uniforms were improved under the new collective agreement is unclear. Pages 18–19 of the 1976 collective agreement outline that the company was to provide two uniforms to all workers, but there is no detail as to what the women's uniforms looked like.
105 Dare Foods and Local 264 of the BC&T 1976, Article 3, 12.
106 Dare Foods and Local 264 of the BC&T 1976, Article 3, 7.
107 Dare Foods and Local 264 of the BC&T 1976, Article 3, 17.
108 Dare Foods and Local 264 of the BC&T 1976, Article 3, 19–20.
109 Dare Foods and Local 264 of the BC&T, 1976, Schedule A. According to the final collective agreement between the Dare workers and the UBW in 1974, packers earned $3.76 per hour.
110 Joan Sangster, *Demanding Equality: One Hundred Years of Canadian Feminism* (Vancouver: UBC Press, 2021), 335.
111 Rosemary Warskett, "Can a Disappearing Pie Be Shared Equally? Unions, Women, and Wage 'Fairness,'" in *Women Challenging Unions: Feminism, Democracy, and Militancy*, ed. Linda Briskin and Patricia McDermott (Toronto: University of Toronto Press, 1993), 251–2.
112 Patricia McDermott, "Pay Equity Lessons from Ontario, Canada," in *Women, Work and Inequality: The Challenge of Equal Pay in a Deregulated Labour Market*, ed. Jeanne Gregory, Rosemary Sales, and Ariane Hegewisch (London: Palgrave Macmillan, 1999), 142.

113 Aileen McColgan, "Legislating Equal Pay? Lessons from Canada," *Industrial Law Journal* 22, no. 4 (December 1993): 271.
114 Sangster, *Demanding Equality*, 335–7. Ontario's Pay Equity Act has been recognized by feminist activists and scholars as a significant moment in the ongoing struggle for pay equity but has drawn several criticisms since its introduction. Joan Sangster notes that the bill did not account for workplaces with little or no male job comparators, and that litigation stemming from the act proved expensive for both trade unions and individuals. See also McColgan, "Legislating Equal Pay?," where it is argued (among other things) that no strong or consistent enforcement procedures were mandated by the act, despite its requirement that employers take proactive measures to mitigate pay inequity.
115 Neil Guppy and Jennifer Vincent, "The Evolution of Canadian Pay Equity Legislation and the Social Organization of Public Opinion," *American Review of Canadian Studies* 51, no. 2, (2021): 313–14. See Figure 1 in Guppy and Vincent's study for a quantitative overview of the gender pay gap in Canada since 1967, and table 1 in the same study for national estimates of the gender pay gap in 2019. Guppy and Vincent also provide a critical discussion of recent provincial and federal attempts to legislate pay equity on page 321.
116 Judy Darcy and Catherine Lauzon, "The Right to Strike," in Briskin and Yanz, *Union Sisters*, 179.
117 Darcy and Lauzon, "The Right to Strike," 179.
118 Marjorie Griffin Cohen, "Employment and Economy Issues," in Atcheson and Marsden, *White Gloves Off*, 63.
119 "Why Some Strikes Drag On," *Financial Times*, 28 May 1973, 6.
120 Joan Sangster, "Remembering Texpack: Nationalism, Internationalism, and Militancy in Canadian Unions in the 1970s," *Studies in Political Economy* 78, no. 1 (Autumn 2006): 62.

2 The Poet and the Nun: Class-Struggle Feminism in Windsor, Ontario, during the 1970s

SEAN ANTAYA

A coterie of feminist scholars has recently identified significant problems with the ways that the second-wave feminist movement is portrayed in feminist scholarship and by activists within the broader women's movement.[1] Perhaps most prominently, Joan Sangster and Meg Luxton argue forcefully against what they identify as a historical "amnesia" about the nature of the women's movement in the 1970s that distorts both the class-based and class-focused elements of the movement during this period. They maintain that this amnesia raises several questions around the politics of memory and the decline of class analysis and materialist perspectives in the academy and in activist circles.[2]

This chapter functions as a case study to support and build upon these broader arguments about the second wave of the women's movement and how it has been remembered. I examine the history of the women's movement in the city of Windsor, Ontario, during the 1970s and the ways that women took important leadership roles in the development of New Left organizations in that community, such as the Labour Centre (TLC), which functioned as the Windsor branch of the New Tendency (TNT) – an autonomist Marxist organization active mainly in Southern Ontario and in Winnipeg during the mid-1970s that sought to pursue a more libertarian alternative to the Leninist vanguard party model. To do so, I examine the trajectory of two women who were central to these developments: Pat Noonan and Bronwen Wallace. After demonstrating that the women's movement in Windsor was distinctly interwoven with revolutionary working-class politics, I show how this history has been distorted in biographical works on Wallace and Noonan that tend to downplay or misrepresent the role of class-struggle politics in these women's lives and in the women's movement more broadly.

To support my arguments, I rely primarily on newsletters, pamphlets, and internal documents from the organizations of which Noonan and

Wallace were members. These sources are supplemented by interviews with former members of the TNT that I originally conducted as part of a broader study on the New Left in Windsor. Furthermore, if biography has long been an important method for analysing earlier periods of the women's movement, as Linda Kealey demonstrates in her chapter in this volume, my use of a biographical approach is relatively unique in terms of examining the feminist politics of the 1970s in Canada. Such an approach demonstrates how two women with comparatively different backgrounds and life trajectories were both nevertheless drawn to the working-class feminism of this period and became influential leaders. As a result, this chapter reinforces the degree to which this stream of feminism became a powerful and attractive current throughout the 1970s while also demonstrating the heterogeneity of the New Left's personnel through this period.

Existing Interpretations of the Second Wave

Sangster and Luxton each show that many scholars and activists insist upon an interpretation of second-wave feminism that claims that the movement was merely focused on the concerns of liberal middle-class white women.[3] Yet, as both scholars are quick to point out, such an interpretation bears little resemblance to historical realities. They show that women instead forged a movement that could hardly be described as homogeneous and had representation from various "streams" of feminism – including liberal feminism, radical feminism, socialist feminism, and Marxist feminism.[4] Significant sections of the movement were rooted in New Left and labour mobilizations, and many organizations put forward a politics that reflected working-class women's experiences and interests.[5]

In a collaborative article, Sangster and Luxton direct their critique against Nancy Fraser, who despite her own socialist-feminist politics portrays the 1970s women's movement as a relatively homogeneous phenomenon that was ultimately co-opted by capital and subsequently facilitated the development of neoliberalism.[6] To be sure, Sangster and Luxton themselves acknowledge *liberal* feminism's "explicit, structural compatibility" with neoliberalism and recognize that it is this variant of feminism that has become dominant since the 1970s. However, Sangster and Luxton maintain that Fraser's broader historical description of the second wave's relationship to neoliberalism is historically inaccurate and underestimates the degree to which second-wave activists were embedded in working-class struggles. Furthermore, they argue that Fraser's historical narrative hampers contemporary political formations that might benefit from engaging with earlier socialist-feminist, Marxist-feminist, or otherwise working-class feminist traditions by portraying these earlier orientations as irrelevant or non-existent within the second wave.[7] These missteps are not unique to Fraser, however, and merely reflect a much broader collective misremembering. As Luxton argues, even when scholars do recognize a greater diversity of perspectives within the second wave, they neglect to seriously engage with the theoretical complexity of 1970s Marxist-feminist and socialist-feminist thought, which can lead to mischaracterizations that "rang[e] from caricatures to completely incorrect."[8]

In their rejoinder to Fraser, Sangster and Luxton also emphasize the historical importance of the revolutionary Marxist "ultra-left" in articulating a class-struggle-centred feminism. Though such theoretical engagements between feminism and revolutionary left politics were never straightforward or uncontested, they did often result in successful mobilizations and organizing efforts. These efforts also sustained a political horizon that extended beyond capitalism and pushed the larger political imaginary leftward. The absence of an organized far left since the 1980s has thus contributed to the narrowing of the political imaginary and the conflation of socialism with liberalism, and has reinforced the neoliberal mantra that "there is no alternative" to a society based upon market principles.[9]

Unsurprisingly, the historians who have explored women's struggles during the 1970s are more attuned to the complexities of women's class-struggle politics throughout the period, but these studies still constitute a relatively small body of literature within wider feminist scholarship and are often ignored by activists. Labour historians in particular, including Sangster, have done much to rectify the deficiencies in the dominant feminist literature and unravel the richness of women's organizing throughout this period.[10] However, much of this history still remains to be uncovered and analysed in sufficient depth, especially as women's experiences differed substantially by region, organizational structure, strategy, theoretical orientation, and relationship to the broader New Left. Indeed, Luxton's comments from nearly two decades ago that "more historical work needs to be done" on women, labour, and the New Left in Canada during the 1970s are still more or less accurate even if the tide is finally shifting.[11]

My chronicle of Pat Noonan's and Bronwen Wallace's experiences in Windsor therefore builds upon this body of literature, functioning as a case study that corroborates Luxton and Sangster's broader interventions by highlighting the productive ways that feminists embraced a politics of class struggle in Windsor. Not only did they participate in revolutionary organizations concerned with working-class struggles, Wallace and Noonan provided vital leadership in both on-the-ground organizing and complex theoretical debates. By doing so, they represented a politics that was far from middle class, reformist, or liberal, as some commentators would have it.

Pat Noonan and the Women's Liberation Movement

In many ways, the history of the women's movement in Windsor begins with Pat Noonan. Noonan was born in Windsor in 1930. After an undisclosed incident as a teenager, she was sent away to an all-girls Catholic school in London run by the order of Ursuline nuns. When she turned eighteen, she chose to join the order herself. Despite her rebellious nature, she enjoyed the comradery within the convent and deeply felt a duty to serve the downtrodden. During her time in the convent, Noonan became interested in liberation theology after joining the social-justice-oriented group Observe-Judge-Act.[12] Once she returned to Windsor, she got involved with a group of other younger social-justice-minded nuns and left-wing priests with whom she supported progressive causes such as women's right to access abortion, anti-poverty initiatives, peace activism, and solidarity efforts for socialist groups in Latin America. Though her activism caused controversies with more traditional conservative clergy, the Ursulines supported Noonan and allowed her to continue organizing, though she eventually left the order voluntarily in 1970.[13] Noonan became the co-founder of the Women's Liberation Movement (WLM) group in Windsor in May of that same year. Though initially unable to attract many prospective members, the organization grew quickly after a somewhat sympathetic profile in the *Windsor Star*.[14]

Like women's liberation groups elsewhere, the group held meetings for women to share their experiences and work through both personal problems and structural barriers that they faced, organized public panels and debates, and protested sexism in the community.[15] But Noonan was not only involved in women's organizing, she was also connected to the Young Christian Students, a Catholic youth group that organized around social justice issues. There, she played a central role in politicizing young people and bringing them into New Left politics. She and some of her younger converts to left-wing organizing also briefly joined the New Democratic Party's Waffle faction during this period, believing (like many other Canadian New Leftists) that a transformed NDP could potentially become a vehicle for an "independent socialist Canada." Like Noonan, some members of this young cohort, including

Jim Monk and Mark Buckner, ended up playing important roles in TNT after the Waffle's expulsion from the NDP and the formation of TLC in Windsor.[16]

Bronwen Wallace and Workers' Unity Women

At approximately the same time that Noonan was forging an activist milieu in 1970-1, Bronwen Wallace and her partner Ron Baxter moved to Windsor to link up with a very different grouping – a radical rank-and-file organization that was active on the shop floor of the Chrysler factories called Workers' Unity (WU). Both Baxter and Wallace had attended Queen's University and were heavily involved in New Left politics on campus. In high school, Wallace became politicized by the 1962 Cuban Missile Crisis, and subsequently took up the archetypal New Left trajectory, first joining the Combined Universities Campaign for Nuclear Disarmament and then the Student Union for Peace Action once she began her university studies. Wallace also became deeply involved in the women's movement. Most prominently, she helped to establish a co-op daycare at Queen's, and took part in the famous 1970 Vancouver Women's Caucus Abortion Caravan protests in Ottawa, where she and other activists occupied the House of Commons – with Wallace herself giving a speech during the occupation.[17]

Due to both RCMP repression of student groups at Queen's and the changing theoretical trends within the broader student movement, Wallace and Baxter decided to leave campus politics behind. Inspired by Italian autonomist Marxism and other New Left thinkers such as Andre Gorz, both Baxter and Wallace, like much of the student New Left, began to turn toward working-class organizing while at the same time distancing themselves from Old Left organizations such as the Communist Party, NDP, and the trade union bureaucracy. They decided to visit Windsor after getting in touch with Lucy Dumouchelle, whom they had met through a mutual acquaintance active in Kingston's tenant organizing movement. Though they initially visited Windsor only temporarily in the fall of 1970 to investigate WU as part of a cross-country road trip, Wallace and Baxter soon decided that Windsor and WU offered the best and most interesting opportunity to get involved in working-class organizing.[18]

Workers' Unity was a New Left rank-and-file group focused mainly on critiquing the bureaucratic leadership of the United Auto Workers (UAW) and facilitating direct action on the shop floor, believing that unions ought to be made into vehicles for gaining workers' control of production by establishing workers' councils.[19] In this sense, WU was broadly comparable to other 1970s rank-and-file union opposition groups like the League of Revolutionary Black Workers or Teamsters for a Democratic Union, which, in their own ways, sought to democratize the labour movement and wrest control away from an increasingly detached labour bureaucracy that many workers felt had come to dominate union politics in the postwar era. Like WU, these organizations were often infused with the politics and personnel of an increasingly Marxist-oriented New Left.[20]

Once Wallace got involved in WU, she helped establish a women's caucus within the group called Workers' Unity Women (WUW). Alongside Pat Noonan's WLM, WUW was one of the main feminist groups in Windsor, primarily targeting the wives of autoworkers as potential recruits, though the group remained made up of the wives and partners of the core WU members.[21] With Wallace's help, the group maintained a column in the WU newspaper called Salt of the Earth that dealt directly with the broader problems that women face in capitalist society and in their specific roles as autoworkers' wives, though WUW made sure to note that the articles ought to be read by both "women *and* men." WUW emphasized the group's working-class identity, noting that "we are not the version of Women's Liberation that one is given in the media," instead explaining that all articles were written by "wives and friends of autoworkers."[22] Articles used plain language to illustrate concepts such as social reproduction, describing the ways that so-called "women's work" in the home is "essential to every corporation in this society."[23] One article in particular drew an analogy between the "internal maintenance" done by repair workers and janitors inside the factory and the equally important "external maintenance" done by workers' wives inside the home. The article further explained how the socially necessary domestic labour performed by women is devalued in capitalist society because it does not directly "produce anything" despite ultimately being essential for production.[24]

Other WUW articles advocated for establishing a co-op daycare centre similar to the one Wallace had previously helped found at Queen's, and argued for daycare access to become a core demand for the UAW.[25] Alienation within the family was another topic, as WUW pointed out the ways in which factory work creates a disconnect between working men and their families both due to the nature of shift work, which forces workers to be away for odd hours during the week, and because of the mental and physical toll that the work itself takes on factory labourers. WUW noted that marital problems in working-class families could often be linked to these conditions.[26] Though the initial WUW group did not win a wide base of support, compared to the UAW's mainstream, its analyses and overall project did point to a radically different way of confronting women's issues in capitalist society and in relation to the labour movement by incorporating much-needed Marxist-feminist arguments that Wallace had initially honed in the student movement, where women's issues were similarly too often dismissed as secondary or irrelevant to the broader class struggle.[27]

The New Tendency, the Socialist Women's Caucus, and the Women's Place

Workers' Unity disbanded over political differences at the end of 1971, but the remnants of WUW soon merged with Noonan's WLM to form the Socialist Women's Group (SWG).[28] Not long after, the SWG came together with other activist groups in the community to form an organization called the Labour Centre, which soon became to function as the Windsor branch of the New Tendency after connecting with similar New Left organizations elsewhere.[29] The Labour Centre itself was composed of different working groups focused on different organizing initiatives, including a gay liberation organization, a high-school student newspaper, a Palestinian solidarity group, and a new rank-and-file autoworkers' group. After joining TLC as a women's working group, the SWG became the Socialist Women's Caucus (SWC) within the Windsor New Tendency.

The SWC's emergence within TNT came at a time when working-class feminism was quickly becoming a major current within the women's movement in Canada, represented by myriad organizing initiatives across the country that often varied in purpose, strategy, and scope. In British Columbia, for example, women established the Service, Office, and Retail Workers' Union of Canada as an explicitly socialist-feminist union meant to organize predominantly women workers in sectors that had been long ignored by the Canadian labour movement's mainstream, often coming into conflict with the more bureaucratized Canadian Labour Congress–affiliated unions in the process. Similarly, in Ontario, Organized Working Women (OWW) emerged as a cross-union organization meant to link together women in the labour movement into a common organization to combat sexism on the job and within their unions and to provide support and resources to women workers in their struggles against their employers. Notably, OWW engaged in strike-support activities in many important struggles involving women workers in Ontario throughout the second half of the 1970s, including the major strikes at Fleck, INCO, and Puretex.[30]

Starting in the summer of 1972, respected Detroit radical Martin Glaberman became an important mentor to many members of TLC, including Wallace, and helped lead a reading group on Marx's *Capital* for the Windsor activists.[31] As one of C.L.R. James's closest collaborators, Glaberman espoused a distinctive heterodox Marxism that emphasized the working-class self-activity and everyday resistance that took place outside the established Old Left organizations. For James and Glaberman, trade unions and workers' parties in the postwar era had degenerated into repressive bureaucratic organizations complicit in the administration of capitalism and in suppressing genuine working-class militancy from below. This perspective stressed the importance of investigation to uncover the prefigurative "invading socialist society" that existed on the shop floor that took the form of wildcats, sit-downs, slow-downs, sabotage, and other "counter-planning" that indicated that workers were developing the capacities to exercise control over production. Such practices ostensibly laid the groundwork for workers' councils, which would inevitably emerge in the right revolutionary contexts.[32] James, Glaberman, and their collaborators endorsed conducting workplace ethnographies called "workers' inquiries" into these conditions at the point of production. However, inquiries were also produced to examine the particular oppressions of women, racialized workers, and young people – the struggles of whom were seen as no less essential to building a socialist society than those of factory workers.[33] Glaberman himself helped produce a number of inquiries while he was a member of the dissident Johnson-Forest Tendency (JFT) within the Socialist Workers' Party and later as part of his own organizations, such as the Correspondence Publishing Committee, which eventually became Facing Reality after a series of splits.[34] Such inquiries could be used to demonstrate to workers how they could build power to exercise control over production, which would eventually manifest in workers' councils in revolutionary scenarios. It was ultimately this unique stream of Marxism that Wallace, Noonan, and many others in the Windsor New Tendency found most applicable to the particular conditions of the 1970s.[35]

Members of TNT were also informed by the emerging Marxist-feminist debates around social reproduction theory and particularly the theorists associated with the Wages for Housework (WFH) perspective such as Selma James, Mariarosa Dalla Costa, and Sylvia Federici, with whom TNT maintained close contact throughout its existence.[36] One-time wife to C.L.R. James, Selma James had herself been a member of the JFT and had written workers' inquiries on women's oppression and struggles in the home before collaborating with Dalla Costa and Federici.[37] Also influenced by debates within Italian autonomist Marxism, these theorists argued that the women's movement ought to demand wages to compensate for the disproportionate amount of domestic labour performed by women in capitalist society, and later helped create a global WFH network.[38] As in the broader New Left, such perspectives sparked substantial debate within TNT around domestic labour, social reproduction, and how women could best combat sexism and oppression.[39]

On a more concrete level, most of the women in TNT still felt that the previous feminist organizing in Windsor involving the earlier WLM had not sufficiently dealt with economic issues, and they remained unhappy with the popular perception of feminism as a middle-class movement. As a result, the SWC began to become more directly involved in working-class women's struggles and held weekly open meetings that any woman could attend without being a member. At the meetings, the women discussed pamphlets and articles of Marxist-feminist orientation, held guest lectures, and attempted to raise women's consciousness by directly confronting personal problems and linking them to larger issues relating to women's place in society.[40] One of the SWC's first initiatives was the formation of a daycare collective in TLC's headquarters. As noted above, Bronwen Wallace had long promoted the benefits of affordable daycare for women and had experience organizing a co-op daycare at Queen's. Indeed, the daycare collective enabled women to participate in SWC open meetings who otherwise would not have been able to attend due to familial obligations.[41]

During this period, the group also directly supported strikes involving women workers, including the much-publicized Dare Foods strike in Kitchener. As Mason Godden describes in his chapter in this collection, the Dare strike was a *cause célèbre* for the Canadian New Leftists who reoriented toward labour struggles in this period. The Dare workers struck for gender pay equity and improvements to the deplorable working conditions, in which it was not uncommon for workers to faint and vomit while on the job. The picket line, meanwhile, was characterized by "extreme violence," with strikebreakers and police pitted against the strikers and their New Left supporters. When repressive court injunctions stymied strikers' abilities to defend themselves on the picket line, supporters organized a successful boycott of Dare products.[42] In Windsor, the SWC organized the local boycott by picketing and leafletting local grocery stores. The group also arranged for four of the Dare strikers to speak and helped them obtain the "moral and financial support" of the Windsor Labour Council. The SWC, supporters from the open meetings, and male members of TLC also went to

Kitchener to join in a motorcade and support the Dare strikers on the picket line. The SWC similarly joined women workers on the picket line at several strikes in Windsor through this period.[43]

Looking to further broaden and intensify its work, the group founded a women's centre called the Women's Place in early 1973. The Woman's Place deployed a three-pronged strategy of service, education, and research. Service entailed engaging with women's immediate problems and often involved getting women in crisis situations to safety and into contact with lawyers as quickly as possible.[44] The education strategy, meanwhile, was multifaceted. In addition to SWC's continuing study groups geared toward the more dedicated activists, the Women's Place held weekly "drop-in" hours on Tuesday afternoons so that women could stop by to discuss any issues or questions with both Women's Place activists and other non-activist women. Further, the Women's Place held workshops related to domestic labour, sexuality, daycare, and women's experiences at work and in the labour movement. The Women's Place also organized smaller "community day" sessions on similar topics in East Windsor and Downtown Windsor, respectively, to engage with women who would not normally be able to obtain transportation to the TLC office or who felt more comfortable attending events in their own neighbourhoods.[45]

The Women's Place and SWC also conducted detailed investigations into the lives of working-class women. Many of the activists involved in the earlier WLM felt that they had alienated other working-class women with over-the-top rhetoric and actions that did not speak to women's everyday experiences and struggles.[46] Demonstrating the influence of the JFT's workers' inquiries, Women's Place activists sought to learn from the experiences of non-activist women through their open discussions and research. Most prominently, Bronwen Wallace documented her experiences as a white-collar worker in an Unemployment Insurance Commission (UIC) office and as a secretary at the University of Windsor. Wallace sought to identify how white-collar work was equally as repressive as factory work, albeit in different ways, and how white-collar workers might build solidarity with one another to overcome these oppressive conditions. While Wallace's inquiries did not result in any lasting organizing in her workplaces, she did identify important contradictions inherent in office work, particularly in the public sector. At the UIC office, for example, Wallace noted that unlike factory workers, whose on-the-job resistance directly threatened capital, it was the unemployed workers themselves who largely suffered when UIC workers failed to meet their quotas processing claims. This led to a situation where workers would often take their frustrations out on the claimants themselves, and vice versa. The situation was further complicated by the fact that workers with more seniority acted as supervisors, meaning that in many cases union stewards themselves were also supervisors with the ability to discipline workers. Furthermore, Wallace identified a climate of "repressive decorum" wherein supervisors' and managers' ostensibly friendly attitudes masked "whose interests are being served by what." She also took note of the persistent deskilling, automation, and reorganization on the job, which caused layoffs and intensified exploitation for the remaining workers.[47] These discussions on white-collar work reflected broader trends in workplaces and the labour movement during the 1970s as women office workers sought to organize around similar problems across North America.[48] Though Wallace herself was not able to formulate a lasting organizing strategy to counter these conditions, her documentation and inquiries remain prescient in the current economic climate, which is increasingly characterized by so-called "unskilled" jobs in the service sector and where austerity has only intensified the above-identified contradictions in the public sector.

In all the SWC's activities and in TLC generally, Wallace and Noonan played key roles in guiding the direction of the group, writing and editing articles and leaflets, organizing discussions, and recruiting members.[49] However, they believed that social transformation was ultimately a collective and participatory process and always emphasized that it would be the masses of working-class women themselves, and not activist leaders, who had the capacity to transform society in struggles against oppression and exploitation. For this reason, they remained cautious about formulating prescriptive solutions, instead opting to augment and document already-existing struggles and try to build women's capacity to fight collectively for a better world.

Within TNT more broadly, there were tensions between a number of competing theoretical perspectives throughout the life of the organization that were never resolved, and the Socialist Women's Caucus was no different.[50] By mid-1974, a group of women in the organization had become more directly involved with the emerging WFH network and felt that they needed to form an organization completely autonomous from the broader TLC, believing that they would not be able to adequately develop the movement in a "mixed" organization with men, which would involve "male mediation of the struggle."[51] Bronwen Wallace, Pat Noonan, and other women in what would essentially become the Martin Glaberman–aligned faction – called Out of the Driver's Seat – did have some concerns about what they felt was an overemphasis on factory work, which Wallace termed "blue collar chauvinism," by the

Auto Workers Group (AWG) within the Windsor New Tendency and believed there were some problems of sexism in the organization more generally. However, Wallace and Noonan remained within the broader organization for the time being and argued that the WFH perspective was also flawed and in fact reinforced women's subjugated position in relation to domestic labour.[52] The split in TLC mirrored developments in the Toronto branch of TNT, where women similarly left the organization to link up with the global WFH network. While the Toronto WFH enjoyed some organizing successes in the late 1970s, particularly among immigrant women and lesbians, the Windsor branch seems to have fizzled out sometime after 1975.[53]

Radical Legacies and the Politics of Memory

The WFH split signalled the beginning of the end of TNT, which formally disbanded in March of 1975.[54] However, both Noonan and Wallace continued to organize around working-class women's issues and were undeniably shaped by the politics and organizing of this era. In the early 1980s, for example, Pat Noonan put together a popular Feminist Theatre project that promoted feminist ideals in Windsor through both theatre performances and innovative guerilla pop-up performances throughout the community. These performances got rave reviews in local media and garnered a popular following. Noonan continued to fight for a better society her whole life, focusing especially on antiwar and environmental activism in her later years.[55]

Post-New Tendency, Wallace similarly continued organizing around women's issues, though she never joined another socialist organization. Instead, Wallace focused more heavily on her writing, eventually becoming one of Canada's leading poets. When one reads Wallace's poetry, it is clear her time in TNT had a profound impact on her life. The writings bear the mark of her earlier activism and the personal and political relationships that thrived in this period of her life. For example, the Windsor-focused poem "Reclaiming the City" can be read to be as much of a Marxist-feminist statement on men's and women's alienation from their families under capitalism as it is a lament for a former relationship in a particular time and place.[56] "Things" describes a car that TNT member Mike Longmoore kindly helped piece together out of spare parts for Wallace.[57] Most directly, "Food," dedicated to Martin and Jessie Glaberman, fondly recounts the time spent at the Glaberman household discussing organizing and Marxist theory around the dinner table, "where a union man from Bologna might meet up with a woman from a feminist commune in New Mexico." The poem also directly mentions the *Capital* reading group that had been such a formative experience for many members of TLC, recalling the ways in which Martin Glaberman "warmed" the old tome's "cold theory."[58] Her other writings of course convey her continued feminist convictions and perceptiveness to the everyday plight of the working-class that was once the focus of her workers' inquiries and activism within the Women's Place. Wallace also continued to engage with the *Radical America* milieu associated with Glaberman, publishing her poetry in the journal during the early 1980s.[59]

For both Noonan and Wallace, however, these histories of class-struggle feminism have been distorted in ways that contribute to the already-existing inaccurate narratives of the second wave. A valuable recent documentary on Noonan, for example, has relatively little to say about the 1970s despite that period being the high point for feminist organizing in Windsor, with Noonan at the forefront. The documentary does examine Noonan's time in the convent and then her founding of the WLM in 1970. However, after some discussion on the WLM's early organizing experiences, the narrative skips to the 1980s and the founding of the Feminist Theatre project. The only reference to Marxism or class struggle comes in passing, when Noonan recalls that she and other women in the WLM faced intimidation from the RCMP, who accused her of being a Maoist. It is at this point that Noonan offhandedly mentions that she had been a member of a Marxist study group at the time.[60] But the viewer learns nothing explicit about the Socialist Women's Group, TNT, TLC, or the Women's Place or the ways these particular organizations intervened in workplaces and the broader community despite Noonan playing a leading role in these various groupings throughout the 1970s. Such omissions, even if unintentional, misrepresent the nature of the women's movement in the 1970s and the milieu in which these activists were embedded by obfuscating the crucial connections to the New Left and the politics of class struggle.

In Wallace's case, her later activism and literary focus on working-class experience, and particularly the experiences of working-class women, has of course been recognized by biographers and literary critics alike.[61] But her involvement within TLC and TNT still tends to be de-emphasized, portrayed inaccurately, or simply misunderstood if it is discussed at all. A special issue on Wallace in the feminist literary journal *Open Letter*, for example, neglects to explicitly mention TNT or her working-class organizing in Windsor.[62] Her early engagements with Marxism and involvement in revolutionary political organizations are only vaguely referenced in passing.[63] In this narrative, such youthful commitments inevitably gave way to an ostensibly enlightened poststructuralist feminism that necessarily rejected Marxism's "totalizing" framework.[64] It is true that Wallace eventually broke from any overt Marxist perspective later in life, but nothing about this process was inevitable. The framing and dismissals of her earlier Marxism are misplaced, as they tend to juxtapose Wallace's youthful revolutionary activism as completely at odds with her later feminism, implying that her Marxist experiences were incompatible with a feminist analysis and that such politics lacked "gender awareness."[65] Yet, as we have seen, Wallace's women's organizing through the 1970s was always fundamentally intertwined with, rather than opposed to, her heterodox Marxist politics. Wallace herself remained just as critical of overly theoretical "academic feminists" and poststructuralists as she was of Marxists.[66] Also absent in the issue are any references to her earlier workers' inquiries, theorizations of social reproduction, and the explicitly Jamesian political perspectives that highlighted the importance of investigation and prefigurative politics, all of which seem to have played a significant role in her literary development and her poetry, in which documentations of working-class experience became such an important focus.

A better but still flawed presentation of Wallace's politics comes across in the work of Gloria Nixon-John. In her otherwise comprehensive study of the relationship between Wallace's poetry, country music, and working-class experience, Nixon-John simply describes "the Labour Centre Organization" as a group that "infiltrated the factory to report about conditions to the Labor Commission (UIC)."[67] But this statement is ultimately a serious misrepresentation of TNT's activities, as TNT activists did not "infiltrate" factories. Most of the members who worked at the factories did so because those were simply the best jobs that they could get in Windsor at that time and were relatively easy to obtain; even some of the members who did have university educations, such as Mike Longmoore, ended up working in the factories their entire lives long after the TNT had disbanded.[68] Even more egregious is the claim that the workers' inquiries were reports for a government commission – the UIC was simply the unemployment insurance office that Wallace worked at – they were a particular method of Marxist organizing that had originated in the JFT as noted above. Finally, Wallace herself wrote nearly as much about white-collar work and domestic labour as other members wrote about factory work.

In her longer biography of Wallace, upon which the above article is based, Nixon-John does recognize the influence of Marxism on Wallace's early development.[69] However, as in the *Open Letter* analyses, she largely misunderstands the variant of Marxism that Wallace actually practised, again often framing the seemingly earlier Marxism and later feminism in opposition with one another.[70] A serious engagement with James and Glaberman's distinct theoretical orientation is entirely absent in the biography; indeed, despite Glaberman's crucial influence on and close friendship with Wallace, his name does not appear once. Such errors and omissions thus reveal an inability to seriously engage with the complexities that characterize the historical relationships between labour, feminism, and the left and with the historic juncture in which Wallace was engaged – an unfortunately common trend among the scholarship identified above by Sangster and Luxton.

Crucially, in both Noonan and Wallace's instances, the distinctly *revolutionary* nature of their politics is also seriously diminished. For New Left organizations like TNT, despite their small size and often modest organizing results, the ultimate goal was nothing short of the total socialist transformation of society. These politics are completely misrepresented when they are collapsed into an amorphous "activism." Such seemingly innocuous characterizations in fact desaturate and warp readers' perceptions of the past and its complexities and only further limit political imaginations in the present.

It is clear, then, that the inaccuracies and lacunae that characterize the biographical work on Noonan and Wallace ultimately reinforce historical amnesia about the nature of the feminist movement during the 1970s discussed at the start of the chapter. Scholars must therefore remain vigilant and push back against these erroneous misunderstandings of the second wave while undertaking further case studies and comparative analyses of women's organizing experiences during this period. It is only by doing so that we can appreciate the full breadth of the second wave and successfully write the histories of the many remarkable women who have been at the forefront of class-struggle politics in their respective communities.

NOTES

1 Throughout the chapter I use "second wave" as a shorthand for the women's movement in the 1970s. However, drawing on the work of other historians, I am otherwise critical of the "wave" periodization. See, e.g., Joan Sangster, "Radical Ruptures: Feminism, Labor, and the Left in the Long Sixties in Canada," *American Journal of Canadian Studies* 40, no. 1 (2010): 2.

2 Both Luxton and Sangster address this problem in multiple articles. See Meg Luxton, "Feminism as a Class Act: Working-Class Feminism

and the Women's Movement in Canada," *Labour/Le Travail* 48 (2001): 63–88; Meg Luxton, "Marxist-Feminism and Anti-capitalism: Reclaiming Our History, Reanimating Our Politics," *Studies in Political Economy* 94 (2014): 137–60; Sangster, "Radical Ruptures"; Joan Sangster, "Creating Popular Histories: Reinterpreting 'Second-Wave' Canadian Feminism," *Dialectical Anthropology* 39 (2015): 381–404; Joan Sangster and Meg Luxton, "Feminism, Co-Optation, and the Problems of Amnesia: A Response to Nancy Fraser," *Socialist Register* 49 (2013): 288–309. See also the responses to some of these arguments: Susan Ferguson, "A Response to Meg Luxton's 'Marxist-Feminism and Anti-capitalism,'," *Studies in Political Economy* 95 (2015): 161–8; Rebecca Schein, "Hegemony Not Co-optation: For a Usable History of Feminism," *Studies in Political Economy* 94 (2014): 169–76; Linda Carty, "A Genealogy of Marxist Feminism in Canada," *Studies in Political Economy* 94 (2014): 177–84; Luxton's subsequent reply, Meg Luxton, "Reclaiming Marxist Feminism: A Response," *Studies in Political Economy* 95 (2015): 161–72. Also useful is Leah Vosko, "The Pasts (and Futures) of Feminist Political Economy in Canada: Reviving the Debate," *Studies in Political Economy* 68 (2002): 55–83. Earlier attempts to grapple with historical mischaracterizations of the women's movement in the 1970s include Lise Vogel, "Telling Tales: Historians of Our Own Lives," *Journal of Women's History* 2, no. 3 (1991): 89–101.

3 Sangster, "Creating Popular Histories," 384; Luxton, "Marxist-Feminism and Anti-capitalism," 140. Targets of their criticisms include, e.g., Victoria Bromley, *Feminisms Matter: Debates, Theories, Activism* (Toronto: University of Toronto Press, 2012); Vanaja Dhruvarajan and Jill Vickers, *Gender, Race, and Nation: A Global Perspective* (Toronto: University of Toronto Press, 2002); Janine Brodie, *Politics on the Margins: Restructuring and the Canadian Women's Movement* (Halifax: Fernwood Press, 1995).

4 This is a central theme in Sangster, "Radical Ruptures"; Sangster, "Creating Popular Histories"; Luxton, "Marxist-Feminism and Anti-capitalism."

5 Luxton, "Feminism as a Class Act."

6 Sangster and Luxton, "Feminism, Co-optation, and the Problems of Amnesia"; see also Nancy Fraser, "Feminism, Capitalism and the Cunning of History," *New Left Review* 2, no. 56 (2009): 97–117.

7 Sangster and Luxton, "Feminism, Co-optation, and the Problems of Amnesia," 288–96, 300–4. Rebecca Schein points out that the historical amnesia identified by Sangster and Luxton is itself the product of liberal feminism's hegemony in the neoliberal era. See Schein, "Hegemony Not Co-optation," 170–3.

8 Luxton, "Marxist-Feminism and Anti-capitalism," 140.

9 Sangster and Luxton, "Feminism, Co-optation, and the Problems of Amnesia," 300–4.

10 Writing on women and labour in the 1970s in Canada includes Joan Sangster, "Remembering Texpack: Nationalism, Internationalism, and Militancy in Canadian Unions in the 1970s," *Studies in Political Economy* 78 (2006): 41–66; Julia Smith, "An 'Entirely Different' Kind of Union: The Service, Office, and Retail Workers' Union of Canada (SORWUC), 1972–1986," *Labour/Le Travail* 73 (2014): 23–65; Heather Jon Maroney, "Feminism at Work," *New Left Review* 141 (1983): 51–71; Julie White, *Mail & Female: Women and the Canadian Union of Postal Workers* (Toronto: Thompson Education, 1990); Pamela Sugiman, *Labour's Dilemma: The Gender Politics of Auto Workers in Canada, 1937–1979* (Toronto: University of Toronto Press, 1994); Linda Briskin and Lynda Yanz, eds., *Union Sisters: Women in the Labour Movement* (Brampton: Charters, 1983).

11 Luxton, "Feminism as a Class Act," 84. Recent writing on the Canadian New Left more broadly includes Peter Graham and Ian McKay, *Radical Ambition: The New Left in Toronto* (Toronto: Between the Lines, 2019); Ian Milligan, *Rebel Youth: 1960s Labour Unrest, Young Workers, and New Leftists in English Canada* (Vancouver: UBC Press, 2014); Bryan Palmer, *Canada's 1960s: The Ironies of Identity in a Rebellious Era* (Toronto: University of Toronto Press, 2009), 245–309.

12 Observe-Judge-Act (sometimes written See-Judge-Act) was originally a social justice method and slogan developed by the left-leaning Belgian Catholic clergyman Joseph Cardijn, founder of the Young Christian Workers. See Michael de la Bedoyere, *The Cardijn Story* (London: Catholic Book Club, 1958).

13 Jim Monk, interview by the author, Amherstburg, Ontario, 2 May2, 2017; Mike Longmoore, interview by the author, Windsor, Ontario, 29 June 29, 2017; and the documentary on Noonan's life, *This Is What a Feminist Sounds Like*, directed by Audra Macintyre and Kim Nelson (Windsor, 2012), http://www.thisiswhatafeministsoundslike.com/#film.

14 *This Is What a Feminist Sounds Like*.

15 *This Is What a Feminist Sounds Like*. On the women's liberation movement in Ontario more broadly, see, e.g., Nancy Adamson, "Feminists, Libbers, Lefties, and Radicals: The Emergence of the Women's Liberation Movement," in *A Diversity of Women: Ontario, 1945–1980*, ed. Joy Parr (Toronto: University of Toronto Press, 1995), 252–80.

16 Monk interview. On the Waffle, see John Bullen, "The Ontario Waffle and the Struggle for an Independent Socialist Canada: Conflict within the NDP," *Canadian Historical Review* 64, no. 2 (1983): 189–215.

17 Bronwen Wallace, "The Cuban Missile Crisis and Me," in *Arguments with the World*, ed. Joanne Page (Kingston: Quarry Press, 1992), 26–37; Gloria Nixon-John, "A Place of Rupture: The Life and Poetry of Bronwen Wallace" (PhD diss., Michigan State University, 2001), 169. On the

significance of the Abortion Caravan protests, see Christabelle Sethna and Steve Hewitt, "Clandestine Operations: The Vancouver Women's Caucus, the Abortion Caravan, and the RCMP," *Canadian Historical Review* 90, no. 3 (2009): 463–95.

18 Ron Baxter, interview by the author, Windsor, Ontario, 31 May 2017.
19 Sean Antaya, "The New Left at Work: Workers' Unity, the New Tendency, and Rank-and-File Organizing in Windsor, Ontario, in the 1970s," *Labour/Le Travail* 85 (2020): 60–72.
20 See, e.g., the collection by Aaron Brenner, Robert Brenner, and Cal Winslow, eds., *Rebel Rank and File: Labor Militancy and Revolt from Below During the Long 1970s* (New York: Verso, 2010).
21 [Bronwen Wallace?], Workers' Unity Timeline, internal TNT document, Windsor, n.d. [1973], personal collection of Gary Kinsman (hereafter PCGK); and "Jane Doe Study Group – HerStory," internal Labour Centre document, Windsor, n.d. [1973?], PCGK.
22 Salt of the Earth, *Workers' Unity*, May 1971.
23 The quote is from "Two for the Price of One," Salt of the Earth, *Workers' Unity*, June 1971. However, this was a general theme across most Salt of the Earth articles.
24 "Two for the Price of One."
25 Salt of the Earth, May 1971; "Daycare Soon," Salt of the Earth, *Workers' Unity*, September 1971.
26 Salt of the Earth, May 1971.
27 For a comprehensive history of sexism on the shop floor and within the UAW itself and the ways in which women fought to improve these conditions, see Sugiman, *Labour's Dilemma*. On women's struggles against sexism within the New Left, see Palmer, *Canada's 1960s*, 297–304.
28 "Jane Doe Study Group – HerStory."
29 On TNT, see Antaya, "The New Left at Work"; John Huot, "Autonomist Marxism and Workplace Organizing in Canada in the 1970s," *Upping the Anti* 18 (2016), http://uppingtheanti.org/journal/article/18-autonomist-marxism/; Gary Kinsman, "The Politics of Revolution: Learning from Autonomist Marxism," *Upping the Anti* 1 (2005): 44–53; Gary Kinsman, "Recovering the History of Canadian Autonomist Marxism," *Upping the Anti* 19 (2017), http://uppingtheanti.org/journal/article/19-recovering-the-history-of-canadian-autonomist-marxism/.
30 For a general assessment of this working-class feminist current, see Maroney, "Feminism at Work," 51–71. Of course, earlier periods of women's organizing also saw strong linkages at times between working-class politics, the left, and struggles for women's emancipation, as the chapters by Linda Kealey and June Hannam in this volume make clear.
31 Monk interview; Baxter interview.

32 See, e.g., C.L.R. James, Grace Lee, and Pierre Chaulieu, *Facing Reality* (Detroit: Bewick Editions, 1974); C.L.R. James, *State Capitalism and World Revolution* (Chicago: Charles H. Kerr, 1986).
33 On the history of workers' inquiries, see Jamie Woodcock, "The Workers' Inquiry from Trotskyism to Operaismo: A Political Methodology for Investigating the Workplace," *Ephemera: Theory and Politics in Organization* 14, no. 3 (2014): 493–513.
34 Kent Worcester, "C.L.R. James and the American Century," in *C.L.R. James: His Intellectual Legacies*, ed. Selwyn R. Cudjoe and William E. Cain (Boston: University of Massachusetts Press, 1995), 176.
35 See the discussion in Antaya, "The New Left at Work," 74–6; and the pamphlet by Ron Baxter, Mark Buckner, Sheila Dillon, Jim Monk, Pat Noonan, Stephen Sherriffs, Bronwen Wallace, and David Walsh, *Out of the Driver's Seat: Marxism in North America Today* (Windsor: Mile One, 1974).
36 Wally Dougherty and Suzy Vanderloop, "Leadership, Collective Practise & the New Tendency," *Newsletter* 3 (1973): 11.
37 See, for instance, Mary Brant and Ellen Santori (pseud. of Selma James), *A Woman's Place* (Detroit: Correspondence, 1954).
38 Mariarosa Dalla Costa and Selma James, *The Power of Women and the Subversion of the Community* (Bristol: Falling Wall Press, 1975); Christina Rousseau, "Housework and Social Subversion: Wages, Housework, and Feminist Activism, in 1970s Italy and Canada" (PhD thesis, York University, 2016).
39 The questions around social reproduction and domestic labour provoked vigorous debate on the left throughout the late 1970s and 1980s. Arguably the most productive of these debates occurred in Canada. See the collections by Michele Barrett and Roberta Hamilton, eds., *The Politics of Diversity: Feminism, Marxism, and Nationalism* (London: Verso, 1986); Bonnie Fox, ed., *Hidden in the Household: Women's Domestic Labour under Capitalism* (Toronto: Women's Press, 1980); and the earlier provocations by Margaret Benston, "The Political Economy of Women's Liberation," *Monthly Review* 21, no. 4 (1969): 13–27; Charnie Guettel, *Marxism & Feminism* (Toronto: Women's Press, 1974).
40 Pat Noonan, "The Women's Movement," internal TLC document (Windsor, 1974), PCGK; "Jane Doe Study Group – HerStory."
41 "Jane Doe Study Group – HerStory."
42 Milligan, *Rebel Youth*, 131–2.
43 "Jane Doe Study Group – HerStory"; Baxter et al., *Out of the Driver's Seat*, 11–12.
44 "Working Group Report: The Women's Place," internal TLC document (Windsor, 1973), PCGK.
45 "Working Group Report: The Women's Place."

46 Baxter et al., *Out of the Driver's Seat*, 8–12.
47 Bronwen Wallace, "White Collar Blues," *Newsletter* 2 (1973): 2–8; Bronwen Wallace, "White Collar Blues Part II," internal TLC document (Windsor, 1973), PCGK; Baxter et al., *Out of the Driver's Seat*, 42–6.
48 See, e.g., Lane Windham, *Knocking on Labor's Door: Union Organizing in the 1970s and the Roots of a New Economic Divide* (Chapel Hill: University of North Carolina Press, 2017), 152–77.
49 "Jane Doe Study Group – HerStory"; Noonan, "The Women's Movement"; Baxter interview; Monk interview.
50 On these different theoretical orientations, see Antaya, "The New Left at Work," 84–7.
51 Windsor Auto Workers Group, "Notes on Acknowledging the Class Perspective: Wages for Housework – Documents #2," internal AWG document (Windsor, 1975), 2, PCGK.
52 Bronwen Wallace, "A Typewriter Is Not a Punch Press but …," *Newsletter* 5 (1974): 18; "The Labour Centre Meeting, January 20, 1974," internal TLC document (Windsor, 1974), PCGK; "Notes from the Underground," internal TLC document (Windsor, n.d. [1973?]), PCGK; "The Labour Centre Meeting Minutes of December 9, 1973," internal TLC document (Windsor, 1973), PCGK; Jim Monk, "Marxism and Historical Movements," internal TLC document (Windsor, 1974), PCGK.
53 On the Toronto WFH and the offshoot, Wages Due Lesbians, see Rousseau, "Housework and Social Subversion," 148–88; Christina Rousseau, "Wages Due Lesbians: Visibility and Feminist Organizing in 1970s Canada," *Gender, Work, & Organization* 22, no. 4 (2015): 364–74. Due to the lack of remaining textual sources, it is difficult to determine exactly when the Windsor WFH branch dissolved, though two documents confirm it was still active through 1975. See Windsor Auto Workers Group, "Notes on Acknowledging the Class Perspective," 10; Windsor Wages for Housework Collective, "Portrait of a Canadian Housewife," *Activist* 15, nos. 1–2 (1975): 10–20.
54 Antaya, "The New Left at Work," 84.
55 "This Is What a Feminist Sounds Like"; Baxter interview.
56 Bronwen Wallace, *Common Magic* (Ottawa: Oberon Press, 1985), 68–71. "Nightwork" draws on similar themes. See Bronwen Wallace, *The Stubborn Particulars of Grace* (Toronto: McLelland & Stewart, 1987), 92–4.
57 Wallace, *The Stubborn Particulars of Grace*, 95–8.
58 Wallace, *The Stubborn Particulars of Grace*, 50–3.
59 See Bronwen Wallace, "Nightshift No. 2 and Overtime No. 3," *Radical America* 16, nos. 1–2 (1982): 99; Bronwen Wallace, "The Housewife's Poem and These Things Happen," *Radical America* 16, no. 4–5 (1982): 45; Bronwen Wallace, "Shopping Around," *Radical America* 16, no. 6 (1982): 45.
60 *This Is What a Feminist Sounds Like.*

61 See, e.g., Gloria Nixon-John, "A Place of Rupture," 167–80; Gloria Nixon-John, "Getting the Word Out: The Country of Bronwen Wallace and Emmylou Harris," in *The Women of Country Music: A Reader*, ed. Charles Wolfe and James Akenson (Lexington: University Press of Kentucky, 2003), 46–60; Debb Hurlock, "Cadences of Voices, Conversations of Change: The Poetry of Bronwen Wallace" (MA thesis, Lakehead University, 1996).
62 Susan Rudy Dorscht and Eric Savoy, eds., "Particular Arguments: A Special Issue on Bronwen Wallace," *Open Letter* 7, no. 9 (Winter 1991).
63 Mary di Michele and Barbara Godard, "'Patterns of Their Own Particular Ceremonies': A Conversation in an Elegiac Mode," *Open Letter* 7, no. 9 (Winter 1991): 43–5.
64 Di Michele and Godard, "Patterns," 55; Susan Rudy Dorscht and Eric Savoy, "Introduction," *Open Letter* 7, no. 9 (Winter 1991): 6.
65 Di Michele and Godard, "Patterns," 44.
66 Janice Williamson, "'The Landscape from How I See My Poems Moving': An Interview with Bronwen Wallace," *Open Letter* 7, no. 9 (Winter 1991): 29–30.
67 Nixon-John, "Getting the Word Out," 48. A few paragraphs later Nixon-John erroneously repeats that the group would "infiltrate and spy" for the government commission.
68 Antaya, "The New Left at Work," 78, 84, 87; Longmoore interview.
69 Nixon-John, "A Place of Rupture."
70 Nixon-John, "Getting the Word Out," 8–17, 170–7.

3 "Most Women Would Prefer to Keep Their Mouths Shut": Challenging Sexual Harassment within the Canadian Broadcasting Corporation, 1981-1986

BARBARA M. FREEMAN

In the 1970s and 1980s, human rights decisions and changing labour legislation and policies supported improved working conditions for women in the federal public service, Crown corporations, and other government-regulated agencies, as well as in the professions and private industry, mainly because of pressure from the women's movement.[1] Feminists inside and outside of the Canadian Broadcasting Corporation (CBC) successfully lobbied for an equal opportunity employment policy there that included a modified affirmative action plan, and for an end to sexist attitudes in their offices and in programming.[2] The next step was a policy to end sexual harassment within the CBC, which management treated as a separate issue, beginning in 1981.

At the time, sexual harassment in the workplace was becoming a contentious issue, so much so that by the late 1980s, the federal and provincial human rights commissions were banning it, courts were hearing litigious cases, and unions were producing strategies to combat it.[3] This chapter will examine the earliest drafts of the CBC's sexual harassment policy, with their emphases on definitions and procedures, because they affected the way management handled internal complaints for decades afterwards. The policy did not protect CBC personnel of any rank from harassment from outsiders, a gap that has repercussions today.

This chapter is part of a larger research project on women broadcast journalists who worked in English news and current affairs from the 1940s to the turn of the twenty-first century. The CBC's employment policies aligned with developing government procedures and laws that it was obliged to follow as a Crown corporation.[4] Nevertheless, my research has found that bureaucratic delays in formulating and implementing an effective sexual harassment policy meant that, in the interim, its female employees, including the journalists, remained vulnerable. Their complaints were resolved only if managers listened to them and then followed the procedures designed to deal with them effectively.

Joan Sangster's evolving feminist-materialist approach to the history of Canadian women in the labour force and the women's movements has influenced my own research, even though I focus on predominantly middle-class media workers rather than working-class women and their occupations.[5] Capitalism, government control, and patriarchy have all shaped the lives of female journalists, much as they have wage-earning women in other industries. As a historian and former news reporter, I examine gender issues in context, grounded in the lively interplay between the women's movements and female newsworkers in the media during the nineteenth and twentieth centuries.[6]

In the 1970s and early 1980s, CBC managers and the women in news, current affairs, and related departments were predominantly white. The female journalists regarded sexism as the main barrier to equality and sexual harassment as a threat that undermined their ambitions. As Sangster has pointed out, the feminist activists of the day were aware of the inequities of class, race, and other forms of discrimination that hurt women.[7] However, that perspective did not really register in the upper echelons of the CBC, where the rhetoric of non-discrimination, "regardless of such considerations" as sex, race, and religion, merely signalled acknowledgment of contemporary human rights legislation rather than pre-1980s concepts of what we now refer to as the intersectionality of more than one identity in one person.[8]

The sexual harassment of female journalists has not been the subject of historical study in Canada before now, although it has been a factor in their careers anecdotally.[9] The academic literature has centred on the work they produced and the constraints they experienced as women in the print media, or has directly compared gender equity in newspaper and television newsrooms.[10] With the exception of policy and culture, historians have largely neglected broadcasting in English Canada, including the careers of women and minorities in the field.[11] The few published studies demonstrate that male broadcasting executives, with their traditional attitudes toward the sexes, tried, not always successfully, to keep women in their domestic place on the air and in the studio.[12]

The CBC management documents in Library and Archives Canada (LAC), some of them newly released, reveal that senior managers started formulating a sexual harassment policy in 1981, one that took many drafts over the next five years. While this file is not very extensive, the policy versions in it clearly map out the process, and the time it took, and are important for that reason.[13] Although CBC employees belonged to several unions and associations, these records do not track many exchanges with them.[14]

Aside from the management holdings at LAC, the late Betty Zimmerman, the director of Radio Canada International between 1979 and 1989, deposited her papers at Carleton University, including a few that also dealt with sexual harassment.[15] In addition to this material, I have inserted compelling personal narratives from four women who worked at the CBC, a publicist and three journalists. Their supervisors or colleagues sexually harassed and/or assaulted three of them, and the fourth woman observed management's response to similar cases. These accounts are strictly from the women's memories, without supporting documentation. It either does not exist or is not available to researchers because archived personnel records are still confidential.

As Sangster writes, feminist oral history is a methodology that acknowledges the lived experiences of the women who are telling their own stories as they reflect on how they managed their personal and working lives during specific times and within their own cultural circumstances. She has also raised questions of privilege, power, and ethics regarding the researcher's relationships with her subjects.[16] I shared similar career experiences with the journalists I interviewed, but I approach their narratives as an historian, not as a colleague. I have shown them my drafts to make sure they are comfortable with my version of their accounts of sexual harassment. These journalists, who worked as pragmatic fact-finders used to being in the public eye, vividly remembered these unsettling incidents, which still rankle. Specifically, they were also speaking frankly as newswomen who were once a minority in the CBC, where sexual harassment was still an issue even as the overtly sexist culture of journalism was beginning to change.

"Despicable!" The 1970s

Decades before feminists coined the term "sexual harassment," a male boss's sexual coercion of a female employee could be damaging for both of them, especially if he was prominent and it became public knowledge (see Bryden in this collection). More often, however, this common behaviour went unreported or unpunished. In 1979, in the first Canadian book on the subject, Constance Backhouse and Leah Cohen defined sexual harassment as "any sexually-oriented practice that endangers a woman's job, undermines her job performance and threatens her economic livelihood."[17] They explained that it was a rampant product of unequal power relations in the workplace, and ranged from sexist innuendo and unwanted attention to sexual assault. If rejected, the harassers suddenly complained about their accusers' work performances or otherwise tried to undermine them.[18] Backhouse later recalled that most of their female interview subjects either remained silent when harassed or strove to maintain their privacy through anonymity and other strategies. The men saw it as harmless flirtation, accused women of using their sexuality to their advantage, or claimed they were lying.[19]

There were no official policies against sexual harassment at the CBC or anywhere else in the federal public service in the early 1970s. As Sangster has revealed, the Royal Commission on the Status of Women (1967–70) heard about it only privately, mostly in letters from misogynist men who defended their behaviour.[20] In 1975, a task force at the CBC completed a report on equal opportunities for women there, but there was no mention of sexual harassment in its recommendations.[21]

In 1976, Jennifer Fry, then in her early twenties, accepted a job as an assistant to the producer at the CBC in Ottawa. Her duties included researching news items, contacting potential interviewees, and otherwise helping to organize the program. From the moment she arrived, a particular man targeted her for attention, touching her, putting his arm around her, or caressing her, even after she asked him to stop. These incidents occurred in front of colleagues. "I had people around who never came to my rescue." Fry did not know what to do about this man, who was older than she was with an established, respectable reputation.

One Saturday morning, a year into her job, he phoned her at her apartment. He claimed that someone had just offered him an attractive new position, he was very torn about it, and he wanted to discuss it with her privately right away. She told him to wait until Monday at the office, but he sounded tearful, so she relented. She phoned a friend and asked her to call her after he arrived to make sure she was okay. His visit went well at first, and when the friend called, Fry signalled that she was fine. When she hung up, he asked if that was someone checking on her. She denied it, and then he attacked her. "So he started to hit on me, physically. I physically had to push him off, physically push him away. And he kept coming at me. I said, 'I share a wall with my next-door neighbours and I'm going to bang on the wall and start to scream if you don't leave.' But he kept going, so I said, 'I'm going to call your wife and tell your wife what you are doing. Right now.' And he finally left."

At work the following Monday, a supervisor took Fry aside and told her that the same man had complained that she was not pulling her weight, was too slow, and was neglecting some of her duties. "I just looked at him and I said, 'What are you talking about?' ... I was doing what I was supposed to be doing, big time ... I just thought, my God, I'd better up my game." While she confided in close friends, she kept silent at work about the assault because she was afraid that her colleagues either would not believe her or would blame her.

Her attacker never bothered her again, even when they had to work together later on. "He knew better. I would *physically* hurt him ... I used to think, you are dirt beneath my feet ... So that was a terrible experience for me, and I say it because *my father had recently died*, I was in my own apartment for the first time, and I was really naïve, obviously, and this person – he was so despicable to have picked on someone like me. Despicable!"[22]

It would be another five years before management decided to implement a policy to deal with such occurrences, the succeeding drafts slowly following changes in the law. Legally, sexual harassment was, for a time, considered a form of gender discrimination and, beginning in 1977, contrary to federal human rights legislation. In time, the provinces followed its lead.[23]

A "Totally Unacceptable" Form of Intimidation, 1981-2

In December 1981, the assistant general manager of the CBC's English Services Division, Clive Mason, sent a *proposed* policy on sexual harassment to the managers in charge of human resources (HR), and to its Office of Equal Opportunity (OEO), which management established after the CBC Task Force on Women recommended it. Mason referred to this first proposal as "a sequel to the equal opportunity policy and affirmative action program," confirming that it was never a part of those particular initiatives.

Mason noted that sexual harassment had become "a subject of increasing public discussion and concern," but that there were problems in developing a policy. They involved the definition of sexual harassment, how to explain the procedures so that management and staff understood them, and the line of responsibility for handling these cases. He asked the managers to circulate the draft and provide him with feedback, including "the viewpoint of a representative group of women." The CBC was a largely male-dominated institution, but, starting in the early 1970s, female employees in several cities had organized themselves locally and then nationally, the better to approach management about their workplace concerns.[24]

Initially, the HR policymakers clearly demonstrated blind spots, assuring their director, R.J. Gurney, that the word "repeatedly" in reference to acts of sexual harassment was important to the definition of it.

The use of the word would "preclude accidental acts from being misinterpreted." Furthermore, regarding "an act that has been consciously rebuffed and never repeated: given the benefit of the doubt for its intent, is not considered to be harassment." The final point, reflecting a common bias against women, stated, "It is not unknown for females to register complaints in retaliation for some other management action. Accordingly, the definition has been arrived at to protect both parties."[25]

There were other cultural assumptions in play as well, which might have left Indigenous women even less protected. One regional manager had advised Gurney not to engage employees in the CBC Northern Service in the consulting process in the same way as the staff working in other regions. In a separate note to Mason, Gurney said this manager told him that, because of "cultural differences with Indigenous employees," the draft policy would probably "not be relevant to them" and their opinions "could probably be better gleaned through individual input as opposed to group sessions." The note did not mention how many Indigenous women worked for the Northern Service, or in what capacity, or explain their perceived cultural differences.[26]

This first sexual harassment policy consisted of four paragraphs. It stated that sexual harassment was a "totally unacceptable" form of intimidation that the CBC would not tolerate. "Sexual harassment is any conduct of a sexual nature – gestures, comments, advances, requests or threats – which is repeatedly imposed on another person and which creates discomfort, embarrassment, anxiety, or physical, mental or moral suffering." It promised confidentiality to what it termed "victims" of sexual harassment, and left it up to senior managers and the HR department to make sure that all employees adhered to the policy.[27]

Karen Flanagan McCarthy, then a twenty-seven-year-old publicist for TV Current Affairs in Toronto, sent a memo to her immediate supervisor, Maureen O'Donnell, who had circulated the draft to her staff. Within the previous eighteen months, a senior male executive had subjected Flanagan McCarthy to crude, masturbatory comments during a telephone call, whereupon she immediately hung up in shock. Afterwards, he acted as if it had never happened, and did not harass her again, but she heard later that he was behaving just as badly with other women. Eventually, after some women complained, the man left the CBC, but management did not tell them why.[28]

Flanagan McCarthy did not mention him in her memo to O'Donnell, but she did object to giving responsibility for enforcing the sexual harassment policy to senior managers. She compared it to "registering complaints of police brutality with the police department. The victim has little chance of a just redress." She went on to point out that "sexual harassment is directly related to power." Most people can deal themselves with sexual harassment from a peer, she wrote, but it was more difficult to rebuff a supervisor, who is often the person who would recommend a female employee for professional advancement, whether she was on staff, working as a casual, or on contract. She wondered how the managers could guarantee confidentiality in such circumstances. She declared, "Most women would prefer to keep their mouths shut rather than risk losing their jobs, or jeopardizing their chances of advancement." Even if the woman stayed quiet about the harassment, she said, there was no guarantee of protection.

Flanagan McCarthy also argued that the word "repeatedly" should be deleted from the policy because, otherwise, instances of one-time abuse would not qualify as harassment; for example, when a supervisor turned down a job seeker because that person refused to provide sexual favours. While she found it encouraging that the CBC considered it a "totally unacceptable form of intimidation," she added, "(Are there acceptable forms?)." She wanted the CBC to recognize that there was a problem with sexual harassment and that it was serious about enforcing a policy. She suggested the appointment of an independent ombudsman, as recommended in the 1975 *Report of the CBC Task Force on the Status of Women*. She also said that she had discussed this policy draft with other female colleagues but wanted it circulated more widely. "It will be valuable, I think, to hear from the greatest number of employees possible before any definite policy is written."[29] Her response to the initial draft is worth noting because it was the most detailed of the few responses from female employees that are available in the CBC archives for the period and possibly influenced subsequent changes in definition at least.

"An Abuse of Power," 1982–3

It appears that management circulated the version that Flanagan McCarthy saw, or possibly the next draft, to more female and male employees. A month later, the manager of career opportunity, Sylvia Moss, told Gurney in HR that "the response to the policy was surprisingly voluminous, articulate and supportive." Most of the feedback involved its application, who would take responsibility for it, and how to handle complaints. Moss attached an updated version sent to the directors of each CBC region. As Flanagan McCarthy had suggested, the policy writers had deleted the words "repeatedly" and "unacceptable" in reference to sexual harassment.[30]

This updated draft did not use the expression "abuse of power," but it covered two types of scenarios where it was evident: first, instances where "submission to or rejection of such conduct by an individual affects, either explicitly or implicitly, employment or conditions of employment of the individual"; second, when "such conduct has the purpose or effect of interfering with an individual's work, performance, or creating an intimidating, hostile, offensive/or embarrassing working environment."[31] This particular wording was similar to the language used in the developing case law on sexual harassment.[32]

At the CBC, this definition or close approximations of it survived subsequent drafts and essentially became the template, but the line of managerial responsibility for examining these complaints, and recommended ways of enforcing the policy, changed over several versions. There were still fears that some women might make false or mistaken accusations, so this draft stated the importance of considering the positions of both parties. It deleted the word "victims" and replaced it with "employees who believe they have been subjected to sexual harassment." It promised them "prompt action," but the CBC would also "exercise extreme care to protect and respect the rights of both the alleged offenders and those registering complaints."

However, there would be some feminist oversight in the process. Perhaps in response to Flanagan McCarthy's concerns, this draft also said that complaints would not go directly to managers, but to the head of the OEO or to its directors in the various CBC regions or divisions. The OEO would investigate these cases and recommend to the senior manager in the relevant location whether the complaint was valid. As Moss explained to Gurney, the "appropriate disciplinary action" covered a range of remedies from "consultation to dismissal, depending on the gravity of the incident, or perhaps, on the number of times a person has been reprimanded."[33]

In the CBC newsroom in St. John's, Newfoundland, both the management and the staff members of the Wire Services Guild reviewed the latest draft and recommended deleting only one sentence: "Wilful abuse of this policy may also be considered grounds for dismissal." The document already covered that potential in proven cases, but the employees were mostly afraid that OEO directors or managers would apply this vague phrase, "wilful abuse," to the complainant if they did not believe her, another deterrent for her.[34] The CBC women's group in the Prairies, after some discussion, endorsed this latest draft as it stood, however. "We are pleased to see that we have such a policy; it seems to be what we need at the present time and we support it."[35]

However, no firm policy was immediately forthcoming, despite these discussions. That vacuum left the handling of sexual harassment complaints up to immediate supervisors, who may have been acquainted with the policymaking process but still had no official guidance. At the time, Judy Morrison was a CBC News reporter on Parliament Hill. One day, while she was discussing one of her stories with a male colleague, another man sitting close by abruptly leaned over, put his hand up her dress, and grabbed her on her buttocks. "Just like that," Morrison recalled. "And I was *stunned*. I was angry. I was furious, and I said, 'What the hell are you doing?'" Both men laughed and her abuser told her he meant it as a joke and that she had no sense of humour. "And I said, 'You're damn right I don't have a sense of humour. That was wrong.'" Morrison complained to his supervisor, who told her that his behaviour was "a firing offence" and asked her what she wanted him to do about it. Morrison felt "it should not have been up to me," but she suggested a written apology because she did not want her abuser's family to suffer the loss of his income due to his "disgusting" behaviour. When he tossed his inadequate apology on her desk – "I am sorry if I offended you" – she read it quickly and threw it into the waste bucket. "It was adding insult to injury in a sense."[36]

"A Strict Liability," 1983

In 1983, the Canadian Human Rights Commission adopted a definition of sexual harassment, including conditions that would have covered Morrison's case: practical jokes that caused embarrassment and unnecessary physical contact up to and including assault.[37] However, at the CBC, a memo from Guy Coderre, vice-president of human resources and administration, revealed that, although its latest draft policy incorporated "extensive suggestions and revisions from the field," the top executives on the management committee had still not given the sexual harassment policy their final approval. Furthermore, there was a new complication, Coderre wrote: "As you probably know, there is somewhat more urgency to this than originally anticipated as recent human rights decisions have made it clear that employers have a strict liability to set up sexual harassment policies."[38] The Canadian Human Rights Tribunal had recently found that employers could be liable if they did not have a sexual harassment policy, at least in cases involving misconduct by supervisors, did not act on complaints, and did not make the policy known to all staff.[39] Clearly, it was past time for the CBC to clear all the bureaucratic hurdles, if only because of legal considerations.

The next draft policy dropped the idea of feminist oversight in the process. It said that the complainant was to go to her immediate supervisor or local human resources manager, not the OEO. HR managers were to be in charge of investigating the accusation and expected the OEO to cooperate with them, as well as advise the complainant if she wished. The findings would then go to the senior line manager in charge of her area, who would decide on disciplinary action.[40] This version of the procedure went straight back for a rewrite. In the next version, there was no mention of the OEO. The employee was to take her complaint directly to the HR manager, who would carry out the investigation and report to senior management in the relevant department for action.

At this point, the procedure became more precise. Upon receiving a written complaint, the HR manager was to arrange for separate, confidential, and detailed interviews with both the complainant and the accused in order to establish whether anything inappropriate had occurred. The HR representative would tell the complainant that although her case must be discussed with one or more of her managers or supervisors, "every effort will be made to maintain discretion and confidentiality." Both parties would learn that interviewing witnesses might be necessary but, in the interests of privacy, "kept to a minimum in order to avoid creating an emotional public issue as well as to minimize the publicity for the parties concerned." The accused person would have "appropriate representation at any further meetings or discussions."

Possibly the most alarming proviso for the complainant was what would happen if the managers decided that her allegations were "unfounded." The policy said, "The actions of the complainant must be considered in terms of degree of the content and the type and level of effect on the persons complained about"; in other words, the harm that her accusations caused the accused person. She could be suspended or dismissed from her job, or at least warned to cease and desist, even if her allegations were true but she could not prove them.[41]

"I Wouldn't Get Past Paragraph 3": Personal Harassment, 1983–4

A month later, a memo from Norn Garriock, the assistant general manager of CBC Television, revealed that there was to be a completely new CBC policy that focused on "personal harassment" of various kinds related to any of the prohibited federal grounds of discrimination, including race, sex, and physical disability. A separate section of the policy dealt with sexual harassment specifically.[42]

While the HR department would still oversee complaints, the new policy also called for a "review committee of senior managers" at the local level to examine the evidence and either determine the outcome or pass their recommendations on to someone with more authority. HR might ask the OEO for its input on a given complaint, but its primary job was to educate managers and employees with "information, guidance and/or training ... to equip them to deal effectively with incidents of harassment in the workplace." The draft did state that any employee involved in these cases had the right to "appropriate union representation." Nevertheless, it still left open the possibility of punishment for complainants who could not prove their allegations of personal or sexual harassment.[43]

The proposal prompted a somewhat acerbic response from Anna Whitley, the supervisor of manpower planning and administration. She noted that, outside of sexual harassment, the draft did not address power imbalances that would affect conditions of employment if one belonged to a racial or religious minority, for example. Whitley was particularly critical of the application and procedure sections of the personal harassment policy. To her, they appeared very "bureaucratic. I think if I was upset about discriminatory behaviour and wanted to know what to do ... I wouldn't get past paragraph 3." She asked for "an equal opportunity policy with a simple procedure" rather than "our present hodgepodge of H.R. staffing policy, collective agreement language, affirmative-action leaflets, etc. etc." Neither Whitley nor anyone involved in drafting the policy noted that sexual harassment of any woman who belonged to a minority group would require an advanced level of sensitivity on the part of HR and senior management to determine a just remedy; in fact, she did not criticize the section on sexual harassment at all. She did want to know if the policy drafters were avoiding any mention of "sexual orientation," which was already covered under the CBC's employment policy, but not yet under federal human rights legislation.[44]

A year later, another memo in the CBC files suggested that if there was, finally, an official policy on sexual harassment, in compliance with the new Canada Labour Code, the management and staff seemed not to be aware of it. In Toronto, a group of female producers in TV Current Affairs asked for information meetings with senior managers to discuss employment issues, including sexual harassment. Trina McQueen, the director of CBC Network Television, met twice with their representatives and then wrote a memo to her supervisor, the vice-president of the English TV network. "They have some interesting things to say on pay and promotion; and on sexual harassment. (Apparently we have a policy which has never been published; and no procedure to follow when the policy is violated.)"[45] McQueen does not remember her meetings with the women, but said that she always believed in hearing people out. In the late 1960s, she had been the CBC's first female TV news reporter and then had worked her way into senior management positions, becoming one of the few women in the CBC boardroom.[46] It is possible that the women producers considered her an ally with influence, even though she was not directly involved with personnel decisions when they approached her.

"He Was Frog-Marched Out of There," 1986

By 1985, the federal and provincial human rights commissions had declared sexual harassment on the job illegal.[47] The final piece of documentary evidence regarding the CBC's approach to harassment is from 1986. While the first draft, in 1981, contained four *paragraphs* on sexual harassment, this latest version, covering personal harassment in general, was four *pages* long, mostly on procedure. The language became very general – as personal harassment on any grounds. It did not use human rights language that specifically protected minorities, possibly because management thought the latest federal Employment Equity Act covered them.[48]

The section describing sexual harassment was essentially the same as in the previous version. However, a new clause stated that people experiencing either personal or sexual harassment should talk back "immediately and directly" to their harassers with "well thought out" responses, document everything, and be comfortable reporting it to their supervisors. Again, HR would investigate, and senior management would decide on punishment. There were alternative reporting routes if any manager was the one accused, but no arbitrator, such as the OEO. There was no longer a clause regarding punishment for unproven allegations, but the procedure now called for destruction of records in those cases. HR was to keep the documents about the proven cases in confidential files.[49] The policy still put the onus on the employee, allowing management to overlook personal or sexual harassment, especially if a victim was afraid to speak up, reluctant to follow the stated procedures, or felt ignored or disbelieved. On the other hand, when managers paid attention, the policy could be very effective.

Deborah Woolway was on the CBC staff in Halifax in the late 1980s, where, she recalled, there was "a nasty upset" when a male newcomer, "who came with a reputation," began sexually harassing other women on the staff. "He hit on the wrong people," and they made individual complaints against him. She felt that the male senior management in the region was slow to intervene. "But when they did, he was frog-marched out of there with his stuff in a box ... We all got sexual harassment training after that ... sensitivity and respect in the workplace." The staff joked that the man in question was the one who had actually needed the training, and these sessions were just taking away from their work time. In retrospect, Woolway saw the value in them as they helped embed the policy. Several years later, a female regional manager had to deal with one of the males in the Maritimes and a female reporter under his authority. "She [the manager] dealt with that so fast your head would spin," Woolway recalled.[50] Clearly, management's willingness to confront the issue, with policy and procedures to follow, made a difference in these cases.

Conclusion

The CBC documents demonstrate that management conferred with the employees regarding a sexual harassment policy, and a number of them, especially women, made suggestions that had some influence, but not enough. The HR department responded with different drafts, in all cases trying to ensure that there was a balance between the rights of the accused and the rights of the complainant. This was not really an equal contest in that women could have a lot to lose if they did speak up, as Flanagan McCarthy had observed. The experiences of Jennifer Fry and Judy Morrison illustrate the reasons why women still felt at a disadvantage – supervisors might disbelieve them or ask them to determine the nature of the punishment. Deborah Woolway's anecdotes illustrate that when managers really listened to complaints and followed the policy properly, they were able to punish the offenders and the staff learned from the experience.

Nevertheless, the strategy to include personal and sexual harassment in one document might have made the overall policy far too complicated and intimidating because the onus to complain was on the employees and the supervisors were still the final judges. We may never know whether the new, all-encompassing version helped Indigenous women in the North or any other minority person who complained of sexual harassment because the personnel records are inaccessible to researchers. Furthermore, by deleting unproved cases from the records, management made it more difficult to conduct internal studies to determine whether their policy worked for people complaining of sexual harassment, or was a deterrent, or why women in the CBC might still just prefer to keep their mouths shut. What began as a defensive management attempt at dealing with sexual harassment took five years of procedural complications that left the power in the mostly male management's hands – without formal, feminist intervention from the

Office of Equal Opportunity – and may have discouraged rather than encouraged women to come forward.

The CBC's personal harassment policy, including sexual harassment, has survived into the twenty-first century, but according to an official investigation, failed dismally in the well-publicized Jian Ghomeshi scandal because the CBC managers and the union involved mishandled the case, neglecting to follow the proper procedures.[51] The CBC continues to revise its policy, but the latest version, updated in February 2024, does not substantially differ from the drafts of the 1980s, although some of the language is now more inclusive and targets workplace violence as well as harassment. It also says management can discipline anyone lodging an *"intentional* false or frivolous" accusation, which could again leave complainants vulnerable to management judgments. However, if there is no resolution, management can appoint an outside investigator.[52] With a few notable exceptions, CBC News and Current Affairs did not start actively recruiting news workers who were Indigenous, Black, or other people of colour until the late 1980s. Further research should focus on the reasons it has taken the CBC and other news media so long to implement diversity hiring properly,[53] and on CBC journalists' own stories about the effectiveness, or not, of personal/sexual harassment policies in their work lives.

Today, employees of the CBC and other news media are struggling with personal and sexual harassment from members of the public. TV journalists have been the targets of crude comments from male passersby trying to disrupt their interviews, and more insults and threats come from telephone callers and online trolls.[54] According to a recent Canadian survey from Ipsos, the online aggressors target mostly journalists who are female and/or identify as Indigenous, a person of colour, or a minority in terms of their sexual orientation or gender identity.[55] The CBC has said it is collaborating with other news media and journalists' organizations in Canada and abroad to pressure social media companies and government regulators to protect all journalists better.[56] The CBC should bring the same concern about safeguarding its employees from outsiders to the next versions of its personal and sexual harassment policies and guidelines.

NOTES

1 Gail Cuthbert Brandt, Naomi Black, Paula Bourne, and Magda Fahrni, *Canadian Women: A History*, 3rd ed. (Toronto: Nelson Education, 2011), 530–43; Jacquetta Newman and Linda A. White, *Women, Politics, and Public Policy*, 2nd ed. (Toronto: Oxford University Press, 2012); Jill Vickers,

Pauline Rankin, and Christine Appelle, *Politics as If Women Mattered* (Toronto: University of Toronto Press, 1993).
2 The most pertinent files regarding the development of the equal opportunity policy are in Library and Archives Canada (hereafter LAC), RG 41, Canadian Broadcasting Corporation (CBC), under accession numbers 2000-01349-X and 2005-00370-0. The "affirmative action" program was in line with federal policy that stipulated goals but not quotas for hiring and promoting women. Barbara M. Freeman, "'Suddenly It Was a Real Thing': The Feminist Fight for Equal Opportunities in the Canadian Broadcasting Corporation, 1971–1981," *Journal of the Canadian Historical Association/Revue de la Société historique du Canada* 30, no. 2 (2019): 121–48.
3 Constance Backhouse, "Sexual Harassment: A Feminist Phrase That Transformed the Workplace," *Canadian Journal of Women and the Law* 24, no. 2 (2012): 296–8, https://www.utpjournals.press/doi/abs/10.3138/cjwl.24.2.275.
4 Louise Dulude, "The Status of Women in Federal Crown Corporations," Advisory Council on the Status of Women, March 1977, copy in Carleton University Reader's Digest Resource Centre, Special Collections (hereafter CU-RDRC), Elizabeth Zimmerman Papers, file F710.
5 Joan Sangster, "Introduction," in *Through Feminist Eyes: Essays on Canadian Women's History* (Edmonton: University of Athabasca Press, 2011), 1–48; Joan Sangster, *Transforming Labour: Women and Work in Post-war Canada* (Toronto: University of Toronto Press, 2010).
6 Barbara M. Freeman, *Beyond Bylines: Media Workers and Women's Rights in Canada* (Kitchener-Waterloo, ON: Wilfrid Laurier University Press, 2011).
7 Joan Sangster, "Creating Popular Histories: Re-interpreting 'Second Wave' Canadian Feminism," *Dialectical Anthropology* 39, no. 4 (November 2015): 381–404, https://doi.org/10.1007/s10624-015-9403-4.
8 CU-RDRC, Elizabeth Zimmerman Papers, file F714, copy of CBC Secretariat, "Equal Opportunity of Employment in the CBC," Corporate Policy, CP No. 6, effective 25 October 1977, distributed 31 October 1977. Workplace policies did not then recognize the importance of interconnected gender and racial identities, nor other markers, such as family origins, migration, and "life-course perspectives." See Karen Flynn, *Moving beyond Borders: A History of Black Canadian and Caribbean Women in the Diaspora* (Toronto: University of Toronto Press, 2011), 4–5.
9 See, e.g., Barbara M. Freeman, "'You Will Have a Good Career Here, but Not a Great Career': Male Mentoring and the Women Journalists at the Canadian Press News Cooperative, 1965–2000," *Labour/Le Travail* 78 (Fall 2016): 237–64; Vivian Smith, *Outsiders Still: Why Women Journalists Love – and Leave – Their Newspaper Careers* (Toronto: University of Toronto Press, 2015), 168, 215; Simma Holt, *Memoirs of a Loose Cannon* (Hamilton, ON: Seraphim Editions, 2008), 91–112.

10 Smith, *Outsiders Still*; Marjory Lang, *Women Who Made the News: Female Journalists in Canada 1880–1945* (Montreal and Kingston: McGill-Queen's University Press, 1999); Gertrude J. Robinson, *Gender, Journalism and Equity: Canadian, US and European Perspectives* (Cresskill, NJ: Hampton Press, 2005).

11 Mary Vipond, "Whence and Whither? The Historiography of Canadian Broadcasting," in *Communicating in Canada's Past: Essays in Media History*, ed. Gene Allen and Daniel J. Robinson (Toronto: University of Toronto Press, 2009), 233–56; Mary Vipond, "Nationalism and Communication," *Canadian Historical Review* 93, no. 3 (September 2017): 568–90.

12 Anne F. MacLennan, "Women, Radio and the Depression: A 'Captive' Audience from Household Hints to Story Time and Serials," *Women's Studies: An Interdisciplinary Journal* 37, no. 6 (July–August 2008): 616–33; Barbara M. Freeman, "We Were Only Women: Elizabeth Long, Equality Feminism and CBC Radio, 1938–1956," in *Beyond Bylines*, 93–121; Barbara M. Freeman, "A Desk in the Corridor: Marjorie McEnaney and Married Women in the Canadian Broadcasting Corporation, 1940s–1960s," in *Women in Radio: Unfiltered Voices from Canada*, ed. Geneviève A. Bonin-Labelle (Ottawa: Ottawa University Press, 2020), 24–42; Laurie Laplanche, "Le Service des émissions féminines télévisées au réseau francophone de la Société Radio Canada (1965–1982): Une histoire du genre dans les organizations," *Journal of the Canadian Historical Association/Revue de la Société historique du Canada* 26, no. 1 (2015): 225–54.

13 LAC, RG 41, CBC, accession nos. 2005-00370-0, vol. 59, file "CBC Women and Sexual Harassment, 1980s" (hereafter CBC Papers).

14 The bargaining units included the Wire Services Guild, for staff journalists, and the (then named) Association of Canadian Radio and Television Artists, for hosts and journalists in radio and television public affairs, most of them on renewable contracts. In addition, there was the Canadian Union of Public Employees, for the secretarial, clerical, and some production staff, the National Association of Broadcast Employees and Technicians, and the radio and TV producers' associations.

15 CU-RDRC, Elizabeth Zimmerman Papers, especially files F710, F714, and F725.

16 Joan Sangster, "Telling Our Stories: Feminist Debates and the Use of Oral History," in *Through Feminist Eyes*, 214, 219–22.

17 Constance Backhouse and Leah Cohen, *The Secret Oppression: Sexual Harassment of Working Women* (Toronto: Macmillan, 1979), 38.

18 Backhouse and Cohen, *The Secret Oppression*, 38–39.

19 Backhouse, "Sexual Harassment," 283–4.

20 Joan Sangster, *Transforming Labour*, 263.

21 CBC, *Women in the CBC: Report of the CBC Task Force on the Status of Women* (Toronto: Canadian Broadcasting Corporation, 1975).

22 Jennifer Fry interview with Barbara Freeman, Gatineau, Québec, 17 September 2019. Account edited by Jennifer Fry in an email to Barbara Freeman, 15 June 2020. Her edits to her cited narrative are in italics.
23 Dominique Clément, *Human Rights in Canada: A History* (Kitchener-Waterloo, ON: Wilfrid Laurier University Press, 2016), 107; Deborah Ann Campbell, *The Evolution of Sexual Harassment Case Law in Canada* (Kingston, ON: IRC Press, Queen's University Industrial Relations Centre, 1992), 1–5, https://irc.queensu.ca/sites/default/files/articles/campbell-the-evolution-of-sexual-harassment-case-law-in-canada_0.pdf.
24 CBC Papers, memo on "Sexual Harassment Proposed Policy," from Clive Mason, assistant general manager, English Services Division (ESD), to Don Goodwin, regional director, Toronto, 17 December 1981, with the attached proposed policy, copied to R.J. Gurney, director of human resources, and to the director of the OEO, Helen McVey. On the women's groups, see CBC, *Women in the CBC*, 1–3; Laplanche, "Le Service des émissions féminines televises," 228.
25 CBC Papers, memo re: sexual harassment from R.J. Gurney, director of human resources, ESD, to Clive Mason, assistant general manager, ESD, 28 December 1981.
26 CBC Papers, a separate note from R.J. Gurney, director of human resources, ESD, to Clive Mason, assistant general manager, ESD, 28 December 1981. He was responding to a query from Mason, 14 December 1981.
27 CBC Papers, policy document attached to memo of 17 December 1981 from Clive Mason to Goodwin and HR managers.
28 Karen Flanagan McCarthy telephone interview from Gatineau, Québec, with Barbara Freeman in Ottawa, 26 August 2020.
29 CBC Papers, copy of memo re: "Proposed Policy on Sexual Harassment" from Karen Flanagan McCarthy, publicist, TV Current Affairs, to Maureen O'Donnell, director, TV Publicity and Promotion, 27 January 1982, copied to Clive Mason. On the ombudsman, who would be independent of the HR department, including the OEO, see CBC, *Women in the CBC*, 190.
30 CBC Papers, memo re: "Sexual Harassment" from Sylvia M. Moss, manager, career opportunity, to R.J. Gurney, director of human resources, ESD, 15 March 1982, with an updated policy draft.
31 CBC Papers, updated policy draft from Sylvia M. Moss to R.J. Gurney, 15 March 1982.
32 Campbell, *The Evolution of Sexual Harassment Case Law*, 10.
33 CBC Papers, updated policy draft and memo from Moss to Gurney, 15 March 1982.
34 CBC Papers, telex to Clive Mason from W.S. Sheppard on behalf of J. Power, copied to J. Power and R.J. Gurney, 17 June 1982.

35 CBC Papers, memo from Lynne Kellner, chairperson, Working Women's Support Group, to Don Bennett, regional director, 23 June 1982, and forwarded from Bennett to Clive Mason, R.J. Gurney, and D. Chomiak, regional human resources manager, Winnipeg, 9 July 1982.
36 Emphasis hers. Judy Morrison interview with Barbara Freeman, Ottawa, 30 October 2019.
37 Campbell, *The Evolution of Sexual Harassment Case Law*, 10.
38 CBC Papers, memo from Guy Coderre, vice-president of human resources and administration, 9 June 1983, with a copy of the draft policy. Copy in CU-RDRC, Zimmerman Papers, file F725, "Sexual Harassment Policy."
39 H.C. Jain and P. Andiappan, "Sexual Harassment in Employment in Canada: Issues and Policies," *Relations industrielles/Industrial Relations* 41, no. 4 (1986): 772–3, https://doi.org/10.7202/050258ar.
40 CBC Papers, "Sexual Harassment Policy," draft policy, 9 June 1983.
41 CBC Papers, another draft of the sexual harassment policy, with a handwritten note on it, dated June 27, 1983, saying that a revision was due on July 4, 1983.
42 CBC Papers, memo for general distribution from Norn Garriock, assistant general manager, television, 28 July 1983, with the draft "Personal Harassment Policy" attached.
43 CBC Papers, draft "Personal Harassment Policy," 28 July 1983.
44 CBC Papers, memo from Anna Whitley, supervisor, manpower planning and administration, to Don Goodwin, director for the Province of Ontario, 21 September 1983. CU-RDRC, Zimmerman Papers, F714, copy of CBC Secretariat, "Equal Opportunity of Employment in the CBC," Corporate Policy, CP No. 6, effective 25 October 1977, distributed 31 October 1977. The policy was in line with human rights legislation in Québec, the first jurisdiction to include sexual orientation. Clément, *Human Rights in Canada*, 116–17.
45 CBC Papers, Trina McQueen, director of Network Television, to Denis Harvey, vice-president, English Television Network, 5 November 1984. On the labour code, see Jain and Andiappan, "Sexual Harassment in Employment in Canada," 773.
46 Trina McQueen interview with Barbara Freeman, Toronto, 1 November 2019.
47 Backhouse, "Sexual Harassment," 296.
48 In 1986, the federal Employment Equity Act regarding hiring and promotions of women, Aboriginal peoples, persons with disabilities, and members of visible minorities came into force, following a 1985 royal commission inquiry headed by Judge Rosalie Abella. Crown corporations, federal agencies, government-owned businesses, and federally regulated companies had to report on their annual progress to the Canadian Human

Rights Commission. Commission on Equality in Employment, "Equality in Employment: A Royal Commission Report – General Summary," *Canadian Women's Studies* 6, no. 4 (Winter 1985): 5–7; Government of Canada, Employment Equity Act, S.C. 1986, c. 31.

49 CU-RDRC, Zimmerman Papers, file F725, "Policy on Harassment," a memo to Zimmerman and other CBC managers from Anthony S. Manera, vice-president of human resources, 28 November 1986.
50 Deborah Woolway interview with Barbara Freeman, Dartmouth, Nova Scotia, 3 June 2011.
51 CBC News, "CBC Inquiry Concludes Management Mishandled Jian Ghomeshi," 16 April 2015, https://www.cbc.ca/news/cbc-inquiry-concludes-management-mishandled-jian-ghomeshi-1.3035574.
52 Italics mine. CBC/Radio-Canada, "Prevention of Workplace Harassment and Violence," 15 June 2021, https://cbc.radio-canada.ca/en/vision/governance/corporate-policies/health-safety-enviro/violence.
53 Andrea Hunter, "From the Women's Page to the Digital Age: Women in Journalism," in *Working Women in Canada: An Intersectional Approach*, ed. Leslie Nichols (Toronto: Women's Press, 2019), 296–7.
54 Hunter, "From the Women's Page to the Digital Age," 298–9.
55 Ipsos, "Online Harassment against Journalists and Media Professionals Is on the Rise," November 2021, https://www.ipsos.com/en-ca./news-polls/Online_Harm_in_Journalism.
56 Ipsos, *Online Harm in Journalism: Research Report*, 9 November 2021, https://site-cbc.radio-canada.ca/documents/media-centre/Ipsos-Online-Harm-in-Journalism-Report.pdf.

4 The 1995 Calgary Laundry Workers' Strike: A Case Study on the Power and Limits of Racialized Women's Class Struggle

ANDREA SAMOIL

On 14 November 1995, sixty laundry workers at Calgary General Hospital's Bow Valley Centre were called into the cafeteria to be told their jobs would be terminated in the next two weeks. They would have no severance payments, despite many working there for years or even decades. Their work was being contracted out to K-Bro Linen of Edmonton, a company that had also recently won the bid for all the hospital laundry in Edmonton through a questionable bidding process and after K-Bro was sold some new, state-of-the-art industrial laundry equipment by the Alberta government for a fraction of its original cost.[1]

Laundry worker Edna McMullan described how it felt to be told her job was gone. "It's kind of funny. They thought we'd just go back and finish [our shift] ... we said, 'We'll walk.' It was great, because no one suspected anything. They thought we'd just roll over and take it."[2] The workers seized on the notion to go home in a sick-out. By the evening they were voting to wildcat, outraged that the 28 per cent pay cut they had taken two years before, with the implicit understanding it would save their jobs from being contracted out, had been for nothing.[3] The next morning at 5:30 a.m., Calgary laundry workers struck for the first time, bringing their union, the Canadian Union of Public Employees (CUPE) Local 8, with them. The following day, sixty workers from the Foothills Hospital laundry, members of the Alberta Union of Provincial Employees (AUPE) Local 55, whose jobs were also being contracted out, struck as well. The 120 Calgary hospital laundry workers, many with no prior experience with unions or workplace action, were determined to not be dismissed without a fight.[4]

These workers ignored two Alberta Labour Relations Board (LRB) orders to return to work. The strike was illegal twice over: first because their contract was still in force, and second because workers were defying a 1983 law that made all hospital strikes illegal at any time in the province. Under the draconian Labour Statutes Amendment Act, laundry workers could be subject to individual fines and jail time, while their unions faced the prospect of punitive fines and even decertification. This law did not deter them. These workers, mainly women, predominantly immigrant and racialized, many of them single parents or older workers, were among the most vulnerable and exploited in the labour force in general. As some of the lowest paid in the hospital, with their jobs already gone, these workers had nothing to lose in walking off.

The ensuing laundry workers' strike and its visible support from the public marked the first concerted public sector fightback against Premier Ralph Klein's neoliberal assault on the working class. For two years a shell-shocked labour movement had been in full retreat, with public sector unions accepting wage cutbacks and other concessions in a futile effort to save their members' jobs; the mass layoffs from privatization and service reductions continued anyway. The strike continued to grow over the next eight days, with hundreds of support workers walking out at the five main acute care hospitals in Calgary. Workers at extended care and nursing homes also joined. All of them had been coerced into accepting pay cuts, concessions, and added work. They, too, were facing the possibility of contracting out.[5]

The public sector in Canada since the 1970s has been subject to what Leo Panitch and Donald Swartz have called a state of permanent exceptionalism, as free collective bargaining was suspended by federal and provincial governments that issued back-to-work orders to end strikes, imposed wage freezes, excluded numerous items from collective bargaining, and declared ever-increasing numbers of public sector workers essential, stripping them of the right to strike.[6] In the 1990s, even as women, racialized workers, and students were organized, union density was falling and union protections weakening.[7] The early 1990s saw few public sector strikes, but that was about to change. From December 1995 through 1996, a series of one-day broad-based rotating strikes in different cities known as the Days of Action took place in Ontario. From 1996 to 2001 strikes by healthcare workers and nurses occurred in six provinces and were met with heavy-handed legislative intervention.[8] Outside of the social worker and correctional officer strikes in 1990, and the laundry workers' strike in 1995, Alberta's public sector workers were quiet until 1997, when energy revenue rose and the provincial government once more posted surpluses.[9]

Alberta has a long political history of conservative governments hostile to workers, particularly those in the public sector.[10] The laundry workers' strike fits into a longer historical pattern of job action in the public sector, as well as union women fighting for recognition of the value of their labour. Notably, there were five previous hospital strikes, but by registered nurses, beginning in 1977 and culminating in the famous 1988 United Nurses of Alberta extralegal province-wide strike, which resulted in record-setting fines for the union but won the nurses their wage demands.

That it was laundry workers who dealt the first blow to Klein's political agenda seems at first unexpected. That hospitals ground to a halt without fresh laundry is, however, very easy to understand. Despite being poorly paid and underappreciated by their employer, laundry workers and their labour were essential to the healthcare system. Their strike challenged the logic that occupying the bottom of the occupational hierarchy justified their livelihoods being sacrificed in the name of deficit reduction. Ken Ogata argues that because the government breached the implied social contract by targeting the most vulnerable workers, Albertans fought back.[11] The militancy of these laundry workers changed the overall public attitude toward government funding cuts in the province and inspired the working class across the province to join their resistance. They are widely credited with making Premier Klein slow his cuts, not just in healthcare but across the board.

It should not be a surprise that women created a moment of crisis in Alberta. It is not just men confronting employer and police violence on picket lines who have shaped the labour history of Canada. The 1995 laundry workers' strike demonstrates the agency of these workers as well as the power of immigrant and racialized women's class struggles. As the strike built, the possibility of a public and private sector general strike emerged. That a general strike did not materialize during this moment of broader class consciousness speaks to how the labour movement's efforts at solidarity remain constrained by hierarchies of race and gender. Joan Sangster's dedication to women's and working-class history has influenced my own work. By choosing to examine the laundry workers' strike, with its questions of agency, the complexities of class and gender and race, and how hierarchies of power and privilege play out in the labour market and the labour movement, I am seeking to contribute to the still useful "add women and stir" studies.[12]

Neoliberal Cutbacks and Contracting Out

Massive public sector cutbacks were not restricted to Alberta in the 1990s but were part of a Canadian and global trend that prioritized reducing public debt at the expense of citizens' well-being by drastically cutting both government services and personnel. Under Klein, the Alberta government drastically reduced the size of government through cutbacks and privatization, with the justification that the private sector would automatically provide higher-quality services at a lower price.

All government workers were subject to a 5 per cent wage rollback in the fall of 1993, followed by a two-year wage freeze, and department budgets were to be reduced by 20 per cent within three years. Estimates put the provincial public sector job losses between 1993 and 1996 at ten thousand. The vehicle for the deepest cuts in healthcare was the restructuring of Alberta's health sector into regional health authorities (RHAs), which passed provincial cuts down to hospitals, who then downloaded them further onto their most vulnerable workers.[13] Labour costs are a major health expenditure, and workers were squeezed through wage cuts, layoffs, and contracting out.[14] Ancillary care workers (non-medical support staff), who perform laundry, housekeeping, and food services, are predominantly immigrant and racialized women. When their work is contracted out, these women lose union and government guarantees around equal pay and protections from discrimination based on race.

In 1993, the Bow Valley facility demanded a 10 per cent wage rollback from laundry workers to reduce the cost of laundry from $1.20 per pound to $0.95.[15] Further wage and benefit cuts in 1994 reduced laundry workers' wages by 18 to 40 per cent of their pre-1992 levels, in order to secure a guarantee against contracting out until March 1995.[16] Many public sector workers at the time accepted massive concessions for fear of losing their jobs to contracting out. Laundry work might have been hard, but it was a career for many of the women who had worked there for decades. For Nadia Turcato, who was fifty-seven years old when the strike occurred and had worked in the laundry for twenty-six years, the prospects for retraining and being hired for another job were grim.[17]

Work in the laundry was hard, hot, and potentially dangerous given the industrial-sized washing, drying, and pressing machines capable of doing hundreds of bags of laundry.[18] The laundry was divided between clean and dirty sides. On the clean side, workers caught the clean laundry coming out of the pressing rollers and meticulously folded items. On the dirty side, the work was arduous as workers lifted and threw heavy bags of soiled linens to empty them onto a belt line for sorting.[19] Laundry coming from isolation (and therefore potentially contagious) patients was placed in yellow bags, and workers had to wear protective gowns, gloves, and masks to handle these. Bags coming from the operating rooms contained biohazards such as blood, as well as the potential for other unpleasant surprises: "Sometimes we'd get [surgical] instruments. I never really run into body parts or anything like that but some people did."[20]

Despite meeting the per-pound goal for laundry costs at Bow Valley, the RHA informed CUPE and AUPE in June 1995 it would be putting the laundry out to tender. Although both unions put in bids to keep laundry in-house, the winning bid belonged to K-Bro Linen. K-Bro planned to truck the Calgary laundry up to its facilities in Edmonton, where the company was already cleaning the capital region's hospital laundry. It would reputedly save the RHA $2 million over five years.[21]

Walking Out

In the early afternoon of 14 November 1995, the laundry workers at the Bow Valley Centre, along with their CUPE representatives, were called in to a meeting in the upstairs cafeteria. Workers were given their two weeks' notice. They would not be given severance or any support to find new jobs. After the sacrifices workers had made, the news was described as a slap in the face. Management representatives left to deliver the same news to the laundry workers at Foothills Hospital, and union reps suggested a sick-out for the rest of the day, as surely everyone must be so upset it would be unsafe for them to return to work.[22]

At a meeting that evening at Bridgeland community hall, Bow Valley workers were angry as they discussed job action, including information pickets or work to rule.[23] Some workers were hesitant to strike: After their wage cut few had any financial cushion to fall back on, while many had dependants. Yvette Lynch, a thirty-seven-year-old single mother of two, had worked at the laundry for fourteen years, and her wages had been reduced to $8.83 an hour.[24] She spoke out strongly in favour of striking. The decision for a full walkout the next morning at 5:30 a.m. was near unanimous, and many workers were excited to go on strike.[25] The next morning, in the dark of early winter, laundry workers prevented trucks from entering to collect clean laundry and deliver it to other hospitals. Shortly after sunrise, around 8:00 a.m., the workers dispersed, needing a break after the emotionally taxing and tumultuous twenty-odd hours from their layoff notice to their first successful, and illegal, job action.

That evening CUPE reps were invited to an AUPE meeting of equally frustrated Foothills laundry workers. One member declared that the employer could take their jobs, but not their dignity. When union representatives warned that the strike would be illegal, "the common refrain was, we don't care. We know we're losing our job, but they can't just simply take it without a fight."[26] Just like at Bow Valley, the laundry workers at Foothills showed up in force the next morning to picket. Striker Lilia Blasetti recalls: "You could hear cheering. People were just so excited. They were finally saying that enough is enough, and they were not afraid to do it."²⁷ Union activists were amazed and inspired by the courage and solidarity that developed on the picket line.

It should not be a surprise that these women were the ones to confront the Alberta government over its neoliberal policy of contracting out government services to the private sector. Neoliberalism is, after all, a highly gendered class offensive. As Susan Braedley and Meg Luxton have argued, neoliberalism formally treats women as un-gendered market actors while simultaneously utilizing a patriarchal system in which women are overwhelmingly responsible for the social reproduction of labour. Women's familial and domestic responsibilities are unacknowledged and rendered invisible by treating women as un-gendered workers, while they are commonly remunerated for their paid work at a lesser rate.²⁸

Further, neoliberal attacks on the public sector have affected women in a multitude of ways. First, the public sector is a major employer of women and one of the few places where tangible progress on equal pay and pay equity have been seen.²⁹ The loss of public sector jobs to layoffs and contracting out has meant the loss of secure jobs with benefits and union protections for women. Second, cutbacks in government social support and welfare services have made the working class more precarious in general and have had serious consequences for women in particular.³⁰ As Monica Townson has noted, neoliberal attacks on the welfare state have disproportionately affected women as they use social services more in general and have higher rates of poverty within vulnerable populations.³¹ Cutbacks and more stringent restrictions on social assistance, unemployment insurance, public housing, and disability pensions in the 1990s left many Alberta women in dire financial straits.³² Third, due to patriarchal norms women have picked up the familial and community responsibilities the government has ceased to fulfill, such as care for the sick, elderly, or disabled.³³ Given the proportion of healthcare workers who are women – in Alberta in 2014, for example, 82 per cent of the workforce engaged in healthcare and social assistance was women – and the burden a deteriorating health system places on women in terms of unpaid care work, it is hardly surprising that laundry workers would be the people to spark a revolt against Klein's cuts.³⁴

Support for the Strike Grows

The announcement that laundry workers' jobs were being contracted out prompted widespread outrage in Calgary and the province at large. It acted as a flashpoint for the pervasive unhappiness with the deteriorating state of the healthcare system. The public, in classic quixotic

Alberta fashion, made one of its wide swings from the populist right to the populist near left. Calgary, the more conservative of Alberta's two largest cities, was unexpectedly on side with strikers, as call-ins to radio shows, newspaper editorials, and letters to the editor demonstrated. One caller to the local CBC station reported he had always been a Klein supporter but was now disillusioned. Even the normally right-wing talk radio shows were inundated with pro-strike callers, undoubtedly significantly aided by prominent anti-union host Dave Rutherford being on vacation the first week. Atypically, the unions and their arguments were given preferential coverage by news outlets, and the strike dominated Calgary's news.[35]

The idea that money could be saved by trucking laundry back and forth from Edmonton "was on the face of it so absurd that it heightened the sense of outrage both on the part of the workers in Calgary laundries and the public."[36] Nor was losing jobs to Edmonton popular. A public opinion poll placed 72 per cent of Calgarians in favour of the strikers, an astonishing level of support in a city where Klein had been mayor.[37] So many doughnuts were delivered to the picket line that strikers became sick of them. People driving by the picket lines, including on the busy Memorial Drive, honked in support in large numbers, a welcome change from the insults and invectives picketers could more frequently expect.[38] People also donated groceries and money to the strikers.[39]

The laundry workers tapped a well of discontent, as workers, both organized and unorganized, had faced massive wage rollbacks and layoffs in the early 1990s.[40] By striking in the face of a hopeless situation, the laundry workers' struggle sparked a moment of class consciousness in Alberta. According to Alberta Federation of Labour researcher Jim Selby, "there had been a fatalistic acceptance of the Klein agenda, but people were angry and discontented and this gave them a chance to show it."[41] By supporting the laundry workers, Albertans felt that they could send Klein a message that cutbacks had gone too far.

The speed at which hospitals entered a crisis state demonstrated to the RHA and public the true worth of the laundry workers' undervalued labour. By the second day of the strike, hospitals were struggling to cope. Clean linens were being rationed. Bedsheets were no longer changed daily, and patients were told to keep their hospital gowns.[42] Management staff struggled to keep the laundry plant at Bow Valley operating. As CUPE Local 8's president, Len Fagnan, noted, "the administration believed, oh well we don't need the laundry workers, we'll just go in and do it ourselves. It didn't take them long to find out that's not possible." Hospital workers were drawn to the picket lines the first few days to talk to the strikers, learning about their working conditions and reasons for striking. From there, workers from different areas in the hospital began to walk out to join the laundry workers.[43]

It is hardly surprising that the regional health authority's first effort to end the strike was through coercive measures via the Alberta LRB. On 16 November, the LRB ordered an end to the strike, which only spurred further defiance. On Friday 17 November hundreds more AUPE and CUPE members in Calgary hospitals walked off their jobs, despite the LRB order. Among them were kitchen staff, housekeepers, clerks, porters, paramedics, and those responsible for maintenance, admitting, and equipment sterilization. Many of them also faced the threat of contracting out.

All but the children's hospital were hard hit: The expanding wildcat forced elective surgery to be cancelled, admissions limited, and patients discharged. In an attempt to curtail the growing wildcat, Klein called for a six-month reprieve from contracting out laundry services.[44] This marked an important turning point, as Klein and the provincial government had successfully maintained their popularity by convincing Albertans that the regional health authorities were divorced from the premier and his cabinet.[45] By intervening directly, Klein was admitting what his critics had been saying all along: The provincial government was the one ultimately responsible for the cuts and chaos taking place in healthcare.

The premier's intervention was unsuccessful in halting the strike; it was too little, too late. On Saturday 18 November the walkout grew larger, with an estimated 2,500 CUPE, AUPE, and sympathetic workers out. Picket lines in Calgary grew as supporters in Calgary and from elsewhere in the province answered the Alberta Federation of Labour's call for solidarity.[46] Even more important was the wildcat jumping the city's boundaries as laundry workers in Lethbridge walked off the job. On Sunday 19 November, CUPE and AUPE members in Calgary formally voted to walk out in support. A meeting between RHA officials and the unions resulted in a proposal for amnesty and $1.2 million in severance and retraining, which laundry workers rejected. This was the first time since Klein's cutbacks started that severance was offered to contracted-out workers.

On Monday 20 November, the Calgary RHA requested that the LRB declare the broad walkout illegal, and the following day the RHA announced it would pursue legal action against workers. The Labour Statutes Amendment Act of 1983 prohibited strikes in healthcare and attached extreme penalties for any violation. It was aimed primarily at the registered nurses' union, the United Nurses of Alberta (UNA), which had struck hospitals effectively three times between its formation in 1977 and 1983. The amendment was part of a broader effort to discipline government workers and turn back the labour relations clock to a time when public service organizations were in effect company unions. The amendment allowed the LRB to suspend a union's dues collection for six months as a financial deterrent against striking, while the provision to directly fine individuals was intended to break solidarity and intimidate members from publicly supporting their union. The amendment also gave the provincial cabinet the power to decertify a union, an even grosser misuse of the power against unions than normally occurred in Alberta.

Yet, because of the massive public support, injunctions and other intimidation tactics did not work the way the government or RHA would have liked. Calgary and District Labour Council president Gord Christie noted that once people are in the street "you can have all the injunctions in the world but it doesn't mean a thing."[47] The health authority tried to salvage public trust by requesting the provincial auditor-general examine the contract awarding Calgary's laundry to K-Bro as rumours of political corruption abounded due to connections between RHA board members and K-Bro's shareholders and directors.

The health authority was extremely reluctant to disclose the details of the winning bid, with spokesperson Judy Williams merely stating that she could "guarantee that [K-Bro's submission] was the lowest cost-bid."[48] Vencap Equities, a provincial government-funded investment firm, owned 60 per cent of K-Bro. Calgary RHA chair John "Bud" McCaig was a member of the Vencap board until he resigned in the summer of 1995 because another company McCaig controlled was attempting to take over Vencap. McCaig was appointed by the provincial government as the chair of the fifteen-member Calgary RHA board in 1994 at the request of Premier Klein, undoubtedly due to his status as a Tory insider and member of the finance committee.[49] Clear ties existed between the RHA chair and the largest shareholder of K-Bro.

Although the auditor-general, Peter Valentine, reported on 11 December that K-Bro had the lowest bid, clearing the RHA board and staff of any conflict of interest and criticizing the media for inaccurate and incomplete reporting on contracts, this did not lessen suspicions of corruption given the RHA's continued lack of transparency.[50] As Lorna Stefanick has commented, the Alberta Progressive Conservatives' record of ethics and public accountability, including separating the public interest from political and economic interests, was questionable.[51]

Attempts to stifle the political nature of the wildcat and to focus the issue solely on the laundry workers and not the overall crisis in healthcare were unsuccessful. The strike had turned into a referendum on cutbacks and contracting out, and workers across the province were voting by walking off their jobs. Inspired by the stand the laundry workers in Calgary were taking and with the news that discussions were already underway to contract out housekeeping at the Royal Alexandra, University of Alberta, and Glenrose hospitals in Edmonton, hospital workers and supporters in Edmonton staged demonstrations on 20 November.

Registered nurses with UNA, 4,500 of whom worked in Calgary, were set to meet on the evening of 21 November. Rowland Nichol, acting president of the Calgary Regional Medical Staff Association, stated, "If nurses join the strike, hospitals will be closed outright." Further, he told the press that doctors were sympathetic to the strike and might take action. Nichol clearly framed the strike as a protest against healthcare cutbacks, a symptom of the immense stresses placed on the healthcare system by cuts and job loss, and not merely a localized labour issue.[52]

Five days in, with 3,500 hospital workers now on strike and more in Edmonton talking about walking off the job, there were predictions that Klein would be forced to announce a moratorium on healthcare cuts. RHA spokesperson Judy Williams reported that Klein had "indicated to us that there may be some room there in terms of finances," a far cry from the blustering premier's declaration at the beginning of the cuts in 1993: "You can produce all the billboard signs you want and all the placards. And you can call me every rotten, stinking name under the sun, but I ain't going to blink."[53]

Klein Blinks

Klein was forced to cancel a trip to Edmonton in order to meet with the RHA board. Calgary mayor Al Duerr pleaded with the premier to pause the cuts and analyse the effects existing cuts had had on healthcare. On the evening of 21 November, Minister of Labour Stockwell Day met with representatives of the RHA, CUPE, and AUPE in an attempt to end a strike that showed no signs of stopping and every sign of continuing to grow. The next day Minister of Health Shirley McClellan announced the cancellation of $53 million of the scheduled healthcare cuts for the next fiscal year. More remarkable was a promise of a funding increase of $40 million for home care.[54] Klein, rather ridiculously, claimed that the cancelled cuts were not related to the strike.

The first setback of the strike came on Tuesday 21 November, when UNA decided not to join the walkout, followed the next day by a failed strike vote by the Health Sciences Association of Alberta (HSAA) (which includes imaging and laboratory technicians, dieticians, and social workers, among others). Nonetheless, momentum continued to build. The week-old strike was no longer confined to Calgary hospitals. Workers struck at fourteen hospitals and extended care facilities in the province. Licensed practical nurses and nursing aids, members of the Canadian Health Care Guild, supported the strike by working to rule or walking around their facilities with picket signs on their breaks. A few extended care facilities were struck fully, and their administration warned families to prepare for patients being discharged.[55] On 23 November, 200 members of HSAA walked off their jobs despite their union's decision not to join the strike. A province-wide healthcare wildcat appeared imminent as Edmonton hospital workers demanded an end to contracting out. That evening, AUPE, CUPE, and Calgary RHA representatives met for an emergency overnight negotiation to halt the strike by reaching an agreement for the laundry workers.

The next morning, Friday 24 November, a deal was reached. A yearlong moratorium was placed on contracting out laundry jobs in Calgary, and workers would receive severance pay when their jobs were inevitably lost. Further, no strikers would be prosecuted for their illegal walkout nor face disciplinary measures or dismissal when they returned to work – an important consideration given the employer had been photographing people on the picket line. Some workers were anxious not just about taking illegal action but also about how long they could survive financially.[56] By the end of the strike, some had already returned to work, dismayed at the lack of progress.[57] The laundry workers voted to accept the deal.

That same morning the support staff set to walk out at the University of Alberta and Charles Camsell hospitals in Edmonton – some of them already on picket lines – were told to go back to work. The Alberta Federation of Labour's motion passed that morning to work toward a general strike was now irrelevant. On Saturday 25 November, Calgary laundry workers and others returned to their jobs.

While other hospital workers were granted a brief reprieve in the form of a six-month moratorium on contracting out, the settlement was hardly a great victory.[58] The most significant aspect of the deal was the first-ever severance offered to workers who would lose their jobs due to cuts. The government acknowledged that the Calgary settlement set a provincial precedent and all healthcare workers in the future who were laid off due to contracting out in hospitals would also receive severance.

More broadly, however, the strike forced the government to re-evaluate its cutback campaign. Ogata has argued that in the aftermath of the laundry workers' strike, "the government's resolve seemed to evaporate. Once he started blinking, Klein couldn't stop." A $100 million cut to physician services was cancelled following the strike, and in year-end interviews Klein acknowledged that healthcare cuts had been too deep.[59] Although already-in-motion privatization and service cuts continued, no new aggressive cutbacks were announced. Jason Foster argues that the strike turned the tide of public sector labour relations and emboldened public sector unions.[60] CUPE national president Judy Darcy said, "I've never seen a strike affect the policy decision of the government before."[61]

Darcy, who was part of the final bargaining from Thursday night through Friday morning, did concede that the union did not get all it wanted but stated it was still a victory for workers. It is true that laundry workers kept their jobs in the short term. Paula Gotell told the CBC from the picket line, "We were told we would keep our jobs. I want my job back," so we should not dismiss how important it was that strikers could return to their jobs without issue.[62] Less tangibly, but undoubtedly important, was a broader recognition of the critical nature of the laundry workers' labour and continuing respect accorded to these workers by fellow healthcare workers and by management. Without laundry workers, hospitals could not operate. Now everyone knew it.

It bears noting, however, that laundry workers were given "working severance," which meant that the employer would deduct the weeks worked after the notice of termination of employment from the final severance payout. For example, if a worker had ten years of service and was entitled to two weeks of pay per year for a total of twenty weeks, then if they were given sixteen weeks' notice, they would be entitled to only the remaining four weeks as severance. If an employer gave long enough notice, it would not have to pay workers anything when their employment ended. While some workers were happy to have any form of severance as a recognition of their years of service, it is no wonder Len Fagnan described laundry workers as overall "not pleased with the deal. They felt that in consideration of everything they went through, it did not give them their job security they were looking for."[63]

The impact of these racialized women's relatively brief moment of overt class struggle was immense. Beyond winning a brief reprieve from contracting out healthcare and the introduction of severance in their sector, the laundry workers inspired workers across the province to strike in sympathy with their struggle and to stand up for themselves. The laundry workers' bravery and willingness to fight for fair treatment after their disproportionately large sacrifices sparked a referendum on healthcare and cutbacks. It forced the government to reverse course on cutbacks in healthcare and generally. Lastly, it demonstrated, however briefly, the centrality and importance of often-dismissed ancillary work to the healthcare system. Yet only two years later, Calgary hospital laundry was privatized and K-Bro Linen won 90 per cent of the contract. Being the ones credited with turning the tide of Klein's neoliberal revolution did nothing to ultimately save the laundry workers' jobs.

Tackling the Limits of Racialized Women's Class Struggle

The marginalized position of the laundry workers within the political economy (including higher rates of poverty and unemployment) and the replication of that marginalization within the labour movement limited the success of their struggle. The predominantly female, racialized workers of the laundry strike were typical of the low-paid and growing section of the public sector that was underrepresented in its unions.[64] The laundry workers' lack of status inside their unions highlights that although unions have been feminized in terms of members, the labour movement itself has not become feminist in practice.[65] The hopes of a "reinvigorated working-class movement, transformed by feminism and committed to a broadly based politic of liberation for oppressed peoples," have not been realized despite what has now been a half century of struggle by feminist union activists.[66]

In order to combat the systemic inequalities that limited the possibilities of success for the laundry workers, efforts to remake unions into feminist organizations must continue. In particular, unions need to fight broadly for women's issues, challenge the gendered and racialized divisions of labour, and meaningfully democratize. Unions need to explicitly connect women's unpaid work and the inequalities in their paid work. Collective bargaining for childcare, paid family leave, and reduced work hours without reduced pay can all help to alleviate the burden of unequally shared unpaid work on women.[67] Such measures allow women to more easily participate in their unions and generate a union climate that embraces issues that affect women at work and outside of it, including abortion and violence.[68] As past feminist and antiracist efforts within the labour movement demonstrate, union support for broader social justice issues can build solidarity with unorganized members of the working class, strengthening support for overt forms of class struggle. The 1972 Dare strike discussed by Mason Godden in this book demonstrates that feminist and other political allies can be vital sources of solidarity, even if such relationships are complicated. Especially in public sector strikes, such as the 1988 UNA strike, support from feminist organizations outside the labour movement can be crucial to their success.

Moreover, to remove limitations on future racialized women's class struggle, the gendered and racialized division of labour and the dismissal of the value of what has traditionally been women's work must be combated. In the healthcare sector, "out-of-care" or ancillary work done by housekeepers, dieticians, and laundry workers, typically performed by women of colour, is undervalued and often invisible. Given the association of these jobs with women's unpaid domestic work, the skills, effort, and responsibilities required to perform them are rarely acknowledged by employers, their own unions, and society more generally. As scholars have argued, many of the "unskilled" (and essentialized as natural) jobs that women perform in the labour market can be viewed as the end of an apprenticeship that begins at an early age with the unpaid domestic labour performed by girls in their family homes.[69]

The denial of the dignity of this type of work, both privately in the domestic sphere and publicly in the wage-labour market, is used to justify low wages and inferior benefits by employers to their workers. This denial of the worth of the work is implicitly upheld by unions, for example by negotiating wage increases in percentages, which compounds the wage gap between bottom and top earners.[70] For true justice for the laundry workers, a radical and systemic change in attitudes around the value of women's work would be needed.

The abrupt, disappointing end of the laundry workers' strike reveals the limits of the transformational capacity of affirmative action if it is not paired with efforts to eliminate systemic inequality. The often begrudging "just add women" approach to union power structures has not made the labour movement less hierarchical, more egalitarian, more committed to equity, or less bound to ideas of preserving the union as an institution at the expense of the members.[71] Karen Bentham notes that historical union structures continue to perpetuate male privilege.[72] The tenacity of existing institutional culture, in this case business unionism, is hardly a surprise as this sort of institutional inertia is not unique to unions.[73] Increased rank-and-file control, a flattening of hierarchies, prioritization of the needs of the most vulnerable members, and a revolutionary vision of uplifting the entire working class are needed to empower racialized women in their class struggle.[74]

In response to the lack of progress made on these fronts despite the hard work done by activists, too frequently detractors point to the presence of women in executive positions as proof unions have done enough.[75] If "add women at the top" was all it took to feminize unions, we might have expected that the fact that CUPE's national president, Judy Darcy, and AUPE's president, Carol-Anne Dean, were women would have led to a different result in 1995, even if it was simply unions willing to see the struggle of their most vulnerable members through to the end, regardless of the risk to the union.[76] Decertification, as the 1972 Dare strike shows, does not preclude workers from winning substantial improvements with their new union.[77] If having women in positions of power was sufficient to make a union feminist, we might have expected non-compromising support for the striking laundry workers' brave stand. Instead, what happened was the all-too-common and disappointing story of a swell of class consciousness and militancy around a call for a general strike, only for the labour leadership to step in and settle the small-scale dispute instead of trying to make headway on the larger-scale working-class issue, in this case contracting out.[78]

The labour movement in Alberta, as even the outside observers could see, was poised to walk out in a general strike.[79] Workers at Edmonton hospitals were gearing up, the building trades were talking about walking out, the Alberta Federation of Labour was preparing for a general strike, and six thousand healthcare workers were already out. The Canadian Labour Congress and unions across the country had pledged support for the laundry workers.[80] The moment to push back hard against Klein's neoliberal reforms seemed to materialize overnight, there to be seized.

But all the healthcare unions involved were clearly intimidated by the example of the massive fines levied against UNA in its 1988 extralegal strike. AUPE was in debt, and its membership was dropping precipitously with contracting out and layoffs. In 1992, when Carol-Anne Dean was elected president, the union was over $1 million in debt. More than 4,700 AUPE members lost their jobs between August 1990 and 1993.[81] By 1995 the total membership had declined to around 35,000, all of whom were facing wage cutbacks, which meant declining union dues. The union was struggling to stay afloat, and the potential fines from an illegal hospital strike might have been enough to pull it under.

What the leaders of the healthcare unions seemed to forget was that the record-setting $425,000 fine levied against UNA in 1988 was paid entirely by the Friends of Alberta Nurses Society, which collected donations from across the country from the labour movement, women's groups, church groups, and the New Democratic Party. For a struggle so clearly understood by the general public as a fight against injustice, the Canadian labour movement and other organizations could be counted on for substantive financial support. In cases like this, where a union is faced with an apparent choice between financial ruin and protecting its members, the question arises: If a union cannot protect its members, what is its purpose?

Conclusion

If there is one thing workers in Alberta might take away from the laundry workers' strike, it is that direct action is an effective tool for class struggle. In 1995 doctors, protesting Klein's cuts to healthcare spending, had little effect with their publicity campaign with the tag line of "Tell us where it hurts." Likewise, the broader coalitions on healthcare the labour movement organized in the early 1990s, which held rallies and demos, had little political effect, with Klein referring to them dismissively as rent-a-crowds.[82] Yet 120 laundry workers managed to bring the operations of the Calgary Regional Health Authority to a grinding halt and make Klein slow his healthcare cuts.

One need not look to those workers with the most institutional power within the workplace to lead: To do so is to allow employers to mystify the true value of workers' labour, reinforcing hierarchies of race and gender and allowing the stratification of the labour force to be replicated within the labour movement. If, on the other hand, we recognize the dignity of all people and their work, then the power even the most economically vulnerable and socially marginalized workers have from the simple fact of their work is easy to recognize. Such workers do not need someone to save them, but they could use a lot more solidarity and a good dose of democratization and feminization of their union practices.

NOTES

1 Alberta Labour History Institute (hereafter ALHI) group discussion with Dave Werlin, Jim Selby, Winston Gereluk, and Tom Fuller, 28 January 2010, Edmonton, Alberta.
2 Allan Chambers, *Fighting Back: The 1995 Calgary Laundry Workers Strike* (Edmonton: Alberta Labour History Institute, 2012), 6.
3 Alanna Mitchell, "Calgary Strike Threatens Hospitals: Workers Set to Walk in Edmonton," *Globe and Mail*, 21 November 1995.
4 Chambers, *Fighting Back*, 18.
5 Collette Singh, ALHI interview by Susan Keeley, 30 April 2009, Calgary, Alberta.
6 Leo Panitch and Donald Swartz, *From Consent to Coercion: The Assault on Trade Union Freedoms*, 3rd ed. (Toronto: University of Toronto Press, 2009).
7 Donald Swartz and Rosemary Warskett, "Canadian Labour and the Crisis of Solidarity," in *Rethinking the Politics of Labour in Canada*, ed. Stephanie Ross and Larry Savage (Winnipeg: Fernwood, 2012), 29.

8 For more details of public sector strikes in the 1990s, see Leo Panitch and Donald Swartz, "Neo-liberalism, Labour, and the Canadian State," in *From Consent to Coercion: The Assault on Trade Union Freedoms*, ed. Leo Panitch and Donald Swartz, 3rd ed. (Toronto: University of Toronto Press, 2009), 183–222.
9 For more on Alberta in the nineties, see Jason Foster, "Revolution, Retrenchment, and the New Normal: The 1990s and Beyond," in *Working People in Alberta: A History*, ed. Alvin Finkel (Edmonton: Athabasca University Press, 2012), 205–41.
10 Alvin Finkel, "The Boomers Become the Workers: Alberta, 1960–1980," in *Working People in Alberta: A History*, ed. Alvin Finkel (Edmonton: Athabasca University Press, 2012), 144.
11 Ken Ogata, "Stakeholder Responses to Government Austerity: What Happens When Strong Stakeholders Fail to React?," *International Review of Administrative Sciences* 83, no. 1 (2017): 129–48.
12 Joan Sangster, "Feminism and the Making of Canadian Working-Class History: Exploring the Past, Present and Future," *Labour/Le Travail* 46 (Fall 2000): 148.
13 Foster, "Revolution, Retrenchment, and the New Normal," 209, 211–12; Brian Bergman, "Fallout from the Klein Revolution," *Maclean's* 109, no. 11 (1996): 20.
14 Healthcare work is landlocked: it cannot be outsourced overseas. Linda Briskin, "Resistance, Mobilization and Militancy: Nurses on Strike," *Nursing Inquiry* 19, no. 4 (December 2012): 290.
15 Len Fagnan, ALHI interview by Dave Werlin, 24 and 30 April 2009, Calgary, Alberta.
16 Pat Armstrong, Hugh Armstrong, and Krista Scott-Dixon, *Critical to Care: The Invisible Women in Health Services* (Toronto: University of Toronto Press, 2008), 115; Foster, "Revolution, Retrenchment, and the New Normal," 212.
17 Anne McGrath and Dean Neu, "Washing Our Blues Away: The Laundry Worker's Strike (Alberta)," *Our Times* 15, no. 1 (March–April 1996): 25–6.
18 Susan Keeley, ALHI interview by Dave Werlin and Winston Gereluk, 3 March 2007, Calgary, Alberta.
19 Yvette Lynch, ALHI interview by Susan Keeley, 29 April 2009, Calgary, Alberta.
20 Lynch, ALHI interview, 2009.
21 Robert Walker, "Authority Backed on Laundry," *Calgary Herald*, 12 December 1995.
22 Keeley, ALHI interview, 2007.
23 Keeley, ALHI interview, 2007.
24 Dave Pommer, "Dirty Laundry," *Calgary Herald*, 26 November 1995.
25 Lynch, ALHI interview, 2009.

26 Sean McManus, ALHI interview, 29 April 2009.
27 Chambers, *Fighting Back*, 7.
28 Susan Braedley and Meg Luxton, *Neoliberalism and Everyday Life* (Montreal: McGill-Queen's University Press, 2010), 7, 13–14.
29 Kate McInturff and Paul Tulloch, *Narrowing the Gap: The Difference That Public Sector Wages Make* (Ottawa: Canadian Centre for Policy Alternatives, 2014), 6.
30 Amanda Coles and Charlotte A.B. Yates, "Unions, Gender Equity and Neoconservative Politics," in *Rethinking the Politics of Labour in Canada*, ed. Stephanie Ross and Larry Savage (Halifax: Fernwood, 2012), 107.
31 Monica Townson, *Women's Poverty and Recession* (Ottawa: Canadian Centre for Policy Alternatives, 2009), 6.
32 Klein reduced provincial spending by 28 per cent in real per capita in a mere three years. Foster, "Revolution, Retrenchment, and the New Normal," 218.
33 Alexandra Dobrowolsky, *Women and Public Policy in Canada: Neoliberalism and After* (Toronto: Oxford University Press, 2009), 8.
34 Government of Alberta, *Alberta Labour Force Profiles: Women 2014* (Edmonton: Government of Alberta, 2015).
35 McGrath and Neu, "Washing Our Blues Away," 25–6; Mitchell, "Workers Set to Walk"; Fagnan, ALHI interview, 2009.
36 Fuller, ALHI group discussion, 2010.
37 McGrath and Neu, "Washing Our Blues Away," 25–6.
38 McManus, ALHI interview, 2009.
39 Lynch, ALHI interview, 2009.
40 Gordon Christie, ALHI interview by Winston Gereluk, 2008.
41 ALHI group discussion with Werlin, Selby, Gereluk, and Fuller, 2010; Steve Patten, "The Politics of Alberta's One-Party State," in *Transforming Provincial Politics: The Political Economy of Canada's Provinces and Territories in the Neoliberal Era*, ed. Bryan M. Evans and Charles W. Smith (Toronto: University of Toronto Press, 2015), 278.
42 Dave Pommer, "Hospital Laundry Workers' Strike May Expand," *Calgary Herald*, 16 November 1995.
43 Fagnan, ALHI interview, 2009; McManus, ALHI interview, 2009.
44 Pommer, "Dirty Laundry."
45 Cathy Lord, "Where Does It Hurt?," *Edmonton Journal*, 16 July 1995.
46 Christie, ALHI interview, 2008.
47 Christie, ALHI interview, 2008.
48 Walker, "Authority Backed on Laundry."
49 McCaig was the co-owner of the National Hockey League's Calgary Flames team and also founder, CEO, and board chair of the transport and drilling company Trimac Ltd., which unsuccessfully bid to buy Vencap.

"John Robert (Bud) McCaig (1929–2005)," *Alberta Champions*, http://albertachampions.org/Champions/john-robert-bud-mccaig-1929-2005/; Robert Walker, "Prominent Tory Gets Health Job," *Calgary Herald*, 10 June 1994.

50 Walker, "Authority Backed on Laundry."
51 The Multi-Corp scandal in November 1995 reinforced the perception that accountability offices and procedures in Alberta were non-functional. Lorna Stefanick, "Blurring the Boundaries of Private, Partisan, and Public Interests: Accountability in an Oil Economy," in *Alberta Oil and the Decline of Democracy in Canada*, ed. Meenal Shrivastava and Lorna Stefanick (Edmonton: Athabasca University Press, 2015), 383; Maureen Macuso, Michael M. Atkinson, André Blais, Ian Greene, and Neil Nevitte, *A Question of Ethics: Canadians Speak Out* (Don Mills: Oxford University Press Canada, 1998), 63–4.
52 Mitchell, "Workers Set to Walk."
53 Mitchell, "Workers Set to Walk"; Richard Cuthbertson, "Klein's Education Legacy: Deep Cuts, but More Choice," *Calgary Herald*, 2 April 2013.
54 It should be noted, $123 million was originally slated to be cut in April 1996, meaning $30 million was still cut after the reprieve. Alberta Health, *Annual Report, 1995–96*, 31 March 1996.
55 Singh, ALHI interview, 2009.
56 McManus, ALHI interview, 2009.
57 Lynch, ALHI interview, 2009.
58 Alanna Mitchell, "Hospital Workers End Wildcat Strike: Alberta Freezes $53-Million in Cuts, Promises Health Authorities an Extra $40-Million," *Globe and Mail*, 25 November 1995.
59 Ogata, "Stakeholder Responses to Government Austerity," 138.
60 Foster, "Revolution, Retrenchment, and the New Normal," 226.
61 Mitchell, "Hospital Workers End Wildcat."
62 Mitchell, "Workers Set to Walk."
63 Fagnan, ALHI interview, 2009.
64 Tania Das Gupta, "Racism and the Labour Movement," in *Equity, Diversity and Canadian Labour*, ed. Gerald Hunt and David Rayside (Toronto: University of Toronto Press, 2007), 181–207.
65 On the failure to organize, represent, or win wage increases for women, see Charlotte Yates, "Women Are Key to Union Renewal: Lessons from the Canadian Labour Movement," in *Paths to Union Renewal: Canadian Experiences*, ed. Pradeep Kumar and Chrisopher Schenk (Peterborough, ON: Broadview Press, 2006), 103.
66 Sangster, "Feminism and the Making of Canadian Working-Class History," 128.
67 Coles and Yates, "Unions, Gender Equity and Neoconservative Politics," 114.

68 Karen Bentham, "Labour's Collective Bargaining Record on Women's and Family Issues," in *Equity, Diversity and Canadian Labour*, ed. Gerald Hunt and David Rayside (Toronto: University of Toronto Press, 2007), 106.
69 Because the skills associated with women's work are not typically acquired in a formalized educational setting, nor result in some form of accreditation, these skills have less prestige and command less pay. Armstrong, Armstrong, and Scott-Dixon, *Critical to Care*, 92–4.
70 Rosemary Warskett, "Can a Disappearing Pie Be Shared Equally? Unions, Women, and the Wage 'Fairness,'" in *Women Challenging Unions: Feminism, Democracy, and Militancy* (Toronto: University of Toronto Press, 1993), 252.
71 Coles and Yates argue that women in leadership have contributed to changing internal culture and priorities, but unions continue to have a complex, contradictory, relationship to women's and equity issues. Coles and Yates, "Unions, Gender Equity and Neoconservative Politics," 103–6; Gerald Hunt, "Introduction," in *Equity, Diversity and Canadian Labour*, ed. Gerald Hunt and David Rayside (Toronto: University of Toronto Press, 2007), 21.
72 Bentham, "Labour's Collective Bargaining Record," 127.
73 Gill Kirton and Geraldine Healy, "'Lift as You Rise': Union Women's Leadership Talk," *Human Relations* 65, no. 8 (August 2012): 979–99.
74 For a discussion of gendering union democracy, see Linda Briskin, "Gendering Union Democracy," *Canadian Woman Studies* 18, no. 1 (Spring 1998): 35–8; on using feminist models to empower workers, see Das Gupta, "Racism and the Labour Movement," 194; and on the link between union democracy and class struggle, see David Camfield, "How to Reinvent the Movement," in *Canadian Labour in Crisis: Reinventing the Workers' Movement* (Halifax: Fernwood, 2011), 111–37.
75 For a more detailed story of women's struggles within the labour movement, see Rosemary Warskett, "The Politics of Difference and Inclusiveness within the Canadian Labour Movement," *Economic and Industrial Democracy* 17 (1996): 587–625.
76 Bentham, "Labour's Collective Bargaining Record," 125.
77 Mason Godden, "'Don't Dare': Labour, Feminism, and the Left on Strike at Dare Foods, 1972–1973," in this volume.
78 General strikes are, of course, not guaranteed to materialize, let alone win the central demands of the strike. For a very similar case of racialized women healthcare workers winning public support in their protest against neoliberal government cuts and the momentum building to a general strike being undercut by labour brass, see David Camfield, "Neoliberalism and Working-Class Resistance in British Columbia: The Hospital Employees' Union Struggle, 2002–2004," *Labour/Le Travail* 57 (Spring 2006): 9–41.

79 Mitchell, "Hospital Workers End Wildcat."
80 Chambers, *Fighting Back*, 15.
81 AUPE membership was around forty thousand in 1990. Penney Kome, "Common Front de-Kleins Cutbacks," *Herizons* 9, no. 1 (Spring 1995): 12–13.
82 Selby, ALHI group discussion, 2010.

PART TWO

Gender and Politics

5 "Giving Women a Voice": Annie Townley, the Labour Party, and Women's Politicization in South-West England in the Interwar Years

JUNE HANNAM

In 1937 Annie Townley, a woman organizer for the Labour Party in the South West of England, wrote that the aim of the women's sections of the party was to "work to get beautiful, healthy and happy human beings" and that the women of Bristol, Plymouth, and other centres were "coming to realise the part they can play in making these areas strong for Socialism and Peace."[1] Her socialist comrade, Mabel Tothill, the first woman to sit on the Bristol City Council, claimed that "housing problems were a disgrace to the city. If they cared for a better world and the future of the younger generation they must alter things."[2]

These statements express the hopes and desires for change of women active in the labour movement from the First World War through the interwar period. They wanted to work for a better world – to end poverty and war, but also to promote happiness and beauty in people's lives. For them, involvement in mixed-sex socialist politics was the best way to achieve their aims. Speaking at a meeting in Bristol, Ruby Part, an organizer for the Workers' Union and a candidate in the municipal elections, did not apologize for coming forward "either as a labour representative or a woman candidate. If they wanted to make the city a real city, and a city of happy homes, and a city better for the children, surely it was well for men and women to work together."[3]

Women who worked within the male-dominated Labour Party faced many constraints in trying to get their voices heard, but as Pat Thane has reminded us, they also found opportunities there to develop their own political skills and to make a difference in women's lives.[4] In their rhetoric they do not necessarily refer overtly to gender and the position of women, but, it will be argued here, in their practice this was often at the forefront of their activities. This chapter will explore some of complex ways in which labour women carried out their politics through an in-depth look at the work of Townley, a paid organizer for the Labour

Party in Bristol and the South West of England. As suffrage historians have long argued, it is important to look beyond national leaders to "include a wide cast of characters who represent the diversity and scope of the movement where it actually happened."[5] It will be suggested here that a focus on the political journey of one local activist, and her relationship with rank-and-file members, can provide insights into the texture of day-to-day campaigning work in the interwar years and into what attracted women to Labour Party politics and what kept them involved. It will be argued that the reasons that women supported labour politics and took the decision to become active citizens can be found not just in structural explanations but also in feelings, emotional experience, and personal relationships.

Historiography

The nature of women's engagement in British labour politics has long been the subject of debate among historians. Pioneering work by Pat Thane and Pamela Graves in the 1990s showed the extent to which women were involved in Labour Party politics in the interwar years, how they battled the party on issues such as birth control and family allowances, and how they had an influence on welfare policies.[6] Graves suggests that there was a shift between the 1920s, when there was still a space for women to raise issues that could challenge male authority, and the 1930s, when the threat of depression, fascism, and war led to a focus on class rather than gender.[7] She argues that although welfare became central to the Labour Party's agenda, the arguments used were couched in the language of class and covered welfare issues that were less controversial than birth control had been.

This standard account has been challenged in subsequent studies that have questioned the use of binary oppositions, whether between sex and class or between feminism and socialism. They have pointed to the fluidity of these concepts and examined the complex ways in which class, gender, and to some extent ethnicity intersected in the development of political identities.[8] It can be argued that socialist women did not just abandon their feminist perspective in favour of the class struggle, but instead found ways to work through the complex relationship between the two in the new context of the interwar years. Linda Kealey also points to this complexity in her chapter in this volume exploring the lives of five Canadian women engaged in left politics in this period. She argues that an in-depth look at women's lives can broaden our view of what is radical about their politics and suggest that our political categorizations are perhaps too rigid.[9] A biographical approach has certainly been significant in revealing the complexities of labour women's politics in Britain and in challenging dominant narratives.[10] Laura Beers's recent biography of the Labour MP Ellen Wilkinson, for example, shows how her quest for social justice and her commitment to the importance of international affairs defined her political outlook. She was passionate in support of feminist and left-wing causes, which could lead to conflicts with the Labour Party leadership, but she could also be pragmatic if that was necessary to achieve change or to consolidate the party's position.[11]

A new feature of the interwar years was the development of a "mass electorate." All men over twenty-one and most women over thirty were enfranchised by the Representation of the People Act of 1918, while women finally achieved equal voting rights with men in 1928. This had an impact on both the theory and practice of politics in this period.[12] Historians of the women's movement in particular have asked what it meant in this new context to be an active citizen, how and whether women became politicized, and what spaces women used to express their aims.[13]

Our understanding of women's involvement in Labour Party politics has also been affected by these concerns. Studies by Laura Beers, Adrian Bingham, and Jon Lawrence have focused on political culture, using the national press to discuss representation of the new woman voter, in particular the housewife, as being a key source of support.[14] They suggest that the image of the housewife deployed by political parties played an important part in defining the nature of women's political engagement. This claim has been important in raising the significance of the gendering of politics in this period, but, as Karen Hunt notes, there is a danger in seeing the housewife as homogeneous. Examining the column "The Housewife" in *Labour Woman*, an official publication of the Labour Party edited by the chief woman officer, she directs our attention to different representations of the housewife, including the drudgery of working-class women's lives. She suggests that the column provided a space for activists to reach "the woman in the home" and that "everyday life was the terrain where such interactions could begin." When issues such as the cost of living were raised, it was in a class context and implied that working-class housewives could use their agency to bring about change through political campaigns and by ensuring such issues were given political priority.[15]

Local Political Activism between the Wars

One way of examining women's activism in the Labour Party, in all its "diversity and ambiguity," has been to refocus attention away from high politics toward a study of the social-political development of the party at a local level.¹⁶ After the 1918 Representation of the People Act, the number of male and female voters in local elections increased, almost doubling the electorate in many areas. Women and men were now able to join the Labour Party as individual members, and women were seen as an important resource for campaigning and building up grass-roots support in this new context of a "mass electorate." Women could belong to the mixed-sex branches but could also join women's sections, and they did so in large numbers. At its height in 1927, there were 250,000 to 300,000 women members of the women's sections.¹⁷ Women contributed to labour politics in many different ways. Activists stood for election to public office, spoke at meetings, and were office holders within mixed-sex branches. In addition, members of women's sections attended meetings, held fund-raising events, and canvassed door to door during elections. There were variations in the extent to which women could exert any influence on decision-making and also how they did so. Local studies have shown the complex ways in which social, cultural, and economic factors combined with gender to influence the character of local labour politics.¹⁸ Women could usually exert more influence in areas where there was a strong tradition of women's public service combined with extensive female employment, such as parts of Lancashire and Liverpool, or where the socialist group the Independent Labour Party predominated. In some constituencies, pressure from women's sections was responsible for putting welfare on the agenda, while in others it was individual women activists such as city councillors or organizers, working with labour men, who were responsible for achieving reforms.¹⁹

It is at the level of the local that historians have been able to explore what attracted women to labour politics and the process by which they were politicized. Activities such as social events, fund-raising, and the creation of links with the neighbourhood and the broader community have been reassessed and seen as important for both strengthening the Labour Party and politicizing women.²⁰ Anne Marie Hughes's study of women in Scotland, for example, argues that it was working-class women's experience of everyday life, rather than abstract ideas of social justice, that politicized them.²¹ Women were often drawn into working for the Labour Party because their emotions were engaged, and this engagement could also help to maintain their loyalty. Neil Evans and Dot Jones, for example, claim that in South Wales the Labour Party "stirred feelings" for women and that these were "an essential ingredient in the operation of the women's networks."²² For Pamela Graves, women were "the conscience of the Labour Party on peace and humanitarian issues," which in turn could increase its appeal to other women.²³ As this suggests, women active at a local level were drawn into international events; for example, they helped refugees from Spain or attended rallies for world peace.

With local studies, of course, a challenge is in how to bring these together to reframe the national story. Matthew Worley's *Labour Inside the Gate* is one of the few texts to look at the Labour Party's national history in a different way by bringing to the fore the "complex matrix of organisations, alliances, personalities and regional variations that made up the party at a grass roots level," which in turn highlights women's specific experiences.²⁴

In an article published in 2013, Karen Hunt and I suggested that we needed to look at localities in ever greater detail in order to develop a new approach to women's politics between the wars. This would entail exploring the different places in which women's politics took place and assessing the role of preceding political cultures and experiences in shaping the possibilities of women's politics in the aftermath of suffrage.²⁵ We argued that the national story of women's politics (and the same could be said of the Labour Party) "will change when it is rebuilt out from the neighbourhood – from the local and the everyday."²⁶ We asked how political activists related to more passive members as well as to women voters; how important bonds of friendship were in sustaining activism; and what the everyday place of political involvement was in working-class women's lives. How did feelings operate in the context of women's everyday political experiences? The political activist might be out canvassing, signing petitions, speaking at meetings, but how did this sit alongside a familial, domestic, and working identity? This chapter explores some of these questions in the context of Townley's work in Bristol and the South West.

Annie Townley: Organizing Women in the South West

Annie Townley occupied a distinct position within the structure of local labour politics in Bristol and the South West. When the Labour Party restructured after the First World War, she was one of nine women appointed as paid regional organizers.²⁷ Her role was to encourage women to become involved in Labour politics and to provide loyal, grass-roots supporters. Nonetheless, as a member of the prewar suffrage generation, whose life was influenced by the women's suffrage campaign, she also aimed to give women a voice within both the party and wider political life. Her task was not an easy one. Outside the large city of Bristol, the South West region was predominantly an area based on agriculture, small-scale manufacture, and the leisure industry, with weak trade union organization and few opportunities for married women's employment. It took Townley seven hours to travel from one end to the other as she attempted to attract women in small towns and villages to attend meetings. She had to take a hands-on approach, assisting local women to set up new groups, providing training and education, and also offering emotional support when life was difficult.[28] It will be suggested here that her day-to-day activities provide insights into the process by which women became involved in labour politics at the grass roots and what this meant in their own lives, as well as for the Labour Party, in a period in which local activism was seen as a valuable way to build party strength.

The new post of regional organizer represented a significant career opportunity for Townley, although it built upon her previous employment and experience. At the time of the 1911 census, she was recorded as a housewife, aged thirty-six, living with her husband, Ernest, a textile worker aged thirty-four, in Blackburn, Lancashire. They had been married ten years and had two young daughters, Kathleen and Florence, aged eight and six, respectively.[29] Only a year later this was to change. Townley, who was a member of the socialist group the Independent Labour Party (ILP) and an experienced political worker, gained employment as an organizer for the Election Fighting Fund (EFF) of the National Union of Women's Suffrage Societies (NUWSS). In 1912 the NUWSS adopted a new policy of support for Labour Party candidates in selected seats where the Liberal MP or candidate was opposed to women's suffrage.[30] To ensure that trade unions and other labour organizations backed this new initiative, women from socialist and labour backgrounds were recruited as organizers to work for the EFF. This enabled Townley, as well as many other working-class women, to combine paid work with their political activism.

Townley's first post was in the Lancashire town of Rotherham, where her talents as an organizer were quickly recognized. It was reported in *Common Cause* that she had done "much canvassing, especially of prominent trade unionists," had formed an EFF committee from members of the local suffrage society and others, and had "collected and tabulated information of all kinds which will be useful to the organizer at an election." It was noted that she had to operate in "trying circumstances" since the committee rooms were not the "healthiest or pleasantest" and that she had had to endure many trials in this "dreary district." But a glimpse was then given of her personality, or at least of the qualities expected of an organizer, since it was claimed that she had emerged from her trials "all smiling and always ready to return to the fray."[31] It might have been because her work was thought "invaluable" that she was found a new post in Bristol in 1913.

The EFF decided to give financial and other support to the Labour Party candidate in the East Bristol constituency, where the Liberal Party MP and minister Charles Hobhouse was an outspoken opponent of women's suffrage. The local branch of the NUWSS, which contained many committed Liberals, was not sympathetic to the new policy, and therefore Townley worked through a separate group, the East Bristol Women's Suffrage Society. This was comprised largely of ILP members and local working-class women.[32]

The Independent Labour Party, which was affiliated with the Labour Party at a national level, was a significant group within Bristol labour politics. As a port city with a mixed employment base, Bristol's trade union organization was weaker and more dispersed than in areas of heavy industry. This made it more possible for the ILP, which had a strong ward organization, to exert an influence within the local Labour Party. The Bristol ILP was one of the strongest branches in the country with over six hundred members in 1911, including many active female members.[33] A number of prominent ILP members threw their support behind the campaign to support women's suffrage and the Labour candidate in East Bristol. Those with whom Townley worked closely at this time were to remain comrades and friends well into the 1920s. They included Walter Ayles, the charismatic organizer of the Bristol ILP who was a city councillor and then the candidate for East Bristol in 1913, and his wife, Bertha, a part-time organizer for the Women's Labour League (WLL) in the South West and president of the Bristol WLL.[34] They were both strong supporters of women's rights and lived in the same street as the Townleys. Another husband-and-wife team, Tommy and Hannah Higgins, who had two young daughters, also worked closely with Townley. Tommy was a coach painter, and both he and his wife were active in the ILP, while Hannah was also an office holder in the Bristol WLL.[35] Mabel Tothill, the president of the East Bristol Women's Suffrage Society, was from a very different background. A middle-class Quaker and suffragist, she had helped to establish, and was a resident of, the university settlement in East Bristol and had also joined the ILP.[36]

Townley's brief was the same as it had been in Rotherham. She had to gain support from local labour groups, conduct door-to-door canvassing, and carry out registration work to ensure that working-class men could vote. She put energy and enthusiasm into her task and was described by Walter Ayles as "a fine speaker and a fine worker" whose "tact and ability" were crucial in enabling her to persuade others to give support.[37] As in the case of many socialist women before the First World War, Townley believed that voting rights would enable working-class women to have a voice in social and economic questions that affected their lives. She also argued that the most effective way to achieve their long-term goals would be through the Labour Party. The EFF campaign merely reinforced this view. Mabel Tothill, for example, claimed that "in many cases the interests of women were closely allied with the interests of the Labour Party and many of those things for which women [who] were working [for] the Labour Party were working for as well."[38]

The link between labour politics and women's suffrage in Bristol was maintained during the First World War. Although active suffrage campaigning had ceased, Townley was still employed as an EFF organizer. There was opposition from NUWSS leaders who had never supported the 1912 policy and who were critical of Walter Ayles because of his stand against conscription. There was a stormy meeting in London, where Townley, Walter Ayles, and Mabel Tothill all argued that Ayles would not have come forward as a candidate without the promise of NUWSS support and that all the good work they had done before the war would be destroyed. Townley left the meeting "feeling awfully sick of the NU" and thought that "Mrs Fawcett [Millicent Fawcett, president of the NUWSS] was hopeless."[39] Nonetheless, Ayles continued to receive financial support.

During the war Townley consolidated her position as a key figure within the local labour movement. Alongside many other ILP members, she opposed the war and was active in campaigning for peace, both through the ILP, the WLL, and the Women's International League, and also organized the Bristol contribution to the Women's Peace Crusade of 1917. From 1916, when Walter Ayles was imprisoned as a conscientious objector, she was effectively the organizer of the ILP in Bristol.[40] Once the Representation of the People Act was passed early in 1918, Townley started political propaganda and registration work for the Labour Party in earnest. She managed to persuade the Bristol Labour Party to set up a shop in East Bristol to act as a focal point for political campaigning, and members of the East Bristol Women's Suffrage Society held their meetings in the same place.[41] Townley was chosen for the position of election agent for Walter Ayles, and in 1920 she was vice-chair of the Bristol Labour Party.[42]

It is therefore perhaps not surprising that Townley was appointed as a woman organizer when the Labour Party's structure was reorganized after the war. As we have seen, she already had a wealth of experience as a political organizer and was well known and respected in the local world of labour and socialist politics. She was a socialist, a suffragist, and a peace campaigner, all of which made up her political identity and her motivation. It is interesting here to consider her role as a married woman activist with a young family. The importance of family involvement in the socialist and labour movement – its role in both drawing men and women into the movement and sustaining their commitment – has often been noted. We rarely have insights, however, into what this meant for day-to-day life. A glimpse is provided of the impact of political activism on the Higgins family in a portrait of Tommy that appeared in the *Labour Leader*. It was noted here that "four nights out of every week he gives to the work of the ILP ... posting bills, giving them out, M.C. at a dance (and he is one of our most popular ones), discussing matters at the [executive committee] – he is always there."[43] Hannah Higgins also attended ILP meetings in the evening as well as those of the Bristol WLL during the day.

In the Townley family it was Annie who was the most prominent activist. Ernest Townley came with her from Blackburn and therefore must have left his paid employment. It is unclear what he did when he came to Bristol. He was active in the local ILP but took on tasks such as literature secretary rather than leadership positions. Annie and Ernest went to many antiwar meetings and conferences together during the war, but Ernest's health was damaged when he was "knocked about" at a demonstration in London in 1916. It was reported in the *Labour Leader* that "he has never been quite well since."[44] He was imprisoned as a conscientious objector in 1918 and asked for a few hours' remand because his wife was attending a Labour Party conference in Nottingham. He was granted twenty-four hours.

This suggests that Ernest was supportive of his wife's activities and shared many of her views. Annie emphasized how important it was for women to have the vote so that they could mitigate the worst effects of the war on wages and work conditions and could claim the right to sit on committees dealing with health, welfare, and maternity.[45] Ernest used similar arguments in a letter written to the NUWSS newspaper *Common Cause* in 1916: "In the crisis all kinds of nice things are being said about women and their adaptability ... In the future there will be great problems and without the co-operation of women many of the problems will never be solved at all. The present time is opportune for giving women (whose claims are long overdue) the human rights of citizenship and political equality."[46] Annie's decision to work for the Labour Party was also endorsed by her husband. He urged ILP members who wanted to concentrate on carrying out socialist propaganda to take a more active part in the Labour Party so that they could liven it up and increase its effectiveness.[47]

Townley's work for the Labour Party, which started in November 1920, meant that she could no longer play such a prominent role in the ILP. At the end of the year, she gave up the position of chairman of the branch, which was taken on by Mabel Tothill. It would have been difficult to hold office in the ILP in case there were conflicts with Labour Party policy, but also the sheer demands of her work as an organizer must have made it impossible to combine both roles. She faced constraints as a paid employee, but the work also enabled her to focus on the needs of working-class women and to link the achievement of their goals to Labour Party politics. These had been her twin aims since her prewar suffrage campaigning.

A key part of Townley's role was to encourage the growth of women's sections in her region. The women's sections were always controversial. Some activists thought that they sidelined women and reduced their potential influence. Most of their members were married women, and there was scepticism, especially from men in the party, about whether housewives could, or even should, become politicized. Activists were far more familiar with the idea that paid work and trade unionism was the main route to politicization.[48]

Townley disagreed with this argument. Before her appointment as a paid organizer, she was secretary of the Bristol women's sections and argued that women-only spaces would draw in those who had little experience of collective action. She believed that women in the home, as much as waged workers, had the potential to take an interest in politics if their needs were recognized and if the right approach was taken. In the South West, the Labour Party would need to recruit such women since, outside the major cities of Bristol and Plymouth, few women were engaged in industrial employment or attached to trade unions.[49] Townley did not want to just provide the Labour Party with fund-raisers and canvassers, but to also bring change to women's own lives. She argued consistently that women needed to have a voice in order to change conditions at home and in the workplace. During the war she linked this to women gaining the vote, but later she saw it as part of active citizenship.[50] For example, in an article on the importance of training women for work on city councils, written in the late 1930s, she included a section entitled "Women Find Their Voices."[51]

But what could be done to get women interested in politics? One way was to show the connections between politics, in particular local politics, and women's everyday lives. In the early 1920s, Townley and her ILP friends, including Bertha Ayles and Mabel Tothill, put forward this message in their writings and their speeches. One article by Townley in *Bristol Labour Weekly* was entitled "Your Money or Your Life." In this she urged women to take account of a candidate's views on health and welfare rather than just their arguments about saving money on the rates. She suggested that the lowering of rates was a false economy if it meant local councils would have less money to spend on welfare and therefore made it more difficult for mothers to get free milk, which could endanger their own lives or those of their children.[52] Articles in the labour press, however, tended to be read by those who were already active. It was public meetings, on topics of interest to working-class women, that were more likely to reach a broader audience. Townley was responsible for organizing many of these meetings, inviting popular speakers such as Ruby Part, who, at one event, appealed to women's specific characteristics that she thought made them ideally suited to support the Labour Party. She claimed that if it was true that man "speaks with his head and woman with her heart," then the Labour Party's municipal policies must appeal to women since they dealt with things closest to their hearts: "home and children, peace and happiness."[53]

In 1923 Townley arranged for the labour candidate Walter Baker and his wife to spend a week in East Bristol, where they held a series of daily meetings aimed at women. Mrs. Walter Baker, JP, argued that "married working women were the hardest worked members of the community because they had to perform all of the duties and work in the home in the absence of up to date appliances and without proper assistance." Townley added that the Labour Party was the friend of women in every way and believed, with writer and philosopher John Ruskin, that "there is no wealth but life."[54] The week concluded with a rally and social event.

Personal contact was important for attracting new female members, and the Labour Party shop played a role in this. The significance of a shop for a political movement was recognized before the war by Margaret Robertson, coordinator of the EFF organizers, when she described the East Bristol suffrage shop: "Many people call at the shop, and the talks carried on there and outside the works are probably as valuable as the meetings in terms of propaganda."[55] Leafleting, door-to-door canvassing, and personal contact within communities could also be crucial. Marge Evans, the daughter of committed trade unionists, was affected by the depression of the early 1920s and thought of joining the Communist Party. "But Florrie Brown, who lived in the same street, persuaded her to join the Labour Party. She did join in 1922, her first job "carrying the tea urn upstairs at meetings."[56] In the early 1930s the East Bristol branch used a new system of canvassers, paid on a commission basis, and street collectors, which drew more women into the party.[57] The personal touch was always significant. Townley, for example, encouraged those who were active in women's sections in small towns and villages to visit other members at least once a year to ensure that they rejoined the party.[58]

At other times it could be a significant national issue that made a difference. Many women were inspired to become involved in the miners' strike of 1926. They were keen to give practical support to miners' families and were crucial in raising money through collecting door to door. Members of the Woman's Quarterly Conference in Bristol, formed to coordinate the local women's sections, assisted at least 160 families in the first few months of the strike and raised money for relief funds.[59] Once events such as these were over, however, it was important to retain women's interest. Townley was full of ideas about how to do this, and she always started from women's day-to-day lives and experiences. Some of her ideas were structural. She praised the different constituencies in Bristol who were "busy educating their members in the duties of citizenship and politics, particularly as affecting women" but was concerned that hundreds of women members were not attached to women's sections. Her aim was to bring the "unattached women together." Special meetings needed to be followed up with more regular ones, which should be held in the afternoon.[60] Townley knew the rhythm of women's lives in her region and planned accordingly. Although few women continued with industrial work after marriage, in holiday centres some had a full-time job in the summer months catering for visitors. In this context Townley accepted that sections in those areas needed to shut down for three months.[61] As preparations increased for war in the late 1930s, women were needed to make gas masks, which meant more work for married women. In Trowbridge and Melksham, therefore, it was decided to "arrange meetings alternately afternoons and evenings" to cater to those at work and to young mothers with children.[62]

Meetings needed to be attractive and welcoming: "Obviously the method is not to try to teach these women the particular Party programme, but first to attract the women to cheerful meetings, as bright as possible – with always a cup of tea. So dull and dreary becomes the life of the average working-class mother, so over worked is she, that only by providing some relaxation and real change can we gain her interest."[63] Townley believed that the women's sections would not simply encourage women to retain their interest in labour politics but would also have the potential to change women's personal lives. There "the housewife can meet other women with the same domestic ties and troubles (many of the latter can be abolished through attending these women's meetings) as her own," and "for an hour she can feel the sense of responsibility as a citizen."[64]

This reminds us of the significant relationship between political activism and sociability. Plays, music, and poetry were all seen as significant for the local Labour Party, along with children's outings and the socials that ended many meetings and rallies. These were not just an add-on to the politics but enabled members to develop firm friendships that then underpinned their loyalties to the party, as well as providing "pleasure" along with the more serious political activities.[65] There was a comfortable, familial feel to these gatherings. Florence Caruth, who took over from Townley as organizer when the latter retired, recalled that there was a "happy and friendly spirit" at the meetings of the joint Labour Women's Sections Committee. There was always a cup of tea and a "real fire in winter," while Mrs. Florence Brown, who was to become the first woman mayor of Bristol, "made rock cakes in the kitchen" when supplies ran low.[66] Affective relationships in the home and the neighbourhood were reinforced in weekly meetings as many of the same family might attend. Townley's own daughter Kathleen was heavily involved. She was secretary of the Bristol Labour Women's Advisory Council, organized many weekend schools that provided talks and training classes, and was appointed editor of the women's column in *Bristol Labour Weekly* in 1932.[67]

There could be a problem if the social side of the sections became too significant. Townley thought that if women were going to have a political voice, then it was crucial to develop their understanding of current policies and of the political process. Her strength lay in offering educational classes and training sessions to build women's confidence to stand as municipal candidates and to increase their effectiveness if they were elected. Training was usually provided through a series of weekly meetings or weekend schools. A more ambitious and complex project was the organization of a mock city council in Bristol, which entailed preparing reports for different subcommittees, discussing the findings, and playing the parts of different officials.

As always, Townley put thought into how to engage the members. She found that doing something practical, such as walking around the ward to note what needed doing, "loosens the tongue of even the silent members." Arousing discussion on what women themselves wanted was a better way to create an interest in council work than a vague talk about local government. She found that "by using simple language, easily understood and by dealing with day-to-day problems that are familiar, we can encourage the expression of views on the part of the shyest member." There was role play to help with canvassing. Members pretended to be industrial workers, shopkeepers, or Tories, and in the comfort of their own meetings canvassers could try out their arguments. This in turn compelled them to read some literature. These methods were not just educational but also "great fun" and caused much "amusement," words that Townley used frequently to avoid the view that meetings were dull.[68]

As women-only spaces, the sections enabled women to express their emotions – these might be anger or distress about the problems that they saw around them or issues in their own family lives. Townley noted that "listeners" meetings, where individual women spoke while others listened, enabled a woman to express what was "pent up inside her."[69] This helped to enable women to find a voice and a political identity. At the same time, these feelings could be channelled through, and help to reinforce, a sense of belonging to a movement. Local party work was located in the community and the neighbourhood, but members could reach out to a wider community through reading *Labour Woman*, listening to charismatic national leaders, and taking part in activities that had national or international significance such as aid for children during the Spanish Civil War.[70]

In all of this process, the role of the organizer was crucial. She gave emotional as well as practical support to members. This was vital in maintaining local sections during the difficult years of the 1930s, when the defeat of the Labour government, depression, and threat of war undermined morale, in particular in small towns and villages. This can be seen in the reports of organizers to the chief woman officer, which only survive for 1937. As Stephanie Ward has suggested in an unpublished paper, these have been a neglected source, used only for the occasional quote rather than being interrogated in depth for what they show about everyday political life.[71] The reports made to the chief woman officer were private documents that allowed organizers to express their feelings in a way that would have been difficult when they wrote for the labour press. Although in her report for *Labour Woman* Townley noted that a planned meeting at the women's section Box "was very small but the committee are determined to carry on," in her private organizer's report she expressed how the secretary had been "very disheartened."[72] Townley had "to talk very gently to them all to get the committee to feel it worthwhile going on," and she tried to encourage those present to go on trying. Similarly in Castle Combe, members of the Chippenham central committee had a picnic and distributed notices of an evening meeting with Townley and the prospective labour candidate as speakers. Not many turned up to the meeting. She wrote in *Labour Woman* that "although small, the effort was well worth-while," but her organizer's report noted "we had all the women peering from their windows and doors, but they would not come near us."[73] The active members were "very discouraged" by the low turnout, and she had to "buck them up."[74]

A great deal of time was spent smoothing troubled waters to keep members on board. There were conflicts that came from national issues, in particular over whether or not support should be given to the Popular Front or to the Left Book Club. These were organizations that sought to bring parties on the left together, including the Communist Party, and it had been decided at the Labour Party's conference that members should not be involved in them. Townley found it difficult to explain this decision to the few members in Melksham and Limpley Stoke "who wanted to attend meetings of the Left Book Club ... it is difficult to say they ought not to have joined ... I made it clear just what the party decisions meant, and appealed to the women to concentrate on our own work."[75] Other problems were far more local. She had promised to give a series of lectures to members of the Corsham section. Only six members turned up to the first lecture. Other members, who had arrived from Wales to live in the town, were more interested in organizing concerts than in listening to "serious subjects." Those who were at the meeting were annoyed and urged Townley to give the remainder of her lectures. She agreed to do this but also argued that in small places such as Corsham, "the social element should not be discouraged."[76] A month later there were still tensions in the group. The secretary had resigned in spite of Townley's offer to "let me try to help." Those present, who were all Wiltshire women, agreed to try to revive the section by visiting all old members, and the organizer could only hope this might be successful.[77] Private lives could also become a matter of public concern and emotional conflict. Irene Chilcott, secretary of the Wootton Bassett women's section, was married to the Labour Party candidate for South Molton. In 1935 the marriage broke down, and when she came up for re-election some members refrained from voting for her. At a meeting Townley recorded that "one of the women said that she did not vote because of all the trouble that was caused by the secretary. I asked her to tell us about it and it transpired that some of the women were bothering themselves about the divorce. I said that members' private lives did not concern the section unless they were in some way injuring the movement."[78] Here party loyalty and efficiency overcame concern about conventional moral codes.

   This chapter has provided a glimpse, through the work of one local organizer, into the ways in which women at the grass-roots level, who were primarily identified with the home, could be persuaded to take part in political activity. This involved sensitivity about their day-to-day experiences and concerns and a recognition that emotions were a key part of this – whether in inspiring their political involvement or in providing the kind of support needed to sustain it. Although it was difficult, in particular outside Bristol, to persuade women to take an active interest in politics, Annie Townley was consistent in arguing that women in the home could and should be politicized. She wanted not just to provide grass-roots supporters for the Labour Party but also to ensure that women would have a voice in bringing about change in their own lives.

In 2013, at a time when young people in particular appeared to be disillusioned with politics, Karen Hunt and I argued that "today when the political process seems more and more remote from people's lives, it is instructive to examine a period in which emphasis was placed on encouraging active citizenship with a focus on immediate concerns that could then link to broader political perspectives."[79] Since then, the revival of interest in Labour Party politics in Britain, the involvement of young people in environmental issues, and the Black Lives Matter movement have seen a resurgence in large political meetings, demonstrations, direct action, and organizing at the local level. It seems timely, therefore, to focus attention on the interwar years, a period characterized by grass-roots activism, to provide an inspiration for more contemporary struggles for political and social change.[80]

NOTES

1. Annie Townley, "Labour Women in the South West," *Labour Woman* (September 1937): 131.
2. *Western Daily Press*, 21 October 1921.
3. *Western Daily Press*, 29 October 1921.
4. Pat Thane, "Women in the British Labour Party and the Construction of State Welfare, 1906–39," in *Mothers of a New World: Maternalist Politics and the Origins of Welfare States*, ed. Seth Koven and Sonya Michel (London: Routledge, 1993), 352–53; Pat Thane, "Women and Political Participation in England, 1918–1970," in *Women and Citizenship in Britain and Ireland in the Twentieth Century*, ed. Esther Breitenbach and Pat Thane (London: Continuum, 2010), 14–15.
5. Susan Ware, "Why We Need More Biographies of Suffragists," *OUP Blog*, 21 August 2019, https://blog.oup.com/2019/08/why-we-need-more-biographies-of-suffragists/?utm_source=adestra&utm_medium=email&utm_content=whyweneedmorebiographiesofsuffragistslink&utm_campaign=oupac-campaign%3A760044.
6. Thane, "Women in the British Labour Party"; Pamela Graves, *Labour Women* (Cambridge: Cambridge University Press, 1994).
7. Pamela Graves, "An Experiment in Women-Centered Socialism: Labour Women in Britain," in *Women and Socialism: Socialism and Women*, ed. Helmut Gruber and Pamela Graves (Oxford: Berghahn, 1998), 203–10.

8 Martin Francis, "Labour and Gender," in *Labour's First Century*, ed. Duncan Tanner, Pat Thane, and Nick Tiratsoo (Cambridge: Cambridge University Press, 2000); June Hannam and Karen Hunt, *Socialist Women: Britain 1880s to 1920s* (London: Routledge, 2002); Amy Black and Stephen Brooke, "The Labour Party, Women and the Problem of Gender, 1951–66," *Journal of British Studies* 36 (1997): 419–52. Joan Sangster has of course been very influential in developing new approaches. See, e.g., Joan Sangster, "Feminism and the Making of Canadian Working-Class History: Exploring the Past, Present and Future," *Labour/Le Travail* 16 (Fall 2000): 127–65.
9 Linda Kealey, "From Dreams of Equality to One Hundred Years of Struggle: Radical Women's Biographies in the History of Canadian Politics," in this volume.
10 See, e.g., Marian Goronwy-Roberts, *A Woman of Vision: A Life of Marion Phillips, MP* (Wrexham: Bridge Books, 2000); Graham Taylor, *Ada Salter: Pioneer of Ethical Socialism* (London: Lawrence & Wishart, 2016); Angela V. John, *Rocking the Boat: Welsh Women Who Championed Equality* (Cardigan: Parthian, 2018), chap. 3, "The Good Life of Edith Picton-Turbervill," chap. 5, "1922: A Year in the Remarkable Life of Lady Rhondda."
11 Laura Beers, *Red Ellen: The Life of Ellen Wilkinson, Socialist, Feminist, Internationalist* (Cambridge, MA: Harvard University Press, 2016).
12 See, e.g., Adrian Bingham, *Gender, Modernity and the Popular Press in Interwar Britain* (Oxford: Oxford University Press, 2004); Julie V. Gottlieb and Richard Toye, eds., *The Aftermath of Suffrage* (Houndmills, Basingstoke: Palgrave Macmillan, 2013).
13 Caitriona Beaumont, *Housewives and Citizens* (Manchester: Manchester University Press, 2013); Breitenbach and Thane, *Women and Citizenship in Britain and Ireland*.
14 Bingham, *Gender, Modernity and the Popular Press*; Laura Beers, *Your Britain: Media and the Making of the Labour Party* (Cambridge, MA: Harvard University Press, 2010); Jon Lawrence, "The Transformation of Party Politics after the First World War," *Past and Present* 190 (2006): 185–216.
15 Karen Hunt, "Labour Woman and the Housewife," in *Women's Periodicals and Print Culture in Britain, 1918–1939*, ed. Catherine Clay, Maria DiCenzo, Barbara Green, and Fiona Hackney (Edinburgh: Edinburgh University Press, 2018), 250.
16 Francis, "Labour and Gender," 199.
17 Pat Thane, "The Women of the British Labour Party and Feminism," in *British Feminism in the Twentieth Century*, ed. Harold L. Smith (London: Edward Elgar, 1990), 125.
18 See, e.g., Matthew Worley, ed., *Labour's Grass Roots: Essays on the Activities and Experiences of Local Labour Parties and Members, 1918–45* (Aldershot: Aldgate, 2005).

19 Duncan Tanner, "Gender, Civic Culture and Politics in South Wales: Explaining Labour Municipal Policy, 1918–39," in *Labour's Grass Roots: Essays on the Activities and Experiences of Local Labour Parties and Members, 1918–45*, ed. Matthew Worley (Aldershot: Aldgate, 2005); Lowri Newman, "'Providing an Opportunity to Exercise Their Energies': The Role of the Labour Women's Sections in Shaping Political Identities, South Wales, 1918–1939," in *Women and Citizenship in Britain and Ireland in the Twentieth Century*, ed. Esther Breitenbach and Pat Thane (London: Continuum, 2010).
20 Neil Evans and Dot Jones, "Help Forward the Great Work of Humanity: Women in the Labour Party in Wales," in *The Labour Party in Wales, 1900–2000*, ed. Duncan Tanner, Chris Williams, and Deian Hopkins (Cardiff: University of Wales Press, 2000).
21 Annemarie Hughes, *Gender and Political Identities in Scotland, 1918–39* (Edinburgh: Edinburgh University Press, 2010).
22 Evans and Jones, "Help Forward the Great Work of Humanity," 225.
23 Graves, *Labour Women*, 157–9.
24 Matthew Worley, *Labour Inside the Gate: A History of the British Labour Party Between the Wars* (London: IB Tauris, 2005).
25 Karen Hunt and June Hannam, "Towards an Archaeology of Inter-war Women's Politics: The Local and the Everyday," in *The Aftermath of Suffrage*, ed. Julie V. Gottlieb and Richard Toye (Houndmills, Basingstoke: Palgrave Macmillan, 2013), 125.
26 Hunt and Hannam, "Towards an Archaeology," 138.
27 For an account of the day-to-day activities of paid organizers, see June Hannam, "Women as Paid Organisers and Propagandists for the British Labour Party between the Wars," *International Labor and Working-Class History* 77 (Spring 2010): 69–88.
28 Annie Townley, "Organising in South West: 1920–1943," *Labour Woman* (September 1943): 91.
29 Ancestry.com, *1911 England Census* (Provo, UT: Ancestry.com Operations, 2011).
30 Sandra Stanley Holton, *Feminism and Democracy: Women's Suffrage and Reform Politics in Britain, 1900–1918* (Cambridge: Cambridge University Press, 1986).
31 *Common Cause*, 12 September 1912.
32 For a detailed account of the activities of the suffrage-labour alliance in East Bristol, see June Hannam, "'To Make the World a Better Place': Socialist Women and Women's Suffrage in Bristol, 1910–1920," in *Suffrage Outside Suffragism: Women's Vote in Britain, 1880–1914*, ed. Miriam Boussahba-Bravard (Houndmills, Basingstoke: Palgrave Macmillan, 2007).
33 June Hannam, *Bristol Independent Labour Party: Men, Women and the Opposition to War* (Bristol: Bristol Radical Pamphleteer 31, 2014), 7–10.

34 John Saville and Bob Whitfield, "Ayles, Walter Henry (1879–1953): Trade Unionist, Pacifist and Labour MP," in *Dictionary of Labour Biography*, vol. 5, ed. John Saville and Joyce Bellamy (Houndmills, Basingstoke: Palgrave Macmillan, 1979). The Women's Labour League was set up in 1906 to encourage working-class women to support the Labour Party. Its branches formed the basis of the women's sections in 1918.
35 Ancestry.com, *1911 England Census*; W.H.A., "Tommy Higgins of Bristol," *Labour Leader*, 14 March 1914.
36 June Hannam, *Mabel Tothill: Feminist, Socialist, Pacifist* (Bristol: Bristol Radical Pamphleteer 45, 1919).
37 *Common Cause*, 3 October and 13 May 1913.
38 *Western Daily Press*, 19 April 1913.
39 Holton, *Feminism and Democracy*, 141.
40 Bristol ILP Branch Minutes 1915–18, Bristol University Archives, Special Collections. Ayles was imprisoned almost continuously from 1916 to 1919.
41 *Common Cause*, 21 June 1918.
42 Bristol ILP Branch Minutes, Executive Committee, 12 March 1919; Annual General Meeting, 25 April 1920.
43 W.H.A., "Tommy Higgins."
44 *Labour Leader*, 31 January 1918.
45 A.T., "Women's Notes," *Bristol Forward*, July 1916.
46 *Common Cause*, 18 August 1916.
47 Bristol ILP Branch Minutes, 1 October 1919.
48 Hannam, "Women as Paid Organisers," 72.
49 Townley, "Labour Women in the South West." For a discussion of the difficulties of generating support for the Labour Party in the South West, see Andrew Thorpe, "'One of the Most Backward Areas of the Country': The Labour Party's Grass Roots in South West England, 1918–45," in *Labour's Grass Roots: Essays on the Activities and Experiences of Local Labour Parties and Members, 1918–45*, ed. Matthew Worley (Aldershot: Aldgate, 2005). Detailed figures exist only for Bristol East Division. In the 1920s there were 1,000 members, 200 of whom were women, and in 1931 there were 2,494 members, including 325 women, but in 1938 out of 1,650 members, 715 were women. Bristol East Divisional Labour Party, 40488/M/3 Bristol Record Office.
50 A.T., "Women's Notes."
51 Annie Townley, "Training for Council Work," *Labour Woman* (June 1939): 83.
52 *Bristol Labour Weekly*, 22 October 1926.
53 *Bristol Labour Weekly*, 29 October 1926.
54 *Western Daily Press*, 27 September 1923.
55 *Common Cause*, 18 July 1912.

56 David Parker, "A Proper Joiner: Marge Evans – Memories of the Bristol Labour Movement," in *Placards and Pin Money: Another Look at Bristol's History* (Bristol: Bristol Broadsides Co-op, 1986), 2.
57 "How East Bristol Makes Members," *Labour Organiser*, May 1931, 84–5.
58 Organizer's reports, 22 February 1937 and 27 March 1937, LP/WORG/37/36, Labour History Archive & Study Centre, People's History Museum, Manchester.
59 Bristol East Divisional Labour Party, 40488/M/3/1, 6 October 1926.
60 *Bristol Labour Weekly*, 10 September 1926.
61 Townley, "Labour Women in the South West."
62 Organizer's report, 12 July 1937, LP/WORG/37/31, Labour History Archive & Study Centre, People's History Museum, Manchester.
63 Annie Towney, "A Woman's Page," *Labour Organiser*, January 1922.
64 *West Bristol Labour Weekly*, 24 September 1926.
65 For a discussion of the importance of social events for women's trade unionism, see Cathy Hunt, "Dancing and Days Out: The Role of Social Events in British Women's Trade Unionism in the Early Twentieth Century," *Labour History Review* 76, no. 2 (August 2011): 104–20. For day-to-day activities in the Bristol women's sections, see Tanya Sinnett, "The Labour Party in Bristol, 1918–29" (unpublished PhD thesis, University of the West of England, 2006).
66 Florence Caruth, "Ship Shape and Bristol Fashion," *Labour Woman*, October 1956, 15.
67 *Bristol Labour Weekly*, 26 May 1934.
68 Townley, "Training for Council Work."
69 Townley, "Training for Council Work."
70 St. George West Ward Women's Section Minutes, 1930s, 40488/M/9, Bristol Record Office.
71 Stephanie Ward, "Friends and Fellow Workers: Emotions in Inter-war Working-Class Women's Politics" (unpublished paper), 26 April 1937, 22.
72 Organizer's report, 25 April 1973, LP/WORG/37/6, Labour History Archive & Study Centre, People's History Museum, Manchester.
73 Organizer's report, 1 July 1937, Labour History Archive & Study Centre, People's History Museum, LP/WORG/27/4.
74 *Labour Woman*, August 1937; organizer's report, 5 July 1937, LP/WORG/37/4, Labour History Archive & Study Centre, People's History Museum, Manchester.
75 Organizer's report, 25 October 1937, LP/WORG/37/29, Labour History Archive & Study Centre, People's History Museum, Manchester.
76 Organizer's report, 8 February 1937, LP/WORG/37/15, Labour History Archive & Study Centre, People's History Museum, Manchester.

77 Organizer's report, 27 March 1937, LP/WORG/37/9, Labour History Archive & Study Centre, People's History Museum, Manchester.
78 Organizer's report, LP/WORG/37/37, Labour History Archive, People's History Museum, Manchester.
79 Hunt and Hannam, "Towards an Archaeology," 126.
80 Local labour history groups such as Bristol Radical History and North West Labour History emphasize the relationship between an understanding of working-class and women's history and contemporary politics.

6 *Centros de Madres*: From Their Origins to Their Radicalization under Salvador Allende's Government

GABRIELA CASTILLO

They sent me a letter
by the morning mail
in this letter they told me
that my brother was imprisoned
and without compassion, with shackles,
they dragged him through the street.

The letter said the reason
that Robert was arrested
was that he supported the strike
that had already been settled.
If this is really the reason
I'm going to prison too, Sergeant.

I find myself so far away
Awaiting news
The letter comes to me and says
that in my country there is no justice.
The hungry ask for bread,
the militia gives them bullets.

– Violeta Parra [1,2]

The words of Violeta Parra, the famous Chilean singer-songwriter and visual artist, might seem crude and harsh, but that does not make them untrue. Like her, many underprivileged and low-income women saw with astonishment how the Chilean establishment turned its back on their dreams and sorrows through most of the late nineteenth and twentieth centuries. However, this trend did not apply just to destitute women; in a strongly patriarchal society like the Chilean one, women of all classes tended to be spectators, a complement to the male presence.

Until the second half of the twentieth century, there were few spaces in Chile where women were able to develop their interests beyond the realm of the household. One of those places was the *centro de madres* (mothers' centre). These centres were non-profit private corporations originally founded by the Chilean government to turn low-income women into what it deemed to be "better" mothers and wives and, by extension, better citizens. As part of a public policy, these centres carried out cultural, social, and technical training activities that were set up according to the needs and interests of their members. Thus, *centros de madres* were where women went to learn about a number of things, such as the spiritual origins of life, the importance of well-constituted families within society, knitting, first aid, and more. The *centros* also connected women with other governmental institutions and charities, which meant they were liminal spaces between the private and the public sphere.

From a historiographical perspective, studying *centros de madres* offers a window into the everyday lives of Chilean women who were often overlooked because of the place they occupied in society; after all, low-income women were at the bottom of the hierarchy, and, since they did not produce the traditional kinds of archival sources on which historians so often rely, it is relatively difficult to tell stories about their day-to-day lives. There are many interesting aspects of this institution, but this paper will look at how *centros de madres* were instrumentalized by a series of governments until their radicalization under Salvador Allende. At the same time, I will examine the ways in which women made use of the tools they were given at *centros de madres* to challenge the roles they were originally expected to fulfil. Thus, this paper will illustrate the rough and treacherous path that *centros de madres* underwent and how difficult it was for their members to challenge the deeply ingrained traditional notions of gender within Chilean society. Despite these challenges, I argue, *centros de madres* up to and including the Allende period were important sites for women's politicization and their commitment to fight for justice.

History of Women and Women in History

Understanding women's role in Chilean society during the late nineteenth and early twentieth centuries requires an acknowledgment of the power of the patriarchy and men's dominance in the public sphere. This paradigm also extended to and was replicated by Chilean historiography. For decades, the way in which Chileans learned about their history was through the lives of generals, statesmen, presidents, and the like. When labour history emerged in Chile around the celebration of the centennial (1910), workers were added into the picture of the country's history. However, most of the subjects from these stories – and the historians who told them – were men. It was not until the tumultuous decades of 1970s and 1980s (between the rise and fall of Salvador Allende's government and the eruption of Pinochet's dictatorship) that a significant group of women entered the field of academic history.[3] Female historians introduced new themes and new perspectives to the discipline. In very broad terms, this is what Chilean feminist historiography has called the "history of women and gender perspectives"[4] since these histories introduced, for example, works on women in politics and public spaces and on women and labour, as well as women in private spaces. Writing about women by women was a slow process that nevertheless turned women into the protagonists of their own stories.

This was not just happening in Chile, of course. As Joan Sangster notes in her introduction to *Through Feminist Eyes: Essays on Canadian Women's History*, "writing on women and gender has been intimately connected to, and stimulated by, movements for social change, most notably, (but not only) the women's movement. Whether it was challenges to the gendered division of labour, patriarchal legal structures, or the regulation of women's bodies, feminist critiques of existing power structures have had an inestimable impact on women's history. In turn, feminist efforts to construct our own 'herstory' offered insights into, and also lent weight to, specific political struggles."[5] This historiographical trend was amplified in Chile, where historians highlighted women's fight for political and juridical equality.[6] Another equally relevant current of the scholarship explored private spaces, where women tended to prevail. This is the case of the groundbreaking work of Teresa Valdés, "Centros de madres 1973–1989: Solo disciplinamiento?" (Mothers' centres 1973–1989: Just disciplining?), published by FLACSO (Facultad Latinoamericana de Ciencias Sociales/Latin American Social Sciences Institute) in 1989. In this work, Valdés explores the characteristics of mothers' centres under the Pinochet regime and long-time members' perceptions of them. Valdés notes how *centros de madres* changed when militaries came to power; once places of companionship and support, the *centros* became places where women were indoctrinated and judged if they were not willing to serve the Junta's idea of nation. In doing so, she unveils the ways in which the state had built relationships with destitute women through the different political projects instated since

1938. Furthermore, she points toward the forms of patronage exercised by Pinochet supporters installed in the *centros* and how they consolidated forms of espionage and control through the networks established by the *centros*. Her scholarship came at a key moment in Chilean history; by the time Valdés published her study, Pinochet's dictatorship was ending and the "return" to democracy was imminent. She took that opportunity to diagnose the changes *centros de madres* needed to undergo in order to be effective agents of change. First and foremost, she argued, they needed to be a feminist institution, instead of a subsidiary replica of the patriarchal society.[7]

Another important work that explores women's private lives is Jadwiga E. Pieper Mooney's *The Politics of Motherhood: Maternity and Women's Rights in Twentieth-Century Chile*.[8] In this study, Pieper Mooney explores the politics of health and political rights through a gendered lens, especially focusing on birth control, healthcare, and motherhood as public policy. Even though this book is not solely about *centros de madres*, chapters such as "Planning Motherhood under Christian Democracy" dedicate an important part of the analysis to the *centros*, helping to contextualize their nature. In this chapter, Pieper Mooney's main concern regarding *centros de madres* is the way in which governments prior to Salvador Allende set their mission as advancing women within the boundaries of a "female" sphere, meaning developing female skills (such as knitting, sewing, etc.) and female bonding around ideas of motherhood without women/members becoming politically active. According to Pieper Mooney, even though *centros de madres* replicated gendered practices ingrained in Chilean historical tradition, this did not prevent women from enrolling in them.

Both Teresa Valdés's and Jadwiga Pieper Mooney's scholarship highlight the importance of *centros de madres* as places where low-income women built networks outside their homes. At the same time, they both recognize the structural influence of the patriarchy in the creation of *centros de madres*; women existed in the spaces they were "allowed to" and made the best of it, resisting their subjugation while expanding their aspirations. Both Valdés and Pieper Mooney study *centros de madres* located in the Santiago Metropolitan Region, specifically Santiago, Chile's capital. Considering that the over-portrayal of the capital is one of Chile's persistent problems when it comes to representation, Fabiola Bahamondes's paper "Centros de madres en el Chile rural: Un espacio de seguridad" (Mothers' centres in rural Chile: A secure space) illuminates the reality of women in *centros de madres* located beyond urban settings. For Bahamondes, rural Chile is, geographically and historiographically speaking, uncharted territory. Following the ideas of

Michel de Certau, Bahamondes argues that *centros de madres* were the only instance where low-income women could socialize through everyday life tasks while building their own strategies of resistance through solidarity and companionship. For Bahamondes, women in rural Chile were interacting with the state via *centros de madres* on their own terms, through their own strategies of support.[9]

This paper offers a comprehensive review of the birth of and changes undergone by *centros de madres* up to the end of the Allende period. Most importantly, by focusing on the women, individuals, and policies of *centros de madres* over time, I emphasize the complexity of the entire system as well as its deep patriarchal roots. I argue that *centros de madres* radicalized women under Allende and helped them become active political agents as part of a socialist political agenda. I also argue, however, that this radicalization highlighted women's agency but that it did not stop reproducing traditional gender roles; it only made them less rigid.

Centros de Madres as Public Policy: From Civilizing Tool to Emancipating Network

Chile was a society designed mostly for men ... until it wasn't anymore. *Centros de madres* developed timidly among this patriarchal space as a project where women – the *pobladoras*, "those who were not directly tied to the production process and [had] marginal political orientation"[10] – could take part. *Centros de madres* were a public space, though filled with intimacy, where low-income Chilean women experienced political and labour consciousness that flourished in their everyday lives.

Chilean historians still debate the nature and birth of *centros de madres*. In this chapter, I take as my starting point the explanation for the roots of *centros de madres* offered by feminist social historians like Teresa Valdés[11] and María Soledad Zarate.[12] They argue that the *centros* emerged in an unofficial way in the early twentieth century and were a product of elite Chilean women's response to the crisis produced by the emergence of industrial society. *Centros de madres* did not just materialize on a specific date as a finalized product. Instead, they developed in stages. In the first stage, from the late nineteenth century to the 1930s, different charities run by the elite targeted low-income women in an atomized manner. This period was followed, from the 1930s, by a slow process of institutionalization with the consolidation of the women's movement and the fight for voting rights, which marked the "official" foundation of the organization in 1952. In this second stage, the Chilean government initially funded and later grouped together several charities, including "wardrobes of the people," the "Association of Housewives," and "housewives' committees" (*roperos del pueblo, Asociación de Dueñas de Casa*, and *comités de dueñas de casas*). Since this initiative was proposed by President Ibañez's wife, the new association was named Foundation Graciela Letelier Velasco de Ibañez, CEMA Chile. A third period came with the 1960s, under Eduardo Frei Montalva's Christian Democracy and his "Revolution in Liberty," which saw the development of a more politicized understanding of the role of women in the household. Finally, when Allende came to power in the 1970s, *centros de madres* became the epitome of radicalization for *pobladoras*.

The Early Stages: Paternalism as the Norm

In the late nineteenth and early twentieth centuries, *centros de madres* were established and overseen by women of a higher social class. The turn of the century found Chile undergoing an eruption of mass society; a decline of the sense of community went hand in hand with rapid industrialization and rapid urbanization.[13] Elite women were motivated to serve those who suffered under these conditions, but their service also has to be understood as a product of their instrumentalization by the Catholic Church. The notion of service was reinforced within Catholicism after the publication of the *Rerum novarum* encyclical in 1891,[14] which inspired a more socially inclined Roman Catholicism.[15] What this revision brought to the role of Catholic Chilean elites was an understanding of responsibility where the rich would oversee the care and well-being – both material and spiritual – of those in need through education, assistance, and justice. Broadly, this movement saw the social question as a result of a moral crisis that had diminished the authoritative and protective role of the Chilean elite. This might seem like a small change, yet it implied an emphasis on social work and changes at a foundational level rather than simply charity.

Chilean historian María Soledad Zárate addressed this subject in her paper "Mujeres viciosas, mujeres virtuosas" (Vicious women, virtuous women).[16] According to Zárate, women were to be "rescued" from moral deviance and taught what and how to teach their children in order to comply with society's expectations. This demonstrates the extent to which religion dictated the lives of women and their place in society. In the case of Chile, the Catholic Church saw as its duty the imposition of the preservation of "female values" such as virginity, sexual honour, and maternity. According to Zárate, nineteenth-century Chilean society widely and firmly believed that a woman's mission in the world was to serve God, her husband, and her children.[17] A virtuous woman, in this rendering, had little say about her life, since her biological-reproductive nature determined the way others viewed her and regulated her aspirations and desires.

As Zárate describes, the counterpoint of the virtuous woman was the vicious woman. A vicious woman was a working woman, one who lived her life beyond the realms of the home and, in the case of Chilean society, had "undesirable" contact with the opposite sex. However, Zárate shows that this stereotype quickly evolved. Over time, fewer women were labelled as licentious, but they were still vicious if they were seamstresses, industrial garment workers, cooks, or washerwomen. Voting rights were not part of their concerns. Thus, the key element that distinguished these two types of women was clear: Virtuous women did not have an occupation outside their homes, while vicious women did.

The elites' call to service materialized through spontaneous initiatives started by groups of women from the higher class who felt the need to gather and talk to low-income women about their experiences, while teaching them how to be better housewives. In the beginning, these groups lacked organization and clear objectives, but it was not long before the state and the Catholic Church took control of them, with both the state and the church playing an essential role in the development of these groups. The *centros de madres* were considered by the church and the state to be successful in indoctrinating low-income women, because they would "improve" the moral and material well-being of families.

Centros de madres had undeniable gender and class implications, since they were paternalist institutions that targeted poor women in order to instruct them in the proper ways of being respectable. The aim of these institutions was to model, educate, and reform each member of these groups according to the principles of progress, hygiene, and moral rectitude. In this sense, they can be read through a Foucauldian lens. During the early twentieth century, Chilean women were conceived by the apparatus as subjects to be "rescued" from moral deviation.[18] These expectations emanated mostly from the moral framework set by the Catholic Church, which saw as its duty the imposition of the preservation of "female values" such as virginity, sexual honour, and maternity.

The 1930s: Fertile Ground for Social Unrest

Into the 1930s, *centros de madres* kept more or less the same approach, with one significant change: The backdrop of Chilean society had turned critical due to the resistance and increasing political participation from the lower classes; this shift in the political arena forced the Chilean government to take concrete actions and provide new solutions, which in the long run translated into public policy that had women as its target subject. Specifically, by 1932, the government had created the Commissariat of Subsistence and Prices (Comisariato de Subsistencia y Precios) in order to satisfy the demands of workers who were clamouring for an immediate improvement to their quality of life.[19] This new organization fixed the prices of essential goods, and it was not long before the government considered that women should be educated as consumers and trained as inspectors to enforce the new law. According to a FLACSO report, this was the first concrete and specific action taken by the state directly benefiting women while identifying them as a separate entity from their husbands. In time, this recognition by the state of women as workers fuelled female popular organizations such as unions and popular presses.[20]

In this context, the Chilean state favoured the spontaneous and organic formation of *centros de madres*, where "indispensable knowledge" would be delivered for the proper care and nurture of children, for the organization of the house and the family, and for the prevalence of a devout home that would subscribe to the moral principles of the Catholic Church. Following this reasoning, better housewives and mothers would be a key component in the making of better citizens. *Centros de madres* provided education to women in areas such as religion, morality, hygiene, and home economics. There was also a juridical component, as low- income women were taught to favour legal and legitimate marital unions. Women of the elite also intervened in female labour by promoting domestic work when possible: Working outside of the home supposedly debilitated the integrity of the family; thus, low-income women were taught to remain faithful to their husbands by pursuing "feminine" work, away from factories and other male-dominated areas. These teachings were reinforced by social workers in the case of every woman who attended the *centros de madres*.

These initiatives of indoctrination and moral reform proved to be effective for the establishment. Chilean historian Teresa Valdés argues that during this period of time, *centros de madres* were more likely to indoctrinate women than to prepare them for life, which can be seen in the way low-income women acted and reacted in the public sphere.[21] For example, as sociologist Julieta Kirkwood[22] explains, when women exercised the right to vote, they showed a profound tendency toward a conservatism that leaned toward independent candidates whose common denominator was their ability to represent conservative authoritarianism, meaning an idea of power that was traditional, hierarchical, disciplined, and moralizing, appealing to the unquestionable image of the patriarch, much like the message that was being delivered by *centros de madres*. These patterns of oppression persisted, and gender roles resembled those of the early years of the twentieth century.

However, things did not last that way much longer. In the 1930s, *centros de madres* were challenged and, to a certain point, taken over by a new organization, the Pro-Emancipation Movement of Chilean Women (Movimiento Pro-Emancipación de las Mujeres de Chile, MEMCh). MEMCh added the fight for equality to the *centros de madres'* agenda, including juridical, political, and work-related equality. In a society in which women's emancipation was considered a synonym of licentiousness, the creation of MEMCh was pivotal when it came to breaking the pattern of female backwardness.[23] The activity and organization of MEMCh rested on the shoulders of the first generation of women from the elite, who had gone to university, and on those who chose to work outside the home, increasing female participation in the public sphere. By combining social and gender struggles, the *MEMChistas* led the way for the fight for female emancipation during the first half of the twentieth century.

This new wave of female political movements embodied in MEMCh was not without problems. Its ideological closeness to the Communist Party successfully linked it to the Popular Front (the ruling political coalition at the time), which in time helped to alter the political agenda of *centros de madres*, pulling them away from a deeply moralist focus. Furthermore, its support for contraception and regulation of clandestine abortions caused some parts of society to accuse MEMCh members of wanting to destroy the traditions of the family. However, we cannot ignore the fact that MEMCh was aligned with bourgeois feminism, which postponed working-class demands (mostly related to improvements in working conditions) and vindication in pursuit of political power, specifically women's right to vote. At the same time, there was a top-down approach that highlighted the differences between low-income women and the women leading the organization, which could be witnessed in the daily interactions through the use of *tú* and *usted*.[24] In spite of these criticisms, MEMCh kept functioning until a wave of anti-communism took over globally during the late 1940s and 1950s and MEMCh began to disappear, eventually dissolving. However, *centros de madres* were still there.

The Years of Christian Democracy's "Revolution in Liberty"

From the 1960s on, with Eduardo Frei Montalva as president, marginalized populations began to take a more decisive role in politics. As a member of the Christian Democratic Party, Frei implemented public policies that were strongly influenced by the social doctrine of the church, which included a special focus on issues such as oppression and the role of the state in promoting social organization and a growing awareness of social justice.[25] Under the premise of "Revolution in Liberty," Frei's government proposed a structural reform that would fight the atomization of marginalized peoples by creating *comunidades de base* (base communities) with a cooperative and mutualist nature.[26] Base communities were grouped into three sections based on their nature – economy related, guild/trade union related, and community related – and then organized under a federation through which they voiced their needs through the official channels of the state. Base community leaders received government training in order to better communicate to the authorities the necessities of their communities on a wide range of issues, such as education and urbanization. In her book *Partners in Conflict: The Politics of Gender, Sexuality, and Labor in the Chilean Agrarian Reform, 1950–1973*, Heidi Tinsman explains that the government understood these base communities as revolutionary

> first, because it will organize the entire community from the base to the highest national level ... Second, because the new society will organize itself and become conscious of the value of self-expression for the first time in history ... Third, because through these organizations the community will participate at all levels of decision making ... Fourth, because the community thus organized will [become] a mobilized and mobilizing force for the new community ... [The community] having power, knowing how to use it, prepared to exercise it, will put pressure on different levels in such a way that it is difficult to imagine the consequences.[27]

Changes to *centros de madres* during this period have to be understood in the context this larger revolutionary impulse. When the female section of Frei's Christian Democratic Party took over the *centros de madres*, it developed a new strategy, which was inspired by a more radical wing of Catholicism: liberation theology.[28] *Centros de madres* first and foremost were considered promoters of social change, albeit social change undeniably influenced by Catholicism. The work of *centros de madres* was explained this way in the remarks from a centre opening in 1962, titled "Cristo Rey" (Christ the King): "By understanding and deepening the High Mission that God has entrusted women, and wishing to collaborate once more with it, we solemnly inaugurate today this Mother's Centre, whose goal is to procure a greater wellbeing and culture to the members that attend these courses."[29] The opening remarks not only invoked God, but also highlighted the importance of the mission that God had placed on the shoulders of women, the cornerstone of the family as well as of society. Women were the moral compass of the village: "Beautiful and Sublime is this mission, but it also entails grave and sublime duties that women must fulfill which require preparation and study in order to succeed in the enterprise. In order to elevate the livelihood of a village, the best method is to gather mothers into groups. With this, one can reach a fundamental organization in the villages, because it is where mothers reside day and night, keeping the sense of life as a whole, creating with their habits and their behavior the ambiance of the village."[30]

Centros de madres aimed to preserve the role of the mother and the housewife, but it was during this time that they also shifted their work to provide women with technical and organizational training to work "from their homes" in order to contribute to the family income.[31] The fact that women were now considered contributors to the family economy was groundbreaking. Before this happened, the money that came from female labour was not technically recognized as it was not formally incorporated in census records. Regardless of the fact that in many cases it was this income that sustained the family, it was considered an anomaly. But during the 1960s, women began to be considered breadwinning mothers. *Centros de madres* also worked to provide women with basic services like water and electricity. The recollections of Inés, a woman from La Legua (one of the poorest areas of Santiago), illustrates the kind of support made available through her *centro de madres* under Frei's government:

> When I got here to La Legua, we immediately founded our *centro de madres* ... we worked fast, right here on the street. I was elected secretary and we had an entire board for the *centro* ... We got here in July and by Christmas, we had already gotten water and electricity. This *centro* lasted until 1962 and it began in 1955 when we got here. When Frei was in charge, they would give us cheese at the *centro*. A big truck came by and they would give it to us. It was a kilo of cheese per family, plus flour and milk. They'd give us fabric on a monthly basis as well.[32]

In the 1960s, *centros de madres* were monitored by a coordinating agency run by the state through the Central Relacionadora de Centros de Madres. Concretely, this meant that *centros de madres* were promoted, institutionalized, systematized, and financed by the state, which confirmed the public recognition of their stature and allowed them to reach an even greater portion of the population. By 1966 there were 3,000 centres in Santiago and 2,500 in the rest of the provinces. By 1969, there were 6,072 centres.[33]

Allende's Peaceful Road to Socialism and the Radicalization of Motherhood

Perhaps the most radical changes to *centros de madres*, however, took place under the government of Salvador Allende. Allende came to power in 1970, and by 1973, when a coup d'état overthrew Allende's government and instated a dictatorship, there were close to twenty thousand *centros de madres* with nearly one million members. The changes amounted to more than just growth, however, and included a transformation of their ideological and practical purposes.

When Allende became president, he did so as the head of the Popular Unity (Unidad Popular, UP), a political coalition formed by socialists, communists, radicals, and a dissident group of Christian Democrats. According to Olivier Compagnon, Popular Unity was a "hybrid of ideological positions, an attempt to pursue the Marxist-Leninist tradition within constitutional norms combined with an ad-hoc Keynesianism and the mystique of revolution."[34] In his victory speech, which was delivered on the morning of 5 September 1970, Allende stated:

> But I know that you, you who put the working class in power, will have the historic task of making reality what Chile longs for: to turn our nation into a country peerless in its progress, in its social justice, in the rights of each man, each woman, each young person of our land. We've triumphed in order to go on to definitively defeat imperialist exploitation, to end monopolies, to bring about a deep and serious agrarian reform, to control the commerce of imports and exports, to nationalize debt, all pillars that will make possible Chile's progress, creating the social capital that will drive our development.[35]

From the beginning, Allende's words signalled the UP's progressiveness, firmly grounded in his socialist roots. The fact that he envisioned a country that strove for equality gave hope to men and women alike. As Pieper Mooney points out, Allende and the UP program were a source of inspiration for women, compelling them to join political action – whether to support him or to protest against him.[36] In fact, women "expanded their political participation even though they were engaged in a class struggle that remained predominantly a male affair."[37] At first glance, Allende's understanding of women's contributions to the public sphere may have seemed similar to that of his predecessors in the Christian Democratic Party. As progressive as the UP political program was, there were very few mentions of specific roles for women and, when women did show up, their roles were inextricably tied to the household and motherhood. Allende's program stated that "full civil status of married women will be established, as will equal legal status for all children whether born in or out of wedlock, as well as adequate divorce legislation which dissolves legal ties and safeguards the woman's and children's rights."[38] Women's status was always linked to their families; in other words, there was a lack of attention to women as citizens independent from their families.

However, as Tinsman states, the UP and the Christian Democrats differed on a crucial point: that of class interests. For those who followed the ideas of the Christian Democrats, women's civic participation was a "means of assisting families, contributing to the community, and deepening democracy"; the UP stressed the importance of female activism to securing class interests and achieving human fulfilment under socialism.[39] That women's work was seen as important to alleviating class injustices was illustrated in the UP's nursery program, which the government saw as facilitating women's work outside of the home: "In order to provide the special requirements needed for the proper development of pre-school age children, and to facilitate the incorporation of women into productive work, we shall rapidly expand our nurseries and nursery school systems, granting priority to the neediest groups in our society. As a result of this policy, the children of urban and rural workers and peasants will be better prepared to start school and continue to benefit right through the normal school system."[40]

Another way in which Allende's government gave room for women to be agents of change was to ensure that *centros de madres* were located as close to a technical school as possible. In a speech from 1971, Allende stated that "mothers' Centres will be able to transform themselves into real centers of training, technical and cultural, allowing women to incorporate themselves into the struggle."[41] *Centros de madres* were officially recognized in the Labour Code as "functional organizations constituted by women who share common interests and whose main objective is the personal growth of its members and the solution of problems inherent to their status and gender within their neighborhood."[42] In concrete terms, this meant that women attended *centros de madres* not only to be with other women but to learn a certified trade and to connect with the world. Women learned about plumbing, heating, and electricity, but also about Chilean labour laws and social realities outside of Chile. Inés Garrido, president of the *centros de madres* of La Cisterna region, fondly recalls how *centros de madres* combined trades training with community building: "In Allende's time we would work inside the parish. There was a lot of affection, a lot of love. We felt free; one would save a little money to buy a few things. With Allende, my daughter learned about sewing and we would make things and we would sell them. People came to teach us courses for free. I learned hairdressing because I never liked sewing. We would be given cards and we would get free food."[43]

Under Allende, several other initiatives were undertaken to strengthen this new role that women would occupy in society. For example, the Allende government instated the National Secretary of Women (Secretaría Nacional de la Mujer), which preceded the creation of the Ministry of Women (Ministerio de la Mujer). This institutional change meant that those who inhabited the margins were now active subjects in politics, capable of managing their own organizations. Women, under this new paradigm, were considered essential revolutionary actors. State discourses about women were transformed. The housewife and mother were now accompanied by the figure of the working woman, not just as a supplementary income earner but as a central instrument and support for social change through her contribution to overcoming poverty. *Centros de madres* were crucial to this transformation. In the words of Allende, "We want to transform Mothers' Centres. Not in a paternalistic way ... but with a different significance, meaning, for women to understand they can and they must have the possibility to access a larger income for them and their own."[44]

During the Allende years, members of *centros* did indeed see their incomes grow and their political opportunities advance. Irene, who lived in an encampment in Santiago, explains the way she embraced her *centro* as a place of solidarity and knowledge:

> I joined *centros de madres* during the Popular Unity, in Saint Nicholas encampment. We had a *centros de madres* there and it was a beautiful thing, delightful, because all the mothers would bring whatever they could, it being bread, two tablespoons of flour or sugar; we would put the kettle on, and we would drink tea. Sometimes we would receive milk at the *centro*, and it wasn't for sale, we would keep it there and drink *mate* with milk, plus everything we would gather among the members. We would talk about our husbands, about our families' ailments, someone would advise another member sending her to a specific place to get help; we would talk about the sociopolitical situation of our country, about how other encampments were doing or what problems they were having ... I joined *centro de madres* because I wanted to learn from my neighbours and maybe they could learn something from me, I wanted to live in a community, share our lives, I wanted to know more things, I wanted to create a JAP [Junta de Abastecimientos y Control de Precios/Committee of Supply and Prices].[45]

The approach taken by the Allende administration paved the way for a much larger liberation and allowed women to exercise levels of agency never seen before. *Centros de madres* became an important link between women and public policies in matters of nutrition, disease prevention, and, most importantly, birth control. According to Fabiola Bahamondes, during the 1970s Chilean women were able to exercise control over their own bodies and regulate their reproductive lives. In her work about rural *centros de madres*, Bahamondes quotes *pobladora* Inés Garrido, who declared in 1971: "We want to end the notion that women get together at *centros de madres* to do knitting and gossiping. Enough of that. We want to be incorporated into current events; we want to learn about culture, about what happens in the world, in other countries where there are women who undergo the same issues and are the same as us. We want to learn what has been denied to us until now."[46] And, for a while, what Inés Garrido and many women like her aspired to achieve became a reality. However, this did not last. As Irene explained, "when the coup came, the encampment was destroyed, we lost everything ... our *centro de madres* died then and there."[47]

After the Coup

The violent coup of 1973 placed the dictator Augusto Pinochet in power. His agenda targeted *centros de madres*. What were once public and effervescent places of gathering and political discussion were turned into private foundations, presided over by Lucía Hiriat, Pinochet's wife. The wives of military officials were installed in these centres, and they were no longer referred to as workers, instead classified as volunteers. The climate was again one of a paternalistic nature, with a strong sense of Catholic morality with the added sinister twist of political surveillance. *Centros de madres* were converted from institutions with policies of support for production to places of social handouts.

The coup, however, could not erase what women had learned and gained at *centros de madres*. They had found their voice and were not going to give it up, despite the cruelty of the Pinochet regime. Inés Garrido recalls confronting the military wives who were uneasy with her "communist voice." She faced them and said: "You, yourself, miss – I told the woman – when you come here, you speak about Christianity, and what's your Christianity, if you yourself come here to support all the wrong things they [the military] do here?" ... Then I was told there were many wrong things about me, that they had an eye on me and that I was on a file. And I told them, 'Sure, the thing is I am asking, I'm demanding my rights, I have my personal dignity.' And then two of us just left."[48] Garrido's recollection illustrates the legacy of *centros de madres*. Their members had to face deeply ingrained notions of gender in Chilean society, but women were politicized through their work and communities at the centres, and they remained committed even in the face of repressive forces. With the coup of 1973 came the persecution, torture, and detention of Allende's sympathizers at the hands of Pinochet's regime. In a time when group meetings of any kind were deemed suspicious and unions were forbidden and considered illegal, *centros de madres* were still functioning. They maintained their enormous network of associations throughout the entire country, now instrumentalized by the regime.

More than just continuing to operate, *centros de madres* became the places where women gathered to find comfort, to socialize, and, in some cases, to form a key arm of the resistance to the Pinochet regime. Yet *centros de madres* were now spaces of indoctrination and latent violence, much like Teresa Valdés has pointed out in her work. After all, living under a violent dictatorship disrupts everything and everyone. However, while *centros de madres* as *institutions* morphed under Pinochet, these changes could not erase the years of bonding and support that women had built through *centros de madres* beyond matters of public policies. Some of these women were the ones who had initially gone to the illegal detention and torture centres such as the National Stadium and demanded news about the whereabouts of their family members; they were also the ones who had created ties with the Chilean Workers' Pastoral Office and gathered international support in the early years of the dictatorship. One of the most emblematic cases of such support was the Asociación de Familiares de Detenidos Desaparecidos (Association of Families of the Detained-Disappeared), which began informally a few days after the military coup in 1973 and is active to this day. Theirs was not a fight for equality anymore, and they were not simply challenging gender stereotypes; they took what they had learned next to other women like them in *centros de madres* and led the fight for justice and democracy, which was (and in many cases, still is) the fight of a lifetime.

NOTES

1 Throughout this chapter, I have provided names and quotations in English, translated from the original Spanish. Unless otherwise indicated, I have translated these materials myself. The names of publications in Spanish have been kept in the notes for accuracy.

2 Violeta Parra, "The Letter," recorded 1971, on *Songs Recovered in Paris*, DICAP Recording Studio, 1971.
3 María Josefina Cabrera Gómez and Javiera Errázuriz Tagle, "Historia, mujeres y género en Chile: La irrupción de las autoras femeninas en las revistas académicas. Los casos de revista historia y cuadernos de historia," *Historia (Santiago)* 48, no. 1 (2015): 279–99, https://doi.org/10.4067/s0717-71942015000100008.
4 Cabrera Gómez and Errázuriz Tagle, "Historia, mujeres y género en Chile."
5 Joan Sangster, *Through Feminist Eyes: Essays on Canadian Women's History* (Edmonton: AU Press, 2011), 4.
6 Some of the most notable works regarding female voting rights in Chile are Julieta Kirkwood, *Ser política en Chile: Las feministas y los partidos* (Santiago: FLACSO, 1982); Diamela Eltit, *Crónica del sufragio femenino en Chile* (Santiago: SERNAM, 1994).
7 Teresa Valdés et al., "Centros de madres 1973–1989: Sólo disciplinamiento?" (working document no. 416, Santiago: FLACSO, 1989).
8 Jadwiga E. Pieper Mooney, *The Politics of Motherhood: Maternity and Women's Rights in Twentieth-Century Chile* (Pittsburgh, PA: University of Pittsburgh Press, 2009).
9 Fabiola Bahamondes, "Centros de madres en el Chile rural: Un espacio de seguridad: 'Cociendo, costureando, entablando un entramado social,'" *Nomadías* 22 (2016): 83–4.
10 William Alexander, *Lost in the Long Transition: Struggles for Social Justice in Neoliberal Chile* (Lanham: Lexington Books, 2009), 160.
11 Valdés et al., "Centros de madres 1973–1989," passim.
12 María Soledad Zárate, "Mujeres viciosas, mujeres virtuosas: La mujer delincuente y la Casa Correccional de Santiago: 1860–1900," in *Disciplina y desacato: Construcción de identidad en Chile: Siglos XIX y XX*, ed. Lorena Godoy et al. (Santiago: SUR: CEDEM, 1995), passim.
13 Josephine Muriel Schofield, "Critique of the Concept of Mass Society" (master's thesis, University of British Columbia, 1971), http://dx.doi.org/10.14288/1.0102019.
14 Pope Leo XIII, *Encyclical Letter of Pope Leo XIII on the Condition of Labor* (New York: Paulist Press, 1940). *Rerum novarum*, or *Rights and Duties of Capital and Labor*, is an encyclical issued by Pope Leo XIII on 15 May 1891. It is an open letter that addresses the condition of the working classes. It discusses the relationships and mutual duties between labour and capital, as well as between government and its citizens.
15 Ana María Stuven, "El 'primer Catolicismo social' ante la cuestión social: Un momento en el proceso de consolidación nacional," *Teol. vida* 49, no. 3 (2008): 483–97, http://dx.doi.org/10.4067/S0049-34492008000200018.

16 Zárate, "Mujeres viciosas, mujeres virtuosas," 329.
17 Zárate, "Mujeres viciosas, mujeres virtuosas," 331.
18 "Apparatus refers to: a thoroughly heterogeneous ensemble consisting of discourses, institutions, architectural forms, regulatory decisions, laws, administrative measures, scientific statements, philosophical, moral and philanthropic propositions – in short, the said as much as the unsaid. Such are the elements of the apparatus. The apparatus itself is the system of relations that can be established between these elements. Secondly, what I am trying to identify in this apparatus is precisely the nature of the connection that can exist between these heterogeneous elements … Thirdly, I understand by the term 'apparatus' a sort of – shall we say – formation which has as its major function at a given historical moment that of responding to an urgent need. The apparatus thus has a dominant strategic function." Michel Foucault and Gordon Colin, *Power-Knowledge: Selected Interviews and Other Writings, 1972–1977* (Hassocks: Harvester Press, 1980), 194.
19 Ministerio del Trabajo, *Decreto ley 520: Crea el Comisariato General de Subsistencias y Precios* (Santiago: Biblioteca del Congreso Nacional de Chile, 1932), https://www.leychile.cl/Navegar?idNorma=6157. This law was derogated in September 1980.
20 Valdés et al., "Centros de madres 1973–1989," 15.
21 Valdés et al., "Centros de madres 1973–1989," 27.
22 Julieta Kirkwood, *Ser política en Chile: Las feministas y los partidos* (Santiago: FLACSO, 1986), 122–32. Later on, in 1944, two hundred women's organizations from a variety of backgrounds gathered in the capital, Santiago, and established the Chilean Federation of Female Institutions (FECHIF). By 1949 FECHIF had accomplished its main objective: the female right to vote in presidential elections.
23 "El Movimiento Pro-Emancipación de las Mujeres de Chile: MEMCH (1935–1953)," Memoria Chilena, Biblioteca Nacional de Chile, accessed 12 October 2019, http://www.memoriachilena.gob.cl/602/w3-article-3611.html.
24 The difference between *tú* and *usted* is mostly cultural. Unlike English, the Spanish language has singular and plural versions of the word "you." The pronoun *tú* is the informal way to say "you." *Tú* is used when one is speaking to someone younger than oneself or to someone who is a close friend. *Usted* is the respectful version of *tú*, used for someone older or higher up in the social hierarchy.
25 "The Social Doctrine of the Church … teaches theological, moral and social education elaborated … by the Catholic Church as an historical answer to social, cultural, economic and political problems through which humanity has lived with the objective of promoting the transformation of the reality

into a more human, just and fraternal society, by means of the respect to the dignity of the human being, human rights and the rights of the people." Ricardo Azael Escobar Delgado, "La doctrina social de la iglesia: Fuentes y principios de los derechos humanos," *Prolegómenos. Derechos y Valores XV* no. 30 (2012): 100. https://www.redalyc.org/articulo.oa?id=87625443006.

26 For more information on Eduardo Frei Montalva's "Revolution in Liberty," see Sebastián Hurtado-Torres, *The Gathering Storm: Eduardo Frei's Revolution in Liberty and Chile's Cold War* (Ithaca and London: Cornell University Press, 2020).

27 Heidi Tinsman, *Partners in Conflict: The Politics of Gender, Sexuality, and Labor in the Chilean Agrarian Reform, 1950–1973* (Durham: Duke University Press, 2002), 131–2.

28 Liberation theology was a "religious movement arising in late 20th-century Roman Catholicism and centred in Latin America. It sought to apply religious faith by aiding the poor and oppressed through involvement in political and civic affairs. It stressed both heightened awareness of the 'sinful' socioeconomic structures that caused social inequities and active participation in changing those structures." *Britannica*, s.v. "liberation theology," last modified 9 June 2024, https://www.britannica.com/topic/liberation-theology.

29 "Charlas para centros de madres," Memoria Chilena, Biblioteca Nacional de Chile, accessed 6 September 2019, http://www.memoriachilena.gob.cl/602/w3-article-60724.html.

30 "Charlas para centros de madres," 7.

31 "MEMCH (1935–1953)."

32 Valdés et al., "Centros de madres 1973–1989," 127.

33 Memoria Chilena, Biblioteca Nacional de Chile, "Los centros de madres en Chile (1930–1989)," accessed 6 September 2019, http://www.memoriachilena.gob.cl/602/w3-article-100688.html.

34 Olivier Compagnon, "Popular Unity: Chile, 1970–1973," in *Encyclopedia of Labor History Worldwide*, vol. 2, ed. Neil Schlager (Detroit: St. James Press, 2004), 128–31.

35 Salvador Allende, "Victory Speech," trans. Marianela D'Aprile (Santiago, 1970), https://www.marxists.org/archive/allende/1970/september/victory-speech.htm.

36 It is worth noting that during the period of 1970–3 there was an enormous anti-Allende, anti-Marxist movement that had strong participation from upper-class women.

37 Pieper Mooney, *The Politics of Motherhood*, 104.

38 Unidad Popular, *Programa básico de gobierno de la Unidad Popular: Candidatura presidencial de Salvador Allende* (Santiago: Instituto Geográfico Militar, 1970).

39 Tinsman, *Partners in Conflict*, 230.
40 Unidad Popular, *Programa básico de gobierno de la Unidad Popular*, 29.
41 Tinsman, *Partners in Conflict*, 230.
42 Valdés et al., "Centros de madres 1973–1989," 32.
43 Valdés et al., "Centros de madres 1973–1989," 130.
44 Salvador Allende, "Discurso en la inauguración de las Jornadas de Discusión Popular, Valparaíso, 11 de enero de 1971," Biblioteca Clodomiro Almeyda, accessed 7 August 2024, https://www.socialismo-chileno.org/PS/APSA/Historia_del_Gobierno_Popular_Tomo_II.pdf.
45 Valdés et al., "Centros de madres 1973–1989," 127.
46 Bahamondes, "Centros de madres en el Chile rural."
47 Valdés et al., "Centros de madres 1973–1989," 127.
48 Valdés et al., "Centros de madres 1973–1989," 127.

7 A Global Turning Point for Equal Pay Struggles: International Women's Year, 1975

SILKE NEUNSINGER AND RAGNHEIÐUR KRISTJÁNSDÓTTIR

On 24 October 1975, United Nations Day, nine out of ten Icelandic women famously walked out of their homes and workplaces to demonstrate the value of their work. The United Nations' International Women's Year (IWY) had brought together various factions of the women's movement – from the most radical to the more conservative – in deliberations about the status of women. The Women's Day Off, as the event was called, was planned by a women's committee formed by a wide range of Icelandic women's organizations to prepare events during IWY.

The IWY is regarded as a watershed in the history of the women's movement around the world.[1] The walkout was momentous and came to have a direct and lasting impact well beyond Iceland. The solidarity of the Icelandic women immediately caught the attention of international media. The following day, readers of *The New York Times* learned that in Iceland almost all women had decided to go on strike. Claiming that many Icelandic men had at first treated the idea as a joke, the paper reported that the women's action had created severe problems not only because there was no one to attend to the women's jobs, but also because the closing of nursery schools had meant that many businessmen were forced to take their children to work with them.[2]

Since 1975, the walkout has been repeated at regular intervals in Iceland, and it has been frequently referred to internationally as an exemplary women's protest.[3] In this chapter we argue that the preparations for and the outcome of IWY were of major importance to globalizing women's struggles in general and the struggles for equal remuneration in particular.

Toward a Microspatial Approach

Historians of global labour history have questioned the nationalism and Eurocentrism of earlier labour history; as Christian G. de Vito and Anne

Gerritsen have shown, there is a tendency to "conflate" the global with the planet and to marginalize the local to the rank of the case study. In an attempt to generalize, global history has looked at structural patterns in predefined spatial units, thus neglecting the diversity of the phenomena and developments under study.[4] Social movement theory offers concepts that connect the local and the global. It can explain why social mobilization processes take place and the mechanisms behind their success or failure. According to Charles Tilly, Doug McAdam, and Sidney Tarrow, mobilization processes depend on the creation and use of political opportunities, the use of specific repertoires of protest, and the process of interpreting and framing grievances to convince the opponent. To understand the emergence of mobilization for equal remuneration in a specific historical setting, it is thus helpful to look at the creation and use of these political opportunity structures. They can materialize at different levels of scale, and we argue that in order to explain equal remuneration struggles around the globe, we need to study the connections between them.[5]

Sidney Tarrow's concept of transnational activism is useful to focus on the mechanisms taking place in the triangular relationship of transnational activists, such as trade unions and women's movements, the state, and international institutions such as the International Labour Organization (ILO), the United Nations (UN), or the European Community. It explains why and how political opportunities emerging either nationally or internationally can be used in the mobilization process. The use of the term "transnational" to highlight border-crossing activities is the result of debates about "methodological nationalism" and aims at moving scholarly analysis beyond the nation state.[6]

In what follows we analyse local and national developments of equal pay struggles in Iceland, India, and South Africa. Each of these societies represents different political and economic situations and different types of labour relations. All three countries entered the United Nations as independent states in the aftermath of the Second World War, and all were members of the ILO. (By the 1970s, however, South Africa was internationally isolated. The country left the ILO in 1964, and ten years later it was suspended from the United Nations because of its apartheid politics.) However, social division differed between the countries. Iceland was a relatively equal society, but because of intersections of caste, race, and gender, South Africa and India had a large population living below the subsistence level. The important differences between the three countries mean that the similarities we find in the struggle for equal remuneration during and around International Women's Year enable us to state that we have found robust global processes that were effective in the fight for wage equality. It is our hope that these findings can then be tested in cases elsewhere.

We start with an outline of the periodization of international political opportunity structures. Thereafter we turn to the different local and national contexts to analyse how the preparations for IWY were used as a mobilization structure in different places in the world. Then we move on to show how the decisions of the 1975 World Conference on Women in Mexico City were used to change national legal frameworks for wage equality. Finally, we demonstrate how legislation and international agreements could be used by individuals, women's organizations, and trade unions to force employers to end wage discrimination against women.

Periodization of International Opportunity Structures before 1975

Even though we focus on the UN IWY of 1975, our analysis is based on our wider understanding of struggles for wage equality during the twentieth century. We argue that global concepts of equal remuneration emerged out of different local and national struggles that served as starting points for the first international struggles for equal pay, but that the international level became increasingly important after the Second World War.[7]

The demand for equal remuneration, independent of who does the job, is probably as old as wage work. As a political aim it was from the outset connected with discussions about democracy, human rights, and citizenship. During the French Revolution, feminists began calling for wage justice between the sexes. On a more practical level, male-dominated trade unions deployed this demand as a strategy to decrease competition between men and women for job opportunities.

The first phase in the development of international opportunity structures spans the beginning of the twentieth century to the end of the Second World War, a period when wage equality was being introduced to the international arena as part and parcel of specific measures to protect women workers. After the First World War, the principle of equal remuneration entered the supranational arena through the Treaty of Versailles (seventh principle of Article 427). The inclusion of the clause was the result of local struggles for equal pay in the Global North. Similarly in 1919, it was due to efforts of labour feminists from the northern transatlantic region that wage equality became a constitutive part of ILO's constitution, and progressively defined as equal remuneration for men and women for work of equal value – instead of the more limited demand of the same wages for the same work.[8] In addition to these international agreements and organizations, the principle of wage equality was during this period channelled through transnational women's and workers' organizations.

During what we see as the second phase, from the end of the Second World War to 1966, equal remuneration became part of three supranational agreements: the UN's Universal Declaration of Human Rights in 1948, the ILO's Equal Renumeration Convention (C100), adopted in 1951, and the European Community's Treaty of Rome in 1957.

The overall development of demands for equal remuneration at all levels – the local, national, and global – had always been related to women's citizenship at the national level. Thus, having gained political and economic citizenship after the First World War, it was women from the Global North who put equal remuneration on the agenda of international organizations, at that time dominated by member states from the Global North, many of which were colonial powers. After the Second World War, however, decolonization entitled most women in the Global South to political citizenship, and it was this group of women that used its strengthened position to push the agenda of international organizations once again toward equal remuneration.

It took until the mid-1970s for international organizations other than the ILO, as well as national legislators, to start adopting the principle of equal remuneration for work of equal value, instead of the much more moderate call for equal remuneration for the same work.[9] By then, feminists from the Global South had gained access to the international arena and brought back the demand for economic and social equality.[10] The impact was now for the first time truly global. The Global South had opened the door for implementation through legal action and trade union negotiations connecting the local, national, and international levels all around the globe. The result was not a unified way of struggling. Rather, we show how IWY, through its preparation and the decisions of international organizations following the 1975 UN women's conference in Mexico City, served as a new impulse for the ongoing equal pay struggles at the local and national levels.

New Supranational Campaigns

In 1974, Leticia Shahani, chair of the UN's Commission on the Status of Women (CSW), claimed that "one of the wonderful things which the UN can do [is] to put pressure on national governments to think and act on global issues which also affect domestic policies."[11]

IWY and the decisions of the 1975 UN women's conference in Mexico were a watershed because as a result the principle of equal pay became a standard included in the agendas of workers' and women's organizations at the international level. During the preparations for IWY, Iceland had, together with India, Hungary, and Mongolia, urged the members of the UN to ratify the ILO's C100.[12] UN conferences had from the outset offered space to discuss the needs of women from the Global South, which influenced the work of the CSW fundamentally, from the drafting of the UN Universal Declaration of Human Rights to programs for development of women that were based on studies by female scholars from the Global South. For the CSW, the right to equal remuneration for work of equal value was as important as political suffrage for men and women.[13] Women from the Global South and the Eastern Bloc demanded economic and social citizenship, while women from the Global North were focusing on political and social citizenship.[14]

The preparations for IWY helped to make discrimination against women more visible. Moreover, during the International Women's Decade (1975–85), the United Nations program promoting equal rights and opportunities for women led to the introduction or reform of equal pay legislation in many countries. This was a period when the visibility of wage discrimination against women together with legal action became one of the most important tools promoting gender equality. A more technocratic and academic approach, to investigate the status of women and collect statistics on women, became important and created key alliances between labour feminists and academics, as many of the studies were carried out at women's studies centres and by women in applied social science.[15] These processes created new political opportunity structures and to some degree also new mobilization structures that both allowed for cross-movement organization between the women's movement and the labour movement on all levels of scale.

Mapping Women: Preparations for IWY in India and Iceland

At the beginning of the 1970s, the UN had initiated national reports on the status of women to prepare for IWY in 1975. These reports became important national mobilization structures for the implementation of equal remuneration as they revealed the continuity of discrimination against women despite national and international agreements to end this discrimination.

India is an important example. Trade unions as well as women's organizations had been involved in equal pay struggles throughout the twentieth century, and as a result the demand for equal pay for men and women became part of the Indian Constitution, adopted in 1949.[16] In 1971, the Commission on the Status of Women in India (CSWI) was set up to assess the impact of constitutional, legal, and administrative provisions that had been important for the status of women and their education and employment. As a result, international opportunity structures were used more widely and changes were made in the national legislation. Two well-known academics who worked closely with Indian women's organizations, Dr. Phulrenu Guha, union minister for social welfare, and Dr. Vina Mazumdar, were appointed as head of and secretary of the CSWI, respectively.[17]

The report of the CSWI, *Towards Equality*, published in 1974, revealed that for a large number of Indian women the situation had become worse after independence.[18] It revealed the huge wage gaps between men and women and other gross violations of the constitution. It showed that most women were still far from enjoying the rights and opportunities guaranteed by the constitution and that independence had affected women adversely: "The social status of women in India is a typical example of this gap between the position and roles accorded to them by the Constitution and the laws, and those imposed on them by social traditions. What is possible for women in theory is seldom within reach."[19] The report brought into clearer focus discrimination against women and not only in India. It was covered by international media and was on the front page of *The New York Times*.[20] This was difficult news for the government. The report framed its claims within the agreements of the ILO's Equal Remuneration Convention and showed that the prevailing policy recommendation was not enough to equalize wages and that prejudice was enforcing different minimum wages for men and women. It criticized earlier surveys and showed that wage differentials were persistent.

The CSWI recommended legislative enactment of Article 39(d) of the Constitution of India, concerning equal pay for equal work – to add the weight of legal sanction to what was only a policy – and recommended the incorporation of this principle in the Minimum Wages Act. Another important result of the investigation was the establishment of the Centre for Women's Development Studies, which still is an important research institute concerned with the status of women in India and continues to maintain the connection between academics and women's movements.[21]

Despite the socio-political differences between Iceland and India, the struggle for equal remuneration has striking similarities. In Iceland too, women's issues were given increased attention during the 1960s and early 1970s. The labour movement had been reluctant to give attention to the principle of wage equality, but Iceland's commitment to new international agreements, as well as transnational second-wave feminism, provided mobilization structures seized by Icelandic campaigners for women's rights. Iceland was party to the European Convention on Human Rights of 1950, the ILO's C100, and the ILO's recommendation 111 on discrimination as regards employment and occupation.

In 1971, the parliament passed a resolution on research concerning the equality of men and women. Conducted by the Department of Social Sciences at the University of Iceland and published in 1975, this research demonstrated that women's occupations were classed as lower paying than those of men and that the difference in income was substantial.[22]

It has been argued that the women's movement in Iceland used the opportunity provided by the UN's International Women's Decade more effectively than women's organizations in many of the neighbouring countries.[23] The Icelandic Red Stocking movement, founded in 1970, launched an attack against traditional views toward women. Inspired by transnational feminist intellectual and political currents from the United States, Europe, and especially Scandinavia, it emphasized women's right to work and education.

Given how radical the Red Stockings were, they caused quite a stir, especially among the older generations, not only men, but also women of previous generations. However, as alluded to at the outset, this radicalism did not stand in the way of cooperation between different factions of the women's movement. In 1974, a wide range of organizations founded a committee to prepare conferences and events during the UN's IWY. The first event was a conference on the conditions of women in the lower income strata,[24] which issued a resolution urging Icelandic women workers to seize the opportunity provided by the IWY. It was there that the idea of holding a women's walkout was introduced.[25]

Meanwhile, in contrast to the women's movement, the Icelandic government was very late in its preparations for IWY. It was not until twelve days before the Mexico conference in June 1975 that the government appointed a committee to oversee Iceland's participation. The three delegates sent on Iceland's behalf had no time to prepare and thus decided to only observe the proceedings of the conference.[26]

The Fruits of 1975: New National Political Opportunity Structures

Iceland and India, like several other countries, had equal pay legislation in place before the ILO's C100 was adopted. This legislation was therefore not necessarily in accordance with the ILO convention, and its scope and reach were limited. As a result of the national reports discussed above, but also following decisions made at the UN women's conference in Mexico in 1975, equal pay legislation changed at the national level. Iceland and India are again illustrating examples; in both countries new equal pay legislation was introduced in 1976.

Wage equality had first been introduced in Icelandic legislation in the early twentieth century, when equal pay was mandated in certain sections of the public sector.[27] In 1961, a law on wage equality in the private sector was introduced, referring to Iceland's obligations to the ILO's C100. The optimistic aim of the legislation was to achieve wage equality by the end of 1967 in occupations where inequality appeared to have been particularly wide and persistent. The specified occupations were industrial labour, work in shops, and office work.[28] Eliminating the gender pay gap proved to be more difficult than expected. The law mandated equal remuneration for the same jobs, but not comparable jobs or jobs of equal value, and there was a continuing tendency to value jobs typically occupied by women less than jobs typically occupied by men.

A turning point was reached in 1973 with a law introducing what was called an equal remuneration board. This was the first Icelandic legislation to mandate the principle of equal remuneration for jobs of equal value, and the accompanying *travaux préparatoires* refer to Iceland's obligations to the ILO's C100 and recommendation 111, as well as the UN's 1966 International Covenant on Economic, Social and Cultural Rights.[29] The bill was introduced by a left-wing parliamentarian, Svava Jakobsdóttir, with direct links to the Red Stocking movement.

In 1976, the government decided to introduce legislation on the equal status and equal rights of women and men, with direct references to the UN's objectives for the Women's Decade. One of the main authors was Guðrún Erlendsdóttir, chairman of the above-mentioned Icelandic IWY committee.[30] Women's position on the labour market was one of the main concerns of the new legislation, which stated that women and men should be provided with equal opportunities for work and education and, as in the legislation from 1973, it clearly stated that women and men should be paid the same wages for comparable jobs and jobs of equal value.[31]

As mentioned, the CSWI recommended new legislation in India. As a result of this, in 1975 the central government adopted an equal remuneration ordinance, which on 8 March 1976 was replaced by the Equal Remuneration Act. The act refers to both the central and state governments. It provides for equal remuneration for men and women workers for work of the same or similar nature.[32] The adoption of the Equal Remuneration Act also changed the Minimum Wages Act and prohibited the earlier possibility of wage differentials for men and women. In 1987 the Equal Renumeration Act was amended, and as a result these exceptions were no longer applicable. Moreover, certain penalties were increased and appropriate jurisdiction for the trial of offences was established, noting that the act shall not be applied to change terms and conditions for the protection of women in certain special situations.

Similarly to Iceland, women's economic citizenship was an important part of this reform, as the amendment provided that the Equal Remuneration Act also included a judicial provision to support women entering occupations they had been excluded from earlier. Moreover, the act granted power to the central and state governments to appoint authorities for hearing and deciding claims and complaints and to appoint labour inspectors to investigate whether employers were violating the act or not, adding to the visibility of discrimination and aimed at ending it. The act provided for penalties, including imprisonment. The Central Industrial Relations Machinery in the Ministry of Labour, as well as the Central Advisory Committee, had the main responsibility for the enforcement of the act.

Legal Action for Implementation

Turning to the extent to which new equal pay legislation offered new political opportunity structures for individuals and workers on the shop floor level, there were differences due to the legal systems and legal literacy in the countries. In India this new political opportunity structure was available only to the few women who had the time and money to go to court, or those whose trade unions had the resources to fund the court proceedings. Given the high numbers of illiterate women in India, legal illiteracy was also widespread among women. However, case law can multiply the effects of a court decision about one leading case to subsequent cases. Moreover, foreign court decisions on leading cases can be used in Indian courts.[33] The wage discrimination case of a female stenographer, Audrey D'Costa, at Mackinnon Mackenzie in Bombay became the case that subsequent cases referred to, and it was even included in the ILO collection of law cases. In this case, a woman confidential stenographer filed a petition as her service was paid less than a male stenographer at her workplace doing the same or similar work. Audrey D'Costa was dismissed on 13 June 1977. She filed an application to the High Court on 5 September 1981. The High Court concluded that this was a clear violation of the Equal Remuneration Act.[34] The company took the case to the Supreme Court, which also decided in favour of the woman secretary. The court decision explained that same or similar work needed to be measured according to skill, effort, and responsibility when performed under similar working conditions, as laid down in the Equal Remuneration Act. The Supreme Court referred to Article 39(d) of the Constitution of India, to the Equal Remuneration Act, to the ILO's C100, and to the British Equal Pay Act of 1970. In addition, the Supreme Court referred to the member states of the European Community that had signed the ILO convention and the European Economic Community Treaty of Rome. To justify equal remuneration for men and women in India, it referred to the equal pay laws of these member states and the precedents of the European Court of Justice to implement equal remuneration for men and women.

This case illustrates the entanglement of an individual case of wage discrimination with national and international opportunity structures. During the case, reference was made to the ILO convention, but in the ongoing critical review of India's implementation of C100 this case also entered the collection of court cases at the ILO. This was used by the Indian government to show that despite a narrow definition in the law of equal remuneration for the same work, the practice of Indian courts showed use of a much broader definition, which was equal remuneration for work of equal value.

In Iceland, the equal rights legislation introduced in 1976 prescribed the establishment of an equal rights council, which should, if needed, file cases on behalf of workers who were considered to have been subject to discrimination.[35] The first such case was brought to court in 1979 on behalf of an unskilled health worker, Guðrún Emilsdóttir, who complained that she had been paid less than men doing the same job at her workplace, a state-run care home for people with disabilities. The case was filed against the Icelandic state by Emilsdóttir herself as well as the equal rights council. A district court adjudicated in her favour. And while the Supreme Court reversed the verdict due to a technical issue,[36] the court ruling stated that paying Emilsdóttir less than her male counterparts was in violation of the equal rights legislation.[37] It was thus clear that with the new legislation, working women in Iceland had been given an effective tool in their struggle for wage equality.

Protests at the International Level

Research has shown that trade unions used international agreements on equal pay to put pressure on multinational companies when national equal pay legislation was absent. But as soon as national legislation was in place, preference was given to using this in demands for equal remuneration.[38] The cases of Iceland and India help to nuance this picture. Iceland's legislation seems to have been relatively progressive, especially the laws adopted in 1973 and 1976. Looking at the comments made by the ILO's CEARC (Committee of Experts on the Application of Conventions and Recommendations) regarding Iceland's implementation of C100 in the 1970s and 1980s, we see that the ILO's specialists acknowledge this. However, Iceland, as many other countries, repeatedly failed to send reports as well as the data specifically asked for.[39] This is an indication that even though the ILO's C100 and the UN's initiatives during the Women's Decade provided important opportunity structures at the national level, neither the government, the unions, nor the employers found reason to refer to the ILO on issues pertaining to equal remuneration. At the same time, it reflects the government's lack of interest in international cooperation on gender equality during this period. As mentioned before, the Icelandic government was very late in its preparations for the Mexico conference in 1975.

The varied relations between the ILO and the member states meant that it was not available as an international arena for protest to workers' representatives from all countries. The national reports on the status of women effected the use of international political opportunity structures. They gave access to international organizations as arenas for protests against gendered wage discrimination. They became useful for public shaming of governments that had not furthered implementation of wage equality legislation, especially when the legal framework was not working.[40] In 1974, the year when the Indian report was published, the Centre of Indian Trade Unions (CITU) wrote a letter of complaint to the ILO with reference to women's experience of systematic wage discrimination, asking for help to investigate the implementation of C100 in various industries both in the organized sector, which is state employment, public employment, and all occupations scheduled under wage boards, and the unorganized sector.[41] For the period between 1973 and 2008, workers' representatives sent their observations regularly to the CEARC, and eight of them concerned C100.[42] Workers used the ILO as an arena for complaints about the lack of implementation, and from 1991 until the present, the government of India has turned to the ILO for technical advice and support in India. This monitoring process affected the implementation of equal remuneration in India twofold: Firstly, the ILO assessed the Indian governments' progress, gave recommendations, and made direct requests on what needed to be done. Secondly, it gave the Indian trade unions an international stage to complain about the lack of implementation by the Indian government.

The reports of the CEARC show how the CITU used the international platform of the ILO, with its formalized structure for complaints, to put pressure on the government of India. As a result, changes were made to the national legislation and control of employers was intensified. Moreover, trade unions and voluntary organizations intensified work on changing the public opinion about women workers through education and brochures on legal literacy. This gave trade unions more influence in India and a better standing in Geneva, where the issues raised by the CITU were turned into direct requests to the Indian government by the CEARC. Moreover, in some of the complaints the CITU brought cases of individual women workers to the knowledge of the ILO. These cases also illustrated in which ways the equalization of wages could hit women workers hard, leading them to lose their jobs or be turned into casual workers. After the complaints of the CITU, the government reported in 1986 that it had taken measures in collaboration with the workers' organizations to absorb the casual women workers into the ordinary workforce.[43]

Mobilization outside the UN Family: South Africa

Even though South Africa was no longer a member of the UN and the ILO, there are indications that IWY affected mobilization structures for equal remuneration in the country. The global emphasis on women's status during the 1970s can be seen in state investigations into the labour market, in steps taken to end wage discrimination in practice, and in suggestions for new legislation. Equal remuneration was included in general agreements concerning international labour standards in South Africa, despite the country having left the ILO in 1964, and these were used by women workers.

When the South African government decided to investigate possible reforms of labour relations through the Commission of Inquiry into Labour Legislation (more commonly known as Wiehahn Commission after its head commissioner, Nicolas Wiehahn), this was a result of protests against apartheid – the Durban strikes of 1973 and the uprisings in townships and especially in Soweto in 1976 – and the decline in foreign investment combined with an economic crisis, as well as foreign and domestic pressure on the South African government.[44] While not primarily aimed at investigating wage discrimination against women, the commission decided to work with a women's study group to investigate the labour situation of women. As a result, the first part of the Wiehahn Commission's report, published in 1979, although critical of the ILO's intervention into South African Apartheid politics, recommended with reference to ILO conventions that wage differences based on sex, age, or marital status should be outlawed, and that all laws contrary to the principle of equal treatment for men and women should be abolished.[45]

In 1981, then, the first South African equal pay legislation was introduced.[46] With reference to a number of international codes, including the ILO's C100 and recommendation 111, the recommendations of the Commission on Transnational Corporations adopted by the UN Economic and Social Council, and the ILO's 1977 Tripartite Declaration of

Principles Concerning Multinational Enterprises and Social Policy, the commission used international themes to frame the need to limit wage discrimination against women. Even though, compared to the intentions and the scope of the international concepts of equal remuneration, the changes applied only to a limited number of women workers covered by industrial councils and only to minimum wages, this was an important and notable step.[47]

Apartheid had also brought to South Africa multinational companies, which had to comply with international soft laws such as the ILO's 1977 declaration, and this opened a connection between the shop floor in South Africa and international and foreign political opportunity structures. The ILO declaration was applicable to workers employed at multinational companies whose main seat was located in an ILO member state, and it included core labour standards, among them C100. South African workers could not use the ILO to put pressure on their own government, but they could use international visibility to put pressure on the multinational companies to keep to rules in their country of origin and not apply the standards of the South African government. In a similar way, international codes of conduct could be used to put pressure on companies with subsidiaries in South Africa.[48] All codes demanded equal pay for work of equal value with reference to the ILO's C100 and recommendation 111.[49] One union that successfully used these soft laws together with workers' protests to put moral pressure on employers was the National Union of Textile Workers in South Africa, which managed to close the wage gap between men and women in the textile plants it had organized all over South Africa. By using the available international instruments, the union thus managed to end one of the most blatant forms of wage discrimination against working women in the industry and create a more transparent wage structure that made wage discrimination of various kinds easier to detect.[50]

Conclusion: 1975 as a Watershed

To be sure, there has always been a gap between the ambitions and outcomes of international labour activism, and the case of the fight for equal remuneration is no exception. Despite narrowed gender wage gaps in most Western countries, women in the twenty-first century earn on a global average between 40 to 90 per cent of men's wages.[51] Yet the examples we have presented above illustrate that during the UN Women's Decade international concepts were used systematically by those women who had knowledge about and access to them and proved to be effective tools in the struggle for wage equality at the national and local levels. Joan Sangster has shown that women did have a voice at the local level, and these local voices were now more connected to international demands.[52]

From the late 1960s onward, ending discrimination against women was an important part of international declarations, conventions, and programs of supra- and international organizations, and the fight for equal remuneration for men and women formed a substantial part of these initiatives. With the initiatives of women from the Global South and the Eastern Bloc, the demand for equal pay received renewed interest within the UN. International Women's Year, with its preparations, its celebration with the 1975 Mexico conference, and the implementation of the decisions made there, changed the struggles for equal remuneration. The standardization of the definition of equal remuneration for the same work and work of equal value and the demand to implement this definition in new or revised laws made the struggles truly global.

In this article we have shown how the UN's Women's Decade and previous work by the ILO impacted diverse repertoires of protest and created new political opportunity structures. Despite its weak standing at the ILO, Icelandic women used C100 and the mobilization for IWY to rally for wage equality and created repertoires of struggle that later had influence well beyond the local level. Moreover, legal improvements directly related to IWY provided them with new means of calling for the implementation of the principle of equal pay for jobs of equal value. Similarly, after the report on the status of women in India, submitted to the Indian government in 1974, and after the Indian Equal Remuneration Act was adopted in 1976, trade unions used the ILO as an official arena to put pressure on the Indian government to implement equal pay legislation and helped women workers who had lost their jobs when equal pay was introduced by protesting at the ILO, with the result that they got their jobs back. And finally, South African women workers were able to refer to international labour standards to introduce equal pay in the textile factories before equal pay legislation was introduced in South Africa. This shows that global concepts were important in personal, local, and national struggles for gender equality in the labour market.

Similarly to what Alvin Finkel writes in his chapter in this volume on the success of feminism in societies where equality is a social goal, we have found that countries with a general goal for equality, such as India after independence and Iceland during the latter half of the twentieth century, have provided a good starting point for equal wage struggles. In South Africa, the struggles for social equality were still ongoing during the fight against apartheid, and equality was at that point in time not a general social goal. However, our research also shows that the struggles for equal remuneration in that country did reinforce general social equality and the strategies used for the implementation of equal pay created more transparent wage structures. As the case of the legal battles in Iceland, textile industry in South Africa, and the court cases in India show, all workers gained from the struggles for equal remuneration.

NOTES

An earlier version of this article has been published in German translation: Silke Neunsinger and Ragnheiður Kristjánsdóttir, "1975: Globaler Wendepunkt für gleichen Lohn? Mikrostudien zur Lohngleichheit," in *Gender Pay Gap. Vom Wert und Unwert von Arbeit in Geschichte und Gegenwart*, ed. Wiebke Wiede, Johanna Wolf, and Rainer Fattmann (Dietz: Bonn, 2023), 261–81.

1 Devaki Jain, *Women, Development and the UN: A Sixty-Year Quest for Equality and Justice* (Bloomington and Indianapolis: Indiana University Press, 2005), 67; Hilkka Pietilä, *Engendering the Global Agenda: The Story of Women and the United Nations* (Geneva: UN Non-governmental Liaison Services, 2002), 30–2; Hilkka Pietilä and Jeanne Vickers, *Making Women Matter: The Role of the United Nations* (London: Zed Books, 1990), 75–6.
2 "Iceland: Women Strike," *New York Times*, 25 October 1975, 34.
3 See "Icelandic Women Strike for Economic and Social Equality," Global Non-violent Action Database, accessed 11 March 2020, https://nvdatabase.swarthmore.edu/content/icelandic-women-strike-economic-and-social-equality-1975; Kirstie Brewer, "The Day Iceland's Women Went on Strike," *BBC News Magazine*, 23 October 2015, https://www.bbc.co.uk/news/magazine-34602822.
4 Christian G. de Vito and Anne Gerritsen, "Micro-spatial Histories of Labour: Towards a New Global History," in *Micro-Spatial Histories of Global Labour*, ed. Christian G. de Vito and Anne Gerritsen (London: Palgrave Macmillan, 2018), 13.
5 Charles Tilly, *From Mobilization to Revolution* (Reading, MA: Addison-Wesley, 1978); Doug McAdam, John D. McCarthy, and Mayer N. Zald, *Comparative Perspectives on Social Movements, Political Opportunities, Mobilizing Structures, and Cultural Framings* (Cambridge: Cambridge University Press, 1996); Sidney Tarrow, *Power in Movement: Social Movements and Contentious Politics* (Cambridge: Cambridge University Press, 1998); Sidney Tarrow, *The New Transnational Activism* (Cambridge: Cambridge University Press, 2005), 23.

6 Marcel van der Linden, *Workers of the World: Essays Toward a Global Labour History* (Leiden and Boston: Brill, 2008), 7; Marcel van der Linden, "Transnationalizing American Labor History," *Journal of American History* 86, no. 2 (1999): 1078–92; Michael Werner and Bénédicte Zimmermann, "Vergleich, Transfer, Verflechtung: der Ansatz der histoire croisée und die Herausforderung des Transnationalen," *Geschichte und Gesellschaft* 28, no. 4 (2002): 6; Silke Neunsinger, "Cross-over! Om komparationer, transferanalyser, histoire croisée och den metodologiska nationalismens problem," *Historisk Tidskrift (Sweden)* 130, no. 1 (2010): 3–24.
7 Silke Neunsinger and Ragnheiður Kristjánsdóttir, "A Grammar of Equal Remuneration Struggles – Global Concepts – Local Negotiations – 1900–1985" (paper presented at "History, Feminism, Theory: Reflections on Women, Gender, Labour, and Colonialism," Traill College, Trent University, 21–2 June 2019).
8 The original 1919 ILO constitution can be found online under Part XIII of the Treaty of Versailles or in International Labour Organization, *Official Bulletin*, vol. 1, 1919–1920, chap. 6, "Part XIII of the Treaty of Peace of Versailles," 332–45. Paula Määttä, *The ILO Principle of Equal Pay and Its Implementation* (Tampere: Tampere University Press, 2008), 88f.; Carol Lubin and Anne Winslow, *Social Justice for Women: The International Labor Organization and Women* (Durham: Duke University Press, 1991), 21–3; Dorothy Sue Cobble, "The Other ILO Founders: 1919 and Its Legacies," in *Women's ILO: Transnational Networks, Global Labour Standards and Gender Equity, 1919 to the Present*, ed. Eileen Boris, Dorothea Hoehtker, and Susan Zimmermann (Leiden and Boston: Brill, 2018), 27–49.
9 Silke Neunsinger, "The Unobtainable Magic of Numbers, Equal Remuneration, the ILO, and the International, Trade Union Movement 1950s–1980s," in *Women's ILO: Transnational Networks, Global Labour Standards and Gender Equity, 1919 to the Present*, ed. Eileen Boris, Dorothea Hoehtker, and Susan Zimmermann (Leiden and Boston: Brill, 2018), 121–48.
10 Jain, *Women, Development and the UN*. Note, though, that at the local level, younger, second wave-Marxist feminists in the north Atlantic region had put economic and social equality back on the agenda.
11 Cited in Jain, *Women, Development and the UN*, 65.
12 Jocelyn Olcott, *International Women's Year: The Greatest Consciousness-Raising Event in History* (Oxford: Oxford University Press, 2017), 22. Olcott refers to the "Report of the Economic and Social Council, Report of the Third Committee," 11 December 1972, A 8928.
13 Jain, *Women, Development and the UN*, 30.
14 Jain, *Women, Development and the UN*.
15 Jain, *Women, Development and the UN*, 69; Silke Neunsinger, "The Unobtainable Magic of Numbers," 121–48.

16 Silke Neunsinger and M.V. Shobhana Warrier, "Transnational Activism and Equal Remuneration in India during the Twentieth Century," in *The Internationalisation of the Labour Question: Ideological Antagonism, Workers' Movements and the ILO since 1919*, ed. Stefano Bellucci and Holger Weiss (Cham: Palgrave, 2020), 329–50.

17 Geraldine Hancock Forbes, *Women in Modern India* (Cambridge: Cambridge University Press, 1996), 226; Vina Mazumdar, *Memories of a Rolling Stone* (New Dehli: Zubaan, 2015); Mala Khullar, "Emergence of the Women's Movement in India," *Asian Journal of Women's Studies* 3, no. 2 (1997): 94–129; Elisabeth Armstrong, *Gender & Neoliberalism: The All India Democratic Women's Association & Globalization Politics* (New Delhi: Routledge, 2013), 47–52.

18 The report was published by the Ministry of Education and Social Welfare under the title *Towards Equality: Report of the Research Committee on the Status of Women in India* and by the Indian Council of Social Science Research (ICSSR) under the title *Status of Women in India: A Synopsis Report of the National Committee (1971–1974)* (New Delhi: ICSSR, 1975).

19 ICSSR, *Status of Women in India*, 13. Cited in Chitra Sinha, *Debating Patriarchy: The Hindu Code Bill Controversy* (New Delhi: Oxford University Press, 2012), 2.

20 Mazumdar, *Memories of a Rolling Stone*.

21 Neunsinger and Warrier, "Transnational Activism and Equal Remuneration in India."

22 *Jafnrétti kynjanna* (Reykjavík: University of Iceland and Örn & Örlygur, 1975), 240–2.

23 Kristín Ástgeirsdóttir, "'Þar sem völdin eru, þar eru konurnar ekki': Kvennaáratugur Sameinuðu þjóðanna og áhrif þeirra á Íslandi 1975–2006," *Saga* 44, no. 2 (2006): 10.

24 "Ráðstefna um kjör láglaunakvenna," *Þjóðviljinn*, 26 January 1975, 4.

25 Guðrún Ágústsdóttir, "Leggjum niður vinnu til að sýna að munar um okkur!," *Þjóðviljinn*, 7 February 1975, 7.

26 Ástgeirsdóttir, "'Þar sem völdin eru,'" 14–19.

27 Public officials (*embættismenn*) in 1911 and schoolteachers (*barnakennarar*) in 1919. See, e.g., Guðrún Erlendsdóttir, "Jafnréttismál og jafnréttislögin," *Konur skrifa til heiðurs Önnu Sigurðardóttur* (Reykjavík: Sögufélag, 1980), 59. Wage equality for other public employees was introduced in legislation in 1945 and 1954, respectively: law no. 60/1945 on public officials; law no. 38/1954 on the rights and duties of public officials.

28 Law no. 60/1961 on the wage equality of men and women (*um launajöfnuð karla og kvenna*).

29 Law no. 37/1973 on an equal remuneration board (*jafnlaunaráð*); *Alþingistíðindi 1972–1973* A, 260–63.

30 Ástgeirsdóttir, "'Þar sem völdin eru,'" 23–6.
31 Law no. 78/1976 on equal status and equal rights of women and men (*jafnrétti kvenna og karla*).
32 Institute of Social Studies Trust (ISST), *The Experience in Implementations of the Equal Remuneration Act (ERA), 1976* (New Delhi: ISST, 2010), 2–4.
33 It was, e.g., used in the ILO training course on C100, held in Delhi in 28 June 1999; see also ISST, *The Experience of Implementing*.
34 Mackinnon Mackenzie and Co. Ltd. vs. Audrey D'Costa (1987) (2) BomCR 654, (1986) 88 BOMLR 516.
35 Article 11 of law no. 78/1976.
36 The women and men at the workplace were members of two different unions and thus paid according to different wage agreements. The majority of the Supreme Court judges claimed that the court could therefore not rule in favour of the woman. A minority disagreed, stating that it should not matter that the women and men were members of different unions.
37 Supreme Court judgement (*Hæstaréttardómur*), 117/1979. On court rulings on equal remuneration in Iceland, see Sif Konráðsdóttir, "Jafnaunareglan í íslenskri dómaframkvæmd og dómum Evrópudómstólsins," in *Guðrúnarbók: Afmælisrit til heiðurs Guðrúnu Erlendsdóttur* (Reykjavík: Hið íslenska bókmenntafélag, 2006), 411–27.
38 Silke Neunsinger, "Translocal Activism and the Implementation of Equal Remuneration for Men and Women: The Case of the South African Textile Industry, 1980–1987," *International Review of Social History* 64, no. 1 (2019): 37–72.
39 The comments can be found online in the ILO database. See "Committee of Experts on the Application of Conventions and Recommendations," accessed 16 April 2020, www.ilo.org.
40 See, e.g., Joan Sangster, *Transforming Labour: Women and Work in Post-war Canada* (Toronto: University of Toronto Press, 2010), 248, on Canada. In the case of South Africa, the international arena was used until national legislation came into place. After the introduction of new legislation, unions went to the courts at home. Neunsinger, "Translocal Activism."
41 Neunsinger and Warrier, "Transnational Activism and Equal Remuneration in India," 329–50.
42 Between 1968 and 2008 the CEACR made 162 observations relating to India, of which 22 observations concerned C100. Two of these (1976 and 1980) were concerned with the proven progress of implementation, while the other 20 were related to non-satisfying implementation of the provisions.
43 Neunsinger and Warrier, "Transnational Activism and the Equal Remuneration in India."
44 See also Alex Lichtenstein, "From Durban to Wiehahn: Black Workers, Employers, and the State in South Africa during the 1970s" (paper

presented at Wits Institute for Social and Economic Research, University of the Witwatersrand, 25 February 2013), cited with kind permission of the author; United Nations General Assembly Resolution 1761, adopted on 6 November 1962. Jacqueline Audrey Kalley, Elna Schoeman, and L.E. Andor, eds., *Southern African Political History: A Chronology of Key Political Events from Independence to Mid-1997* (Westport, CT: Greenwood Press, 1999); Charles H. Feinstein, *An Economic History of South Africa Conquest, Discrimination and Development*, (Cambridge: Cambridge University Press, 2005), 224; Sahkela Buhlungu, *A Paradox of Victory: COSATU and the Democratic Transformation in South Africa* (Scottsville, SA: University of KwaZulu-Natal Press, 2010), 80.

45 The commission cooperated with the Study Group on Women's Employment, which we have not been able to find out more about. Emma Mashinini, representative of the Commercial, Catering and Allied Workers' Union of South Africa at the Wiehahn Commission, has described the commission as an all-male panel in her memoir. Emma Mashinini, *Strikes Have Followed Me All My Life: A South African Biography* (London: Women's Press, 1989), 47.

46 Iris Berger, *Threads of Solidarity: Women in South African Industry 1900–1980* (Bloomington: Indiana University Press, 1992), 261–2.

47 Neunsinger, "Translocal Activism."

48 E.g., the Sullivan Code, the Code of the South African Council of Churches, the Code of the Consultative Committee on Labour Affairs by the South African Council of Trade Unions, and the Fair Labour Code of South Africa, proposed by the Trade Union Council of South Africa. The British government's code of conduct for British corporations operating in South Africa was the result of a series of articles in the *Guardian* by Adam Raphael about the starvation wages paid by British companies in South Africa. The American Sullivan Code was initiated by the American Baptist preacher and labour leader Leon Sullivan, who later also joined the board of General Motors. Grace Davie, *Poverty Knowledge in South Africa: A Social History of Human Science, 1855–2005* (New York: Cambridge University Press, 2015), 202–6; James Sanders, *South Africa and the International Media 1972–1979: A Struggle for Representation* (London: Routledge, 2000), 122–3.

49 Martin Holland, "Disinvestment, Sanctions and the European Community's Code of Conduct in South Africa," *African Affairs* 88 (1989): 539.

50 Neunsinger, "Translocal Activism."

51 See also Määttä, *The ILO Principle of Equal Pay*, 18; Richard Anker, *Gender and Jobs: Sex Segregation of Occupations in the World* (Geneva: ILO, 1998), 30.

52 Sangster, *Transforming Labour*, 246; Joan Sangster, *Dreams of Equality: Women on the Canadian Left 1920–1950* (Toronto: University of Toronto Press, 1989).

8 The Impact of Communism and Socialism on Women's Struggles and Social Entitlements in the Twentieth Century: A Global Overview

ALVIN FINKEL

Joan Sangster's first book examined women within the Co-operative Commonwealth Federation and Communist Party in Canada, addressing their goals and achievements but also patriarchal barriers they faced.[1] This article assesses similar issues for societies governed at various times in the twentieth century by parties proclaiming socialist or communist principles. It explores the gender equality proclaimed by the early Soviet government, influenced by feminist ideologies, and analyses why Soviet governments and their postwar European satellites only partially achieved that promise. The roles of women within political and social life in Communist China, Indochina, and Cuba are also examined. We then examine women's lives after Communist parties either no longer ruled or adopted pro-capitalist policies. Next, we compare the Communist record for women's equality with Global South governments proclaiming socialist agendas, including Communist-led united fronts in Indian states after 1957. Finally, we assess the impact of elected social democratic parties in Western bourgeois democracies on gender equality. Throughout, we examine what factors contribute most to women achieving and retaining equality and social justice in regimes proclaiming social justice goals. We find that the prior presence of feminist organizations matters, but equally important is the catalyst role that socialist organizations, with their proclaimed goals of equality for all, play in causing women to organize to ensure that such equality includes eliminating gender inequality. Our focus is on the extent to which the specific needs of equality-seeking women have been met in struggles for and formulation of social policies. The countries examined are those with considerable, relevant scholarly literature. The sources are mostly secondary, with emphasis on feminist and socialist historians.

The Soviet Case

Men vastly outnumbered women in both parties that formed the post-revolutionary Russian government, and only one woman served in the first cabinet. Nonetheless, Aleksandra Kollontai, people's commissar of social welfare, was the first woman in a cabinet in a parliamentary system anywhere.[2] Kollontai and fellow activists in the Zhenotdel, the women's department of the Communist Party Central Committee, influenced the early revolutionary government to promote gender equality. Five days after the revolution, the government declared a far-reaching, if only aspirational, insurance program for workers. It included coverage for pregnant women, reflecting the dominant Bolshevik view that both genders needed equal access to paid work. Lobbied by the Zhenotdel, the government legalized abortion in 1920, years before any capitalist country.[3]

Kollontai regarded the family as a bourgeois institution that condemned women to either imprisonment in the household or a double workday of paid and household work.[4] Encouraged by the Zhenotdel, the Central Executive Committee of Soviet Russia introduced the Code on Marriage, the Family, and Guardianship in 1918. Aiming to create sexual equality and undermine nuclear families, the code legislated publicly operated childcare, collective laundries, collective kitchens, and child dormitories. In practice, when such institutions were funded, only women were hired.[5]

Practical considerations, popular resistance, and chauvinism within the male leadership undermined Kollontai and the modest feminist movement. Few Russian women supported Kollontai's view that the family ideal was counter-revolutionary. Most ignored collective kitchens and cooked for their families.[6]

Social conditions made survival the goal of individuals, households, and the state, with revolutionary changes relegated to the future. The imperialist world war, followed by the civil war, produced devastated infrastructure, poverty, and widespread famine. Lenin introduced the New Economic Policy (NEP) in 1921. It left political control of the new Soviet Union under Communist Party guidance but allowed petit bourgeois capitalism to prevail outside existing worker-run city factories. Goals of equalization of wealth and gender equality were paused.[7]

Intact families were expected to raise their children, much as in pre-revolutionary times. The only children's dormitories established were for orphans. They bore no resemblance to the orderly, socialist-minded, well-staffed children's homes that Kollontai envisioned. Instead, they mimicked the poorly funded, surveillance-minded orphanages that had functioned since the reign of Peter the Great. Such institutions were supplemented by the paid labour of desperate women in the countryside who contracted to care for abandoned town children. They often used the meagre pay to feed their own children while the foster children died or joined child street armies in the towns. About 80 per cent of infants in state care in the early 1920s died before reaching adulthood.[8]

The historic gender pay gap expanded under the NEP. Cash-strapped Soviets put housing in the control of residents' collectives. Women did most of the work but held only 4 per cent of managerial positions. Even that modest inroad was soon under attack. After Lenin's death in 1924, Joseph Stalin gradually acquired full power and, as party general secretary, expelled old Bolsheviks to create a party that used violence and censorship to impose ever-shifting objectives. Stalin distrusted the relative independence of cooperatives and placed housing under the control of workplaces, over which the party increasingly exercised complete authority. A traditionalist on gender issues, Stalin disbanded the Zhenotdel, cancelling feminist influence on party policy.[9]

Stalin wanted women's cheap paid labour but within a return to pre-revolutionary patriarchy. The Family Code of 1936 recriminalized abortion, toughened divorce laws, and, pro-natalist, provided family allowances to families with six children or more, and a maternity leave of sixty-three days.[10] Growth of the childcare system was minimized and provided substandard care to about six hundred thousand mostly urban children in 1932, rising to four million during harvest season, when it reached rural areas.[11]

Post-Stalin, separate party organizations for women were recreated, but lacked independence from party leaders. While they influenced Soviet authorities to improve services for women and children, priority given to the military and to economic growth restrained social policy funding.

Abortion and divorce were relegalized in the late 1950s. But women's earnings were about half of men's, and women were ghettoized in low-paying occupations. Still, as of 1956, women working outside agriculture were guaranteed a modest pension at age fifty-five, five years earlier than men.[12] A falling birth rate influenced a 1973 decision to provide universal maternity benefits, family allowances for mothers of four or more children, and sixteen weeks' paid maternity leave. In 1974 mothers deemed unable to feed their children received a cash allowance, the first means-tested Soviet program.[13] Affordable daycare programs expanded to include all working mothers via workplace social funds. Paid maternity leave was gradually prolonged to a full year.[14]

Cheap rents also benefited low-income women, but continuous housing shortages relegated most single women, including many divorced mothers with children, to the 20 per cent of households on the waiting list to leave hostels for an apartment in 1985. That year the state abandoned responsibility for housing citizens.[15] Communist Party planning documents continuously promised apartments for all, but the priority assigned to the military and capital-intensive industries, along with corruption and bureaucracy, upended such promises.[16] Feminist groupings outside the rigid, male-dominated party were forbidden.

The achievements of Soviet communism for women should not be understated. The literacy rate for women in Tajikistan in 1925 was .6 per cent. In 1959, it was 100 per cent versus 20 per cent in neighbouring Iran, Turkey, and the Indian subcontinent.[17] Ultimately, however, women, after the early revolutionary years, played a minor role in influencing government programs. Communist suppression of independent feminist organizing limited the ability of women to protect established rights as they entered the harsh post-Communist world.[18] The patriarchal notions that the Communists preserved despite improvements in women's lives proved even more lethal within neoliberal, post-Communist societies.

Central and Eastern Europe

As communism was imposed by the Soviets on Central and Eastern Europe after the Second World War, women there shared similar experiences to Soviet women. On the one hand, they were victims of authoritarian rule by male-controlled parties wary of mass participation in policymaking or policy implementation. On the other hand, they benefited from a state ideology that proclaimed equality of citizens, even though their governments relegated women to lesser equality. Family allowances were introduced after pro-choice legislation in the 1950s caused birth rates to fall. Twenty-five per cent of family income in Hungary and 17 per cent in Poland emanated from that source, far more than in Western Europe.[19] Family allowances contributed to halving infant mortality in the region in the 1950s and increasing life expectancy by five years. But further progress in both areas ceased after that decade.

These countries were not all alike with regards to social policies affecting women. Czechoslovakia, the lone state in the region with more than a passing fling with parliamentary democracy before 1945, and where the Communists won 38 per cent of the vote in a fair election in 1945, invested heavily in social policies. Even before the brief Dubček reform era, each enterprise provided daycare, health services, canteens, and access to holiday resorts. In 1970, the Czech Communists, responding to disillusionment resulting from the Soviet invasion of 1968, introduced reforms that included twenty-eight months of paid maternity leave, a fixed-rate maternity allowance, birth subsidies, and an allowance for families with two or more children.[20]

The German Democratic Republic was at once the most invasive state in areas of individual autonomy and the most generous in social provision. The ideas of Clara Zetkin, a 1920s Communist leader who regarded women's employment and labour activism as the best guarantor of their full citizenship, remained important to German Communists. The GDR enshrined women's right to pregnancy and maternity leave, as well as children's allowances, in the constitution, while placing childcare under central government authority rather than leaving it to enterprises, as was common throughout the Soviet Bloc. Its counterpart was Hungary, which had placed most social policy programs under state management after the 1956 uprising in recognition of existing weaknesses in enterprise-managed social welfare funds. By 1960, just short of half of all three- to six-year-olds in the GDR were enrolled in state-paid childcare, mostly full-day. In 1980, only half of women in the Federal Republic of Germany were in paid employment versus 73 per cent in the GDR.[21]

The relative efficacy of communism over capitalism for women in countries that had been outside the advanced capitalist world before the Communist period became evident after the Communist regimes collapsed. In Bulgaria, a 1994 survey found few Bulgarians who were negative about communism. Among the Pomaks, Slavic Muslims in southern Bulgaria, 88 per cent regarded the Communist period as better than their post-Communist lives. Though some women resented the Communists' atheism, they remembered fondly their provision of maternity leave and childcare. In the early 2000s, as the lead-zinc mines and related industries shuttered, Pomak women's nostalgia for communism grew. Social assistance had virtually disappeared. With medicine and hospitalization privatized, and rent, food, and utilities subject to market pricing, many families felt forced to give their babies to orphanages. Albena, a former cook who had been unemployed for three years, cleaned streets as workfare to receive meagre social assistance to feed her two children in a home without electricity. Her comment: "I will tell you a hundred times ... communism is better than democracy. A hundred times better. For poor people, a hundred times better."[22]

In Hungary too, poverty was more pronounced than under communism. Vilma, an industrial worker, who married fellow worker Miklós in 1988, just before the collapse of communism, provides an example. They received a two-room flat when their first child was born, and Vilma went on paid maternity leave when each of their two children was born. Then came capitalism. Miklós lost his job in 1993, and failing to make a living from music, he abused Vilma, whose low wages forced the family to seek assistance from the Family Support Service Centre. Some food packages were all they received. Under communism, as a worker, Vilma would have been automatically eligible to separate from Miklós and be rehoused. His employer could not fire him under communism without having arranged for another employer to hire him at a similar wage. In late 1994, Vilma was also laid off and turned to sex work to feed her family. Welfare workers threatened to withdraw her meagre financial assistance if she continued with that work. In 1995, beaten and emaciated, she approached the child welfare agency, whose funds and authority had been slashed in the transition from communism to capitalism, and surrendered her two children.[23]

A decline in women's rights and incomes occurred across Central and Eastern Europe after the fall of communism. Across Yugoslavia, abortion had been a free medical service. In post-Communist Croatia, abortion cost two months of an average woman's wages.[24] In Poland, where the Communists made access to abortion almost universal despite Catholic Church opposition, abortions became almost impossible in 2016. By contrast, in Romania, where the Ceauşescu government had banned abortion from 1966 to 1990 for natalist reasons, a new women's movement won a partial restoration of abortion rights.[25]

The overall decline in basic human rights as well as income guarantees for women after communism disappeared reflected a continuing lack of substantive democracy. Top-down Communist governance had made the women's movement an instrument of the male-dominated party leadership. There was considerable noblesse oblige in the parties' policymaking. But their main concerns were how many babies women produced and what women could add to GDP rather than gender equality, or women's right to control their own individual and collective destinies. Women benefited from policies promoting state-subsidized childcare and easy access to abortion and divorce. But, generally, they had not fought for these advances, and were not organized to stop the neoliberal patriarchs of the post-Communist period, who, in the name of nationalism, erased women's and workers' rights while imposing predatory capitalism and patriarchal norms.[26] The equality-seeking aspects of Communist ideology had promoted at least some major rights for women, whereas the disappearance of egalitarian ideology in the post-Communist period made calls for gender equality, to the extent that they continued to persist, appear at loggerheads with the overall patriarchal conservatism that had become the new paradigm.

China and Indochina

The transition for women from guaranteed income earners, if second-class in their wages, to second-class workers with few job or social guarantees also occurred in China as the Communist Party abandoned its early adherence to a dictatorial but still substantive communism. The post-Mao regime was equally dictatorial but adopted a capitalist economic model, though with significant intertwining of state and private profit-making enterprise planning. Former socialist policies evaporated, though the ruling party persisted in maintaining the Communist Party moniker.

The Communists, upon first taking power, scrupulously enforced a pre-existing but often unenforced ban on binding women's feet, and declared gender equality while doing little in policy terms to challenge ingrained patriarchy. As in the Soviet Bloc, however, the view was that all women should engage in paid labour. Women profited from childcare arrangements organized at the levels of enterprises and agricultural communes. Like the men in the cities and towns, they benefited from the "iron rice bowl," which guaranteed all workers free public education, almost-free healthcare, social housing, job tenure, pensions, and elderly care.[27]

All that began to collapse in 1978 as state-owned enterprises (SOEs) began to compete with private enterprises, which were not required to provide social services, leading eventually to SOEs winning the right to cancel benefits. Between 1978 and 2004, the portion of health bills paid by the state dropped from 85 per cent to 16 per cent.[28] Faced with a decline in social guarantees in a still-patriarchal society, Chinese elders looked to sons to provide what the state had once provided to seniors since daughters' services were rendered to their husbands' families. In 1978 the "reformist" government imposed a one-child policy. So, being born a girl became a death sentence for many babies whose parents viewed them as burdens who would never become providers to their birth families. Female feticide, infanticide, and child abandonment had, by 2004, produced "gendercide": 121.4 boys for every 100 girls and in some rural areas 140 for 100.[29]

Vietnam, which financed generous social programs during the period of the struggle for national liberation and its immediate aftermath, using abundant aid from the Soviet Union and the People's Republic of China, had moved away from socialist objectives by the late 1980s, as its former foreign financiers had ended subsidies. Social programs disappeared almost overnight, though in 1999, the Communist government implemented a program for affordable preschools that soon enrolled almost half of eligible children. But there was no state aid for children under three or aid with school fees.[30] Independent feminist organizing remained illegal because of the Communist Party's mistrust of civil society organizations.

Other Communisms

Cuba's revolutionary commitment to egalitarianism, including equality of the sexes, lasted longer than Indochina's and was still intact at the end of the twentieth century. The social security law of 1963 included universal old age pensions, disability pensions, death benefits to families, paid maternity leave, illness leave, and leave for work and home accidents. Men received pensions at sixty-five and women at sixty; in 1970, those were reduced to sixty and fifty-five, respectively. The pension replaced work income 100 per cent. Universal ration cards guaranteed everyone sufficient calories and nutritional food. By 1989, Cuba was setting aside 35 per cent of total current expenditure for its social programs.[31]

Health was seen in terms of social determinants. Universal free education, food rations, low-cost housing, and universal social security were linked, and social programs created jobs that were dominated by women at most levels, though not necessarily the top administrative positions. Popular participation and mobilization in health campaigns also focused on women. Health clinics were established throughout the country and after 1964 converted into area polyclinics. In the 1970s, health professionals were trained to look for the material factors in their communities that contributed to disease. The government established the goal of having physicians on every block and in every agricultural area in the 1980s, with one family doctor and one nurse for every 120 to 150 families (600–700 people). The local physicians made the referrals for polyclinics and hospitals.[32]

But the collapse of the Soviet Union, purchaser of most of Cuba's sugar crop, produced an economic shock in the early 1990s. Cuba maintained most of its social programs. But daycare became means tested, and rations were reduced and ultimately eliminated.[33] Again, while women's participation marked Cuba's Communist experience out from European communism, party control over civic life limited possibilities for independent feminist movements.

Probably the most hopeful Communist regime in terms of women's rights to date has been the one in Kerala, an Indian state of about thirty-five million people. The parliamentary Communist Party of India (Marxist) has been in and out of power since its formation in 1964. Throughout its tenure, it has maintained its bottom-up character despite nominal Leninist structures. The party's origins were in both the national independence movement and trade union and peasant movements, all of which preceded the formation of the party itself.[34] Women's organizations within Kerala, including the women's sections of the CPI(M), are not creatures of either the state or a party with a monopoly on state power. They have had considerable impact in a system of multi-party politics. Nonetheless, in its early years in office, arguably, the CPI(M) and the Left Front improved women's social position without promoting full equality. But the gains for women were huge: A focus on social policy and redistribution of wealth meant improvements in housing, guaranteed food supplies, education, and health. Kerala's social statistics by the 1980s resembled those of an advanced capitalist country more than an Indian state, even though Kerala was in the bottom half of Indian states in per capita income.[35] Like Cuba and Mao-era China, Kerala demonstrated the falsity of American imperialist models of "stages of economic development" that suggested that dizzying economic growth was necessary to produce a society where high rates of infant mortality, low life expectancy, ill health, and low standards of education could be combated.[36] Most noticeable in its social statistics was the ratio of women to men, which contrasted heavily with overall statistics for the country, which showed a dearth of women relative to men.[37] In most of India, girls were a cost that poor parents could not bear since they would soon look after the parents of their husbands. The cost of dowries was an additional worry. In Kerala, where the state, rather than children, would guarantee the survival of older people, such concerns were less important. Ration shops, guaranteed housing, pensions, and free medical care might be rolled back somewhat by Congress-led governments, but in a state where the population was permanently mobilized, a Congress government with a narrow majority could only decelerate the state's move to greater egalitarianism.

Still, women often had the unhealthiest, lowest-paying roles in agriculture, jobs that left them "stooping and bending in the rice field, barefoot in the water that may contain leeches and other parasites, exposed to the monsoon rains."[38] In a state where political mobilization both within and across the socialist-capitalist divide had produced a powerful women's movement, the rival political fronts responded to pressures for programs relating to specific women's demands. In 1994, the Congress-led front funded an experiment in Malappuram, the state's poorest district, to give women-only community development societies funds to develop health, education, and economic programs. This effort produced a large number of latrines, wells, toilets in schools, remedial education for children in poor families, and a decline in cases of cholera, typhoid, and malaria. The Left Front, back in power in 1996, turned that pilot project into a state-wide program that received a generous portion of the state budget, though the funds went to the *Kudumbasree*, women-dominated self-help groups, rather than groups open only to women. Women's greater representation at the level of the *panchayats*, the municipal governments, also became significant as the Left Front increased the portion of the state budget given to *panchayats* to about 40 per cent by 2002.[39]

Though women's rights overall in India are modest relative to what was achieved by Communist-led governments in Kerala, there was a period just after independence from Britain where feminist goals such as equal wages with men for the same work made progress. As Silke Neunsinger and Ragnheiður Kristjánsdóttir point out in their chapter in this collection, "countries with a general goal for equality, such as India after independence and Iceland during the latter half of the twentieth century, have provided a good starting point for equal wages."

Non-Communist Achievements

Movements inspired by socialist and communist ideologies were influential at various times in postcolonial nations. Sometimes, women's efforts to achieve empowerment through community mobilization and acceptance of local knowledge and experimentation over the alleged expertise of international capital and local, male elites yielded gains similar to those experienced in Kerala, if on a smaller scale. For example, the Soils, Food and Healthy Communities project, a pilot project in northern Malawi, led by Ekwendeni Hospital, recorded a substantial decline in malnutrition and underweight babies and young children.[40] But without mass movements of the left and nation-wide movements for women's empowerment, such projects often remain geographically circumscribed.

Examples of Global South countries where mass movements of both the left and of women have made important strides toward gender equality in recent years include Bolivia and Costa Rica. In Bolivia, where women often dominated the Indigenous social movements of the coca growers (*cocaleros*), the government of the Movimentio al Socialismo, in power from 2006 to 2019 and headed by President Evo Morales, acceded to demands for state health clinics, the building of more schools, and free education. The infant mortality rate and levels of inequality fell significantly while literacy rates soared. These progressive policies contrasted sharply with the neoliberal policies of Bolivian governments in the 1980s and 1990s, dictatorships and elected governments alike, that ignored women's demands and peasant and worker demands in favour of attracting foreign investors and trade.[41]

Costa Rica provides an interesting case. Its governments did not label themselves as socialist but were able to legislate a social democratic agenda that was relatively gender-friendly after a decision in the late 1940s to disband the armed forces. At that time, the militaries throughout Latin America dominated government spending and reinforced the patriarchal goals of the Roman Catholic Church. Male breadwinners in nuclear families were deemed guarantors of income for households, and state social spending was restricted to means-tested programs for the destitute. By contrast, Costa Rica put guarantees of universal pensions and health insurance into its constitution in 1961. Ten years later it included all self-employed and rural workers in the system.[42] By 1990, virtually all health expenditures in Costa Rica were public, and preventive care aimed at the rural and urban poor had become the focus of the health system.[43] By then, a women's movement focused on economic security for women and children had influenced the authorities to supplement existing universal programs with pensions for the indigent, a school lunch program, nutritional programs for poor children, and housing subsidies.[44]

In an earlier period, Sri Lanka and Tanzania were additional examples of countries where women's movements won gender-friendly legislation before internal and external factors interfered. Many other countries made progress before American invasions destroyed their social experiments, including greater gender equality: for example, Chile and Uruguay.[45] As Gabriela Castillo argues in this collection, the Popular Unity government of Salvador Allende, which united the socialist forces in Chile and aimed at a revolutionary transformation of the country from capitalism to socialism within an electoral framework, "stressed the importance of female activism to securing class interests and achieving human fulfilment under socialism." Focusing on changes they induced in the long-standing *centros de madres*, Castillo shows that the socialist government radicalized women's sense of agency. While that did not end the reproduction of traditional gender roles, it made those roles less rigid, and the empowerment that women developed in the socialist period allowed them to resist efforts to turn back the clock on women's rights by the right-wing authoritarian, patriarchal military regime that brutally ended the Popular Unity democratic experiment.

Social Democracy in Western Europe

Comparisons of social democracy with Communist regimes are difficult because the former, more than the latter, governed in countries with advantages rooted in colonialist exploitation from both the colonial and neocolonial periods. One early example of a left social democratic regime where women were key policy developers deserves special mention: social democratic Vienna from 1919 to 1934, before fascism destroyed the socialist experiment. The Viennese success, superficially, resulted from a capitalist head start. But the city was bankrupt after the Austro-Hungarian empire collapsed. The new Austria included only 6.5 million people of the former empire's 55 million and had no capital funds for reconstruction, its people having lost all their savings. Vienna, with its 2 million people, had state-level status and extensive taxation and legislative powers. A postwar blockade by the Allied powers during the winter of 1918–19 almost starved Vienna, and it was forced to send tens of thousands of children abroad. There had been no wartime construction, and the city lacked decent housing for its workers, much like the Russian cities. The municipal Socialists focused on creating state-owned but cooperatively managed housing estates similar to those that Stalin had disbanded before they could prove their worth.

Emmy Freundlich, Socialist legislator and president of the International Cooperative Women's Guild, whose organization influenced the Viennese experiment immensely, described these homes as "owned and built by the entire community." Working-class homes in prewar Vienna had lacked most amenities, but these homes, influenced by Socialist women's priorities, "are small parts of the city rather than individual houses. They have courts, gardens, playgrounds for children, electrically equipped kitchens, bathrooms, and other accommodations." By 1930 Vienna had built forty-five thousand lodgings and had planned fifteen thousand more. Once the famine was over, vigorous public health measures reduced infant mortality sharply. The Socialist politicians, with an eye on children because of influence from the women's movement, established twenty-eight child guidance clinics, mostly in schools, on the model initiated by the left-wing Freudian psychiatrist Alfred Adler.[46]

Have women experienced better results in Western countries when they are governed by self-proclaimed social democrats or communists than when conservatives or liberals rule? The social democratic nations of Scandinavia lead the pack among Western democracies for the greatest gender economic equality and better provisions for daycare and maternity leave. In the early 1960s, Sweden stood out as a nation that had both a dominant Social Democratic Party and a strong feminist movement that straddled party formations. A multi-partisan feminist movement that included Social Democrats, Communists, and Liberals influenced the governing Social Democrats to replace the prevailing one-income household ideal with a two-income ideal. Group 222, the most influential women's organization, argued that "traditional sex roles must be changed so that home and family become to an equally great extent men's and women's concern and so that material support and social responsibility become to the same degree men's and women's task."[47] To that end, generous maternity and later paternity leave were added to subsidized daycare as state policies.

The Swedish Social Democratic government reported to the United Nations Commission on the Status of Women in 1968: "Every individual, irrespective of sex, shall have the same practical opportunities, not only for education and employment, but also in principle the same responsibility for the upbringing of children and the upkeep of the home. Eventually to achieve complete equality in these rights and obligations, a radical change in deep-rooted traditions and attitudes must be brought about among both women and men, and active steps must be taken by the community to encourage a change in the roles played by both."[48]

But part of the government motivation to implement universal state-subsidized daycare, the lynchpin of their two-income paradigm, was that the alternative to having more working women was to import more non-white labour. That offended Swedes who cherished a white, European, Christian identity. So, unsurprisingly, in recent years, with the spread of neoliberalism to Scandinavia and the growth of white nationalist populist and patriarchal movements, women's gains have been undermined particularly but not exclusively when the Social Democrats are out of power.[49] In good part, that is because the right-wing alternative parties to the Social Democrats are less committed to equality among citizens as a goal. In their chapter in this volume, Neunsinger and Kristjánsdóttir point out that Iceland's achievements for women in the latter half of the twentieth century have resulted from society adopting more general social equality goals. That such goals are more frequently supported by left-leaning governments helps to explain why programs to benefit women diminish when the right is in power.

The presence of social democrats in governing coalitions in different European countries has not guaranteed policies favouring women's paid work. Feminist calls in Germany for universal childcare were repelled even when the Social Democrats were in government. The

Social Democrats cooperated with conservatives to support tax policies favouring two-parent, single-earner households even as divorce rates soared. In 2006, only 38 per cent of married mothers with children under age twelve were in paid labour versus 86 per cent in Sweden, 77 per cent in Denmark, and 55 per cent in France.[50]

Ironically, single mothers were more likely to be living in poverty in France despite that country's better record on state support for childcare. In the mid-1980s, the figure was 22.8 per cent in France versus 8 per cent in Germany.[51] Germany's social spending much exceeded France's, where participation of Socialists and Communists in government was limited before 1981: 33.5 per cent of GDP versus 23.8.[52] The election of a Socialist-Communist coalition, supported by women's organizations calling for a massive increase in state-subsidized childcare spaces, yielded disappointment when President François Mitterand largely abandoned his promise to open three hundred thousand new daycare spaces.[53]

June Hannam's article in this collection on the British Labour Party points out that women were most influential in areas where women's employment and public services were long established or where the Independent Labour Party, which was far more clearly socialist than the mainstream of the Labour Party, predominated. The more committed Labour Party members were to socialist principles of equality, the more they were prepared to accept that gender equality was an important goal.

In Italy, the Communist Party was the leading force on the left. But it never won a national election. While the Communists defended women's right to work and supported childcare programs, the dominant Christian Democratic Party reinforced the sexism of the Roman Catholic Church. In 1970, only 14 per cent of married Italian women were in the paid workforce.[54]

The contrast between countries where social democrats generally governed, as in Scandinavia, and those where the social democrats failed to win nationally, as in Canada, or were largely irrelevant in national elections, as in the United States, during the period of the greatest advance of the welfare state, is stark. In 1980, single motherhood was almost synonymous with poverty in the United States and Canada. Puritanical commentators claimed that single motherhood, as opposed to a lack of social policies to permit women to raise children on their own, *caused* poverty. In the United States, 42.3 per cent of single mothers lived in poverty versus 11.9 per cent of all people between the ages of twenty-five and fifty-nine. In Canada, it was 42 versus 10.3 per cent. But in Denmark, it was 4.8 per cent versus 4.5; in Finland, 4.5 versus 3; and in Sweden, 4.8 versus 7.7.[55] Significantly, social democratic expenditures that reduced economic burdens on single mothers reflected a commitment not just to gender equality but to equality more generally. This was reflected in the large percentage of gross domestic product that they reserved for social programs in 1980. The United States spent 21 per cent of GDP on social programming; Sweden, 33.5 per cent; and Denmark, 29.1.[56] The Gini coefficient, a broad measure of equality of income in which one person having all wealth yields a Gini of 1 and complete equality yields a 0, averaged .227 in the Scandinavian countries against .335 in the United States.[57]

Attacks on the welfare state since the 1980s have disproportionately harmed women. A continuing sex-segregated labour market concentrates women's jobs in the state or state-subsidized "caring" sectors, including the education, health, and social service sectors, while men's jobs are overwhelmingly in the private sector. So women's jobs come under direct attack during bouts of austerity. When "caring" jobs disappear, the transfer of those services to the home requires women to provide unpaid labour for work that formerly paid incomes to them. Austerity is not gender-neutral, and the partial embrace of austerity by social democrats after the 1970s in most countries demonstrates how gender-unbalanced political parties remained in the late twentieth and early twenty-first centuries.

While austerity policies appeared almost universal over several decades, both the starting points and end points varied across countries. Countries with strong social democratic histories preserved and even extended social policies that created gender equality far more than countries with weak social democratic pasts. Finland, for example, lost 15 per cent of its exports when the USSR collapsed in 1991. It introduced modest user fees for some social services and reduced subsidies for prescriptions, and cut parental benefits for new babies by 12 days, from 275 to 263.[58] But cuts largely ended after the mid-1990s. Meanwhile, in the United States, even today, no national program pays parents that stay home with new babies, and no program provides daycare for older children as parents return to work.[59]

Conclusion

Women's movements in vastly different societies may share common aims.[60] The historical record demonstrates that feminism is most influential in societies where economic equality is already valued. In hunter-gatherer societies, women's equality with men permitted social structures that allowed for complementarity of the sexes, generalized sharing of goods, and guaranteed social protections for the sick and the aged.[61] By the beginning of the twentieth century, few societies exhibited such characteristics. Feminists included both left-wing proponents of such widespread equality as well as liberals who accepted unequal structures but wanted equality of women with men throughout the class structure. The most radical communist and socialist feminists wanted to eliminate all structures that created both unequal distribution of wealth and prescriptive roles for each sex. The actual Communist societies rarely embodied this ideal; they liberated women from the household to work, but for a fraction of men's incomes while earning no income for their continued unequal share of household work. Nonetheless, communism provided social guarantees that allowed women to choose whether to marry, or if married, to choose to divorce. To a degree, the same things were true of social democracy. Interestingly, within parliamentary regimes, both Communist and social democratic, the greatest social gains for women occurred when leftist parties and centrist parties had feminist components with shared goals, such as we have seen in Kerala and Sweden. The calls of feminists for policies that favoured women's economic independence were reinforced by socialist ideologies of equality among individuals within societies, even when many men who promoted those ideologies fought rearguard battles to assert the idea of equality among patriarchal households rather than equality among all citizens, regardless of gender. Socialist feminism often successfully countered such paternalistic traditionalist conceptions of socialism.

Women's ability to advocate for themselves independently was limited in one-party Communist states, where non-party organizations were closely monitored or banned. In capitalist societies, the economic control by private corporations restricted feminist possibilities, though social democratic and Communist parties sometimes responded to feminist pressures to restrict corporate hegemony. Generally, both communism and social democracy have proven friendlier to women's rights than conservatism and liberalism, although independent feminist movements have been more active in liberal North America than in European states where social democrats are strongest. But they have been less successful in achieving women-friendly legislation than their counterparts in Western Europe, which largely work inside traditional left political parties and trade unions. The women who have seen the greatest losses throughout the period of neoliberalism are the women of the former Soviet Union and its satellite states. Largely deprived of influence within ruling Communist parties and disallowed from forming independent women's organizations, they have proved little able in the post-Communist period to mount an effective opposition to the imposition of patriarchy and the stripping of former social policies, both of which have marked the "reform" period of post-communism.

NOTES

1 Joan Sangster, *Dreams of Equality: Women on the Canadian Left, 1920–1950* (Toronto: University of Toronto Press, 1989).
2 Kollontai was elected to this cabinet post at the Second All-Russian Congress of Soviets of Workers' and Soldiers' Deputies. "Prominent Russians: Aleksandra Kollontai," *RT Russiapedia*, https://russiapedia.rt.com/prominent-russians/politics-and-society/aleksandra-kollontai, accessed 17 July 19, 2024
3 Wendy Z. Goldman, *Women, the State, and Revolution: Soviet Family Policy and Social Life, 1917–1936* (Ann Arbor, MI: Cambridge University Press, 1993), 5–12.
4 Elena Iarskaia-Smirnova and Pavel Romanov, "Rhetoric and Practice of Modernisation: Soviet Social Policy," in *Amid Social Contradictions: Towards a History of Social Work in Europe*, ed. Gisela Hauss and Dagmar Schultze (Leverkussen Opladen, Germany: Verlag Barbara Budrich, 2009), 150–1.
5 Goldman, *Women, the State, and Revolution*, 1, 3, 11.
6 Lynne Attwood, *Gender and Housing in Soviet Russia: Private Life in a Public Space* (Manchester: Manchester University Press, 2010), 64.
7 The New Economic Policy is described in detail in a biography of its principal supporter: Stephen F. Cohen, *Bukharin and the Bolshevik Revolution: A Political Biography, 1888–1938* (Oxford: Oxford University Press, 1980). On its impact on women and children, see Goldman, *Women, the State, and Revolution*, 71–83; Iarskaia-Smirnova and Romanov, "Rhetoric and Practice of Modernisation," 151–2.
8 Goldman, *Women, the State, and Revolution*, 67–8; David Tobias, *Moving from Residential Institutions to Community-Based Social Services in Central and Eastern Europe and the Former Soviet Union* (Washington, DC: World Bank Publishers, 2000), 5–6.
9 Attwood, *Gender and Housing in Soviet Russia*, 27–9, 41, 46, 62–71, 89, 102–3, 110; E. Thomas Ewing, "'Life Is a Succession of Disappointments': A Soviet Girl Contends with the Stalinist Dictatorship," in *Girlhood: A Global History*, ed. Jennifer Helgren and Colleen A. Vasconcellos (New Brunswick, NJ: Rutgers University Press, 2010), 148.
10 Yoshie Mitsuyoshi, "Maternalism Soviet-Style: The 'Working Mothers with Many Children' in Post-war Western Ukraine," in *Maternalism Reconsidered: Motherhood, Welfare and Social Policy in the Twentieth Century*, ed. Marian Van der Klein et al. (New York: Berghahn, 2012), 206.

11 Bernice Glatzer Rosenthal, "Love on the Tractor: Women in the Russian Revolution and After," in *Becoming Visible: Women in European History*, ed. Renate Bridenthal and Claudia Koonz (Boston: Houghton Mifflin, 1977), 370–99.
12 Jolanta Aidukaite, "The Formation of Social Insurance Institutions of the Baltic States in the Post-Socialist Era," *Journal of European Social Policy* 16, no. 3 (2006): 259–60.
13 Lynne Haney, *Inventing the Needy: Gender and the Politics of Welfare in Hungary* (Berkeley: University of California Press, 2002), 93.
14 Saul Estrin, "The Inheritance," in *Labor Markets and Social Policy in Eastern Europe: The Transition and Beyond*, ed. N.A. Baer (Oxford: Oxford University Press, 1994), 72.
15 Attwood, *Gender and Housing in Soviet Russia*, 154–60, 170, 180–2, 193–4; Steven E. Harris, "Soviet Mass Housing and the Communist Way of Life," in *Everyday Life in Russia Past and Present*, ed. Choi Chatterjee, David L. Ransel, and Mary Cavender (Bloomington: Indiana University Press, 2015), 181, 190.
16 Anders Aslund, *How Capitalism Was Built: The Transformation of Central and Eastern Europe, Russia and Central Asia* (Cambridge: Cambridge University Press, 2007), 17.
17 Kiril Nourzhanov and Christian Bleuer, *Tajikistan: A Political and Social History* (Acton, Australia: ANU Press, 2013), 2, 4–5, 57–64, 69–71, 77–83.
18 Linda Racioppi and Katherine O'Sullivan, *Women's Activism in Contemporary Russia* (Philadelphia, PA: Temple University Press, 1997).
19 Stephen Haggard and Robert R. Kaufman, *Development, Democracy, and Welfare States: Latin America, East Asia, and Eastern Europe* (Princeton: Princeton University Press, 2008), 150–1, 156.
20 Estrin, "The Inheritance," 61; Haney, *Inventing the Needy*, 93.
21 Patrizia Albanese, *Mothers of the Nation: Women, Families, and Nationalism in Twentieth-Century Europe* (Toronto: University of Toronto Press 2006), 128; Karen Hagemann, "Between Ideology and Economy: The 'Time Politics' of Child Care and Public Education in the Two Germanys," *Social Politics* 13, no. 2 (Summer 2006): 222, 240–1; Éva Bicskei, "'Our Greatest Treasure, the Child': The Politics of Child Care in Hungary, 1945–1956," *Social Politics* 13, no. 2 (Summer 2006): 160–1.
22 Kristen Ghodsee, *Muslim Lives in Eastern Europe: Gender, Ethnicity, and the Transformation of Islam in Postsocialist Bulgaria* (Princeton: Princeton University Press, 2009), 97.
23 Haney, *Inventing the Needy*, 227–8.
24 Albanese, *Mothers of the Nation*, 118.
25 Gail Kligman, *The Politics of Duplicity: Controlling Reproduction in Ceausescu's Romania* (Berkeley, CA: University of California Press, 1998).

26 Barbara Einhorn, *Cinderella Goes to Market: Citizenship, Gender and Women's Movements in East Central Europe* (London: Verso, 1993).
27 Joe C.B. Leung, "The Emergence of Social Assistance in China," *International Journal of Social Welfare* 15, no. 3 (July 2006): 189.
28 Shaoguang Wang, "China's Double Movement in Health Care," in *Morbid Symptoms: Health under Capitalism*, ed. Leo Panitch and Colin Leys (London: Merlin, 2010), 249.
29 Christina Larson, "In China More Girls Are on the Way," *Bloomberg News*, 31 July 2014, https://www.bloomberg.com/news/articles/2014-07-31/chinas-girl-births-ratio-improves-as-country-gets-more-educated.
30 Jody Heymann, *Forgotten Families: Ending the Growing Crisis Confronting Children and Working Parents in the Global Economy* (Oxford: Oxford University Press 2006), 229; Nghiem Tran Dung, *Social Health Insurance in Viet Nam* (Hanoi: Health Insurance Department, Ministry of Health, 2010), http://www.ilo.org/wcmsp5/groups/public/---asia/---ro-bangkok/---ilo-hanoi/documents/presentation/wcms_145792.pdf, retrieved 15 March 2017; "Health Care in Vietnam Limping," *Economist*, 20 September 2014.
31 Claes Brundenius, "Cuba: The Retreat from Entitlement?," in *Exclusion and Engagement: Social Policy in Latin America*, ed. Christopher Abel and Colin M. Lewis (London: Institute of Latin American Studies, 2002), 332–4, 337.
32 Julie Feinsilver, "Cuba's Health Politics at Home and Abroad," in *Morbid Symptoms: Health under Capitalism*, ed. Leo Panitch and Colin Leys (London: Merlin, 2010), 217–19.
33 Brundenius, "Cuba: The Retreat from Entitlement," 334, 337, 348; Feinsilver, "Cuba's Health Politics at Home and Abroad," 222; Gavin Mooney, *The Health of Nations: Towards a New Political Economy* (London: Zed, 2012), 167.
34 Manali Desai, "Indirect British Rule, State Formation, and Welfarism in Kerala, India, 1860–1957," *Social Science History* 29, no. 3 (Fall 2005): 457–88.
35 Richard W. Franke and Barbara H. Chasin, *Kerala: Radical Reform as Development in an Indian State* (n.p.: Institute for Food and Development Policy, 1989), 89; Patrick Heller, "Mobilization and State Intervention: Industrial Workers in Kerala, India," in *State-Society Synergy: Government and Social Capital in Development*, ed. Peter Evans, International and Area Studies Digital Collection (Berkeley: University of California Press, 1997), 48, 94; K.P. Kannan, "Poverty Alleviation as Advancing Basic Human Capabilities: Kerala's Achievements Compared," in *Kerala: The Development Experience: Reflections on Sustainability and Replicability*, ed. Govindan Purayal (London: Zed, 2000), 40.
36 A theory most associated with Walter W. Rostow, advisor to President Kennedy. See Simon Reid-Henry, *The Political Origins of Inequality: Why a More Equal World Is Better for Us All* (Chicago: University of Chicago Press, 2015), 74.

37 Jean Drèze and Amartya Sen, *India: Development and Participation* (Oxford: Oxford University Press, 2002), 85.
38 Franke and Chasin, *Kerala*, 90.
39 Raghav Gaiha and Vani Kukarni, "Panchayats, Communities, and the Rural Poor in India," *Journal of Asian and African Studies* 37, no. 2 (2002): 58–9; Mooney, *The Health of Nations*, 155–8.
40 Raj Patel et al., "Cook, Eat, Man, Woman: Understanding the New Alliance for Food Security, Nutritionism and Its Alternatives from Malawi," *Journal of Peasant Studies* 42, no. 1 (November 2015): 21–44.
41 Sven Harten, *The Rise of Evo Morales and the MAS* (London: Zed, 2011); Martin Sivak, *Evo Morales: The Extraordinary Rise of the First Indigenous President of Bolivia* (London: Palgrave Macmillan, 2010); Roger Burbach, "Update: Communitarian Socialism in Bolivia" (North American Congress on Latin America, 2 April 2010); Benjamin Kohl and Rosalind Bresnahan, "Bolivia under Morales: Consolidating Power, Initiating Decolonization," *Latin American Perspectives* 37, no. 3 (2010): 5–17.
42 Haggard and Kaufman, *Development, Democracy, and Welfare States*, 85.
43 Evelyne Huber, "Globalization and Social Policy Developments in Latin America," in *Globalization and the Future of the Welfare State*, ed. Miguel Glatzer and Dietrich Rueschemeyer (Pittsburgh: University of Pittsburgh Press, 2005), 26, 83, 86.
44 Huber, "Globalization and Social Policy," 83, 87.
45 On Chile and Uruguay, see Haggard and Kaufman, *Development, Democracy, and Welfare States*; on Sri Lanka, William W. Murdoch, *The Poverty of Nations: The Political Economy of Hunger and Population* (Baltimore: Johns Hopkins University Press, 1980), 69–73; on Tanzania, Kjell Havnevik and Aida C. Isinika, eds., *Tanzania in Transition: From Nyerere to Mkapa* (Dar Es Salaam: Mkuki Na Nyota Publishers, 2010).
46 Emmy Freundlich, "Municipal Housing Development in Vienna," *Annals of the American Academy of Political and Social Science* 150 (July 1930): 228; Peter Singer, *Pushing Time Away: My Grandfather and the Tragedy of Jewish Vienna* (London: Granta Books, 2003), 131.
47 Anne-Marie Daune-Richard and Rianne Mahon, "Sweden: Models in Crisis," in *Who Cares? Women's Work, Childcare, and Welfare State Redesign*, ed. Jane Jenson and Mariette Sineau (Toronto: University of Toronto Press, 2001), 151.
48 Monica Townson, *A National System of Fully-Paid Parental Leave for Canada: Policy Choices, Costs, and Funding Mechanisms*, Series A, Equality in the Workplace (Ottawa: Labour Canada, 1983), 21.
49 Kjell Östberg, "Swedish Social Democracy after the Cold War: Whatever Happened to the Movement," in *Social Democracy after the Cold War*, ed. Bryan Evans and Ingo Schmidt (Edmonton: Athabasca University Press, 2012), 205–34.

50 Hagemann, "Between Ideology and Economy."
51 Evelyne Huber and John D. Stephens, *Development and Crisis of the Welfare State: Parties and Policies in Global Markets* (Chicago: University of Chicago Press, 2000), 109.
52 *OECD Bulletin*, no. 146 (January 1984), reprinted in Andrew Armitage, *Social Welfare in Canada: Ideas, Realities and Future Paths*, 2nd ed. (Toronto: McClelland & Stewart, 1988).
53 Kimberley J. Morgan and Kathrin Zippel, "Paid to Care: The Origins and Effects of Care Leave Policies in Western Europe," *Social Politics: International Studies in Gender, State and Society* 10, no. 1 (Spring 2003): 49.
54 Albanese, *Mothers of the Nation*, 149.
55 Huber and Stephens, *Development and Crisis*, 109.
56 *OECD Bulletin*, no. 146, 22.
57 Jens Alber, "The European Social Model and the United States," *European Union Politics* 7, no. 3 (2006): 406.
58 Duane Swank, *Global Capital, Political Institutions, and Policy Change in Developed Welfare States* (Cambridge: Cambridge University Press, 2002), 139–49.
59 Sonya Michel, *Children's Interests/Mothers' Rights: The Shaping of America's Child Care Policy* (New Haven: Yale University Press, 1999).
60 The fight for equal pay, e.g., a focus of the 1975 international conference on women in Mexico City, inspired campaigns in Iceland, India, and South Africa, where feminists confronted very different regimes. Those struggles are the subject of the article by Silke Neunsinger and Ragnheiður Kristjánsdóttir in this book.
61 M. Dyble et al., "Sex Equality Can Explain the Unique Social Structure of Hunter-Gatherer Bands," *Science* 348, no. 6236 (May 2015): 796–8.

PART THREE

Violence and the Law

9 The Seduction of Vivian MacMillan: Scandal, Politics, and Perception in Depression-Era Alberta

P.E. BRYDEN

In September 1933, at either the deepest point of the Great Depression or at the beginning of the recovery – depending on one's vantage point – a brief article on the front page of the Toronto *Globe* announced a suit for "damages on [a] serious charge" against the premier of Alberta. The charge was that of seduction, and John Brownlee had known it was coming; indeed, when informed of the statement of claim, he noted that "while one regrets to have to face a case of this kind, still it will enable me to come to grips with rumours that have been spread abroad through the Province for some weeks."[1] The resulting trial gripped the public's attention through 1934, ended Brownlee's premiership, and played a role in the electoral failure of the United Farmers of Alberta (UFA) in 1935; the subsequent appeal of the original decision and later Supreme Court hearing were somewhat less riveting than the original trial, shorn as they were of the salacious testimony of both the accuser and the accused, but the case itself was not put to rest until 1940.

At the heart of the Brownlee scandal is sexual assault; echoes of the testimony given in 1934 can be heard in courtrooms across the nation and through the decades. Indeed, it finds particular resonance in the twenty-first century "Me Too" movement, but also in thousands of other courtrooms where similar testimony was given in the 1930s, 1940s, and beyond.[2] In addition to the legal issues in which this case traded, however, it was also a political scandal with all the attendant features of concealment, public disapproval, and reputational disintegration.[3] As such, it offers a unique opportunity to examine not only layers of courtroom interpretation, where one person's experience and account of that experience are weighed against another's, but also the evolving public perception of the scandal and of the transgression at its root. In each environment, other factors bear on the outcome. In the court, familiar class and gender biases came into play, whereas in the broader public these were woven more overtly into the tapestry of the larger political and economic environment. Thus the Brownlee case not only sheds light on the legal evolution of sexual assault at the nexus between seduction and rape, but it also underscores the important ways in which public perceptions affected that evolution. As Joan Sangster has argued elsewhere, highly publicized trials "both reflected and constructed public thinking" about, in this case, sexual assault; "legal proceedings and newspaper accounts exposed prevailing social values and stereotypes as well as how legal professionals and observers deployed and redefined these ideas during court proceedings."[4] In the Brownlee scandal, we see a real disjunction between the views of the public and those of the court, clearly delineating the distinction between scandal and crime. Moreover, in the years that followed, the episode was largely forgotten; what was remembered, when it was, was what happened, not what made it a scandal. That little bit of historical forgetfulness has further limited the lessons of the scandal.

A political scandal is a particular sort of event, characterized as much by what people think as by what actually happened. John B. Thompson identifies the key components of scandal, and while other authors may debate the relative significance of each of these elements, few disagree with the general framework. For a situation to be considered a political scandal, there must first be a transgression, which is then concealed; the event must be regarded with disapproval when it is eventually uncovered, by the public or a portion of the public, which denounces the acts, and eventually the "disclosure and condemnation of the actions or events may damage the reputation of the individuals responsible for them."[5] Using this definition, the situation involving Premier Brownlee and Violet MacMillan in the 1930s was clearly a political scandal: There was sex, kept secret for some time, outraging the Alberta public and leading to reputational disintegration.

Sangster and other feminist scholars have urged historians to interrogate the silences, to listen carefully to what is not said, to consider what is not included in the archival record and write histories that are attentive to these gaps and interruptions.[6] A political scandal offers an interesting opportunity to consider silences in a very public, almost cacophonous, episode. In the Brownlee case there are certainly still unanswered questions, issues on which the historical record remains mute and voices that have been rendered dumb through both the passage of time and the constraints of the day. There are also, however, silences that are illuminating in terms of understanding political culture in 1930s Alberta, and voices that, despite efforts to quiet them at the time, offer important correctives to our analysis of the history of sexual violence in Canada. Indeed, it is the very volume of some of the voices that we have remembered as silent that is the most compelling lesson of the Brownlee scandal. The possibility that a very clear, very public message could be all but erased from the collective memory of the event is a clear reminder of the vicissitudes of history.

Sangster has also been critical of the idea of historiographical progress, and of the view that "insight builds on insight" in an ever-upward historical narrative. While admitting her own guilt in offering a "progressive narrative" in, for example, describing labour history as "moving from a narrow focus on male artisans to a more expansive focus that took in women, family and community," Sangster has been continuously attentive to the anti-Whig trajectory of both history and historiography.[7] The Brownlee scandal underlines the failures of a narrative of progress, just as it illuminates the historiographical twists and backsliding that have occurred in the successive reinterpretations of events. Perhaps scandal offers more opportunities for misinterpretation than other political episodes, dependent as it is not on what happened, but on the perception of what happened. Regardless of the reason, however, such has been the re-evaluation of *Brownlee v. MacMillan* over the years that few could continue to imagine an "ever-upward" trajectory of historical insights over time.

To think about Brownlee and Sangster in the same space is to upend the historiographical record and return to the interpretation that was offered in the 1930s – an assessment of the transgression that situated it firmly as a sexual assault, even if that was not the name that was given to it. It is to think about where the record is silent and to imagine the other transgressions that did not become scandals. It is to consider how the voices of women, even when heard loudly and clearly, are more seldom listened to. It is to confront the long, deep history of the early twenty-first century's Me Too movement and the equally lengthy roles played by both institutional limitations – from the court, in this case – and public outrage. In order to get to these places, we will first examine the scandal in all its component parts, and then the ways in which later generations of interpreters have attempted to reframe it as something other than what it was at the time.

The Scandal

Transgression and Concealment

Scandal begins with a transgression; *naming* what lay at the heart of the Brownlee case was a problem for both the law and the voters in 1930s

Alberta, but identifying it as a transgression was difficult only for the legal profession. Indeed, by 1937, everyone, including the former premier, seemed to agree that something quite insalubrious had occurred to Vivian MacMillan while she studied and worked in and around the premier of Alberta's office between 1932 and 1933. That widespread public preoccupation with the saga was at once a result of the economic and political environment of the Great Depression, a reflection of the shortcomings of the law, and a potential impetus for change. In the dry spring of 1934, however, when the trial was conducted in an Edmonton courtroom packed to the rafters, it wasn't the law that lured the audience or even the sex, but rather the stature of the man against whom the charges were brought; it was the entertainment value of a morality play – free for all to see – in the depths of a depression that seemed to know no morality.

Vivian MacMillan had just graduated from high school in Edson, Alberta, when the premier – UFA leader John Brownlee – came to town, the guest of her father. It was the summer of 1930, and Brownlee had been premier for five years. Described as tall and erect and "a model of incorruptibility," he led a government with an impressive record of balancing the budget, reducing expenditures, and wresting control of natural resources from the federal government.[8] He enjoyed a high level of popularity, but the beginning of the Depression and increasing calls for government assistances suggested that Brownlee's support might be precarious. All that was on the horizon, though, when the premier visited Edson in the summer of 1930. During an hour-long drive to a picnic on the McLeod River, Brownlee chatted with Allan MacMillan, the town mayor, his wife, Letha, and their daughter Vivian, and commented at least once and perhaps twice on the beauty of the latter. Brownlee learned that the eighteen-year-old was considering pursuing studies in music. The premier "disapproved" of the scheme and instead "suggested that she go to Edmonton and take a business course."[9] Although her mother thought MacMillan was too young to set out on her own in Edmonton, that was the path that she eventually followed, no doubt using the premier to bolster her case with her parents. By the beginning of September 1930, MacMillan had a room at the Edmonton YWCA and a place in the business program at Alberta College. Within days, the premier was on the phone; "a little birdie" told him that she was in town, and he was calling to invite her over to the Brownlee house for Sunday dinner.

According to MacMillan, that was the beginning of a deep friendship with Florence Brownlee, wife of the premier and the mother of their two teenaged boys, *and* paved the way for the beginning of a coercive sexual relationship with the premier that would last for years. For over two years, MacMillan spent every Thursday and Saturday evening at the Brownlee home. The premier "usually drove her home afterward himself."[10] The drives rapidly turned into meandering treks around the outskirts of Edmonton. The premier early on admitted that "he had been madly in love with [MacMillan] for some time" and that he "was very, very lonely, and that he and Mrs Brownlee had not been living together as man and wife for a good number of years." Brownlee needed MacMillan, he argued, to "give in to him," or he would not be able to go on "as the Premier of Alberta;"[11] he said it was her "duty to show [her] gratitude for having been so kind to [her]."[12] The stakes were even higher: Having sex with Brownlee would also "save Mrs. Brownlee's life, his future and the honor of his family."[13] Within a few days, he "used force on her, during which he partially succeeded in his object" of penetration; MacMillan tried to end her contact with the Brownlee family, but the premier was back within the week, arguing that it was her "duty to save Mrs. Brownlee's life" and ultimately forcing her "down in the backseat of the car." MacMillan later explained that "he had one arm around me, holding me down on the seat of the car. He used his other hand to raise my clothes and undo his own. On that occasion we had complete sexual intercourse."[14] And so began a period of almost three years of coercive sex.

The locations varied: Often, it was in secluded areas of back-roads Edmonton, but occasionally in the Brownlee house itself. In September 1931, Florence Brownlee, accompanied somewhat bizarrely by Vivian MacMillan's mother, travelled to Vancouver for three days; MacMillan stayed in the Brownlee house, again having unwanted sex with the premier. The relationship with the premier had, by this time, become so regular "as to practically constitute a habit."[15] The following summer, another situation arose that eased MacMillan into the Brownlee home: the departure of a live-in maid and the disappearance, therefore, of another set of eyes. Again, the premier insisted on engaging in sex with the young woman. This time, the "connections" between MacMillan and Brownlee occurred while Florence and the premier's two teenaged boys lay sleeping in neighbouring rooms or, in the case of sixteen-year-old Jack, in the *same room*. MacMillan did not attempt to stop Brownlee; while she was not "hypnotized" by the premier, she felt that he "completely domineered" her, manipulating her with arguments about his wife's illness and the suggestion that "if his daughter had lived he would be proud of her if she would do the same thing," presumably in the greater interest of the state.[16]

The physical price MacMillan paid to creep around in the Brownlee household was too much; in the fall of 1932 she collapsed on her way to her position as a secretary in the office of the attorney general. She was taken to University Hospital by the premier's wife, where she remained for three days. Her mother arrived from Edson to take her home to recover for another seven weeks from what MacMillan described as a nervous breakdown.[17] "I was getting very tired," she explained, "and those pills I was taking upset me and I kept getting a very severe pain in my left side. I had lost about thirty pounds."[18] Upon her return to Edmonton, and with some difficulty, she ended her connection with Brownlee, asking for her "freedom" on several occasions before finally wrenching herself out from under what she called "his spell" over her in the summer of 1933.[19]

Little of this was known in the period between 1930 and 1933. By 1933, MacMillan was apparently worried that her late-night drives with the premier were being observed, and by July of that year she was ready to tell her parents about the nature of her connection with Brownlee. There were also apparently rumours in Ottawa that Brownlee was involved in a "triangular affair with [a] stenographer in his office," but there was no real evidence.[20] There seems little reason to believe that the details of the situation were known outside a very small group. The scandal had not yet begun, although the transgression had continued for years.

Public Revelations, Response, and Reputational Disintegration

Everything changed with the filing of seduction charges against the premier by Vivian MacMillan and her father. Each sought damages of $10,000. With these charges, and the ensuing court drama in the summer of 1934, any secrecy was removed, and the details of the contact between the premier and MacMillan were splashed across newspaper front pages from one side of the continent to the other, and given at least passing notice by readers in London and Paris.[21] Not only was the concealment, such a necessary part of a scandal's trajectory, uncovered, but the public responded virtually continuously with opprobrium. This was true when the initial charges were laid, when the trial began, and when the verdict was passed – there was a consistent level of public outrage.

The initial suit was filed in an Edmonton courthouse in September 1933 and covered in detail in *The Globe* in Toronto. The filing, and subsequent newspaper coverage, capped a period of increasing speculation; the premier admitted that the trial would allow him "to come to grips with rumors that have been spread abroad through the Province for some weeks." He went on to maintain that there was "not a word of truth to the allegations."²² Whatever the rumours were, they no doubt fell on receptive ears: Only the previous year, the newspapers had been full of details of the minister of public works' "wife-swapping" deal and his secret divorce.²³ The UFA may have enjoyed a sterling reputation in the early years of governance, but by the early 1930s that was disappearing quickly. The news of this new transgression involving the premier easily eclipsed the earlier scandal and was covered extensively.

There was a great deal to keep the public interested. The original charges were filed in September 1933; the premier responded in November with a counterclaim that purported that Vivian MacMillan and a certain John Caldwell had conspired to extort money from Brownlee.²⁴ This claim was based on information that Brownlee and his team of lawyers had uncovered through the legwork of a private detective. Three people were prepared to testify that Caldwell, a third-year medical student at the University of Alberta and boyfriend of MacMillan, had stated that he would soon be coming into a large sum of money thanks to someone "high up in political life."²⁵ The public chewed over the competing claims for the next several months, waited as the trial was twice delayed, and then watched in anticipation as it began in an Edmonton courthouse in June 1934. Reports from the courtroom, and from the Brownlee home and the back roads around the capital where the jury was taken during the course of the six days of testimony, riveted audiences at home and abroad.²⁶

There is no question that once the transgression became public knowledge, the public cared about it. There was, as Thompson argues, clear public disapproval, demonstrated not only in the somewhat prurient fascination with the details of the trial, but also in more direct ways.²⁷ The Brownlee boys bore the physical brunt of schoolyard opprobrium, returning home enough times with black eyes that they were ultimately sent east to Ontario to weather the remainder of the trial with their grandmother. Politicians demonstrated their disapproval directly to the premier in a number of obvious and more subtle ways: One UFA member publicly refused the honour of moving the Speech from the Throne and instead excoriated the government for failing to shuffle the cabinet portfolios. He then crossed the floor to join the Liberals, bringing another UFA member with him.²⁸ Behind the scenes, a realignment of political forces in Alberta in light of the growing threat of the Social Credit movement was deemed impossible because the premier was "timid and vacillating" and unable to address the "disrepute into which some of [the UFA] members have fallen."²⁹ The trial had not yet begun, but it is clear that the reputation of the premier had already begun its decline.

Once the trial finally got underway, the public was privy to days of intimate details about the relationship – coercive and sexual in the lengthiest version, paternal in the premier's considerably shorter testimony. In many regards, Brownlee's version of events differed little from that offered by MacMillan. He concurred with her account of their meeting in Edson, with much of her tale of moving to Edmonton, with the explanation of the early contact and her regular visits to the Brownlee home. He also admitted to arranging to pick her up late at night in what would appear to be agreed-upon locations, driving out of town with her, and then returning her to darkened street corners some hours later. In fact, he even allowed that she had stayed at the Brownlee home in the absence of his wife. Where his response to MacMillan's testimony differed was to deny many of the details – that he suggested that she stay at the YWCA when she moved to Edmonton, for example, or that "he had ever pushed her out of his car and later phoned his apologies"[30] – but nevertheless leave intact the broad picture of a relationship of considerable intimacy. His efforts to discredit the plaintiff were specifically directed to issues of enticement, or the manner by which she had come to Edmonton in the first place, to the suggestion that he had promised her employment in the legislature, to the question of whether or not he had plied her with pills, and to the health of the girl he described as "gay, bright, happy [and] vivacious."[31] He did not directly deny the accusation that he had had sex with MacMillan, but rather instead confined his defence to the denial of key components of the crime of seduction.[32]

Seduction was a curious charge, but the only avenue really open to MacMillan, and even then somewhat debatably. In the mid-seventeenth century, English common law recognized a tort for damages done to a daughter. Based on law that recognized that an injury done to a servant gave their master the right to sue for loss of services, the "seduction action extended this doctrine by acknowledging a daughter's position in the family as one of servitude."[33] But the law recognized loss of service only as a side effect of pregnancy; "merely seducing the daughter was of no consequence," nor was the father in a position to sue for loss of services if his daughter worked elsewhere.[34] The case that MacMillan and her father brought to trial confronted both of these legal precedents – that the seduction result in a pregnancy, and that the father of the woman seduced be shown to have lost services due to that pregnancy and confinement – while making use of the seduction law as a tool for addressing the sexual assault at the root of the Brownlee scandal.

In using the charge of seduction, MacMillan's lawyers depended on the court's recognition of the evolution of the tort. What had once been an action open only to masters of servants had become an action open to fathers of daughters and, as was proposed in 1930s Alberta, should also be open to the women themselves. In building a case around one law's progression, we can see an implicit recognition that other legal options remained unavailable. Assault or harassment charges would surely have been considered by late twentieth-century legal teams, but that was not the case in the 1930s, when assault was violent and the term "sexual harassment" had yet to be coined.[35] The absence of violence, the appearance of consent, and the length of the connection all pointed to the difficulties in making a case against the premier on the charges of rape. MacMillan's options in the face of sexual predation, like those of so many others, were severely limited; seduction remained, at least for the time, the more likely legal gambit.[36]

The trial itself was over fairly quickly, lasting in total only six days. Here again, however, is evidence of the public reaction to the transgression and the results of that reaction on the premier's reputation. Before jury deliberations began, Brownlee dropped the countercharges against John Caldwell for blackmail. Perhaps that affected the jury's decision. In the end, the jury of six men deliberated for just over four hours, returning to the courtroom to answer the judge's questions: "Did the defendant seduce the plaintiff, Vivian MacMillan?" "Yes," replied the foreman. The second question was when the seduction had occurred, to which the jury foreman replied, "At the time stated by Vivian MacMillan." The jury further found that she had suffered damages, as had her father, and awarded Vivian $10,000 and Allan MacMillan $5,000.[37] There was an "outburst of cheering" in the courtroom following the jury's award, pointing to the widespread public support that MacMillan had amassed over the course of the trial and the clear public sense that the premier had been the one in the wrong.[38] Any rumours of blackmail or suggestions that the accusations were politically motivated remained in the background, far overshadowed by Brownlee's decision to tender his resignation even before the court's decision was reached, which would certainly have been interpreted as an admission of guilt.[39]

The judge, however, was not so convinced of Brownlee's guilt. Indeed, Justice Ives had been quite specific in his charge to the jury, a recitation of the facts as he saw them that took under half an hour:

> It is a question of seduction and that alone is the issue ... I know no better aid that you can have than to test the respective stories told by witnesses in light of reason. How consistent is the conduct they allege with that conduct which you would expect from the average reasonable man

of ordinary habits of mind ... Do not find a verdict upon possibilities. You balance probabilities ... Now, this must be said, that the story of the female plaintiff in so far as this misconduct is concerned is fully and entirely unsupported by any other evidence. It is just her own evidence ... There is this thought that must occur to you: that if this relationship is, as disposed by the plaintiff, extending over a period fully three years and, considering the conspicuous position occupied by the defendant, it is astounding, to my mind, that no one has been found who, in any way, had reason to suspect anything other than a very proper relationship.[40]

Having thus been told what would and would not be "astounding" to think, the jury of six men rapidly came to the opposite decision to that which the judge essentially told them to reach. To have done so points to a certain resoluteness on the part of the jury. After six days of hearings, the men of the jury betrayed little uncertainty: Their decision was unanimous, reached quickly, and after only one further question to the court (regarding the evidence of MacMillan's physical ailments).[41] A furious Justice Ives was not impressed, telling the jurors before he dismissed them "that I strongly disagree with your decision." So strongly, in fact, did he disagree with them that he reserved the verdict and subsequently overturned it, charging court costs to the MacMillans.[42] It was a dramatic and generally unpopular conclusion to a trial in which the majority seemed to side with MacMillan.

Scandal and the Law

There are rarely firm endings to political scandals. Rather than reaching satisfactory conclusions with the drop of a gavel or the resignation of a politician, they fade more slowly from public view, shifting off the front pages and eventually out of sight entirely. Justice Ives's unsatisfactory overruling of the jury's verdict marked, as well as anything can, the beginning of the end of the Brownlee scandal. Most of the issues raised in court were far from resolved, making this an odd moment to mark as an endpoint for the scandal itself. This is particularly true as the ruling occurred at the moment of widespread public outrage, but it is here that the events of the previous few years in and around the Brownlee home shifted from being the subject of public outcry to being about the law, first, and eventually about something else altogether. The scandal, though, had run its course.

Public outrage did not disappear when Justice Ives reserved the ruling of the jury for his own consideration, nor when he overturned the decision, declaring that "no illness resulted from the seduction" and there was "no evidence that the ability of the daughter to render services was in any way interfered with." It did, however, shift its gaze. As far as Justice Ives was concerned, the "law is well settled that damage is the gist of the action," and finding no evidence of damage, he dismissed the case with costs.[43] The immediate response indicated that there was still considerable public support for the MacMillan version of events: Not only was there a speedy collection of a considerable sum of Depression-era money for the MacMillans to mount their appeal, but newspaper editorial writers across the country shook their collective heads at the "unsavoury case."[44] But this reaction was different from the breathless coverage that had characterized the reporting on the trial itself, and it would grow only more sedate and more infrequent as the appeals process continued. The scandal, which at its core was about sex and power, was beginning to disappear, rearranging itself from an exploration of morality into a question about the law and the capacity of the legal framework to evolve. And that latter character was far less interesting, far more commonplace, and ultimately, far less scandalous than the accusations of unwanted sex between the farmer premier and the teenager.

Long before any form of justice was secured, there was a satisfactory conclusion to the sex scandal. Most scholars of scandal recognize the significance of consequences in understanding its trajectory; in political scandals, these generally manifest in reputational disintegration. The trial process had left Brownlee's career in tatters; once the jury delivered its verdict, there was little left for Brownlee to do but resign. He met with the lieutenant governor immediately after the jury's decision and while Justice Ives was still reserving it for his own consideration; in a subsequent statement, Brownlee indicated that he had "notified the Lieutenant-Governor of [his] intention to resign as premier of the province" and asked for a "few days to clean up matter[s]" before formally tendering the resignation.[45] That formality followed three days later, leaving caucus members "dumbfounded by the situation confronting them ... [they] could talk of little else" at the outset of the emergency meeting.[46] Apart from the last spasm of outrage over the judge's intervention in the case, public interest largely shifted to other matters. As a political scandal, the transgression had been made public, condemned, and – significantly, for the purposes of marking its conclusion – resulted in the appropriate reputational collapse. Brownlee had resigned, and the United Farmer government was in tatters. No longer an active scandal, it relatively quickly disappeared from public view.

But as an issue, rather than a scandal, the case was far from resolved. Use of the Alberta Seduction Act as the basis for the legal action complicated matters as far as the law was concerned, even if the public remained clear about who had been in the wrong. Seduction was a charge rarely used in the absence of a pregnancy (and the *MacMillan v. Brownlee* case was the first such case in Alberta history),[47] with damages never awarded to the victim even then, but rather to the man whose "property" had been damaged. The original jury verdict was overturned because damage had not been proved; the Alberta Court of Appeal upheld that decision in February of the following year.[48] But the appeal court was divided, with two of the five judges finding it reasonable that the jury had reached the decision that it had, and therefore unreasonable that it be overturned: "The finding of seduction cannot be disturbed."[49] Those dissenting opinions perhaps gave MacMillan the confidence to press her case to another level, despite the fact that public interest in the case had all but disappeared.[50] Even the results of the Supreme Court appeal, released in 1937, garnered little public attention, despite overturning the decisions of the two lower courts. Chief Justice Lyman Duff found that section 5 of the Seduction Act could apply to a woman "of virtuous life and habits" who had been seduced by a man who had used "enticement" or taken "some unfair advantage ... through which he has induced the woman to have intercourse with him."[51] Moreover, "the verdict of the jury must stand" unless it was one that "no jury, acting judicially, could give." He did not find this to be the case, and thus ordered the return of the $10,000 award to MacMillan and coverage of her costs throughout the entire case. It was a stern blow to Brownlee, who shortly thereafter agreed to settle.[52] After one final, failed, appeal to the Judicial Committee of the Privy Council (JCPC) in an effort to save his reputation, Brownlee gave up.[53] MacMillan emerged victorious, not just in the eyes of the public but also, ultimately, in the opinion of the courts.

This finally marked the end of the scandal and the end of the legal saga. In the first, after the transgression was revealed and public outrage registered, a political punishment was meted out; scandals do not deal in the law, but in perception and reputation, and in this regard the Brownlee scandal was essentially concluded with the premier's resignation. The collapse of the UFA in the election of 1935 and the decision of the JCPC in 1940 were mere formalities, epilogues to the story that ended with the Edmonton jury's decision in favour of MacMillan in 1934. The legal saga carried on beyond that point, as successive courts considered the nature of seduction and the possibility of damages being awarded to the victim, but by 1940 those too had been established with a degree of finality. Despite two separate but equally conclusive endings to the Brownlee case – one as political scandal and the other as point of law – it has not disappeared entirely from the collective consciousness. While the law was firmly set, the scandal itself was too salacious to lie dormant forever. This highlights a curious feature of political scandals, which on the one hand are so ephemeral as to have attracted little scholarly attention, but on the other can be so sensational as to warrant subsequent periodic public airings. But without the original public casting judgment or expressing outrage – with, in other words, an entirely new context – the original message of the scandal is lost. The Brownlee case is a good example of that.

Like most scandals, Brownlee's disappeared from sight pretty quickly. That is, in part, the nature of scandal: Dependent on public interest, they remain scandals only so long as there is a public that cares. In this regard, interest in Brownlee and MacMillan was sustained for a relatively long period as far as scandals are concerned, but it had still nevertheless disappeared by the middle 1930s.[54] This was a political scandal, in the sense that it carried very real political costs for Brownlee and for the UFA, and a sex scandal in that it involved sex rather than financial malfeasance or corruption or any of the other sorts of misdeeds politicians have been known to dally in. Unlike some sex scandals, however, it did not symbolize broader political concerns – or at least, it was not understood that way by the public. As Anna Clark has persuasively shown in the British context, some sex scandals became "intertwined with the politics of the day," largely due to the "instigator's ability to sustain his or her credibility, to use the scandal to symbolize wider political causes and mobilize public opinion."[55] This was not the case in Depression-era Alberta: While MacMillan's credibility remained intact throughout the trial, it was never her intent to link her situation to broader matters of public policy. Initially, there had been some suggestion that the original charge owed something to the interference of Liberal lawyers and financiers; those rumours failed to achieve much traction. Rather, this was at heart a sex scandal with political costs, and any lasting implications would be felt in gender dynamics, views on sexual assault, and the evolution of the concept of consent.

In the afterlife of the Brownlee scandal, amnesia is more apparent than memory. The public reaction to the scandal is regularly underplayed, the final verdict of the Supreme Court and judicial committee ignored, and the power inequity between Brownlee and MacMillan forgotten, whether the episode is reported as history, in art, or in journalism. In fact, the saga is almost never retold in the manner that the jury (and a good portion of the public) heard it in the summer of 1934 – as a case of abuse of power resulting in emotional and physical damages worthy of financial redress. Historians have used the case to illustrate the evolution of seduction law, or to partially explain the downfall of the United Farmers and the rise of Social Credit in Alberta.[56] In these studies, the scandal is less important than either the legal or political repercussions. But to ignore the fact that these events created a scandal is to misread the contemporary context. According to Thorner and Reddekopp, who provide by far the most substantial analysis of the legal implications of *Brownlee v. MacMillan*, the absence of substantial public comment on sexual morality suggests that the case "challenges one of the most compelling characterizations of Alberta as a moralistic, fundamentalist Bible belt."[57] The jury decision, however, was a unanimous indictment of the casual misogyny that tolerated a long-term coercive sexual relationship with a teenager indebted, in Depression-era Alberta, to the premier for a job. Surely there was morality in that determination, but the original jury finding in favour of Vivian MacMillan has received so little attention in the scholarly literature that the conclusions one can draw from it are usually overlooked.

The popular literature has also severed the scandal from its original context, ignoring the public response and retelling the events differently from the way they were heard by Albertans in the summer of 1934. Little, if anything, was written about the scandal for the better part of half a century; the fate of the law was left to wend its way through various courts, occasionally attracting media comment, but after the war the episode seems to have disappeared. Then, in the 1990s, stories about the scandal began appearing in magazines and newspapers. A change to the way the media could report on divorce proceedings led the *Calgary Herald* to suggest that there was finally an "epilogue in the 1934 case of a country girl led astray by the 'flattery and expert love-making' of John Brownlee";[58] other reports recalled Brownlee's depiction at the time as an "immoral urban politician who'd used his sophisticated wiles to lure Vivian into a lengthy, squalid affair."[59] But the initial reports were brief – mere mentions of a scandal that had happened long ago. When President Bill Clinton faced impeachment over his own sexual misconduct south of the border, however, the Brownlee case was reopened as prologue:

> A powerful politician spots a pretty woman, young enough to be his daughter.
>
> The two begin a lengthy, secretive sexual affair. They even carry on in the politician's office. In the end, however, the affair explodes into a sensational court case. The young lady spills out the details, much to the delight of the world's press.

The politician, supported by his wife, denies everything and alleges a conspiracy of his political enemies. Nevertheless, he's found guilty, his reputation ruined.

You don't have to look as far away as Washington, D.C. to find this story. It happened in Canada, in Edmonton, though you have to go back in time, to the 1930s when Alberta Premier John Brownlee was disgraced over his alleged romance with 18-year-old Vivian MacMillan.

In this recounting, it was the "outrage of busybodies" that forced Brownlee's resignation following his "affair." The finding of the jury was ridiculed, MacMillan's allegations described as "a load of baloney," and the situation dismissed as a "personal, not a public, matter."[60] The perspective from the end of the century contrasts with that of the time, as might be expected, but in offering a Clinton-era interpretation of events, the significance of the original outrage is lost. The scandal is retold rather than reconsidered.

Subsequent versions of the Brownlee case only continued to undermine the lessons of the original scandal. Barbara Smith included a highly fictionalized version of the story in a collection of "great Canadian love stories" that casts MacMillan as a lovesick schoolgirl and the premier as "smitten";[61] Janice Tyrwhitt included large portions of the cross-examination in her assessment of the case, but still came to the conclusion that it was a "sordid lawsuit marred by false oaths, reckless decisions, political cross-currents and relentless publicity [from which] no winners emerged." Brownlee's behaviour was "commonplace" throughout history, "without damaging ... [men's] leadership." The biggest losers in this telling were the people of Alberta, "who had lost a capable and accomplished premier."[62] There have even been attempts to turn the events of the early 1930s into entertainment: *Respecting the Action for Seduction* was a play about the trial, offering the possibility that MacMillan had been a woman scorned, seeking revenge on a man who refused to make their love public. It was acclaimed for "wear[ing] [its] history lightly." In this rendition, the Supreme Court decision finally awarding MacMillan (by then married and now Vivian Sorensen) her $10,000 is met with sorrow: "It's over John. I told a better story," Vivian announces.

> JOHN: It's not over. I'm prepared to put in a special request to appeal to the Privy Council of the British Empire.
> VIV: What does it matter, John. You've lost. We've ... lost.[63]

These retellings of the Brownlee episode decades later are not grounded in new research or based on the discovery of new evidence; each uses the same material that was available to the public in the 1930s and reshapes it into a different sort of story. Each, then, revisits the events without appreciating the scandal. But it is in the scandal that there is significance. The fact that this was a political scandal demonstrates the degree to which the transgression was met with public outrage; it was not, as later commentators purported, an exercise of power or desire that was commonplace and unremarkable. To focus only on the events and not on the reaction is to miss the point. That, in 1934, a jury of six men and a province full of hard-strapped Albertans could evaluate the case of a powerful politician having sex repeatedly with a woman who felt unable to resist his pressure, and view it as something outrageous, something demanding some form of punishment, something far different from everyday misogyny, is profoundly important. The fact that this was a scandal is important. The fact that it has all but been forgotten, and when revisited has been instead rewritten, is important. It has not been Vivian MacMillan's voice that time has silenced, or that of John Brownlee, but the collective cry of an outraged public that shouted "shame" and the collective voice of a jury that ruled "guilty" that have been lost; the loudest voices at the time are the ones that have disappeared. The result has been the recurring requirement to see it all over again – the transgressions, the outcries, the reputational disintegrations – before any of the lessons about sex and power are learned. Scandals raise the issues, but history fails to remember.

NOTES

1 "Alberta Premier Sued for Damages on Serious Charge," *Globe*, 23 September 1933, 1.
2 The fits and starts of attention that have been given to sexual assault are examined by Barbara Freeman in the CBC of the 1980s ("'Most Women Would Prefer to Keep Their Mouths Shut': Challenging Sexual Harassment within the Canadian Broadcasting Corporation, 1981–1986") and by Nadia Verrelli and Lori Chambers in the courts of the same period ("Battered Women and Self-Defence before *R. v. Lavallee*: The Forgotten Case of *R. v. Whynot [Stafford]*), both in this collection. There has never been a time when the echoes of the Brownlee case were quiet.
3 John B. Thompson, *Political Scandal: Power and Visibility in the Media Age* (Cambridge: Policy Press, 2000), 13–14.
4 Joan Sangster, "The Meanings of Mercy: Wife Assault and Spousal Murder in Post–Second World War Canada," *Canadian Historical Review* 97, no. 4 (December 2016): 515.

5 Thompson, *Political Scandal*, 13–14.
6 All of Sangster's work explicitly addresses the silence in the historical record when it comes to the lives of women, particularly on the left. See "The 1907 Bell Telephone Strike: Organizing Women Workers," *Labour/Le Travail* 3 (1978): 109–30, which Sangster describes as "very much part of a moment of 'discovery' in Canadian women's history" ("Discovering Women's History," in Joan Sangster, *Through Feminist Eyes: Essays on Canadian Women's History* [Athabasca: Athabasca University Press, 2011], 49); much of her work also addresses and interrogates the archival silences and the absences in the oral history record (see, e.g., "'Pardon Tales' from Magistrate's Court: Women Crime and Count in Peterborough County, 1920–50," *Canadian Historical Review* 74, no. 2 [June 1993]: 161–97; "Invoking Evidence as Experience," *Canadian Historical Review* 92, no. 1 [March 2011]: 135–61).
7 Sangster, "Introduction: Reflections on Thirty Years of Women's History," in *Through Feminist Eyes*, 20.
8 Patrick Brode, *Courted and Abandoned: Seduction in Canadian Law* (Toronto: University of Toronto Press for the Osgoode Society for Legal History, 2002), 149–50.
9 "Vivian MacMillan Tells Her Story," *Lethbridge Herald*, 25 June 1934, 2; see also Janice Tyrwhitt, "She Destroyed a Government and Ended a Premier's Career," in *Fury and Futility: The Onset of the Great Depression*, ed. Ted Byfield (Edmonton: United Western Communications, 1998), 272.
10 "Vivian MacMillan Testifies in Brownlee's Seduction Trial," *Edmonton Bulletin*, 25 June 1934.
11 "Vivian Testifies to Harrowing Ordeal," *Edmonton Bulletin*, 26 June 1934.
12 "Brownlee's Counsel Grills Star Witness," *Calgary Daily Herald*, 26 June 1934.
13 "Vivian Testifies to Harrowing Ordeal."
14 Tyrwhitt, "She Destroyed a Government and Ended a Premier's Career," 285.
15 "Brownlee's Counsel Grills Star Witness."
16 "Hearing of Action against Premier and of Premier's Counterclaim Commences," *United Farmer*, 29 June 1934, 12.
17 "Vivian Testifies to Harrowing Ordeal."
18 Tyrwhitt, "She Destroyed a Government and Ended a Premier's Career," 287.
19 "Vivian MacMillan Recounts to Court Story of Meetings," *Calgary Albertan*, 26 June 1934.
20 Franklin L. Foster, *John E. Brownlee: A Biography* (Lloydminster: Foster Learning, 1981), 215.
21 See, e.g., "Alberta Typist Accuses Premier at Court Hearing: Says She Tried to Get Free of Relationship but Failed," *Globe*, 26 June 1934; "Girl Wins Verdict against Premier," *New York Times*, 1 July 1934, 22; and "Premier

Faces Girl's Charges in Court," *Washington Post*, June 25, 1934, 5. The Paris *Midi* report and that in the London *Daily Mail* are cited in Thomas Thorner and G.N. Reddekopp, "A Question of Seduction: The Case of *MacMillan v. Brownlee*," *Alberta Law Review* 20, no. 3 (1982): 447.
22 "Alberta Premier Sued for Damages on Serious Charge," *Globe*, 23 September 1933, 2.
23 J.F.J. Pereira, "Charges of Wife-Swapping against Brownlee's Public Works Minister Merely a Curtain-Raiser," in *Alberta in the 20th Century: A Journalistic History of the Province in Thirteen Volumes*, ed. Ted Byfield, vol. 6 (Edmonton: United Western Communications, 1998), 278.
24 "Vivian MacMillan and John Caldwell Deny Conspiracy," *Lethbridge Herald*, 20 November 1933, 3.
25 Foster, *John E. Brownlee*, 225–6.
26 "Court Pays Visit to Brownlee Home and Rural Roads," *Globe*, 30 June 1934, 2.
27 Thompson, *Political Scandal*, 14.
28 Foster, *John E. Brownlee*, 234, 229.
29 Conservative Leader Ray Milner to R.B. Bennett, quoted in Franklin L. Foster, *John E. Brownlee: A Biography* (Lloydminster: Foster Learning, 1981), 232.
30 "Premier in His Defence Denies Charges," *Edmonton Bulletin*, 28 June 1934.
31 "Brownlee Defends Self on Stand," *Lethbridge Herald*, 28 June 1934.
32 See Thorner and Reddekopp, "A Question of Seduction: The Case of *MacMillan v. Brownlee*."
33 Brode, *Courted and Abandoned*, 7.
34 Brode, *Courted and Abandoned*, 8.
35 Reva B. Siegel, "A Short History of Sexual Harrassment," in *Directions in Sexual Harrassment Law*, ed. Catherine A. Mackinnon and Reva B. Siegel (New Haven: Yale University Press, 2003), 3–8.
36 See Constance Backhouse, *Carnal Crimes: Sexual Assault and the Law in Canada, 1900–1975* (Toronto: Irwin Law, 2008), 287–96.
37 Brode, *Courted and Abandoned*, 164.
38 "Brownlee, Cabinet Place Resignations in Hands of UFA Party's Caucus," *Edmonton Journal*, 3 July 1934.
39 Thorner and Reddekopp, "A Question of Seduction: The Case of *MacMillan v. Brownlee*," 458–61.
40 "Verdict Is Found against Brownlee; Judge Disagrees," *Globe*, 2 July 1934, 2.
41 "Verdict Is Found against Brownlee; Judge Disagrees," 2.
42 "Verdict of Jury Quashed by Judge in Brownlee Case," *Globe*, 5 July 1934, 1.
43 *Allan D. MacMillan and Vivian MacMillan v. John Edward Brownlee* [1934] 2 W.W.R. 511.

44 Over $2,000 was collected in a drive spearheaded by the *Edmonton Bulletin*. See Foster, *John E. Brownlee*, 261; Brode, *Courted and Abandoned*, 165.
45 "Premier to Stay at Home," *Edmonton Bulletin*, 3 July 1934, 1.
46 "Brownlee and Cabinet Resign," *Edmonton Bulletin*, 3 July 1934, 1.
47 Thorner and Reddekopp, "A Question of Seduction: The Case of *MacMillan v. Brownlee*," 454.
48 *MacMillan v. Brownlee* [1935] 1 DLR 481.
49 *MacMillan v. Brownlee* [1935] 1 DLR 481 at 504.
50 Newspaper coverage of Brownlee disappeared after July 1934, only to resume once the case appeared before the Supreme Court in 1937. It was only Vivian's appeal that was heard by the Supreme Court; her father's Alberta appeal had previously been rejected by all five justices. He did not pursue the matter any further.
51 *McMillan v. Brownlee* [1937] SCR 318 at 324.
52 [1937] SCR 318 at 328; Brode, *Courted and Abandoned*, 171.
53 *McMillan v. Brownlee* [1940] 3 DLR 353.
54 See Ari Adut, *On Scandal: Moral Disturbances in Society, Politics and Art* (Cambridge, UK: Cambridge University Press, 2008), 11–12.
55 See Anna Clark, *Scandal: The Sexual Politics of the British Constitution* (New Jersey: Princeton University Press, 2004), 1–12.
56 See Thorner and Reddekopp, "A Question of Seduction: The Case of *MacMillan v. Brownlee*," 448–9; Brode, *Courted and Abandoned*, 169–70; J.A. Irving, *The Social Credit Movement in Alberta* (Toronto: University of Toronto Press, 1959), 95–96; and John J. Barr, *The Rise and Fall of Social Credit in Alberta* (Toronto: McClelland & Stewart, 1974), 33–6.
57 Thorner and Reddekopp, "A Question of Seduction: The Case of *MacMillan v. Brownlee*," 473.
58 "Media Unmuzzled," *Calgary Herald*, 22 December 1989, A4.
59 "The Premier's Disgrace," *Edmonton Journal*, 14 May 1995, C1.
60 David Staples, "Affairs of the State – Does the Punishment Fit the Crime?," *Edmonton Journal*, 29 January 1998.
61 Barbara Smith, "John Brownlee and Vivian MacMillan," in *Passion and Scandal: Great Canadian Love Stories* (Calgary: Detselig Enterprises, 1997), 187–97.
62 Tyrwhitt, "She Destroyed a Government and Ended a Premier's Career," 303.
63 David Cheoros, Karen Simonson, and Debbie Marshall, *Her Voice, Her Century: Four Plays about Daring Women* (Victoria: Brindle & Glass, 2012), frontispiece, 210.

10 Rehabilitating "the Girls": Women's Employment and Expertise in the Prison for Women, 1949-1965

KATIE-MARIE McNEILL

Introduction

Following the commencement of her role as superintendent of the Prison for Women (P4W) in Kingston, Ontario, in 1960, Isabel Macneill wrote to a prison reformer that "'the girls' accepted me to-day, but of course I am not doing anything yet. I imagine we shall disagree about some things but I hope both sides will be reasonable."[1] Macneill would find that "the girls" were reasonable but could not always say the same for her male Penitentiary Service colleagues, who disagreed with her and her colleagues' approach to prison management. Macneill shared a desire with other professional and volunteer women working in P4W to support the rehabilitation of incarcerated women, which would enable a return to civilian life. Women working in P4W leveraged their positions as middle-class and well-educated women to justify their expertise in criminalized women's rehabilitation.

In this chapter, I explore how women working in P4W, as employees and as volunteers, developed prison rehabilitation programs between 1949 and 1965. Early programs took the form of academic education and were followed with vocational training and recreation. These programs reflected the positions and interests of the middle-class positions the women working and volunteering in P4W came from but were also grounded in the knowledge that incarcerated women would carry stigma following release and needed access to careers that were easier for women to enter. These rehabilitation programs showed success, yet recommendations out of P4W for reforming the Canadian prison system were routinely disregarded by the male-dominated Penitentiary Service. I argue that women working in P4W were perceived as having expertise only in rehabilitating women, not incarcerated people, despite the success of their programs in reducing recidivism and supporting incarcerated women.

The period of 1949–65 spans two thrusts for reform in the Penitentiary Service. These efforts were driven by two commissions investigating the penal system: the 1938 Royal Commission to Investigate the Penal System of Canada and the 1956 Report of a Committee Appointed to Inquire into the Principles and Procedures Followed in the Remission Service of the Department of Justice of Canada, hereafter referred to as the Archambault Commission and the Fauteux Commission, respectively. This period also coincides with the appointment of two commissioners of penitentiaries, Major General R.B Gibson, who began in 1946, and A.J. MacLeod, who began in 1960 following Gibson's appointment as special advisor to the minister of justice.[2]

Additionally, P4W experienced changes in personnel within this wider context of reform between 1949 and 1965. Nineteen forty-nine marked the hiring of the first educational matron, the first dedicated teaching position in P4W's history, and 1965 marked the resignation of the first superintendent of P4W, a position that had been created only five years prior. These new positions enabled the creation of programs, a budget dedicated to education, and coordination with local volunteers to improve the academic and vocational training opportunities for incarcerated women. Prior to 1949, there were no formal programs offered to incarcerated women. Between the move of women from Kingston Penitentiary into P4W in early 1934 and 1949, P4W had women working in laundry, mending uniforms, and sewing new uniforms for federal departments, as well as in daily operations such as cooking and cleaning.[3] It is within these contexts, the Penitentiary Service–wide reforms and the changes in P4W's organizational structure, that women's expertise in prison rehabilitation programs was situated.

The study of the Prison for Women between 1949 and 1965 is also situated within the wider history of prisons in Canada, of which interest ebbs and flows as a part of a wider and well-established legal historiography.[4] A large portion of that history has been written about the nineteenth century, particularly the establishment and early years of Kingston Penitentiary.[5] Women's experiences of incarceration are noted in prison histories, but unless they are the title subject, women receive substantially less attention than incarcerated men. Different explanations for the disparity of attention include women's historically smaller prison population and that women are not seen as normative prisoners.[6]

Academic interest surrounding the incarceration of women and girls in Canada increased in the late 1980s and early 1990s with publications from historians, such as Carolyn Strange, sociologists, such as Ellen

Adelberg and Claudia Currie, and women with lived experience, such as Fran Sugar and Lana Fox.[7] Strange and other historians, including Joan Sangster, soon added their historical perspectives on Canadian women's incarceration.[8] Much of the scholarship exploring the history of women's incarceration in Canada comes from the 1990s to the mid-2000s and explores the different ways in which women and girls were regulated and disciplined.[9] In his chapter in this volume, Ted McCoy details Sangster's contributions to the history of women's incarceration as an extension of the socialist-feminist approach of her wider body of scholarship. The timing of increasing research into criminalized women parallels public interest in P4W following the 1994 Commission into Certain Events at the Prison for Women Kingston, known as the Arbour Report, which led to the eventual closure of the prison in 2000.[10]

This chapter brings together the regulation of criminalized women with women's work, two areas of scholarship to which Joan Sangster has contributed extensively, through archival records from national, provincial, and university collections. Like the hierarchal structure of the prison itself, records regarding P4W are more abundant from those in positions of power and least available from incarcerated women. Isabel Macneill's fonds from the Nova Scotia Archives provide personal reflections on her employment at P4W and what she hoped to accomplish. These records interact with frank correspondence with local Kingston politicians held at Queen's University Archives and reveal Macneill's frustrations about the bureaucratic restrictions surrounding her work, while records from Library and Archives Canada (LAC) detail Penitentiary Service reactions to her tenure. The experiences of other women working at P4W are captured through administrative files from the Correctional Service of Canada fonds from LAC largely through their reporting up the chain of command to their supervisors at Kingston Penitentiary. The creation of the educational matron position also created new reports that offer insight into the day-to-day of P4W and largely support this chapter.

The First Educational Matron and Early Programming

Dr. Helen D. Chataway began as educational matron on 15 August 1949.[11] She was hired following Commissioner Gibson's plan to implement the recommendations from the Archambault Commission, which called for "a complete reorganization of the educational system," in federal prisons.[12] Chataway was believed to be the woman for P4W as she was well educated and respectable. She completed a bachelor of arts in 1923 and a master of science in 1924 at the University of Manitoba before pursuing a PhD in chemistry at McGill in 1926.[13] She went on to have a successful career as a researcher for private companies in Ottawa and authored a book on economics before assuming her position at P4W.[14] Although Dr. Chatatway had no teaching experience, her education and professional background embodied respectable, middle-class womanhood, which made her an attractive candidate to teach at the prison.

Chataway set out immediately to create a school schedule as there had been no formalized programs prior to her position.[15] She interviewed women to gain a better understanding of their educational backgrounds and found that every woman, with the exception of the Doukhobor women, had attended school to at least the third grade.[16] The first challenge Chataway faced was creating a school schedule that accommodated incarcerated women's working schedules. Most women worked in the prison, and their work was prioritized because it facilitated the operation of the prison. Their prison labour was also regarded as a key tool in their rehabilitation.[17] Women who washed laundry worked during the first half of the week, while women who pressed laundry worked the second half, and women who worked in the kitchen had split shifts that revolved around meals, which created scheduling difficulties. Chataway suggested to her superiors, Deputy Commissioner McCulley and Kingston Penitentiary Warden Allen, that the best remedy to scheduling problems was to hold classes in the evenings.[18] Her proposal was rejected as McCulley thought women would not want evening classes, and more importantly, none of the male prisons had evening classes.[19]

Undeterred, Chataway offered eight classes within two months of starting her position.[20] The classes included introductory oral and written English for French-speaking women, introductory English for English-speaking women, introductory arithmetic, and typing. Women with more advanced literacy could take correspondence courses offered by the Ontario Department of Education or the Department of Veterans' Affairs and get academic support on their assignments in the classroom. There were also French classes for English speakers and an art class, which were facilitated by volunteers from the recently established Elizabeth Fry Society of Kingston.[21]

The Elizabeth Fry Society of Kingston (EFK) was established in 1949 when a group of local women concerned with the conditions of prisons came together, inspired by press coverage of an accused young woman and her breakdown due to pretrial incarceration.[22] This group of women met with McCulley in Ottawa to seek guidance on what they could do for incarcerated women. He directed them to reach out to Kathleen "Kaye" Healey, an employee in the Department of Extension at Queen's University who had been involved in volunteering in Kingston-area prisons since the mid-1940s, to discuss options.

Kaye Healey had been involved with prisons through her work supporting distance students, including incarcerated men, taking Queen's University courses, and she had also been more recently involved in P4W. Healey learned of the complete lack of educational programs for women from a friend, Dr. Clarence Crawford, who worked as a psychiatric consultant for Kingston-area prisons.[23] Crawford mentioned to Healey that he wanted to bring educational resources to women to relieve boredom. Healey's employment with the Department of Extension gave her access to a host of educational resources, so she began to bring films into P4W, much to the delight of incarcerated women and the matron staff.[24]

When the group of women and Kaye Healey met, they discussed how to best help incarcerated women and together they formed EFK. The society was established by Kaye Healey, Harriet Selby, Dorothy Bartlett, Vera Cartwright, Elizabeth Harrison, Blossom MacDougall, Eileen Lord, and Jeanne Hughes. Among this group were a lawyer, social worker, artist and art instructor, and a physical education teacher.[25] The Elizabeth Fry Society of Kingston resembled other women's organizations involved with the law as its membership comprised middle-class and well-educated women, many of whom were married.[26] Its position in Kingston facilitated its access to visits to P4W as the members were perceived to be maternal, caregiving mentors who could support and guide their "fallen sisters" who were incarcerated, continuing a tradition of women's prison visiting in other Canadian contexts.[27]

With a growing partnership, Chataway and EFK created opportunities for vocational learning. Their first foray into vocational education was a St. John's Ambulance home nursing course in late 1949. The course was taught by local instructors who were recruited by EFK, who utilized their personal and social networks to organize the course.[28] For eight weeks women participated in biweekly classes to receive certification in home nursing upon the successful completion of exams.[29] Eleven women took the course to completion, and all passed their exams. Chataway and EFK believed that the home nursing training would help incarcerated women's employment opportunities following their release.

Incarcerated women could learn and practise typing skills as another way to prepare for employment after release. However, there was only one typewriter available for practice in November 1949.[30] Chataway ordered a second typewriter almost immediately as there was a high demand to learn typing skills.[31] To maximize the number of women learning, Chataway created a daily schedule of one-hour typing blocks that could be quickly rearranged to ensure the typewriting seat was never empty. Chataway offered short instructional periods before allowing women to practise and provided feedback on typing sheets as women finished them.[32]

Both home nursing and typing offered skills that could translate into women's employment in the early 1950s and aligned with expectations of what women's incarceration should look like to different parties involved in P4W. Firstly, the Penitentiary Service was interested in reforming incarcerated women into productive citizens. Women's citizenship has been historically tied to their performance as mothers and wives and how well they are perceived to perform in these roles.[33] Women working outside the home could maintain their respectability as wives and mothers, and their claim to citizenship, if they adhered to shifting definitions of respectability.[34] Home nursing and typing fit within these constructions and satisfied the Penitentiary Service's desire for women to be productive upon release.

Secondly, through the programming offered, women working in P4W demonstrated their belief that traditionally feminine careers were the most viable employment option for incarcerated women upon release.[35] The women working in P4W understood that incarceration carried stigma and that careers with the least resistance to hiring them could benefit formerly incarcerated women on an already difficult journey. The Penitentiary Service wanted programs to reform women into productive citizens, and the P4W staff and EFK volunteers wanted incarcerated women to increase their levels of education and gain employable skills. Chataway and EFK's early education programs sought to do both.

Dr. Chataway's initial progress was respected by McCulley, but he noted that her reports appeared increasingly discouraged after a few months.[36] McCulley believed her discouragement stemmed from a lack of consistent student participation in classes. He wrote to Kingston Penitentiary's warden to remind Chataway that it was "important, however, for us to keep in mind that very few of these women, by any stretch of the imagination, be called students," and he continued that "the various little pleasures such as the Halloween party, the Christmas concert, etc., will inevitably have more immediate interest for them than educational preparation for the day of release."[37] Chataway reassured him that this was not the case.

Her discouragement was not because of the capacity of her students. Chataway was discouraged because of the demanding six-day workweek.[38] She and the other matrons worked a minimum of forty-eight hours per week, and with their small staff, illnesses and vacations severely impacted their ability to supervise the prison. The matron team often worked unpaid overtime.[39] At this time, some single matrons still lived in the prison in staff quarters, which meant these women worked whenever there was a staffing shortage.[40] Chataway also supervised women in a custodial manner instead of teaching when staffing levels were low. Despite her positive feelings about building relationships with incarcerated women, Chataway suggested to McCulley that she, and the other matrons, work five days a week for a total of forty-four hours to allow sufficient time to rest as the existent schedule did not leave "enough time for renewing of faith in the ultimate verities."[41]

There was also the issue of salaries. Chataway earned the same as a grade one guard, which was the lowest-paid male position in all Canadian prisons.[42] Chataway was by far the most educated prison teacher, if not one of the most educated Penitentiary Service staff members, yet the highest end of her pay scale was 13 per cent less than the starting salary of a male prison schoolteacher, who could be hired with a high school diploma as a qualification.[43] Chataway mentioned the issues surrounding schedules and salaries in her monthly reports, but her professional advice, when recognized, was recognized only in regards to women's education and not beyond the P4W classroom.[44] Chataway's position as an educated, middle-class woman afforded her authority to reform incarcerated women from the perspective of the Penitentiary Service, yet the expertise she developed as a prison worker was ignored when she suggested changes to the systems that structured her work. Dr. Chataway resigned soon after voicing her concerns in January of 1951.

More of the Same and Growing Community Partnerships

Mrs. Vera Hudson was hired to replace Chataway. Her title was changed to "educational officer" to reflect that it was the same position as that of instructors in men's prisons. Hudson was married and had small children, so she adhered to a strict schedule of Monday to Friday, 9:00 a.m. to 6:00 p.m., and Saturday mornings. The hiring of Hudson in a permanent position without the consultation of Ms. Lorraine Burke, the long-standing head matron, created tension.[45] Despite forty-eight-hour workweeks, Burke did not think Hudson was available enough for the position. Burke was frustrated that she had to work more overtime hours for activities such as projecting recreational films on Sunday afternoons and evenings because of Hudson's availability.

Hudson was a model of a respectable woman, but her childcare responsibilities were contentious for her co-workers. The men hiring P4W staff wanted maternal care and maternal characteristics in the women hired to rehabilitate "the girls" but did not recognize the actual responsibilities and labour of mothers in their structuring of positions, rendering invisible Hudson and other women's domestic labour, a pattern that Andrea Samoil, in her chapter in this volume, explains was a problem for women working in hospital laundry rooms decades later in Alberta. These decision-makers also did not account for how these familial responsibilities would impact the staffing levels of the prison, issues that could have been identified through consultation with P4W's senior staff, who had decades of prison experience.

While Hudson did not maintain the same availability as her predecessor, she did maintain similar educational programs. Hudson continued to offer classes to women with elementary-level abilities in literacy and numeracy. She continued to open the classroom space to women taking independent correspondence courses, and she worked with EFK volunteers to offer a wider variety of classes than she alone could offer. Hudson prioritized teaching women with low levels of literacy and numeracy one on one despite calls for standardized teaching from Ottawa as she understood her students' needs better than senior policymakers in the Penitentiary Service did.[46]

Hudson also oversaw an expansion in vocational education options. In January 1952 a pilot program in beauty parlour skills accepted its first cohort of students.[47] The warden of Kingston Penitentiary chose six young women who had applied and who were approaching release to participate in the course.[48] The women were instructed in hairdressing by Mrs. Fuller, an instructor from the community, and were aided by Hudson. For six months the students learned their trade in the evenings after their workday.[49] The course culminated in an exam, which included a written and practical styling component that they completed on each other. All of the students were successful in their exams, which counted as credit toward a hairdressing apprenticeship. Unbeknownst to the students, the rest of the incarcerated women gathered with the matrons and surprised the graduates with a ceremony complete with certificates, corsages, and new nylons purchased by the other women, who had pooled their funds.[50]

The graduation of women from the beauty parlour course was a proud event in the prison and earned a feature article in the women's section of the prisoner publication, *Telescope*, which was published out of Kingston Penitentiary. The images of young, beautiful, white-passing women with their hair and makeup styled beaming into the camera at their graduation ceremony embodied the goals of P4W's education program. Working in a salon was viewed as an employment opportunity that would allow a woman to work anywhere that she chose to relocate to after release, in addition to working in a field dominated by women.[51] The beauty parlour course offered tangible skills that translated directly to a stable job and reinforced other less tangible skills such as personal grooming, polite conversation, and etiquette, which were also valued by the women working in P4W.

In addition to formal education organized by Hudson in the classroom and salon, incarcerated women were taught respectable and feminine behaviours, skills, and hobbies through recreation. The bulk of these recreational activities were supported by EFK volunteers.[52] From 1949 onwards, EFK visited the prison on Thursday evenings to provide companionship, legal advice, and instruction in activities like knitting, sewing, and crafts.[53] As the partnership between the society and P4W grew stronger, volunteers entered the prison more frequently and expanded their offerings of recreational activities to include square dancing, choir, mothercraft (lessons on how to be a better mother), and jewellery-making, which were based on volunteers' personal interests and hobbies. Volunteers instantiated womanly virtues to incarcerated women through their teaching of hobbies and continued to legitimize their expertise about the needs of incarcerated women to the Penitentiary Service through their own performance of gender as respectable women.

EFK's embodiment of respectability and expertise in women's issues was further legitimated by the Penitentiary Service with financial support. The society lobbied Commissioner Gibson to create an honorarium for one of their most dedicated volunteers, the gardening instructor Rowan Patterson.[54] Patterson was a single British immigrant from a middle-class background who was a renowned gardener, and she used her knowledge to aid women with their garden plots. Garden plots created for food production during the Second World War were converted into recreational plots that women could cultivate. It was a popular pastime and one of the few recreational pursuits that appealed to older women.[55] Patterson was referred to as a part-time social worker who worked at P4W, employed by EFK through funding from the Penitentiary Service, which truly symbolizes the complicated relationships between the Penitentiary Service, P4W, and EFK. By 1961, Patterson held the position of rehabilitation officer.[56] The blurring of the lines between women volunteers and paid staff would increase with the hiring of Isabel Macneill as superintendent.

Pushing Boundaries of Definitions of Women's Expertise

A.J. MacLeod began as commissioner in 1960 and had a plan to revitalize the penal system following the recommendation of the 1956 Fauteux Commission that P4W implement "a more intensified system of varied forms of treatment."[57] MacLeod created the position of superintendent of P4W and recruited Isabel J. Macneill to fill it. This new position would oversee the development of all programming and rehabilitation at P4W as well as supervise the team of matrons.[58] The superintendent would report directly to the commissioner of penitentiaries but would copy the warden of Kingston Penitentiary on correspondence. The warden of Kingston Penitentiary still had financial control over the institution, as Kingston Penitentiary and P4W were considered one accounting unit in the Penitentiary Service. The warden was responsible for annual budgeting, accounting, personnel administration, and building maintenance.[59] Yet the superintendent was responsible for "the treatment and training of the inmates and for the direction and discipline of the staff" and was to be "given all of the disciplinary powers of a Warden in relation to Prison for Women, and in addition is given such other powers of a Warden as are necessary for the effective discharge of the Superintendent" as defined by the commissioner.[60] This complicated arrangement dividing authority in P4W would prove to be a point of frustration by the mid-1960s, but did not deter the enthusiasm Macneill initially brought to the role.

Macneill was recruited for her prior experience in leadership roles, particularly in institutions, and for how she embodied respectable womanhood. Macneill had studied fine arts at Mount Saint Vincent University before obtaining her teaching certification and came from a well-established family.[61] She enlisted in the Royal Canadian Women's Naval Service (WRENS) in 1942 and was promoted to the rank of commander of the HMCS *Conestoga*. Macneill was the first woman in the British Commonwealth to reach this rank and was awarded an Order of Empire for her wartime service.[62] She then became the superintendent of the infamous Ontario Training School for Girls (OTSG) between 1948 to 1954, where she was responsible for the care and incarceration of girls aged eight to sixteen.[63]

Macneill found the task of disciplining girls while simultaneously providing a rehabilitative environment to be an impossible paradox given the low staff-to-child ratios. She cited a difference in correctional philosophy as the reason for her resignation from OTSG in 1954.[64] Macneill returned to WRENS for a few years before travelling to Europe to research penal practice. Prior to starting at P4W, she chaired a Nova

Scotia committee on juvenile delinquency. The committee's proposal, which emphasized prevention and avoided detention, was rejected for being "too revolutionary," which was indicative of Macneill's evolving philosophy on correctional institutions.[65]

Macneill began at P4W in 1960 and started working with the prison's team of staff, including Marion Batstone, a social worker, and EFK. Batstone had worked at P4W since 1957 and operated under the personal philosophy that prisons were supposed to "enable as many inmates as possible to live happily in normal society, to produce good citizens, not good prisoners."[66] Soon after in 1961, Margaret Benson, a psychologist, joined the treatment team. Benson had been attracted to P4W because, at the time, it "was one of the bright progressive spots in the Canadian correctional field."[67] Batstone and Benson had expertise in their own professional domains in social work and psychology, respectively, from their education and professional training. Macneill's expertise came from her experience, and when the treatment team's knowledge was combined with the laywomen's expertise from EFK, the prison was primed for change following the Fauteux Commission's report.

Macneill made school attendance equivalent to full-time prison work as one of her first reforms. Seventeen women enrolled full time immediately following the change.[68] This change signalled that Macneill valued incarcerated women's education equally to their production of goods for the Penitentiary Service. This stance differed substantially from that of others in the Penitentiary Service who saw prison labour as integral for prisoners to repay their debt to society for the figurative cost of their crime and literal cost of their incarceration. Over 90 per cent of women, with the exception of unwell and elderly women, worked or attended school full time under Macneill's new programming.[69] Other educational additions included a business course. The business course included bookkeeping and other office skills, expanding upon the years of typing practice previously offered. One of the most popular opportunities introduced by Macneill, however, was learning domestic skills in the Housekeeping Cottage.

The Housekeeping Cottage was a fully furnished model home within prison grounds built by incarcerated men in trades education programs at Collins Bay Penitentiary and installed by men incarcerated at Kingston Penitentiary.[70] P4W hired Mrs. Betty Hof, a former restaurant manager with a post-secondary education in household science, to teach women how to cook, clean, and keep a house.[71] Hof's authority came from her education, professional background, and status as a married woman. The course was an instant hit, especially with younger women, and a wait list was started to accommodate interest. Women in the course spent ten weeks learning domestic skills including polishing silverware, setting a formal dinner table, cleaning hardwood floors, deep-cleaning bathrooms, grocery shopping on a budget for a family, and cooking family-sized dinners. On Sundays, the classes practised cooking a large meal to share in the dining room, emulating the idealized nuclear family dinner.[72]

Pre-release Program Development

With Macneill's support, EFK initiated more programs to better meet the needs of women, knowledge of which came from over a decade of working with incarcerated women. One such need was a pre-release program. The pre-release program helped women who were approaching release reintegrate into the Kingston community. The development of a pre-release program was a specific recommendation from the Fauteux Commission, and P4W was the first to implement such a program.[73]

Initially, the program began with volunteers escorting women out of the prison for the day to visit friends and family, eat at restaurants, and shop for groceries, and for other daily activities that were absent in prison.[74] These trips were intended to help women readjust to civilian life. One volunteer remembered the first time she took a woman to a grocery store. As she walked toward the store entrance, she realized the woman was sitting patiently in the car's passenger seat. The volunteer walked back, opened the door, and then realized that her companion had not opened a door for herself for the last few years of her life locked inside P4W.[75]

The pre-release program grew to include work placements where women could apply skills gained in vocational training programs and prison employment. Interested women could be placed in a full-time position for four to six weeks before release, which was arranged in collaboration by P4W staff and EFK. Some examples of placements included administrative and secretarial work, waitressing, nursing, babysitting, and housekeeping.[76] While these jobs were traditionally feminine, EFK and Macneill were pragmatic in the fields they suggested. They wanted to find jobs that were readily accessible to women in multiple locations to give women as many options as possible following their release.

Women, particularly young women and first offenders, were also encouraged to work on their coping skills and mental health to prepare for release. Counselling, group therapy, psychotherapy, Alcoholics Anonymous meetings, peer-led groups, and consultation with chaplains were offered to support women emotionally and psychologically. Macneill and the staff at P4W saw great improvements from therapy participation, and by 1965, over 50 per cent of the population was participating in one or more types of therapy.[77] The overall success of this treatment-based approach, in which education and therapy were key components, was reflected in a reduction in the recidivism rate from 47 per cent to 24 per cent between 1961 and 1966.[78]

The Beginning of the End of Women's Leadership

Despite P4W's success, the relationship between Macneill and the Penitentiary Service strained from her frequent ideas on reform. Wardens of larger, male prisons felt they could not implement intensive types of therapy and educational programs, and some felt as though P4W was lacking in discipline. The Penitentiary Service responded by slowly eroding Macneill's powers as superintendent, giving some authority to the Regional Headquarters office in 1962 following amendments to the Penitentiary Act and placing P4W under Collins Bay Penitentiary's supervision instead of Kingston Penitentiary's.[79] The Collins Bay warden, Victor S.J. Richmond, and his staff expressed their displeasure with Macneill's leadership in a variety of ways. With this change in hierarchy, Collins Bay assumed control of rations and rotten produce and wormy fish were delivered regularly, and the warden would conveniently become unavailable via phone until hours later to resolve the issue. Macneill described that "this cat and mouse procedure can go on all day! And is extremely frustrating."[80] Despite the reduction in recidivism by a remarkable 50 per cent in two years, Macneill's unorthodox treatment of prisoners was met with suspicion and sabotage by her colleagues.

A proposal to move P4W from Kingston to Cornwall in 1964 further signalled the lack of respect for the work done by Macneill, the treatment team, and the volunteers of EFK. The proposal was met with vigorous and organized opposition. Letters from P4W, EFK, the Elizabeth Fry Society of Toronto, the John Howard Society of Ontario, the John Howard Society of Kingston, local politicians, and Kingston community members voiced support for keeping P4W in Kingston.[81] As Macneill wrote to personal friend and Kingston member of Parliament John R. Matheson, "although most of Canada looks upon me as an authority on the female offender I have not found the Penitentiary Service willing to listen, and follow my recommendations."[82] Ultimately P4W remained in Kingston, but distrust between P4W and the Penitentiary Service grew.

With tensions mounting, Commissioner MacLeod offered a patronizing solution to Macneill that was supposed to appease all his senior staff. In May 1965, MacLeod offered Macneill a new position at headquarters in Ottawa to develop a female prison program, female staff-training program, and programs for families of offenders. She would have no direct authority in prisons and would advise other prisons on these matters because MacLeod thought a "feminine point of view" would benefit all programming decisions.[83] MacLeod explained that there was "value of the feminine touch and talents in these matters," which only Macneill could provide despite having never married and having no children, unlike the vast majority of her married male colleagues with families.[84] Macneill declined the job.

Additional administrative changes through directives signalled further deterioration in the relationship between Macneill and the Penitentiary Service.[85] The Ontario Regional Headquarters assumed authority over the training of incarcerated women and the discipline of women and staff, stopping just short of eliminating the need for a superintendent.[86] There was a theoretical divide between the treatment team at P4W and the rest of the Penitentiary Service on how to approach rehabilitation. The Penitentiary Service dismissed the successes of P4W's treatment programs because it did not believe that these treatments were harsh enough, especially for incarcerated men.

This decision was met with protest from Macneill, staff, and EFK, who argued that P4W was a separate institution and should be recognized as such by the Penitentiary Service giving Macneill the same full authority as other wardens, not by adding yet another layer of bureaucracy and effectively removing her leadership. When this proposal was stonewalled, Macneill resigned.

Macneill explained to the solicitor general, "In [my] final analysis, my conflict is not only with the treatment of female offenders, but with the Penitentiary Service in general. What has been done in Prison for Women, with a deplorable plant, a mixed population, and limited staff to reduce recidivism could have been done throughout the service."[87] Macneill's ambition to reform P4W and incarceration in Canada was the main reason she was hired as superintendent, but also contributed to her resignation as the Penitentiary Service did not appreciate her different approach to prison management. Initiatives such as individualized treatment plans including education and therapy, working with community partners, and pre-release programs were fought for through a bureaucratic maze and resulted in a drastic reduction in recidivism and were largely unappreciated by the male leadership of the Penitentiary Service. Macneill stopped working at P4W on 1 December 1965.[88] Her formal tongue-in-cheek resignation letter to the solicitor general stated that she was "an unqualified abolitionist" who did not "believe in corporal punishment, or humiliating practices in institutional discipline" and was therefore unfit to lead P4W under the current philosophy of the Penitentiary Service.[89] Her resignation prompted a Special Joint Committee on Penitentiaries investigation and was followed by the resignation of other key staff, including Marion Batstone and Margaret Benson.

Batstone explained in her resignation letter, "I have resigned as Social Worker in the Prison for women because the philosophy of rehabilitation of female inmates for which I have worked continuously since 1957 has been abandoned."[90] As a social worker, Batstone had classified women, managed work release placements, and helped women to achieve and maintain sobriety – something that other federal drug treatment centres had failed miserably in doing.[91] Batstone and Benson explained during the investigation how the decisions to remove Macneill's authority and philosophy from P4W had reduced the efficiency of programs, destroyed trust between staff and incarcerated women, and destroyed the culture of rehabilitation they had fostered, all while requiring a higher operating budget for staffing because of a new emphasis on discipline.[92] Batstone identified what she thought was the conflict between the Penitentiary Service and P4W's successful although different methods: "The Canadian Penitentiary Service has no real desire to retain well qualified professional staff, unless they are obedient and non-critical."[93]

The Elizabeth Fry Society of Kingston also sent a statement to the Special Joint Committee that directly questioned the actions and motivations of the Penitentiary Service in pushing out Macneill:

> The Penitentiaries Service, in the last ten years, has increased penitentiary staff, has built new buildings, has provided greatly improved training programs and has provided additional amenities and recreation in its male institutions, all at considerable expense to the taxpayer. And it still had little or no effect on the recidivist rate of approximately 7 out of 10.
>
> Why then has the Penitentiaries Service rejected, rather than extended, the one philosophy and program of individual treatment and counselling which actually produced excellent results in the Prison for Women?[94]

Macneill, Batstone, Benson, and EFK volunteers worked together to develop an individualized approach to rehabilitating "the girls" in their custody, building upon the earlier efforts of educators Hudson and Chataway. Their successes in the reduction of recidivism and supporting women through aftercare programs were ignored by the Penitentiary Service, who favoured instead the complaints of male wardens who found the treatment of incarcerated women to be too different from that of incarcerated men. When wider reforms were suggested, women working at P4W were not seen as experts by their male peers, despite their outcomes, because the Penitentiary Service recognized their authority to come from only their embodiment as respectable women. The Penitentiary Service found P4W's methods not punitive enough, even though these rehabilitation-focused programs occurred in a maximum-security federal prison and showed promising results for incarcerated women who participated.

Conclusion

In 1949, the Penitentiary Service of Canada sought respectable women's expertise to create educational programming to reform incarcerated women with the creation of the educational matron position and hiring of Dr. Helen Chataway. Chataway developed basic literacy and numeracy classes for incarcerated women, which were supplemented with vocational training. These efforts were encouraged and supported by EFK volunteers, who were typically middle-class, well-educated, and married women from the Kingston area. A partnership between P4W staff with professional knowledge and volunteer women whose authority came from their positions in the community allowed for a wider variety of programs in the prison.

In 1960, Isabel Macneill's hiring as the superintendent allowed for the staff and volunteers to collaborate on, develop, and implement new rehabilitative programs based on professional knowledge and years of experience working with incarcerated women. The Penitentiary Service hired Macneill to usher in reforms, yet Penitentiary Service leaders were unimpressed when she and her team initiated a series of changes to women's incarceration. Programs that included full-time education instead of prison labour, pre-release employment placements, and therapy reduced rates of recidivism in half to 24 per cent in fewer than five years, while the average recidivism rate across men's federal prisons remained around 70 per cent.[95] Macneill, staff, and women volunteering at P4W found that by 1965 their expertise was still recognized by the Penitentiary Service only because of its perception of them as good women. These women's innovative ideas in rehabilitation and their recommendations for prison reform were not recognized by the rest of the Canadian prison system because they challenged, ever so slightly, the philosophy of the prison system, which was designed by men for men.

NOTES

1 Archives Ontario, John Howard Society of Ontario fonds, Prison for Women 1961–1971, letter from Macneill to Kirkpatrick, 1 December 1960.
2 Dominion of Canada, *Annual Report of the Commissioner of Penitentiaries for the Fiscal Year Ending March 31, 1961* (Kingston: Kingston Penitentiary, 1961), 13.
3 Dominion of Canada, *Annual Report of the Superintendent of Penitentiaries for the Fiscal Year Ending March 31, 1934* (Ottawa: Printer to the Queen, 1934), 11. Construction concluded in 1932, but riots and overcrowding at Kingston Penitentiary resulted in men being held in P4W between 1932 and 1934.
4 Philip Girard, "Who's Afraid of Canadian Legal History?," *University of Toronto Law Journal* 57, no. 4 (2007): 727–9.
5 See Roger Neufeld, "Cabals, Quarrels, Strikes, and Impudence: Kingston Penitentiary, 1890–1914," *Histoire Sociale* 31, no. 61 (1998): 96. Neufeld states that most Kingston Penitentiary history focuses on the Brown Commission; Peter Oliver's *"Terror to Evil-doers": Prisons and Punishment in Nineteenth-Century Ontario* (Toronto: University of Toronto Press, 1998) offers a comprehensive history of punishment pre-penitentiary, the political actors involved in the establishment of Kingston Penitentiary, and its early years, including the Brown Commission (see 139–44 for commission); and Ted McCoy brings a Foucauldian lens to the early period of Kingston Penitentiary and the Brown Commission in *Hard Time: Reforming the Penitentiary in Nineteenth-Century Canada* (Edmonton: Athabasca University Press, 2012).
6 Sheelagh Cooper, "The Evolution of Federal Women's Prison," in *In Conflict with the Law: Women and the Canadian Justice System*, ed. Ellen Adelberg and Claudia Currie (Vancouver: Press Gang, 1993), 33; Kelly Hannah-Moffat, *Punishment in Disguise: Penal Governance and Federal Imprisonment of Women in Canada* (Toronto: University of Toronto Press, 2001), 72. Cooper suggests that incarcerated women are neglected because of insignificant population size, whereas Hannah-Moffat argues that incarcerated women are ignored because prison administrators do not understand how to govern the non-normative prisoner and scholarship reflects that inability to comprehend.
7 Carolyn Strange, "'The Criminal and Fallen of Their Sex': The Establishment of Canada's First Women's Prison, 1874–1901," *Canadian Journal of Women and the Law* 1 (1985): 79–92; Ellen Adelberg and Claudia Currie, eds., *Too Few to Count: Canadian Women in Conflict with the Law* (Vancouver: Press Gang, 1987); Ellen Adelberg and Claudia Currie, eds., *In Conflict with the Law: Women and the Canadian Justice System* (Vancouver:

Press Gang, 1993) – this collection revisited concerns from the 1987 publication; Karlene Faith, *Unruly Women: The Politics of Confinement and Resistance* (Vancouver: Press Gang, 1993) – Faith was a contributor to both collections and expanded her ideas in this monograph; Fran Sugar and Lana Fox, "Nistum Peyako Séht'wawin Iskwewak: Breaking Chains," *Canadian Journal of Women and the Law* 3 (1989–1990): 465–82.

8   Joan Sangster, "Incarcerating 'Bad Girls': The Regulation of Sexuality through the Female Refuges Act in Ontario 1920–1945," *Journal of the History of Sexuality* 7, no 2 (Fall 1996): 239–75; "Criminalizing the Colonized: Ontario Native Women Confront the Criminal Justice System, 1920–1960," *Canadian Historical Review* 80, no. 1 (1999): 32–60; Carolyn Strange, *Toronto's Girl Problems: The Perils and Pleasures of the City, 1880–1930* (Toronto: University of Toronto Press, 1995).

9   Joan Sangster, "Girl in Conflict with the Law: Exploring the Construction of Female 'Delinquency' in Ontario, 1940–1960," *Canadian Journal of Women and the Law* 12, no. 1 (2000): 1–35; Joan Sangster and Tamara Myers, "Retorts, Runaways, and Riots: Patterns of Resistance in Canadian Reform Schools for Girls, 1930–60," *Journal of Social History* (Spring 2001): 669–97; Joan Sangster, "'She Is Hostile to Our Ways': First Nation Girls Sentenced to the Ontario Training School for Girls, 1930–1960," *Law and History Review* 20, no. 1 (Spring 2002): 59–96; *Girl Trouble: Female Delinquency in English Canada* (Toronto: Between the Lines, 2002); "Reforming Women's Reformatories: Elizabeth Fry, Penal Reform and the State 1950–1970," *Canadian Historical Review* 85, no. 2 (2004): 227–52.

10 Louise Arbour, *Commission of Inquiry into Certain Events at the Prison for Women in Kingston* (Ottawa: Public Works and Government Services Canada, 1996).

11 Library and Archives Canada (hereafter LAC), RG 73 4-17-7 vol. 108, school report, 17 October 1949, 1.

12 Joseph Archambault, R.W. Craig, and J.C. McRuer, *Report of the Royal Commission to Investigate the Penal System of Canada* (Ottawa: Printer to the King's Most Excellent Majesty, 1938), 354–61; R.B. Gibson, "The Penitentiaries Move Forward" (an address given to the Canadian Penal Congress, Kingston, Ontario, 21 June 1949).

13 Helen Drinkwater Chataway, "The Sulphuration of Fatty Acids" (PhD diss., McGill University, 1926); Helen Drinkwater Chataway, "The Photo Bromination of P-Nitro Toluene" and "The Effect of a Magnetic Field on Organic Synthesis" (master's thesis, University of Manitoba, 1924).

14 Helen Drinkwater Chataway, *Economics and Life* (Toronto: Ryerson Press, 1948).

15 Women could take correspondence courses with the Department of Veterans' Affairs and the Ontario Department of Education from late

1947, when Kingston Penitentiary's schoolteacher volunteered to process enrolments and coursework on an ad hoc basis.
16 LAC, RG 73 4-17-7 vol. 108, school report, 4 March 1950, 2. The Doukhobor women were eventually transferred to Agassiz Mountain Prison, which had been built for members of the Sons of Freedom. For more on the Doukhobors, see Gregory J. Cran's *Negotiating Buck Naked: Doukhobors, Public Policy, and Conflict Resolution* (Vancouver: UBC Press, 2006).
17 Those who were ill or too old to work were exempted. Dominion of Canada, *Annual Report of the Commissioner of Penitentiaries for the Fiscal Year Ending March 31, 1951* (Ottawa: Printer to the King's Most Excellent Majesty, 1952), 7–8; see also Ted McCoy's chapter "Labour" in *Hard Time: Reforming the Penitentiary in Nineteenth-Century Canada* (Edmonton: Athabasca University Press, 2012), 19–60, for more discussion about the connection between labour and rehabilitation in Canadian penology.
18 LAC, RG 73 4-17-7 vol. 108, school report, 17 October 1949, 3.
19 LAC, RG 73 4-17-7 vol. 108, McCulley to Kingston Penitentiary, 4 November 1949, 1. By 1957, the educational staff at Kingston Penitentiary had recommended that classes move to the evening to allow for more flexibility in men's schooling. See also Shirley Tillotson, *The Public at Play: Gender and the Politics of Recreation in Post-war Ontario* (Toronto: University of Toronto Press, 2000), 129, for a discussion of how women were similarly seen as "helpers rather than policy makers" in municipal services.
20 LAC, RG 73 4-17-7 vol. 108, school report, 17 October 1949, 2.
21 LAC, RG 73 4-17-7 vol. 108, school report, 17 October 1949, 2.
22 Queen's University Archives, Dean of Women Oral History Project, box 3, file 38, Kathleen Healey, interview by Susan Jackson, 2 August 1977, interview 38, transcript and recording.
23 Healey, interview by Susan Jackson, 2 August 1977.
24 Faith Avis, *Women in Cages: The Prison for Women and the Elizabeth Fry Society* (Markham: Quarry Press, 2002), 57.
25 Hannah-Moffat, *Punishment in Disguise*, 109.
26 Sangster, "Reforming Women's Reformatories," 231; Felice Batlan, *Women and Justice for the Poor: A History of Legal Aid, 1863–1945* (New York: Cambridge University Press, 2015), 49–52.
27 Lee Stewart, *Women Who Volunteer to Go to Prison: A History of the Elizabeth Fry Society of British Columbia, 1939–89* (Victoria: Orca Books, 1993), 21–2; Strange, "The Criminal and Fallen of Their Sex," 81.
28 LAC, RG 73 4-17-7 vol. 108, school report, 4 March 1950.
29 LAC, RG 73 4-17-7 vol. 108, school report, 9 December 1949, 1; 4 April 1950, 2.

30 LAC, RG 73 4-17-7 vol. 108, school report, 9 December 1949.
31 LAC, RG 73 4-17-7 vol. 108, school report, 4 March 1950.
32 LAC, RG 73 4-17-7 vol. 108, Special Report of the Work of One Day, 28 March 1950.
33 Lara Campbell, *Respectable Citizens: Gender, Family, and Unemployment in Ontario's Great Depression* (Toronto: University of Toronto Press, 2009), 12; Mona Gleason, *Normalizing the Ideal: Psychology, Schooling, and the Family in Postwar Canada* (Toronto: University of Toronto Press, 1999), 78.
34 Joan Sangster, *Earning Respect: The Lives of Working Women in Small-Town Ontario, 1920–1960* (Toronto: University of Toronto Press, 1995), 114–15.
35 Joan Sangster, *Transforming Labour: Women and Work in Post-war Canada* (Toronto: University of Toronto Press, 2010), 20.
36 LAC, RG 73 4-17-7 vol. 108, McCulley to Kingston Penitentiary, 4 November 1949, 3.
37 LAC, RG 73, 4-17-7 vol. 108, memo to Kingston Penitentiary, 22 November 1951.
38 LAC, RG 73 4-17-7 vol. 108, Special Report of the Work of One Day, 28 March 1950.
39 LAC, RG 73 4-17-7 vol. 108, memo to Commissioner, 22 March 1950, 4.
40 LAC, RG 73 4-17-7 vol. 108, memo to Commissioner, 22 March 1950, 3.
41 LAC, RG 73 4–17–7 vol. 108, monthly report, 12 January 1950.
42 Dominion of Canada, *Annual Report of the Commissioner of Penitentiaries for the Fiscal Year Ending March 31, 1949* (Ottawa: Printer to the King's Most Excellent Majesty, 1950), 10.
43 Dominion of Canada, *Annual Report of the Commissioner of Penitentiaries for the Fiscal Year Ending March 31, 1949*, 11.
44 LAC, RG 73 4-17-7 vol. 108, school report, 9 February 1950, 2.
45 LAC, RG 73 4-17-7 vol. 108, Deputy Commissioner to Commissioner, 25 May 1953.
46 LAC, RG 73 4-17-7 vol. 108, school report, January 1955.
47 Penny McCormack, "Vocational Training – A Beauty Parlour," *Telescope*, September 1952, 26.
48 McCormack, "Vocational Training – A Beauty Parlour," 27.
49 McCormack, "Vocational Training – A Beauty Parlour," 26–7.
50 McCormack, "Vocational Training – A Beauty Parlour," 27.
51 Mary Jane Logan McCallum, *Indigenous Women, Work, and History, 1940–1980* (Winnipeg: University of Manitoba Press, 2014), 97–8.
52 Tillotson, *The Public at Play*, 131.
53 LAC RG 73 4-17-7 vol. 108, monthly report, 4 March 1950.
54 LAC RG 73, 1-25-119 vol. 86, letter to Commissioner from E. Fry, Kingston, 21 February 1962.

55 LAC, RG 73 4-17-7 vol. 108, school report, 11 August 1952.
56 LAC, RG 73 1-25-119 vol. 86, annual report, 1961–2, 8.
57 Gerald Fauteux et al., *Report of a Committee Appointed to Inquire into the Principles and Procedures Followed in the Remission of Service of the Department of Justice of Canada* (Ottawa: Queen's Printer and Controller of Stationary, 1956), 88; Government of Canada, *The Annual Report of the Commissioner of Penitentiaries for the Fiscal Year Ended March 31, 1961* (Kingston: Kingston Penitentiary, 1961), 1.
58 Nova Scotia Archives (hereafter NSA), Isabel Macneill fonds, MG1 vol. 3649, file 2, Prison for Women – Superintendent – Terms of Reference from Commissioner of Penitentiaries, circa 1960.
59 NSA, Macneill fonds, MG1 vol. 3649, file 2, Prison for Women – Superintendent – Terms of Reference from Commissioner of Penitentiaries, circa 1960.
60 NSA, Macneill fonds, MG1 vol. 3649, file 2, Prison for Women – Superintendent – Terms of Reference from Commissioner of Penitentiaries, circa 1960.
61 B.M. Greene, ed., *Who's Who in Canada 1940–41* (Toronto: International Press Limited, 1941), 476. Her father was head of mathematics at Dalhousie University, and her grandfather was a judge.
62 NSA, Macneill fonds, MG1 vol. 3649, file 4, appendix B – resume to Dr. Barbara Kay, 11 July 1966.
63 See Sangster's *Girl Trouble* and "'She Is Hostile to Our Ways': First Nation Girls Sentenced to the Ontario Training School for Girls, 1930–1960" for in-depth studies of OTSG.
64 NSA, Macneill fonds, MG1 vol. 3649, file 3, "Some comments on my conflict with the Penitentiary Service," n.d.
65 NSA, Macneill fonds, MG1 vol. 3649, file 4, appendix B – resume to Kay, 11 July 1966.
66 LAC, Watson fonds, MG 32 C69 vol. 86, second statement by Batstone, 23 November 1966, 1.
67 LAC, Watson fonds, MG 32 C69 vol. 86, statement by Benson, October 1966, 1.
68 Peter Sypnowich, "Inside Canada's Prison for Women," *Star Weekly Magazine*, 10 August 1963, 2.
69 NSA, Macneill fonds, MG1 vol. 3649, file 2, narrative report, Prison for Women, April 1964–March 1965, 3.
70 "Get Bungalow: Prisoners to Study Home EC," *Globe and Mail*, 21 April 1962.
71 Jean Webb, "Not by Salads Alone," *Federal Corrections* 4, no. 3 (1965): 1–4.
72 Webb, "Not by Salads Alone," 1–4.

73 Fauteux et al., *Report of a Committee Appointed to Inquire into the Principles and Procedures Followed in the Remission of Service of the Department of Justice of Canada*, 89.
74 Isabel Macneill, "The Addict as a Prisoner," *Federal Corrections* 3, no. 3 (1964): 4–5.
75 Avis, *Women in Cages*, 70.
76 Queen's University Archives (hereafter QUA), Matheson fonds, file 201, letter to Macneill, 11 June 1963; Avis, *Women in Cages*, 68.
77 NSA, Macneill fonds, MG1 vol. 3649, file 2, narrative report, Prison for Women, April 1964–March 1965, 3.
78 QUA, Matheson fonds, file 202, confidential letter from Macneill, 26 May 1965.
79 NSA, Macneill fonds, MG1 vol. 3649, file 3, "Some comments on my conflict with the Penitentiary Service," n.d.
80 NSA, Macneill fonds, MG 1 vol. 3649, file 1, letter to MacLeod, 8 July, circa 1965.
81 QUA, Matheson fonds, file 202, confidential letter from Macneill, 26 May 1965.
82 QUA, Matheson fonds, file 202, confidential letter from Macneill, 26 May 1965.
83 NSA, Macneill fonds, MG 1 vol. 3649, file 1, letter from MacLeod, 3 May 1965, 1–2.
84 NSA, Isabel Macneill fonds, MG 1 vol. 3649, file 1, letter from MacLeod, 3 May 1965, 1–2.
85 LAC, Watson fonds, MG 32 C69 vol. 86, statement by Macneill, 27 October 1966, 6.
86 LAC, Watson fonds, MG 32 C69 vol. 86, second statement by Batstone to Committee, 23 November 1966, 2.
87 NSA, Macneill fonds, MG 1 vol. 3649, file 1, letter to Solicitor General, 9 February 1966.
88 LAC, Watson fonds, MG 32 C69 vol. 86, statement by Macneill, 27 October 1966, 2.
89 NSA, Macneill fonds, MG1 vol. 3649, file 1, resignation to Solicitor General, 9 February 1966.
90 LAC, Watson fonds, MG 32 C69 vol. 86, first statement by Batstone to Committee, 27 October 1966, 1.
91 LAC, Watson fonds, MG 32 C69 vol. 86, second statement by Batstone to Committee, 23 November 1966, 4. Her comparisons are to the Matsqui Centre, a treatment centre for addiction, which struggled despite four million dollars in government investment.
92 LAC, Watson fonds, MG 32 C69 vol. 86, second statement by Batstone to Committee, 23 November 1966; statement by Benson, October 1966, 3.

93 LAC, Watson fonds, MG 32 C69 vol. 86, first statement by Batstone to Committee, 27 October 1966, 2.
94 LAC, Watson fonds, MG 32 C69 vol. 86, statement by EFK on P4W and the Penitentiary Service, 27 October 1966, 2.
95 LAC, Watson fonds, MG 32 C69 vol. 86, statement by Benson, October 1966, 2.

11 Battered Women and Self-Defence before *R. v. Lavallee*: The Forgotten Case of *R. v. Whynot (Stafford)*

NADIA VERRELLI AND LORI CHAMBERS[1]

Introduction

On 11 March 1982, in Bangs Falls, Nova Scotia, Jane Hurshman, then known as both Jane Stafford and Jane Whynot,[2] shot and killed her common law husband, Billy Stafford, while he slept in their truck, an act that lacked the traditional element of imminent threat required in self-defence.[3] In November 1982, Hurshman was acquitted by jury on charges of first-degree murder. The Court of Appeal later vacated the acquittal and ordered a new trial.[4] At Hurshman's request, her lawyer, Alan Ferrier, negotiated a plea bargain of manslaughter, and she served a short sentence in jail. The case attracted extensive national media attention, and Hurshman became a celebrity in the movement to end violence against women in Canada.[5]

The Hurshman/Stafford/*Whynot* case is interesting not only in its own right, but also because it foreshadowed the Supreme Court of Canada decision in *R. v. Lavallee*,[6] in which a battered woman who shot her partner in the back was acquitted by jury. In *Lavallee*, the acquittal was also vacated on appeal, but the accused appealed and the case advanced to the Supreme Court of Canada. The *Lavallee* decision, written by Madame Justice Bertha Wilson, the first woman appointed to the Supreme Court of Canada, explicitly referenced the decision in *R. v. Whynot* when she asserted that a battered woman could not be expected to wait for "an uplifted knife" to protect herself, noting that this would condemn her to "death by instalment."[7] This decision endorsed the view taken by the jury; in the *Whynot* case, arguments presented by Ferrier for the defence and Justice Burchell's charge to the jury provided a preview of the interpretation of self-defence that would be successful in *Lavallee*. Perhaps surprisingly, however, the *Whynot* case is now all but forgotten.[8] Our aim in this paper is simple: Using primarily the original trial transcript, we tell the story of *R. v. Whynot* and of Jane Hurshman herself.[9] Providing a widely accessible account of this case is important as the transcript is not publicly available, the appeal decision is not accessible to the non-legal community,[10] and biographies of Hurshman, written by journalists, not only lack legal (and historical) analysis but also are now out of print.[11] The story below makes an important contribution to historiography about legal responses to intimate partner violence in Canada and helps to fill a chronological gap in our knowledge of women who strike back against their abusers: The majority of existing historical work on this subject is about policing and courts in the nineteenth century,[12] the case of Angelina Napolitano in 1911,[13] the creation of shelters in the late twentieth century, which notably occurred after Hurshman's case,[14] and developments in law since the *Lavallee* decision.[15]

The Background to Stafford's Death

Jane Hurshman was born on 25 January 1949. Her father served in the army, and the family had lived in Gagetown, New Brunswick, Germany, and Winnipeg, Manitoba.[16] Her father was a heavy drinker, and, until Hurshman was in her teens, was also physically violent toward her mother.[17] She left her family in 1964 and moved to Nova Scotia to live with her grandmother. At the age of fifteen, she became pregnant by her boyfriend[18] and married him soon thereafter.[19] While her husband was not physically abusive, he was an alcoholic who eventually lost his job and was openly unfaithful; she wanted out of the marriage.[20] When he refused to divorce her, she set out to have an affair to give herself grounds for divorce. In late 1976 or early 1977, she met Billy Stafford, who promised, "I will protect you always. You won't be hurt anymore."[21]

Lamonte William "Billy" Stafford was born on 13 February 1941. He was first married to Pauline Oickle, whom he abused relentlessly. She eventually filed for divorce on the grounds of cruelty and fled to Ontario to escape him.[22] This was followed by a brief common law relationship with Faith Hatt. Hatt, pregnant and afraid of Stafford, also left him, moving to Calgary.[23] When Hurshman met Stafford, he was charming and attentive. She "had no knowledge of this man's cruel past."[24] Within weeks, they were living together, and within months, she was pregnant. Soon thereafter he made her stop taking birth control, despite the fact she had almost bled to death after the birth of their only son together, Darren.[25] Darren's birth was difficult, and to prevent further pregnancies, Hurshman went ahead with a tubal ligation.[26] Although Stafford's permission was technically not required because they were not legally married, her decision nonetheless made him very angry.[27]

By this time, Hurshman had realized Stafford was a dangerous man: He had lost his licence several times for dangerous driving and for drinking and driving, yet continued to drive in defiance of the law; he always carried a gun in the truck, and if he saw a deer he shot it, whatever the time of year and the status of the hunting season; and he hated the RCMP, toward whom he was "totally hostile."[28] Within two years of the couple living together, Stafford was no longer working on the boats from which he had been expelled due to violence.[29] Hurshman worked as a cook at a local care home and supported the family. As she described at trial, because of the "beatings, and the mental abuse, just the hooting and hollering day in and day out, it was a joy just to go to work, to get away from it all."[30]

Stafford established total control over Hurshman's life. He did not allow her to go anywhere unless it was to work or run errands for him, and then she always had time limits; she was not allowed to have a Bible, go to church, or have pictures of her family in the home. She endured constant surveillance, humiliation, and criticism.[31] He subjected her to what would now be described as coercive control. Evan Stark, the author who has popularized this theory of abuse, asserts that "the main means used to establish control is the micro-regulation of everyday behaviors associated with stereotypic female roles, such as how women dress, cook, clean, socialize, care for their children, or perform sexually."[32] Men who exercise coercive control will not give up and allow women to leave, and coercive control "is more predictive of intimate homicide than the severity or frequency of physical violence."[33]

This risk of femicide was in plain sight in the Hurshman case, as she was subjected to unrelenting violence by Stafford, who was known in the community as a very aggressive and volatile man. Hurshman first experienced physical abuse in 1977.[34] The violence quickly escalated as Stafford continued to be emboldened – he was not afraid to hit her in front of neighbours and friends. He shot at her while she was bent over the stove; he tormented her by sleeping all day and then keeping her awake at night; he deliberately wet the bed and left garbage everywhere.[35] He yelled and screamed, pushed and shoved. As Hurshman described it during the trial, the abuse was constant: "On better days, even though you weren't getting beat bad you'd get slapped around or yelled at and treated like a dog."[36] Stafford engaged in "perverted sexual abuse that ranged from ... bestiality to torture."[37] As she noted at trial, "whenever I did get a beating, he would always tell me it was my fault; I was the one that started it. You hear it so much that after a while you being to believe it is something you say or do."[38]

This reign of terror did not end with Hurshman. Stafford started abusing their son, Darren, when he was a baby.[39] He pointed guns at Darren's head, held a butcher knife to his throat, threatened him, and imposed intense, sadistic controls on his eating and activities.[40] As Hurshman later told Brian Vallee, "the only thing Bill ever taught Darren was 'to be a man' to fight and hate."[41] Hurshman's fifteen-year-old son, Allen Whynot, and Stafford's live-in friend, Ronny Wamboldt, were also victims.[42]

Sadly, as noted by one of her biographers, "people, including family and friends, knew what was happening in the Stafford household, but no one helped."[43] There was nowhere for Hurshman to go as shelters did not yet exist in Nova Scotia. Further, "the police were aware of Stafford's violent tendencies and his ability to avoid the law, but the authorities seemed powerless to assist Hurshman."[44] As they admitted at trial, family, friends, and police were deeply afraid of Stafford themselves.[45] Hurshman wanted to leave, but could not as he constantly threatened her (and her family).[46] She considered suicide, but did not want to abandon Darren to his father's sole custody.[47] She thought about killing Stafford, but always stopped herself because of the thought of leaving Darren without a mother by going to jail.[48] She also thought of hiring someone to kill him, even approaching an acquaintance to ask for his help, but the friend refused.[49] It was in this context, and after explicit, imminent, threats to the lives of her friend and neighbour, Margaret Joudry, and her son Allen that Hurshman killed Stafford.

Death of Billy Stafford and Police Investigation

On the day Hurshman killed Stafford, he had sexually abused her and fought with their neighbour Margaret Joudry.[50] That evening on their way out, Stafford threatened to deal with their neighbour by dumping five gallons of gas on her trailer and "watch[ing] them [Margaret and her tenant] burn."[51] He also threatened to kill Hurshman's son Allen.[52] When they returned home, Stafford fell asleep, or passed out, in the truck. It was one of his rules that Hurshman had to stay in the truck with him until he woke up.[53] That night, however, she defied him. She cautiously blew the horn to bring Allen outside and asked him to get her the gun. She then put the shotgun barrel through the window, rested it against Stafford's left ear, and pulled the trigger.[54] She gave the gun to her son and asked him to get her clean clothes, to clean up the mess in the driveway, and to call his grandfather to meet her and pick her up.[55] She climbed in the truck with Stafford's body, still unsure if she had killed him, and abandoned the truck on a nearby road. She was then picked up by her parents, showered at their house, and returned home, refusing to tell them anything about what had happened.[56] Allen, with the help of Joudry's tenant, broke the gun down, cleaned up the bloody tissue from the driveway, and dropped the gun, rags, and blood-covered rocks in the river.[57] When Hurshman returned, together they burnt all her clothes, towel, and facecloth in the woodstove.[58]

On 12 March 1982, Stafford's parked truck was found by a local man, who called the police. One of the officers called to the scene immediately recognized that Stafford had been shot and it was not a suicide.[59] When Staff Sergeant Williamson arrived and was told the victim was Billy Stafford, he thought, "It couldn't have happened to a better guy."[60] They did not have an immediate suspect as "there were a lot of people who felt threatened by him. He intimidated most everyone he knew."[61] When they drove to the Stafford home and informed Hurshman that Stafford was dead, she fainted. She later stated, "At that moment I really knew that he couldn't hurt any of us anymore."[62]

On 13 March, the RCMP arrived at Hurshman's house with a search warrant, and she was taken to Liverpool for interrogation.[63] After a long night in which she was relentlessly interrogated and denied sleep, she asked to speak with Lamonte Stafford, Billy's father.[64] She first confessed to him and then told the police what had happened, detailing the abuse. For whatever reason, however, the information about violence in the house was not included in the statement that was prepared detailing her confession.[65] She was officially charged with murder on 16 March 1982.[66] Alan Ferrier, a young legal aid practitioner, was appointed her lawyer. Distressed at the prospect of leaving her youngest son without a mother by going to jail, she told the police that her son Allen had killed Stafford while protecting her from an ongoing physical attack in the cab of the truck. She thought the police would not arrest Allen because of his age. However, the RCMP did not accept her new story. She was arrested and sent to the provincial jail.[67] When Allen was also arrested, she agreed to take a lie detector test. This revealed that she had not told the truth about Allen's involvement.[68] After the polygraph, she provided a new statement for the police in which she admitted that she, and not Allen, had killed Stafford. She was freed on bail on 29 March.[69] On 7 June, she was committed to stand trial and all charges against Allen were dropped.[70] Hurshman and Ferrier were willing to enter a plea of manslaughter. The Crown, however, chose explicitly to charge her with first-degree murder, which is planned and deliberate.

She faced a potential twenty-five-year jail sentence if convicted.[71] Five months later, in November 1982, Jane Hurshman would go to trial.

R. v. Whynot

R. v. Whynot began on 2 November 1982 with a true bill from the grand jury, attesting that the Crown had sufficient evidence to proceed.[72] Ferrier represented Jane Hurshman; Blaine Allaby presented the evidence for the Crown; the case was heard by Justice Burchell.[73] *R. v. Whynot* attracted "nationwide attention," and from the beginning of the trial the courtroom in Liverpool was packed.[74] Perhaps not surprisingly, given roughly concurrent public debates about sexual harassment in the workplace as detailed by Barbara Freeman in this volume, the press was watching this murder trial closely.

The pretrial motions in the case were extensive and time consuming. During the *voir dire* Justice Burchell determined that Hurshman's confession from 14 March would be excluded. The interrogations on the night of 13 March and morning of 14 March had been, as Ferrier put it, "designed to tire and frustrate a woman who is obviously very placid and quiet, who was under the influence of drugs" (sedatives administered to her by a doctor after Stafford's death was confirmed).[75] Most importantly, by excluding her extensive evidence regarding abuse from her statement, the police had deliberately rendered it incomplete.[76] The second, and false, admission, which blamed Allen, was ruled admissible as it had been made freely and in the presence of Hurshman's lawyer. Justice Burchell confirmed that the polygraph was inadmissible (under general rules of the court), and the officer who had performed it could not discuss the procedure itself if called to the stand. Her third admission, obtained in the aftermath of the polygraph, would be admitted as evidence despite the exclusion of the polygraph itself.[77] Further, although Allaby sought to preclude Ferrier from advancing evidence of Stafford's history of abuse of Hurshman, Justice Burchell found that the witnesses could be called: "Evidence of past abuse is relevant to the issue of motive."[78] Importantly, and illustrating the degree to which decisions are variable based upon judicial discretion, in these pretrial decisions Justice Burchell had set parameters for the case that would allow Ferrier to explore evidence and issues many other judges might have excluded from the outset.

Allaby then began the case for the prosecution: He set out to prove the murder was planned. He noted for the jury that his evidence would be presented in three parts. First, he would bring a witness to prove Hurshman had previously considered having Stafford killed. Second, he would provide detail about events on the night of Stafford's death. Third, he would present expert evidence from the RCMP.[79] He followed this plan to the letter; nonetheless, his witnesses provided support for the defence by noting Stafford's constant violence and Hurshman's fear and desperation.

Allaby's first witness was Beverley Taylor, a local man who admitted that Hurshman had attempted to hire him to kill Stafford. He had refused to comply, fearing Stafford was trying to set him up for a failed drug deal as he had threatened those who had given evidence against him in other cases. Allaby asserted that this evidence pointed to Hurshman having a long-term plan to kill Stafford. Taylor, however, noted that she appeared "desperate" and "trapped" and stated "I asked her why she didn't go to the police, she said they wouldn't help her. I asked her why she didn't go to a lawyer, she said she'd never run far enough to get away from him."[80] The battle lines of the trial had already been drawn by this first witness: There was no question that Hurshman had killed Stafford, but had she believed herself to have any other option?

Next, Allaby provided evidence of the sequence of events on the night of Stafford's death. Witnesses admitted that Hurshman had solicited their help, and Allaby asserted that this pointed to the deliberate and planned nature of her actions. Allen, her son, detailed his attempts to clean up the driveway,[81] and Roger Manthorne, a neighbour and Joudry's tenant, admitted having helped break down and dispose of the gun.[82] Maurice Hurshman, her father, described picking her up on the night of Stafford's death, but said she was clearly in shock and didn't tell him, or her mother, what had happened.[83] Under cross-examination, however, these very same witnesses provided evidence confirming Stafford's violence and suggesting Hurshman was in a constant state of fear, evidence that would not help the prosecution.

Ronny Wamboldt, an impoverished and alcoholic live-in friend, remembered how often he had been physically and verbally abused by Stafford. Asked why he did not go to the police after being assaulted, Wamboldt responded he was "afraid I might get more."[84] He also asserted that Hurshman "was a beautiful mother," but Stafford would "bully her around at least twice, three times a day."[85]

Allen Whynot testified about the abuse he had suffered, confirmed Stafford had also physically abused young Darren,[86] and described the constant abuse to which his mother had been subjected. He recalled Stafford telling his mother that if she left "he would kill her mother, father, sisters, and that he would find and kill her." He also noted that things had been getting worse.[87] On redirect, Allaby tried to minimize the damage of this testimony, asserting that "there were a few good times in the house." But Allen responded, "Not for us."[88] Hurshman's parents also admitted that they had been frightened of Stafford, who had attacked Maurice Hurshman and damaged their home. Her father noted, "I don't think he wanted her to come around that much. Apparently, he picked her friends."[89] Hurshman, this testimony illustrated, was experiencing violence daily, and no one appeared able or willing to help her to bring this violence to an end.

Fifteen police officers then gave testimony regarding the collection of forensic evidence and the search of the house,[90] the workings of the gun that had killed Stafford,[91] the serology reports on Hurshman's blood and that of the victim,[92] the pictures taken of the crime scene, the house and Hurshman's bruises,[93] the interrogation of Hurshman as a suspect,[94] the dealings of the police with Stafford over the years,[95] and the statement taken after the polygraph.[96] Staff Sergeant Williamson admitted that he had always ordered his men to go to the Stafford home well armed and in pairs, noted that Stafford "had made threats against several of my members,"[97] and testified that he had said to other officers that "she deserved a medal"[98] because "maybe a couple of our members may have been shot in the future time by Mr. Stafford."[99] While the evidence from the police established without a doubt that Hurshman had killed Stafford, the police themselves seemed sympathetic to her plight and unable to control his violence.

The only witness to contest the picture of Stafford as a violent tyrant was Margaret Joudry, the neighbour Hurshman maintained had been threatened on the night of Stafford's death. Joudry admitted that she was angry with Hurshman because of being forced to come to court as a witness: "She got me mixed up in this and there is no need of it."[100] She admitted that Hurshman had complained about Stafford's violence but attempted to undermine sympathy for her, asserting that she "didn't pay any attention to her. I heard so many lies."[101] When Ferrier cross-examined Joudry, however, "the courtroom became a verbal battleground"; she was belligerent, asserting to Ferrier "it's none of your business," only to be ordered by Burchell: "It is the business of this Court and the business of the jury ... it's not for you to say. You must answer the questions."[102] Joudry's hostility to Hurshman was palpable, and the jury would have considered her evidence with much caution. It is hard to imagine that anyone would have disagreed with Ferrier's later assertion, in his closing statement, that Joudry's "motives, frankly, make her a suspect witness."[103]

On 16 November 1982, the defence began presentation of their witnesses. Ferrier's argument was that Hurshman had been provoked and "acted in the heat of passion," "as an impulsive reaction to what

[Stafford] had said about taking care of Allen and Margaret." There had been no premeditation, and therefore she could not be guilty of first-degree murder. At most, she was guilty of manslaughter.[104] Like Allaby, Ferrier had a three-pronged approach to his argument. First, he provided extensive evidence of abuse by putting Hurshman herself on the stand for "over four hours," during which time she detailed "the most intimate and painful details of her life to the spectator-packed courtroom."[105] Allaby tried to preclude Hurshman from speaking about Stafford's actions against other people that she had not witnessed directly, asserting that such evidence was "hearsay." Ferrier argued, however, that Stafford's bragging about violence he had inflicted on others was "admissible in respect to evidence which shows the state of mind of the accused in respect to the deceased." Justice Burchell agreed and admitted the testimony in its entirety.[106] Next, Ferrier introduced psychiatric evidence suggesting that Hurshman believed herself not to have any alternative way of escaping from Stafford. And finally, he called witnesses who reinforced that this belief was not simply subjective, as others were also deeply afraid of Stafford, including police themselves. His argument was that no one had helped Hurshman or stopped Stafford's violence and, provoked by an immediate threat, she had responded in the heat of passion to save her son and neighbour.

On the stand, Hurshman testified that when Stafford would go into rages "his face would get just blood red and his eyes would get right big and bulge out and ... he would froth from the mouth just like an animal."[107] When asked why she didn't leave, she stated, "There was no leaving him." She "didn't really think anybody would believe just how bad we lived in that house."[108] He "often bragged to her about killing a fellow fisherman ... and that he had gotten away with it";[109] it was a fact that he had been on a ship from which a young man had disappeared in 1974, and he was widely suspected in the community of having killed him. This was why he had lost his job and been banned from the boats. He repeatedly threatened Hurshman that "wherever you go old woman you'll be back ... I'll just start with your mother and father and sisters until you come back."[110] On the night of Stafford's death, when he had threated to kill both Joudry and her son, Hurshman believed he would do it.[111] She hit a breaking point: "I just said to hell with everything. I'm just not living like this anymore."[112] She believed that if she had left, or if she had not killed Stafford that night, "there would have been a lot more people killed than Bill."[113] On cross-examination, Allaby attempted to minimize the abuse and asserted that Hurshman had been planning the murder for some time. However, on redirect she stated clearly, "No, I didn't. I didn't think I had enough guts to do it."[114]

Ferrier then called expert witnesses to attest to Hurshman's state of mind. Dr. Rose Mary Sampson, a clinical psychologist from Halifax, had interviewed Hurshman six weeks before the trial and found her to be extremely depressed and "showing considerable suicidal ideation."[115] She also noted that Hurshman had "extremely low self-concept" and limited planning ability, which, "even in the best of times [which the night of the killing was certainly not], [was] problematic,"[116] suggesting that she would have been incapable of a planned and deliberate (first-degree) murder. Dr. Carol Abbott, a Halifax doctor of psychiatry, had assessed Hurshman in three meetings in May and June and found her "nervous and tense."[117] Abbott argued that Hurshman had been in a situation of forced passivity and that the killing was "quite inconsistent with a deliberate plan that is well thought out and what you call cold-blooded murder."[118] She also affirmed that Hurshman's inability to get away from Stafford was not about personality weaknesses because "there were very good reasons why this lady couldn't get out of the situation she was in ... there was a threat to the lives of people that were very dear to her and I don't think that she had much doubt that there was a very, very high chance of her husband carrying out his threats."[119] Dr. John Dimock, a forensic and child psychiatrist with extensive background in child abuse, had examined Darren, who showed clear signs of abuse and described his father as a "bad man who hit him."[120]

The last group of witnesses for the defence were neighbours and community members who testified about Stafford's violence.[121] Marsha Freeman recounted the story of Stafford trying to drive into her while she was walking with her baby. When he was fined, he shot bullets into the house she and her husband were building.[122] Marilyn Fisher, a neighbour, had reported Stafford in 1979 for threatening her after she had called the RCMP when he shot her dog. She asserted that he "looked like a wild man ... he scared me."[123] Stafford also punched and shot visitors to the home for no apparent reason,[124] and forced another man to perjure himself to allow him to be acquitted on a deer-jacking charge.[125] Andrea Wamboldt, Ronny's ex-wife, both confirmed, "I saw him beat her up many times,"[126] and testified that Stafford had put a gun to her head and forced her to leave the Stafford house, in the middle of the night, in the middle of winter, without a coat.[127] Both Faith Hatt and Pauline Oickle, Stafford's ex-partners and the mothers of his other children, gave evidence about the abuse they had suffered when they lived with him. Faith Hatt asserted, "I couldn't just break off with him and stay here in town."[128] Pauline Stafford testified, "He beat me quite often with anything he could get a hold of."[129] She had charged him once and thought there would be a peace bond, but he just beat her again as punishment, choking her until she passed out.[130] Afraid she might be killed, she fled to live with a cousin in Ontario.[131] Together, these witnesses painted a picture of a violent man whom police and the community had been unable to control. How then was Hurshman, a small woman, to protect herself against her three-hundred-pound, six-foot-tall husband and his guns and knives?

During his closing statement, Ferrier described self-defence as the justification available to all "in using force to defend himself or any-one under his protection from assault if he uses no more force than is necessary to prevent the assault or the repetition of it," and asserted that the jury would have to consider whether the threat to Hurshman – or to those over whom she had a duty of protection, in particular her son Allen – was real, or perceived by her to be real.[132] Ferrier reminded the jury that it would have to weigh whether her actions were more forceful than necessary in response to the threat.[133] But his main effort focused on manslaughter. He quoted section 215 of the Criminal Code: "Culpable homicide that would otherwise be murder may be reduced to manslaughter if the person who committed it did so in the heat of passion caused by sudden provocation."[134] He argued that Hurshman had shot Stafford impulsively, in response to his threats to kill her son and their neighbour.[135] He urged the jury to "consider the syndrome of a battered wife": "We don't know what it was like to live in that household. We don't know what it was like to be subjected to the kind of violence and abuse and sadomasochistic sexual practices that would drive anybody over the wall."[136] He suggested that all members of the jury, in her shoes, "would [have] take[n] him seriously,"[137] and noted she "felt imprisoned"[138] and "was firmly of the belief that this man could get away with anything."[139]

Blaine Allaby countered that Hurshman should be found guilty of first-degree murder. He suggested that she had waited, calculatingly, for "the opportunity"[140] to kill Stafford. While he admitted that Stafford "was a bully,"[141] he asserted, "Billy Stafford, perhaps unfortunately, is not the one who is on trial."[142] He argued, "We may sympathize with Jane Stafford in her situation but ... I would submit that in this case we have to say that we sympathize but what you did was planned and deliberate, was not provoked."[143] He concluded, "The law is the law."[144]

On 19 November 1982, Justice Burchell charged the jury; his explanation and review of the evidence took seven and a half hours. Unlike Ferrier, who focused largely on reducing the offence to manslaughter, he emphasized the possibility that Hurshman had acted in self-defence, and his argument provided a preview of the decision in *R. v. Lavallee*. He began his explanation of the law with a definition of culpable homicide, noting that the first stage in the inquiry is to determine the factual matter of whether the accused committed the crime. He then explored the defences available to the accused. He explained that the law of self-defence proceeds from necessity, "from the instinctive and intuitive necessity to preserve oneself."[145] He reminded the jury, "If you have any reasonable doubt as to whether the accused acted in self-defence ... then the Crown will have failed to prove the homicide was culpable."[146] The question before the jury with regard to self-defence was thus whether the "killing of Mr. Stafford was objectively or actually a necessity."[147] If the jury found that self-defence applied, this would constitute a full defence to the crime and Ms. Whynot would be not guilty. If self-defence did not apply, it still had to consider the partial defence of provocation. Justice Burchell explained that provocation applied in cases of culpable homicide committed in the heat of passion.[148] The test for provocation, he explained, was both objective and subjective: "Was the threat enough to deprive an ordinary person of self-control and did the actual circumstances deprive this accused of self-control"?[149] Only if neither of these defences were to apply would the jury proceed to a consideration of whether the accused was guilty of first-degree murder – that which is planned and deliberate – or second-degree murder. Burchell noted, "Deliberate for this purpose has been held to mean carefully thought out, not hasty or rash."[150] He told the jury that it could decide between four verdicts: guilty of first-degree murder, guilty of second-degree murder, guilty of manslaughter, or not guilty.[151] But the order of consideration should be: Did the murder occur; do any of the defences apply, considering first the full and then the partial defence; and only if not, what is the degree of the murder?[152] The jury deliberated for eighteen hours and returned with a not-guilty verdict.[153]

The Crown successfully appealed. The five-man panel of the Court of Appeal ordered a new trial,[154] and Justice Burchell was mildly reprimanded for going over the evidence in too much detail in his charge to the jury. The Court of Appeal found that character evidence about Billy Stafford should have been excluded as "it served only to create sympathy for the respondent."[155] The court took issue with Justice Burchell's definition of self-defence, describing it as "broad enough to say that a person is justified in killing anyone who has threatened them and is likely to carry out such a threat."[156] No assault was underway when Stafford was killed; thus the jury should not, it asserted, have been given self-defence as an option. Consequently, the Court of Appeal found that the jury had been improperly instructed and otherwise might have come to a different conclusion.[157] Unlike the jury, the

Court of Appeal evidenced no understanding of the abusive context in which Hurshman had lived and acted, or at least considered such evidence irrelevant to the law.

The date for Hurshman's new trial was set for 14 February 1984, but she decided to plead guilty to manslaughter instead. The Crown agreed, urging a jail sentence as a deterrent.[158] Justice Nunn found that Hurshman had lived a tragic life but had acted as "judge, jury and executioner." Hurshman was sentenced to six months in prison, plus two years of probation, but was allowed to continue her schooling while in jail.[159] She opted not to appeal this sentence. On 14 April 1984, she was released from jail and immediately asked Alan Ferrier to start the legal work to change her name, and Darren's, back to Hurshman.[160]

Aftermath

After completing her sentence, Hurshman lived with her sons in Halifax. She took a job at the Halifax Rehabilitation Centre, where she would work for eight years, helping older people with behavioural issues.[161] She worked the night shift because of her difficulty sleeping in the aftermath of abuse.[162] She "became a highly visible person in Nova Scotia by speaking out against domestic violence."[163] She was also interviewed extensively by journalist Brian Vallee, who was deeply moved by her story.

In 1986, Vallee's biography of Hurshman, *Life with Billy*, was published. Vallee explicitly endorsed the decision of the jury and condemned the Court of Appeal for failing to understand the context of intimate partner violence. The book sold well and Hurshman did dozens of interviews, including for *The Journal, Front Page Challenge, Morningside,* and *The Fifth Estate*. She felt most comfortable, however, speaking with other battered women, stating, "It's therapeutic for me to be with others who have suffered what I suffered ...We feel safe enough to share, to cry, to laugh."[164] She wanted to break the silence about domestic violence: "It is wrong to ignore battering ... if you ignore it, it continues to spread like a cancer."[165] She lamented, "In my community everyone knew I was being abused, yet no one acknowledged that fact. No one spoke about it out loud," and argued, "Battering isn't taboo – talking about it is."[166] With regard to the failure of the police to help, she asserted, "The police admitted they were afraid of Billy Stafford, yet I lived with him for [five] years and took the beatings. If I knew these policemen were not going to deal with Bill, what was I supposed to do?"[167] She called on society to do better, insisting abused women "deserve to live life with dignity, free of pain and without having to worry every day about what will happen next ... until this changes more and more women will continue to suffer in silence and more will continue to die."[168]

When Hurshman killed Stafford, no services were available for battered women in her community, but this changed in the aftermath of her case. Second Story Women's Centre, a resource centre for women, opened in Lunenburg in January 1983;[169] a hotline for assaulted women was established in 1984; and Harbour House (now known as South Shore Transition House),[170] a shelter for abused women, opened in the mid-1980s.[171] As a high-profile woman who had experienced incarceration, Hurshman served on the board of the Halifax branch of the Elizabeth Fry Society and was appointed to the solicitor general's Special Committee on Provincially Incarcerated Women in 1991.[172] In the spring of 1991, plans were underway to make a movie of her life for CBC with Brian Vallee and using his book. While she did not want celebrity status, Hurshman told her biographer Vernon L. Oickle: "I believe it will be very beneficial to tell this story in a movie because of the public awareness it will create ... everyone watches TV and if it helps them, then that's great."[173] Yet she noted that speaking about her story was difficult: "Every time I do, it brings back all the bad memories. You do it because you want to make a change – to stop the violence."[174] Her work on behalf of battered women took its toll on Hurshman, who had to keep confronting all those who had failed to help her. She also had to keep confronting herself and her guilt for having killed Stafford.[175]

Hurshman struggled with guilt over having killed Stafford and with kleptomania, which her doctors asserted was caused by disassociation related to her abuse. She was a deeply religious person; she felt that her ongoing problem with stealing was a sin and that she was an embarrassment to her family.[176] Each time she was arrested for shoplifting, she made headlines. She started treatment with John Curtis, a psychiatrist specializing in kleptomania, but the treatment seemed not to be working as she kept being arrested for shoplifting.[177] Hurshman was once again due in court in March 1992 when, on 22 February, she failed to show up for work.[178]

The next day her body was found in her parked car. She was slumped over and had a gun in her hand.[179] Forensic tests and an autopsy determined the death to be by suicide.[180] Her funeral was held on 28 February 1992.[181] Three days later a candlelight vigil was held in Halifax.[182] On 8 June 1992, Halifax police officially closed the file on Hurshman's death.[183] Ultimately, Stafford still managed to kill Hurshman, despite the actions she had taken in self-defence and in defence of her children and neighbours.

Conclusion

This case is important for many reasons, but most of all because of the legal arguments made by Justice Burchell in his charge to the jury. The subsequent acquittal of Hurshman endorsed precisely the definition of self-defence that would be upheld by Justice Bertha Wilson and the Supreme Court of Canada in *R. v. Lavallee*. While Hurshman herself ultimately still had to go to jail, her case provided essential evidence of the problem of intimate partner violence and the failure of police, and courts, to protect women from violent men. Beyond the legal legacy of the case, it is important to honour Hurshman. She was a powerful advocate for other battered women, and her story prompted the creation of the first services for battered women in Nova Scotia. In her introduction to *Life with Billy*, she described the impact of coercive control and violence on her life: "I couldn't understand why I was being beaten ... I lost everything: my confidence, my self-esteem, my pride – with time, I even lost the ability to care or feel."[184] She asserted that only by talking about violence would other women be saved the pain she had suffered: "I don't think a day goes by when I don't get up with that thought going through my head: I wonder who and where, right at this minute, it is happening to?"[185] Sadly, her case, and her advocacy, have largely been forgotten. But both deserve to be remembered, particularly in a context in which the problem of intimate partner abuse is far from eliminated in current Canadian society. We hope this article fills a gap in historiography regarding the legal treatment of women who fight back against their abusers, provides background to help understand the decision in *R. v. Lavallee*, and honours Hurshman and her advocacy on behalf of all assaulted and coerced women.

NOTES

1 We would like to acknowledge the support of the Social Sciences and Humanities Research Council of Canada in completing this work: 435-2019-0032.
2 Stafford was her common law husband's name. Whynot was her legal and married name. In 1984 she changed her name to Hurshman, her maiden name, and out of respect for this choice, this is how we refer to her throughout this paper: Brian Vallee, *Life with Billy: The Crime That Shocked a Nation, the Abused Wife Who Struck Back* (Toronto: Seal Books, 1986), 208.
3 The notion of imminence created now well-understood obstacles for women who killed in self-defence: Elizabeth Sheehy, *Defending Battered*

Women on Trial: Lessons from the Transcripts (Vancouver: UBC Press, 2014), 23. These self-defence standards were first challenged in the United States in *State v. Wanrow* (1977), 559 P2d 548 (Wash S Ct) and *State v. Kelly* (1984), A2d 364 (NJ S Ct).

4 *R. v. Whynot (Stafford)* (1983) 61 NSR (2d) 33 (CA).

5 Vernon L. Oickle, *Jane Hurshman-Corkum: Life and Death after Billy* (Halifax: Nimbus, 1993), xii. After Stafford's death, Hurshman married again, hence the name Hurshman-Corkum.

6 *R. v. Lavallee* [1990] 1 SCR 852. See Martha Shaffer, "The Battered Woman Syndrome Revisited: Some Complicating Thoughts Five Years after *R. v. Lavallee*," *University of Toronto Law Journal* 47 (1997): 1–33; Elizabeth Sheehy, "Developments in Canadian Law after *R. v. Lavallee*," in *Women, Male Violence and the Law*, ed. Julie Stubbs (Sydney: Institute of Criminology, 1994), 174–91, https://ssrn.com/abstract=2328826; and Sheehy, *Defending Battered Women on Trial*, 1–56.

7 *R. v. Lavallee*, at 883. Madame Justice Bertha Wilson's biographer asserts that she had to work hard to convince the rest of the court of her reasoning: Ellen Anderson, *Judging Bertha Wilson: Law as Large as Life* (Toronto: University of Toronto Press, 2001), 219.

8 The only explicit reference to this case in recent commentary on intimate partner violence and the law in Canada is in Elizabeth Sheehy's excellent book *Defending Battered Women on Trial*, in which she provides a three-page summary of Hurshman's story.

9 Our central source for this article is the original transcript from *R. v. Whynot*. The case was heard in Liverpool, Nova Scotia, in November 1982 in the Supreme Court of Nova Scotia, Trial Division. Alan Ferrier kept the paper copy of his appeal books, submitted in 1983 to the Nova Scotia Court of Appeal. He agreed to provide us with a copy of the file in its entirety. For this, we are extremely grateful.

10 In fact, when the authors searched for this case, at the University of Toronto law library, the nearest paper copy available was in northern New York State.

11 Oickle, *Jane Hurshman-Corkum*; Vallee, *Life with Billy*; Brian Vallee, *Life after Billy: Jane's Story: The Aftermath of Abuse* (Toronto: Seal Books; McClelland Bantam, 1993); and Brian Vallee, *The War on Women: Elly Armour, Jane Hurshman, and Criminal Violence in Canadian Homes* (Toronto: Key Porter Books, 2007).

12 Constance Backhouse, *Petticoats and Prejudice: Women and the Law in Nineteenth-Century Canada* (Toronto: Women's Press, 1991); Lori Chambers and John Weaver, "'The Story of Her Wrongs': Abuse and Desertion in Hamilton, 1859–1892," *Ontario History* 93 (Fall 2001): 107–26; Lori Chambers and John Weaver, "Alimony and Orders of Protection: Escaping

Abuse in Hamilton-Wentworth, 1837–1900," *Ontario History* 95 (Fall 2003): 113–35; Kathryn Harvey, "To Love, Honour and Obey: Wife-Battering in Working-Class Montreal, 1869–1879," *Urban History Review/Revue d'histoire urbaine* 19, no. 2 (1990): 128; Lorna McLean, "Deserving Wives and Drunken Husbands: Wife Beating, Marital Conduct and the Law in Ontario, 1850–1910," *Histoire social/Social History* 35, no. 69 (2002): 63.

13 Karen Dubinsky and Franca Iacovetta, "Murder, Womanly Virtue, and Motherhood: The Case of Angelina Napolitano, 1911–1922," *Canadian Historical Review* 72, no. 4 (December 1991): 505–31.
14 Nancy Janovicek, *No Place to Go: Local Histories of the Battered Women's Shelter Movement* (Vancouver: UBC Press, 2007).
15 Sheehy, *Defending Battered Women on Trial*.
16 Oickle, *Jane Hurshman-Corkum*, 15.
17 Oickle, *Jane Hurshman-Corkum*, 16. For Hurshman, abuse was both normalized and something that might get better over time: appeal book, *R. v. Whynot*, part 2, "Transcript of Evidence," part 2, 5, 39.
18 Oickle, *Jane Hurshman-Corkum*, 16.
19 Vallee, *Life with Billy*, 45.
20 Vallee, *Life with Billy*, 46.
21 Vallee, *Life with Billy*, 51.
22 Oickle, *Jane Hurshman-Corkum*, 16; "Transcript," part 2, 267–76.
23 Oickle, *Jane Hurshman-Corkum*,17; "Transcript," part 2, 261–7.
24 Oickle, *Jane Hurshman-Corkum*, 18.
25 Vallee, *Life with Billy*, 54.
26 Vallee, *Life with Billy*, 57.
27 Stafford was very angry that Hurshman had rendered herself "useless": "Transcript," part 2, 16.
28 Vallee, *Life with Billy*, 84–5.
29 "Transcript," part 2, 16.
30 "Transcript," part 2, 17.
31 Vallee, *Life with Billy*, 90.
32 Evan Stark, *Coercive Control: The Entrapment of Women in Personal Life* (New York: Oxford University Press, 2007), 5.
33 Sheehy, *Defending Battered Women on Trial*, 235.
34 Vallee, *Life with Billy*, 61; "Transcript," part 2, 70.
35 Vallee, *Life with Billy*, 72, 74.
36 "Transcript," part 2, 23.
37 Vallee, *Life with Billy*, 92.
38 "Transcript," part 2, 20.
39 "Transcript," part 2, 65.
40 "Transcript," part 2, 67; part 1, 481–5, 578; part 2, 18.
41 Vallee, *Life with Billy*, 68.

42 Vallee, *Life with Billy*, 69.
43 Oickle, *Jane Hurshman-Corkum*, 26.
44 Oickle, *Jane Hurshman-Corkum*, 26.
45 "Transcript," part 1, 965.
46 Vallee, *Life with Billy*, 75; "Transcript," part 2, 57.
47 "Transcript," part 2, 101.
48 Oickle, *Jane Hurshman-Corkum*, 27.
49 Vallee, *Life with Billy*, 98–9.
50 Vallee, *Life with Billy*, 101.
51 Vallee, *Life with Billy*, 105; "Transcript," part 2, 65–9.
52 Vallee, *Life with Billy*, 105.
53 Vallee, *Life with Billy*, 106.
54 Oickle, *Jane Hurshman-Corkum*, 11.
55 Oickle, *Jane Hurshman-Corkum*, 12.
56 Oickle, *Jane Hurshman-Corkum*, 13.
57 Oickle, *Jane Hurshman-Corkum*, 12.
58 Oickle, *Jane Hurshman-Corkum*, 112; "Transcript," part 2, 69–72.
59 Oickle, *Jane Hurshman-Corkum*, 7.
60 Oickle, *Jane Hurshman-Corkum*, 9.
61 Oickle, *Jane Hurshman-Corkum*, 9.
62 Oickle, *Jane Hurshman-Corkum*, 113.
63 Oickle, *Jane Hurshman-Corkum*, 115.
64 Lamonte Stafford was initially very supportive of her (although he later became distressed by the amount of publicity the case created for his family). This initial support suggests Stafford's family was aware of his violence toward Hurshman and sympathetic to her.
65 Vallee, *Life with Billy*, 118–19.
66 Vallee, *Life with Billy*, 121.
67 Vallee, *Life with Billy*, 123.
68 Vallee, *Life with Billy*, 129.
69 Vallee, *Life with Billy*, 130.
70 Vallee, *Life with Billy*, 131.
71 Oickle, *Jane Hurshman-Corkum*, 29.
72 Oickle, *Jane Hurshman-Corkum*, 30–1.
73 Oickle, *Jane Hurshman-Corkum*, 30.
74 Vallee, *Life with Billy*, 134.
75 Vallee, *Life with Billy*, 135; "Transcript," part 1, 223.
76 "Transcript," part 1, 244.
77 "Transcript," part 1, 320.
78 "Transcript," part 1, 367.
79 "Transcript," part 1, 413.
80 "Transcript," part 1, 425–7.

81 "Transcript," part 1, 529–83.
82 "Transcript," part 1, 598–618.
83 Vallee, *Life with Billy*, 148.
84 "Transcript," part 1, 479.
85 "Transcript," part 1, 464.
86 "Transcript," part 1, 550.
87 "Transcript," part 1, 571–3.
88 "Transcript," part 1, 583.
89 "Transcript," part 1, 717.
90 "Transcript," part 1, 735–45.
91 "Transcript," part 1, 768–92.
92 "Transcript," part 1, 780–805.
93 "Transcript," part 1, 824, 884.
94 "Transcript," part 1, 908–22, 944–9.
95 "Transcript," part 1, 958–69.
96 Transcript, Part I, 971–73.
97 "Transcript," part 1, 958–65.
98 Oickle, *Jane Hurshman-Corkum*, 42; "Transcript," part 1, 968.
99 "Transcript," part 1, 923.
100 Vallee, *Life with Billy*, 143; "Transcript," part 1, 643.
101 "Transcript," part 1, 637.
102 "Transcript," part 1, 657.
103 "Transcript," part 2, 299 (h).
104 Oickle, *Jane Hurshman-Corkum*, 43; "Transcript," part 2, 1–5.
105 Oickle, *Jane Hurshman-Corkum*, 43.
106 "Transcript," part 2, 39–40.
107 "Transcript," part 2, 22.
108 "Transcript," part 2, 75.
109 "Transcript," part 2, 101.
110 "Transcript," part 2, 57.
111 "Transcript," part 2, 47.
112 "Transcript," part 2, 71.
113 Vallee, *Life with Billy*, 162; "Transcript," part 2, 98.
114 "Transcript," part 2, 100.
115 "Transcript," part 2, 107.
116 "Transcript," part 2, 109.
117 "Transcript," part 2, 121.
118 "Transcript," part 2, 126.
119 "Transcript," part 2, 132, 130.
120 "Transcript," part 2, 157.
121 "Transcript," part 2, 130.
122 "Transcript," part 2, 183.

123 "Transcript," part 2, 189.
124 "Transcript," part 2, 193–5.
125 "Transcript," part 2, 200–3, 170.
126 "Transcript," part 2, 226.
127 "Transcript," part 2, 229.
128 "Transcript," part 2, 262.
129 "Transcript," part 2, 267.
130 "Transcript," part 2, 270.
131 "Transcript," part 2, 272.
132 *Criminal Code of Canada*, s. 37.
133 Transcript, Part II, 286.
134 *Criminal Code of Canada*, s. 215.
135 Vallee, *Life with Billy*, 174.
136 Vallee, *Life with Billy*, 175.
137 "Transcript," part 2, 290.
138 "Transcript," part 2, 295.
139 "Transcript," part 2, 295.
140 "Transcript," part 2, 299 (n).
141 "Transcript," part 2, 299 (1).
142 "Transcript," part 2, 299 (m).
143 "Transcript," part 2, 299 (u), 177.
144 "Transcript," part 2, 299 (u).
145 Criminal Code, R.S.C. 1985, c. C-46, s. 37.
146 "Transcript," part 2, "Charge," 50.
147 "Transcript," part 2, "Charge," 53.
148 "Transcript," part 2, "Charge," 54.
149 "Transcript," part 2, "Charge," 57.
150 "Transcript," part 2, "Charge," 60.
151 Oickle, *Jane Hurshman-Corkum*, 49.
152 "Transcript," part 2, "Charge," 72–3.
153 Vallee, *Life with Billy*, 178.
154 *R. v. Whynot (Stafford)* (1983) 61 NSR (2d) 33 (CA).
155 Vallee, *Life with Billy*, 191.
156 Vallee, *Life with Billy*, 191.
157 Vallee, *Life with Billy*, 191.
158 Vallee, *Life with Billy*, 195.
159 Vallee, *Life with Billy*, 199.
160 Vallee, *Life with Billy*, 208.
161 Oickle, *Jane Hurshman-Corkum*, 83; Vallee, *Life after Billy*, 4.
162 Vallee, *Life after Billy*, 4.
163 Oickle, *Jane Hurshman-Corkum*, 83; Vallee, *Life after Billy*, 27.
164 Vallee, *Life after Billy*, 29.

165 Vallee, *Life after Billy*, 30.
166 Vallee, *Life after Billy*, 30.
167 Oickle, *Jane Hurshman-Corkum*, 92.
168 Oickle, *Jane Hurshman-Corkum*, 93.
169 http://www.scstory.com/favicon.html.
170 harbor-house.ca.
171 Oickle, *Jane Hurshman-Corkum*, xiii.
172 Oickle, *Jane Hurshman-Corkum*, 101. In 1992, when the report was issued shortly after her death, it was dedicated to her.
173 Oickle, *Jane Hurshman-Corkum*, 108.
174 Oickle, *Jane Hurshman-Corkum*, 50.
175 Oickle, *Jane Hurshman-Corkum*, 98.
176 Oickle, *Jane Hurshman-Corkum*, 98.
177 Oickle, *Jane Hurshman-Corkum*, 99.
178 Oickle, *Jane Hurshman-Corkum*, 163.
179 Oickle, *Jane Hurshman-Corkum*, 169.
180 Oickle, *Jane Hurshman-Corkum*, 183
181 Oickle, *Jane Hurshman-Corkum*, 202.
182 Oickle, *Jane Hurshman-Corkum*, 206.
183 Oickle, *Jane Hurshman-Corkum*, 210.
184 Jane Hurshman, introduction to *Life with Billy: The Crime That Shocked a Nation, the Abused Wife Who Struck Back*, by Brian Vallee (Toronto: Seal Books, 1986), xi.
185 Vallee, *Life with Billy*, xii.

PART FOUR

Theory and Method

12 From Dreams of Equality to One Hundred Years of Struggle: Radical Women's Biographies in the History of Canadian Politics

LINDA KEALEY

Introduction

In recent years the fascination with women's autobiography has eclipsed biographical studies in terms of critical reflection and discussion. As noted by Hemecker and Saunders (quoting Virginia Woolf) in *Biography in Theory*, biography has often existed in an "ambiguous world between fact and fiction," though it is also viewed as based in trustworthy historical data. Like history, biography is also subject to changing interpretations, notes historian Alice Kessler Harris. As Hemecker and Saunders further observe, for Carolyn Steedman, who wrote a biography of her English working-class mother, biography is also a way into class and gender history. As June Hannam writes in her contribution to this collection, a biographical approach encourages tackling the complex relationships between the two. Writing in 2010, American historian Susan Ware pointed to the "symbiotic" connection between biography and history, especially for the study of women and gender. For feminist biographers, gender is key and underlines the link between the personal and the political, a point made by Sean Antaya in his essay tracing the activism of two working-class feminists in the 1970s. This connection encourages attention to daily lives as well as to public roles. Indeed, as Ware notes, biographies of women in politics have succeeded in broadening the very notion of what constitutes the "political." It is my contention that biographies of activist women on the left also help to broaden our conception of what is "radical" about their activism. With the emergence of women's/gender history in Canada, particularly since the 1980s and the publication of studies of radical women on the left, a small stream of biographical writing on women radicals in Canadian politics has appeared that pays close attention to gender, class, ethnicity, and to a smaller degree, race. These biographical studies stemmed in part from the rediscovery of women's roles in left-wing political formations. Such works include, among others, Joan Sangster's *Dreams of Equality* (1989), Kealey and Sangster's edited collection, *Beyond the Vote* (1989), and Janice Newton's *The Feminist Challenge to the Canadian Left, 1900–18* (1995).[1]

This interest in women's political activism extends to revisionist views on the history of the suffrage movement, which celebrated national and provincial centenaries over the past few years commemorated by the University of British Columbia Press series Women's Suffrage and the Struggle for Democracy, edited by Veronica Strong-Boag. An overview volume by Joan Sangster is accompanied by five regionally focused histories that promise to nuance our views of women's political activism in the nineteenth and twentieth centuries. Tarah Brookfield's 2018 volume on Ontario, for example, integrates information on radical outspoken suffragists such as Flora Macdonald Denison, who campaigned for birth control and sexual freedom for women in addition to suffrage. She also integrates a discussion of socialist women's support for suffrage, thus widening our historical lens on the contributions of working-class and left-wing women to a movement until recently largely attributed to middle- and upper-middle-class women in Canada. These volumes and recent biographical studies of other outspoken women provide us with an opportunity for thinking about the experiences of radical women who engaged in political activism writ large – how they came to embrace the need for radical change that included women, what obstacles they encountered, and how they are, or are not, remembered. Such studies also raise the question of how radicalism is defined and how earlier links to the suffrage movement might have contributed to later identification with and involvement in radical political movements.[2]

My own contribution to the history of women on the left, *Enlisting Women for the Cause: Women, Labour and the Left in Canada, 1890–1920* (1998), examines women socialists of various classes and ethnicities (largely Finnish, Ukrainian, and Jewish women) whose political activities preceded the founding of the Communist Party of Canada (CPC) and the Co-operative Commonwealth Federation (CCF), whose women Sangster writes about in *Dreams of Equality*. While a few Canadian Communist and CCF women leaders have been the subjects of hagiographic accounts over the years, many women on the left who played significant roles have been the subjects of more intense scrutiny only in the last couple of decades. My contribution in this essay draws on the biographies of five Canadian women radicals, all white. Their biographers rarely had access to personal papers; four were able to interview descendants, but sources were primarily public documents or organizational records. These women radicals were activists whose analyses and actions were based to one degree or another on critical understandings of their society's views of gender, class, region, language, or ethnicity. Recognition of racial or ethnic discrimination was sporadic. As Sangster has observed, these intersections often obscured the roles played by activist women and how they were perceived by their comrades in the social and political movements in which they were involved. Perhaps it is time to complicate our understandings of what it meant to be radical in 1919, during the Great Depression, and beyond.[3]

The women: Helen Armstrong, women's leader of the 1919 Winnipeg General Strike (1875–1947); Helena Gutteridge, English immigrant to Vancouver (1879–1960); Rose Henderson, based largely in Montreal (1871–1937); Laura Jamieson, British Columbia (1882–1964); and Jeanne Corbin, French immigrant to Canada, who lived in Edmonton, Toronto, and Northern Ontario (1906–1944).[4]

Helen Armstrong

Unlike the last four, who have received published biographies, Helen Armstrong's strongest source is a documentary film by Winnipeg producer and director Paula Kelly, who diligently followed leads on Armstrong beyond the printed and public sources.[5] We know that Armstrong was the eldest daughter of Alfred Jury, a Toronto tailor, labour activist, freethinker, Knights of Labor supporter, and Lib-Lab candidate in the 1880s; that she had met George Armstrong, a carpenter, in Toronto, and married him in 1897 in Montana, where she came into contact with the US suffrage movement; and that she had four children and settled in Winnipeg in 1905, where she became involved in labour organizing when her eldest daughters could assist with domestic life. She took up the cause of women workers in particular. In the war years, she was involved in the 1917 Woolworth's retail clerks' strike, having helped them to unionize, and that same year was president of the Women's Labour League and participated in anti-conscription leafleting, for which she was arrested. In 1918 she campaigned for minimum wage legislation, and in 1919 became the chief women's organizer of the six-week Winnipeg General Strike, which involved her in picketing, soapbox oratory, and the organization of a soup kitchen for the strikers, particularly the women who had fewer resources to fall back on. She was arrested several times, and her husband, as one of the leaders of the strike, was tried along with other union leaders and sentenced to prison. In the aftermath of the trials and imprisonment, George was elected to the Manitoba legislature. George, however, was blacklisted, so the whole family, including daughters and husband, moved to Chicago in 1924, returning to Winnipeg after the 1929 crash. Helen and George stayed in Winnipeg until the 1940s, eventually moving to California to be near one of their daughters; both died in California.

For the filmmaker so many gaps and questions remained. Paula Kelly persisted and found a great-niece by marriage who had letters, speeches, and press clippings relating to Armstrong. These sources confirmed Armstrong's early American experiences with suffrage, which she brought to her political activism in Winnipeg, urging women to use the power of their votes so that working-class women could have a say in their social, economic, and political futures, a theme echoed in Hannam's discussion in this volume of English suffragist, socialist, and Labour Party organizer Annie Townley. Armstrong herself ran for municipal office unsuccessfully in 1923. Kelly also found Armstrong's granddaughter who remembered her as a fighter and generous to those in need. Armstrong, she remembered, hated housework and corsets and sometimes feigned illness to avoid housework. A grandson turned up in Winnipeg to search for more information on his grandparents and confirmed Armstrong's suffrage activity.

To what extent can we consider Armstrong radical? Clearly, she was class conscious and feminist in her support of women workers and suffrage, but as her granddaughter put it, "Ma was definitely not a socialist." She also advised her, perhaps ironically, not to marry a socialist if she wanted her children to wear shoes! From the available public evidence, it would be logical to conclude that "Ma" Armstrong's political views were socialist as well as feminist. According to David Thompson, who recently published an article on fellow Winnipeg radical Edith Hancox, Armstrong "told a voting audience in 1923 [that] she disagreed with her husband's vanguardism: 'I don't believe the world is going to be saved by putting a handful of scientific socialists at the head of things.'" Oral history and family lore, however, provide another perspective, perhaps one influenced by the passage of time both in Helen Armstrong's life and those of her descendants. Finding personal evidence is often difficult in constructing biographies of women radicals. The authorities, however, considered women like Armstrong "dangerous radicals," especially during the Winnipeg General Strike. Clearly, stepping outside accepted gender roles to engage in "masculine" behavior threatened the social order and resulted in being labelled "radical."[6]

Helena Gutteridge

Like many women political activists, Helena Gutteridge left no personal papers to help the historian-biographer reconstruct her life, although an interview with a niece in Irene Howard's account provides some sense of how others perceived her. Despite Gutteridge's working-class background in England, her niece recalls her own mother's impression of Helena as "hoity toity," assertive, and possessing the good looks of a model.[7] Gutteridge's father was a blacksmith and eventually a builder's foreman who married a labourer's daughter. According to Howard, Gutteridge's childhood experiences exposed her to women reformers and radicals, which led her to Theosophy, a philosophy/religion that embraces a diversity of classes, races, and creeds. Her involvement with Theosophy and the Co-Freemasons encouraged self-improvement and raised her political consciousness; when she joined the Pankhursts and the Women's Social and Political Union, she left these other movements behind and learned public speaking in order to campaign for the vote, even getting arrested at a suffrage demonstration at the British Parliament.[8]

Gutteridge's working-class adolescence also entailed going to work at age fourteen in a ladies' clothing department, where she learned the tailoring trade. Immigrating to Vancouver in 1911 at age thirty-two, she joined the Local Council of Women, the BC Political Equality League (BCPEL), and the Journeyman Tailors Union and soon became a vice-president and delegate to the Vancouver Trades and Labor Council and the BC Federation of Labor. Dissatisfied with the BCPEL's failure to attract working women, Gutteridge set up an "Evening Work Committee" at the Labour Temple under the auspices of the breakaway Pioneer Political Equality League (PPEL). She mingled with other reformers such as Mary Ellen Smith, who became BC's first woman member of the legislative assembly, but essentially did not fit in with the "ladies" of the PPEL. In 1913 she was involved in creating the BC Women's Suffrage League as a working-class women's group, which sought ties with the labour movement and their support for woman's suffrage. Her report for the league in the *BC Federationist* in 1913 declared that "the woman's movement and the labour movement are the expressions of a great revolutionary wave that is passing over the whole world." That same year she testified before the Royal Commission on Labour Conditions in BC, representing the Local Council of Women and pressing for a minimum wage for women. By 1914 she was president of the Tailors' Industrial Union (formerly the Journeymen Tailors) and through the union movement learned about socialism and found contacts in the Socialist Party of Canada (SPC) and the Social Democratic Party (SDP), a breakaway from the SPC. She also met socialist women such as Bertha Merrill Burns, Susie Lane Clark, and Evelyn LeSueur through the league. As Howard notes, it is not clear whether Gutteridge switched to the SDP, but "she was, generically speaking, a socialist." Gutteridge also initiated a coalition of groups to fight for suffrage – the United Suffrage Societies.[9]

Suffrage, however, faded into the background during the war years, though Gutteridge was able to connect women's suffrage to the issues that concerned working women and men at the 1914 convention of the BC Federation of Labor. Unlike some suffrage supporters, she did not believe that women were international peacemakers, nor did she think the Liberal Party would deliver on women's suffrage. Nor was she in favour of conscription, siding with the parts of the labour movement that viewed the war as benefiting capital. Like other suffragists, Gutteridge was furious with the Borden government's enfranchisement of female relatives of those serving in the military – women needed to be enfranchised on the same basis as men. In BC, the Liberals did enact provincial women's suffrage in 1917. For Gutteridge, while suffrage was a political tool, it could not address all the issues of concern to working women and men.[10]

After war was declared, her main focus was on organizing unemployed women, forming the Women's Employment League, which set up a cooperative settlement along British lines to provide work for unemployed women, an organization that lasted until 1915. Dissatisfied with this measure, she organized the Minimum Wage League in 1917, working with Mary Ellen Smith and others to get the Minimum Wage Act passed in 1918 and becoming active in the Federated Labor Party. Gutteridge organized laundry workers that same year, though a strike failed to get a closed shop, throwing eighty women and twenty men out of work; the Minimum Wage Act tribunal, however, won the workers higher wages than the union demanded.[11]

By the later years of the war, the leadership of the Vancouver Trades and Labor Council (VTLC) favoured industrial unionism and the general strike as a means of pushing a progressive agenda. Gutteridge, now a machine operator and delegate from the United Garment Workers (UGW), soon became president of this union, which identified with craft traditions. In the crucible of the Winnipeg General Strike, the labour movement fractured and the VTLC was ousted from the national umbrella organization, the Trades and Labor Congress (TLC); craft unions, including the UGW, reorganized and affiliated with the TLC. Gutteridge attended the National Industrial Conference in the fall of 1919 and pressed for wider legislation limiting hours of work and establishing a minimum wage, reasoning that progressive economic strategies would assist in solving larger social problems, especially for women workers. While Gutteridge married Oliver Fearn, a sheet metal worker, in October 1919, she continued to work in a tailor shop and was active in the labour movement in Vancouver until they moved to the Fraser Valley in 1921 to farm; the marriage, however, did not last, and Gutteridge moved back to Vancouver, where she was listed as a tailor once again, in the early 1930s. Here she became involved in the CCF, where she met other women committed to social reform – Mildred Osterhout, Grace Woodsworth (later MacInnis), Dorothy Gretchen Steeves, and others who espoused more radical views, some active in the BC SPC, which participated in the CCF. Through the League for Social Reconstruction and the CCF clubs, Gutteridge connected with Osterhout, who ran CCF summer camps devoted to adult education featuring speakers such as Steeves on socialized medicine, Gutteridge on trade unions, and Laura Jamieson on proletarian literature. In 1934 the CCF convention tackled unemployment as a priority and pressed for increased relief, sending a delegation to the premier and cabinet in December; by 1935 Gutteridge was on the executive of the CCF's Unemployed Conference and working actively with other women to aid relief camp workers, who eventually organized the On-to-Ottawa Trek of the unemployed.[12]

Divisive politics within the CCF characterized the second half of the 1930s, with clashing views of what the new social order might look like. Gutteridge was heavily involved in the Planning Commission, which investigated social and economic programs pursued by the Labour government in New Zealand, as well as investigating programs in Sweden and Norway. The 1937 convention, however, brought to a head the political tensions between left and right within the party, which refused to cooperate with the CPC, a view that Gutteridge supported. No revolutionist, Helena Gutteridge envisioned a radically different society through constitutional means, although she sometimes sided with more left-wing SPC views. In that same year, she was elected alderman for Vancouver with the support of women from the New Era League and the CCF. In her two and a half years in office, she mainly campaigned for housing reform, including social housing. Defeated in December 1939 and in subsequent elections during the war, partly because of CCF opposition to the war, she worked for the party before taking a position as welfare worker among the interned Japanese for several years. In 1945 she returned to Vancouver and became involved in the reconstituted Women's International League for Peace and Freedom (WILPF) alongside Laura Jamieson, who had served as president of the Vancouver branch before the war. While Jamieson and other CCF women withdrew from the organization because of opposition to NATO and anti-communist tensions, Gutteridge remained with the Vancouver WILPF, and while she often took anti-communist positions, she consistently defended civil liberties, remaining active until her death in 1960.[13]

Rose Henderson

Not all women radicals came from working-class backgrounds. Rose Henderson, an immigrant from Ireland who was subsequently involved in middle-class reform, is the subject of Peter Campbell's 2010 biography, *A Woman for the People*. Many details of her life are missing from the historical record, but she was a prominent social worker, former assistant to the judge of the juvenile court in Montreal, and later an elected member of the Toronto Board of Education. Like many women critical of a system that forced working-class women to leave their families for poorly paid labour that did not live up to the ideal of the breadwinner husband and father, Henderson envisioned a fundamental transformation of the economic, social, and political system. Such a transformation needed men and the labour movement, as well as women's involvement in public life, to make change. Motherhood, however, was key to her vision, though she sought an empowered motherhood. It is only speculation that the death of her husband at an early age led her into activism, but it seems likely; the marriage of her only child in 1908 further coincided with these activities. Similar to Helen Armstrong, perhaps domestic entanglements had to be resolved before she could find time for activism.[14]

Henderson clearly sought out groups that espoused values such as universal brotherhood and peace, joining the Bahá'ís around 1911 and later associating with the Theosophists and finally the Quakers, all of whom shared such general values. She supported women's suffrage and women's agency in general, pushing for mothers' pensions in 1914 and moving into the orbit of organized labour during the First World War. Henderson was involved in the Canadian Labor Party during the war and increasingly saw women's involvement in politics as crucial. At the same time, she joined groups like the National Council of Women, but her move leftward increasingly meant estrangement from these bourgeois women's groups. In the crackdown on labour and the postwar unrest of 1919, her premises were raided and her position at the juvenile court increasingly challenged. An RCMP informant called her a "regular firebrand."[15]

In the 1920s she worked with independent labour parties and ran as a labour candidate in Montreal in the federal election of 1921 and in BC in 1925, though unsuccessfully. Postwar, she was also involved in the women's peace movement. In the 1920s she spent time in Great Britain and Europe, and in late 1923 or early 1924 visited the Soviet Union. Although she praised many aspects of Soviet society, including Lenin's policies on women, she did not describe it as utopian (although she later participated in pro-Soviet cultural activities and wrote letters of introduction for Canadians travelling there).[16]

As part of her commitment to the peace movement and her faith in the power of education to change society, Henderson campaigned against militarism in the schools particularly after she moved to Toronto, where she participated in the creation of the Ontario wing of the CCF. The latter and the labour movement supported her bids for a seat on the school board, which she finally won in 1933. As Campbell explains, Rose participated in a variety of labour parties and in the debates over the formation of the CCF, but she also had links to the CPC, which viewed her as a potential recruit. According to Campbell, she worked cautiously with the CPC while maintaining her ties with other political formations on the left. In many ways her politics were difficult to categorize, though clearly they were based in an idealism that society could be transformed through commitment to a peaceful, egalitarian system.[17]

When Rose Henderson died in 1937, she was claimed by social democrats and Communists alike but then mostly forgotten, perhaps, as Campbell suggests, partially because she did not easily fit customary left categories. Little memory of her existed in the women's groups she participated in, although she is perhaps most remembered for her campaigns to support mothers. Her life also reminds us of the limits of what we can recover from the public record. In Henderson's case, her biographer had, like filmmaker Kelly, access to a descendant, though we know much less about the nature of the information gained. Like Armstrong and Gutteridge, Henderson's commitment to changing the conditions of women as workers and mothers was key to fixing the broader injuries of class oppression. All three women believed women's political activism including suffrage would move this agenda forward.[18]

Laura Jamieson

In the case of Laura Marshall Jamieson, the subject of Veronica Strong-Boag's recent biography, there are similarities but also differences with

Armstrong, Gutteridge, and Henderson. Although known as a BC suffragist, peace activist, juvenile court judge, and champion of the minimum wage for women, as well as the wife of a prominent lawyer, Jamieson came from a rural, hardscrabble background and was orphaned at age nine. Unlike many women of her background, she was able to gain an education, taught school, and graduated from the University of Toronto. She married a classmate in 1911 and had three children; her husband shared many aspects of her politics, in particular commitment to women's suffrage, though he was somewhat more in the liberal reform tradition.[19]

For my purposes, however, it is Jamieson's turn to the left that is of interest. Surely, her own struggle after her parents died, her determination to get an education, and her movement into the middle class through marriage must have shaped her political consciousness, but so too did her activism on women's issues. As Strong-Boag notes, Laura belonged to a small socialist study group that included J.S. Woodsworth, social reformer and founder of the CCF, who advocated for equal pay and citizenship rights. In the 1920s her WILPF/peace activities included links to labour and other progressive groups; like Henderson, she linked peace with the school system and the power of education. With the sudden death of her husband in 1926, she became a part-time juvenile court judge, took in boarders, and ran study groups to keep body and soul together.[20]

Like Henderson, Jamieson faced the dilemma in the 1930s of choosing between alliance with anti-fascists concerned with developments in Europe or acceptance of pacifism at all costs. Jamieson chose the former, linking peace with economic justice, opposing Japanese aggression, and urging admission of Jewish refugees to Canada, while also concerned with protecting civil liberties. During the Depression, she cooperated with women in the CPC in relief efforts but also worked with more mainstream women's groups, although she became disillusioned with their failure to address the needs of domestic workers and to help poorer women with birth control. She also joined a CCF club in Vancouver that linked the tradition of suffragist radicalism to the CCF, in the words of her biographer. Separate women's groups emerged within the CCF with the help of Jamieson and other feminists, who found it difficult to penetrate the male leadership circles.[21]

And in 1939 after resigning as judge, Jamieson ran and was elected to the BC legislature in a by-election. After the 1941 provincial election, BC had five women in the legislature, and while their partisan political views were not aligned, they did work together to bring more women into the realm of politics through the Vancouver Women's School for

Citizenship, which Jamieson founded. The three CCF women in the group – Jamieson, Dorothy Gretchen Steeves, and Grace MacInnis – worked together to support household workers' unionization and fair compensation for domestic work not covered by minimum wage legislation, as well as advocating for equal pay and day nurseries. All three lost in the 1945 election to Liberal-Conservative coalition candidates in the midst of strident anti-communist and racist commentary. As Strong-Boag points out, the loss of these women's voices meant a decided lack of attention to women's issues in the legislature.[22]

Although Jamieson cooperated with women in various parties on issues of common concern, she was not sympathetic to what she saw as dogmatic Marxism. For her, the path forward lay in education, building coalitions, and social democracy. She did not believe in revolution, but she did think the causes of working people and women shared common ground. Jamieson went on to municipal politics in the postwar period. Like Henderson, Gutteridge, and Armstrong, she disappeared from historical memory until labour and women's history rediscovered her. And like the others, few personal papers remained for historians to peruse, though her story lived on in her granddaughters' memories. As her granddaughter Anne remarked about her life of struggle in losing her parents, an infant son, and her husband, these "did not vanquish her indomitable spirit but rather inspired her to work for the betterment of women's lives, for the working class and for all disadvantaged people."[23]

Jeanne Corbin

The final biography discussed here was written by Andrée Lévesque. *Red Travellers* reconstructs the life of Jeanne Corbin, who was prominent in the CPC in the 1920s and 1930s. Her parents migrated from France to Alberta in 1911, attracted by 160 acres of land. Her parents sent her to Edmonton for high school, where she became involved in the Young Communist League and the Young Pioneers, as well as selling the party newspaper, *The Worker*. By 1925 the RCMP had opened a file on her as a dangerous agitator. Corbin spent a year teaching school despite RCMP attempts to prevent her employment; in any case, she was soon fired for teaching socialism in school.[24] In the aftermath, she worked at a leftist bookstore and organized unemployed women in Edmonton before moving to Toronto in 1929 to work for the Central Committee of the CPC and to serve as secretary of the Canadian Labor Defense League (CLDL). She also assisted well-known Communist leader Becky Buhay with the organization of working women; the party was trying to attract them into unions and its Workers' Unity League (which had replaced the Women's Labour Leagues). According to Lévesque, the CPC was also concerned with making sure the Women's Labour Leagues' members (who were mostly ethnic workers' wives) embraced proletarian values.[25] During the "Third Period" after 1928, an era of economic collapse and consequent radicalization of workers, the CPC for a time rejected all collaboration with non-militant groups. Corbin was arrested several times at demonstrations in the 1930s and spent time in Ontario and Quebec penal institutions. She travelled across Canada as business agent for *The Worker* to drum up subscriptions but had little success given the prevailing economic conditions.[26]

In 1930 she was appointed organizer in Montreal, where the party was concerned with getting more French Canadian members in order to balance its heavily ethnic composition of Finns, Ukrainians, and Jews. Her years in Montreal were spent organizing workers in the needle and textile trades.[27] In 1932 she returned to Toronto but was then sent to Timmins in Northern Ontario as secretary for the local CLDL. Corbin was regarded as a perfect fit for the multi-ethnic workforce that was employed in the mining and forestry industries. She spent ten years there and was arrested for her role in supporting striking lumber workers in Rouyn, Quebec. The result was three months in jail. She continued to work with the CLDL and in 1937 became secretary to the manager of the workers' co-op.[28] She suffered increasing ill health that was not diagnosed for several years; hospitalized in 1942 with tuberculosis, she died in May 1944. Dozens attended her funeral, including leaders of the CPC, and according to her biographer she was commemorated as a party heroine. Despite her involvement in organizing women workers and familiarity with the Women's Labour Leagues, Corbin never explicitly identified with women; for her, class, not gender or ethnicity, was what mattered. Perhaps because of that and the fact that she was young, unmarried, and able to give herself wholeheartedly to the party, it was easier to subsume other aspects of her identity under one label – comrade.

Because she left no papers or descendants, we will never know what her thoughts might have been on the situation of women within the CPC. Certainly, her work with Buhay in Toronto might have led her to question the role of women in Communist politics. By the early 1930s, after leading a delegation of women to the Soviet Union, Buhay herself was critical of the party's lack of serious attention to women's issues. As Lévesque notes, the ideal of the new Soviet woman was much touted by the party, stressing the supposedly equal status of women and their roles as both workers and mothers and as the comrades of men. Within the national communist parties as well as the Comintern, the utility of separate women's organizations was questioned during the Third Period, much like the experiences of Annie Townley within the British Labour Party in the interwar years and the Windsor, Ontario, feminists who founded the Socialist Women's Caucus in the 1970s. Women, however, were actively involved in demonstrations, rent strikes, opposition to evictions, and celebrations of International Women's Day. Nevertheless, as Lévesque writes, despite promises of equality, "this man's party controlled female activities and was careful of its power to redirect all specifically feminine issues."[29]

Conclusion

What do these lives tell us about women radicals in the first half of the twentieth century? First, they demonstrate how difficult it is to write life stories without personal papers or oral histories. The connections between the personal and the political are crucial but often obscure. The women radicals discussed here experienced and/or observed inequalities as mothers and in work, pay, and other areas of employment as well as in the political realm. Recognizing the needs of women, including working-class and immigrant women, was often key to the development of a radical politics of class. Secondly, our political categorizations are perhaps too rigid. As a Communist activist and organizer, Corbin most clearly fits the category of woman radical, fighting class injustices, often working with women to recruit them into unions and the party; yet to our knowledge she never embraced a feminist analysis. This is not surprising given left-wing suspicions of feminism and suffrage as "bourgeois." As David Thompson points out in his study of Winnipeg CPC member Edith Hancox, her passionate defence of the dispossessed, of the need to emancipate women workers and to defend children, youth, and the elderly, was eclipsed in the late 1920s by the party's suspicion of her activities in the Women's Labour Leagues, which were dismissed as feminist distractions from the real struggle, a concern within the Socialist Party of Canada and the British Labour Party, among other political groups.[30] From the other four life stories, however, it seems that class, gender, and a keen sense of inequality fostered an oppositional political consciousness that makes them difficult to slot neatly into particular political formations that are often posed as reformist versus revolutionary, social democratic versus communist. Suffrage activism clearly figured in the lives of four of the five, suggesting that their views might be better understood as a mix of "labour feminism" and "labour socialism," the latter term developed by James Naylor in *The Fate of Labour Socialism*.[31] Suffrage was a tool for change that was fought for, not bestowed. The franchise was a tool, though limited, in the struggle to obtain social, economic, and political change. Armstrong, Gutteridge, Henderson, and Jamieson at various points ran for political office in the hope of bringing into being a more just and equal society, not just for women but for all. Third, stepping outside accepted gender roles into public and political life because of personal struggles and identification with working women's inequality might explain individual willingness to push boundaries and embrace radical politics. Armstrong's life and actions appeared to the state to be radical and dangerous; as the Winnipeg magistrate said, "no special protections ... no sympathy" for women who stepped outside their gender roles. As a vocal defender of working women, the vote, and the working class, Armstrong tested the boundaries of gender propriety. On the other hand, Henderson's aspiration included a radical vision of motherhood; freeing women from domestic drudgery would give women the room to participate in political life. Gutteridge's working-class background and employment as well as her early associations with radical suffragists positioned her to become involved in BC's labour, socialist, feminist, and peace movements, consistently fighting for working women within them. Like some women radicals associated with "labour socialism," Gutteridge found a home within the CCF, planning for a new social order that would not be realized. Henderson and Jamieson through marriage and profession lived middle-class lives yet identified with labour, the working class, and working women's challenges to support suffrage and later labour parties, the peace movement, and the CCF. Sometimes these women radicals worked with socialist organizations, including the SPC, the SDP, and the CPC. Their political trajectories were, however, complicated and non-linear, and in general they were forgotten perhaps because of that very fact – they did not fit into stable political categories.

For most of these women, born in the nineteenth century when women's sphere was defined by marriage and motherhood even if working-class women spent time in the labour force, their struggles to obtain the vote, to demand decent pay and working conditions, to stamp out child labour, and to work with male colleagues to achieve a more just society need to be viewed as "radical" for their time. It is speculative but worth thinking about what radical politics might have looked like if women's issues and concerns had been incorporated as central to the social, political, and economic transformations aimed at replacing the industrial capitalist system. Recognition of the exploitation of working-class men, women, and children, including those who were immigrants or racialized others, as well as women more generally, might have challenged and complicated notions of how to make social change. For these women, the suffrage, labour, and left political movements were key to a better, more just future. These biographies suggest that we need to rethink our assumptions about radical credentials and the historical treatment of women radicals in Canada. And our historical understandings of women in left politics would benefit from further biographical studies that include activists from other left political formations.

NOTES

1 On women's autobiography, see Jill Ker Conway, *When Memory Speaks: Reflections on Autobiography* (New York: Knopf, 1998). William Hemecker and Edward Saunders, eds., *Biography in Theory: Key Texts with Commentaries* (Berlin: DeGruyter, 2017), 127; Carolyn Steedman, *Landscape of a Good Woman: A Story of Two Lives* (New Brunswick, NJ: Rutgers University Press, 1987); Alice Kessler Harris, "Why Biography?," *American Historical Review* 114, no. 3 (June 2009): 625; Susan Ware, "Writing Women's Lives: One Historian's Perspective," *Journal of Interdisciplinary History* 11, no. 3 (Winter 2010): 413–14, 421; Joan Sangster, *Dreams of Equality: Women on the Canadian Left, 1920–1950* (Toronto: McClelland & Stewart, 1989); Linda Kealey and Joan Sangster, eds., *Beyond the Vote: Canadian Women and Politics* (Toronto: University of Toronto Press, 1989); Janice Newton, *The Feminist Challenge to the Canadian Left, 1900–18* (Montreal: McGill-Queen's University Press, 1995).
2 Joan Sangster, *One Hundred Years of Struggle: The History of Women and the Vote in Canada* (Vancouver: UBC Press, 2018); Tarah Brookfield, *Our Voices Must Be Heard: Women and the Vote in Ontario* (Vancouver: UBC Press, 2018). Other volumes in the series include Denyse Baillargeon, *To Be Equals in Our Own Country: Women and the Vote in Quebec*, trans. Käthe Roth (2019); Sarah Carter, *Ours by Every Law of Right and Justice: Women and the Vote in the Prairie Provinces* (2020); Lara Campbell, *A Great Revolutionary Wave: Women and the Vote in British Columbia* (2020); Heidi MacDonald, *We Shall Persist: Women and the Vote in the Atlantic Provinces* (2023).
3 Linda Kealey, *Enlisting Women for the Cause: Women, Labour and the Left in Canada, 1890–1920* (Toronto: University of Toronto Press, 1998).
4 These biographies were chosen to examine similarities among women who were of approximately the same generation with ties to labour, socialist movements, and suffrage politics; Corbin is the exception in terms of generation and ties to the suffrage movement. Her life story as

a Communist activist most closely fits the stereotype of women's roles in revolutionary movements.
5 *The Notorious Mrs. Armstrong*, directed by Paula Kelly (Buffalo Gal Pictures, 2001).
6 David Thompson, "More Sugar, Less Salt: Edith Hancox and the Passionate Mobilization of the Dispossessed, 1919–1928," *Labour/Le Travail* 85 (2020): 142. See also Paula Kelly, "Looking for Mrs. Armstrong," *Canada's History Magazine*, 9 January 2016; Kealey, *Enlisting Women for the Cause*, chap. 7, "'No Special Protections … No Sympathy': Postwar Militancy and Labour Politics," 219–52.
7 Irene Howard, *The Struggle for Social Justice in British Columbia: Helena Gutteridge, the Unknown Reformer* (Vancouver: UBC Press, 1992), 29.
8 Howard, *The Struggle for Social Justice*, chaps. 2 and 3. Co-Freemasonry admitted both women and men into the organization and originated in late nineteenth-century France in a period of feminist and suffrage activism.
9 Howard, *The Struggle for Social Justice*, chap. 4, especially 61–70, 76–7. The SPC was hostile to women's suffrage, which it viewed as a bourgeois movement that deflected attention from the class struggle. See also Lara Campbell, *A Great Revolutionary Wave: Women and the Vote in British Columbia* (Vancouver: UBC Press, 2020), especially chap. 6, "Labouring Women."
10 Howard, *The Struggle for Social Justice*, 81–8, 98–9.
11 Howard, *The Struggle for Social Justice*, 108–25.
12 Howard, *The Struggle for Social Justice*, chap. 6, especially 127–35 for the later war years and 1919; chap. 7, 136–9; chap. 8, 155–6, 158, 161–2, 165–70.
13 Howard, *The Struggle for Social Justice*, chap. 8, 175–6, 184, 163; on her aldermanic career, chap. 9, 186; on housing, chap. 9, 195–200; on election losses, chap. 9, 215–17; on return to Vancouver and WILPF involvement, chap. 11. The New Era League was formed in late 1916 to implement much-needed reforms such as mothers' pensions using women's newly won provincial vote.
14 Peter Campbell, *Rose Henderson: A Woman for the People* (Montreal: McGill-Queen's University Press, 2010), 11–12.
15 Campbell, *A Woman for the People*, 43–4, on Bahá'ís, etc. On labour activities, see 54, 80–1; quote, 84.
16 Campbell, *A Woman for the People*, 85 (Montreal election); 118 (BC election); travel to Europe, Russia, 105–9, 121.
17 Campbell, *A Woman for the People*, 143 (Quakers, campaign against militarism); chap. 7, especially 167–71.
18 Campbell, *A Woman for the People*, viii, 189, 276.

19 Veronica Strong-Boag, *The Last Suffragist Standing: The Life and Times of Laura Marshall Jamieson* (Vancouver: UBC Press, 2018), on becoming an orphan, 18; on education and marriage, 28–32, 37–40.
20 Strong-Boag, *The Last Suffragist Standing*, on study group, 71; links between peace and labour movement, 75–6; death of husband and subsequent activities, 78–82.
21 Strong-Boag, *The Last Suffragist Standing*, on anti-fascism and pacifism, 94, 126–7; disillusion with women's groups, 97–101; CCF, 104–6.
22 Strong-Boag, *The Last Suffragist Standing*, on elections, 118, 143 (five women MLAs); school for citizenship, 137–38; Jamieson, Steeves, and MacInnis, 149–50; loss of women's voices, 161.
23 Strong-Boag, *The Last Suffragist Standing*, 217.
24 Andrée Lévesque, *Red Travellers: Jeanne Corbin and Her Comrades* (Montreal: McGill-Queen's University Press, 2006), 16–26.
25 Lévesque, *Red Travellers*, 38–40.
26 Lévesque, *Red Travellers*, 27–29; 42 ff.
27 Lévesque, *Red Travellers*, chap. 3, especially 30–2, 55–7 (organizing the needle and textile trades).
28 Lévesque, *Red Travellers*, chap. 4, especially 101–8, 120.
29 Lévesque, *Red Travellers*, chap. 6, "Women in a Man's Party," 140–2; 152; quote, 155.
30 Thompson, "More Sugar, Less Salt," 160. Hancox was demoted to clerical work for the party and retired from activism partly due to ill health and financial difficulties.
31 James Naylor, *The Fate of Labour Socialism: The Cooperative Commonwealth Federation and the Dream of a Working-Class Future* (Toronto: University of Toronto Press, 2016). Other left-wing movements, such as Trotskyism and anarchism, have to date received little historical attention in Canada, let alone a gendered analysis.

13 Revisiting *Many Tender Ties*: A Materialist Reading of Sylvia Van Kirk's Text

D.Y. TURNER

Introduction

Many have recognized Sylvia Van Kirk's *Many Tender Ties: Women in Fur-Trade Society, 1670–1870* as a significant intervention into fur trade studies from a gender history approach.[1] However, I argue that Van Kirk's contribution should be considered within the historiography of the body for its methodological insights into the affective exchanges between subject, author, and reader, which reveal deep and nuanced theoretical considerations about the archive and the representation of the other. In this chapter I revisit *Many Tender Ties*, locating it in the multiple, complex, and overlapping historiographical currents of Canadian history. Instead of viewing *Many Tender Ties* at the intersection of fur trade studies and feminist theory and from a discursive critique, which is how it has typically been viewed, I argue that it stands out in the Canadian context as a foundational affective text of the study of the body – gendered, laboured, and racialized bodies.

The historiography of body studies, in which I argue that *Many Tender Ties* is embedded, can be viewed as sharing in the same concerns and nascent genealogy of the new materialist field.[2] My own analysis stems from the (new) materialist field, and I use it to critically interrogate, as Susan Yi Sencindiver writes, the "limitations engendered by the prominence given to language, culture, and representation, which has come at the expense of exploring material and somatic realities beyond their ideological articulations and discursive inscriptions."[3] It is important to note that my reading of *Many Tender Ties* uses concepts that, while relatively new for Western academia, are a part of Indigenous knowledge systems that have been maintained for generations. As anthropologist Zoe Todd has pointed out, Indigenous scholars and authors were keenly aware of the significance of the ontological turn well before it became a popular academic paradigm.⁴ Critiques about discourse and representation, and discussions about how to "organize ourselves around and communicate with constituents of complex and contested worlds," have been present in Indigenous thought for centuries.⁵ It is a crucial assumption held by Indigenous scholars that alterity or otherness is not an epistemological difference, but an ontological difference – essentially, a difference between worlds and not world views.⁶

This chapter will begin with a brief overview detailing the historiographical significance of *Many Tender Ties*. I will engage with some longstanding critiques of *Many Tender Ties*, which frame my discussion about the representation of the other through the colonial archive. Lastly, I will outline how theorists Gilles Deleuze and Humberto Maturana can help to recalibrate how historians understand and relate to their subjects and objects of study by emphasizing Van Kirk's attention to the material and somatic realities of the body within historical discourse and practices.

Overlapping Historiographies: *Many Tender Ties* in a Broader Context

Of all the shifts in the new fur trade historiography in the 1980s, the focus on women as agents and actors was – along with a greater focus on Indigenous people – a hallmark of the field.⁷ *Many Tender Ties* (1980) represented a significant intervention in gender and women's history for not only viewing women within the fur trade, but acknowledging their indispensable roles and substantiating the promise of women's history to reinterpret the past overall.⁸

As Jarvis Brownlie and Valerie Korinek note in the introduction of their collection *Finding a Way to the Heart*, Van Kirk's "feminist questions and insights helped pry open the narrow parameters of historical inquiry to expand the areas of life considered worthy of investigation."⁹ Van Kirk's study, along with Jennifer Brown's *Strangers in Blood: Fur Trade Company Families in Indian Country*, published in the same year, influenced a generation of feminist historians. Brown's study of the familial patterns that developed in fur country was a groundbreaking analysis of the social conditions of the fur trade that also considered the role of women.¹⁰ As Van Kirk writes in her introduction, *Many Tender Ties* examines the "role played by Indian, mixed-blood and white women in the development of the fur trade society" in order to reconstruct the "complex, human dimension" of the trade.¹¹ Her work confirmed and proved how the fur trade could not have proceeded without the active participation of Indigenous, mixed, and Métis women.¹² Not only did her revelations about women in the fur trade disrupt decades of inherited knowledge from previous historical work, but her methodology was significant: Relying on the Hudson's Bay Company records, and an array of traveller and trader accounts almost exclusively penned by men, Van Kirk read "against the grain" in order to find crucial insights into the role of women.[13] Women in Van Kirk's work were essential contributors to the spread and functioning of the trade, and witnessed the gradual entrenchment of racist ideology.

By focusing on and researching the lives of women in the fur trade, Van Kirk broke with older scholarship that had traditionally focused on the European men and, to a much lesser extent, their Indigenous male counterparts. Van Kirk's approach differed greatly from Harold A. Innis and Donald G. Creighton's narratives, in which women were non-existent, and from Peter C. Newman's subsequent characterization, which relegated women to the role of mere bedmates of white traders.[14] Understanding that the trade was a hybrid set of cultural values, norms, customary practices, and familial networks throughout North America slowly became the standard.[15] The trade was a complex set of ever-changing practices, undergoing negotiations of meaning and significance, and Indigenous actions and participation therein were never predictable nor preordained. As Van Kirk pointed out, the Indigenous women of the fur trade provided food and pemmican, dressed fur, and made moccasins, snowshoes, canoes, and lodges.[16] They could be hunters, guides, transporters, diplomatic agents, and traders.[17] As "women in between," Indigenous, mixed, and Métis women often helped to ameliorate tensions in the relationships between the men of the fur trade. For these reasons, Van Kirk viewed these women of the fur trade as the architects of the society that dominated northern North America from 1670 to 1870.

We can learn something of Van Kirk's motivations concerning her research in a letter she wrote to Jennifer Brown in 1972. Brown wrote to Van Kirk after being informed by the Hudson's Bay Company archivist of their overlapping archival research. In her first reply, Van Kirk confirmed that women and their marriages "a la façon du pays," or *in the custom of the country*, were important elements to fur trade history; however, she confessed that she was only marginally interested in identifying underlying trends and themes, and her true focus lay with individual experiences. Van Kirk was troubled by the "dehumanized way in which [the] history [had] been written." For this reason, she wrote that her thesis would touch on "the mixed-bloods as a group," but that she was "primarily concerned with the initial relationship between the White trader and his Indian wife, and [would] be dealing with mixed-blood women only in terms of their relationship with White men."[18] Van Kirk would go on to argue that her work supported "the claims of theorists in women's history that sex roles should constitute a category of historical investigation," and that it was necessary to not place women within the male-dominated world of the fur trade in the role of passive victim, but rather to extend the concept of the "active agent" to them.[19] These explanations demonstrate that Van Kirk was conscientious of the feminist and ideological implications of her work and research. A body of resultant work is a testament to how significant this shift has been in fur trade studies. Various scholars have linked the importance of female labour and maternal-familial relations to the working of the fur trade, imperial interconnections, and colonial projects.[20]

Many Tender Ties, then, is widely recognized as an essential contribution to historiographies of the fur trade, as well as to Canadian women's and gender history. It is also, as I and others have argued, part of the historiography of the body.[21] Lisa Helps, Jane Nicholas, and Patrizia Gentile have shown that the historiography of the body in the Canadian context is not straightforward.[22] Considerations of the body have been present since the 1960s and with the rise of the new social history; and since the 1980s, academic study has increasingly focused on the significance and theories of the body. Studies of medicine, religion, colonialism, the law, and education have all produced work that speaks to the importance of the body in Canadian history, including Wendy Mitchinson's *The Nature of Their Bodies*, James Opp's *The Lord for the Body*, and Mona Gleason's "Embodied Negotiations," to name just a few.[23] As these diverse studies show, focusing on the body can make class relations and processes of gender and racialization more tangible.

As Joan Sangster notes, theories of the body, be they Foucauldian or phenomenological, feminist or materialist, have been the catalyst for significant historical productivity, influencing studies of race, sexuality, class, and power.[24] Despite this fecundity, Sangster warns that historians, especially, through their productive dialogues with poststructuralist thought and theory, need to be wary of the persistent "dilution of the material" and of writing that concentrates, to a flaw, "on the body as cultural object or endows discourse and language with inordinate causal weight."[25] As historian Kathleen Canning has noted, body histories have left a historiographic mark by convincing readers that bodies have been significant objects of historical investigation, but have most frequently analyzed bodies as signifiers.[26] Discourse has often overshadowed other methods of analysis. Readings of *Many Tender Ties* have often emanated from a discursive or poststructuralist lens. In so doing, scholars have simultaneously recognized Van Kirk's contribution to women's and gender history, but also how her representation of Indigenous women was problematic.

Critiques of *Many Tender Ties*

Van Kirk's work has not gone without criticism. While acknowledging the crucial work done by *Many Tender Ties*, Jacqueline Peterson and John Afinson write that Van Kirk pays "insufficient attention to the varying tribal and cultural backgrounds of the native women" that she describes.[27] Adele Perry has suggested that *Many Tender Ties* is "a simultaneously ambivalent and inspiring intervention into women's, aboriginal, and fur trade historiography."[28] Perry elaborates that *Many Tender Ties*, like other social histories of the 1970s and 80s, reflects Van Kirk's desire to acknowledge her subjects as "active agents who made choices about their own lives and histories. But locating agency in fur trade marriages can rub readers attenuated to the complex and enduring legacies of colonialism, sexuality, and gender the wrong way." For Perry, "the extent to which *Many Tender Ties* was wedded to a liberal feminism and grounded in a positivist naivete that falls on particularly rough ground in the messy context of the colonial archive" would become increasingly problematic in the 1990s.[29]

Perry's critiques follow from literary scholar Julia Emberley's 1990 article that interrogates the study of "Native women" in literature and history.[30] Focusing on Van Kirk's discussion of the "Slave Woman" Thanadelthur, Emberley critiques both Van Kirk's use of the archive as well as her representation of the other and the place of the subaltern.[31] Emberley suggests that the "Native woman informant" was appropriated by historians like Van Kirk to explain "colonial confrontation," an appropriation that was determined by "the assumptions that govern how the archive is read and sociopolitical pressures [bearing] on the historian to make use of certain interpretive strategies." Van Kirk was caught between the practices of "the self-determined decolonization struggle of native people living in the geopolitical territory known as Canada and materialist-feminist concerns for articulating a theory of gender subordination with a class analysis informed by an antiracist and anti-imperialist ethicopolitics."[32] Between these juxtaposed practices, Emberley views Van Kirk as transferring the problems of her materialist feminism into the study of Indigenous women and decolonial struggle.[33]

Specifically, Emberley views Van Kirk as subsuming the Indigenous decolonial struggle, aims, and practices into her "first world" feminism, thereby obscuring them.[34] For Emberley, Van Kirk deploys the colonial archive to establish the legitimacy of the colonizer through a process that erased Indigenous people and nations and used them as tools in an ongoing process to achieve colonization. Historians like Van Kirk, who fetishize the colonial archive as the only source of the real Canadian past, obscure the imperial violence of which historical discourse was never capable of escaping.

Emberley's critiques mirror Gayatri Spivak's influential work "Can the Subaltern Speak?" Echoing Spivak's sentiment that "white men are saving brown women from brown men,"[35] Emberley asserts that the relationship of the liberal feminist academic to her new colonized subject of study – "Native women" – does not differ significantly from an earlier benevolent view of Native-European confrontation.[36] In this way, the newly found, active agent as Native woman functions in the same role in the colonialist discursive system as she ever did, but with a new opposite, the first-world feminist. The relationship has been transformed into white women saving brown women from white men.

Emberley's critiques form an essential part of the equation for understanding the body in history. Discursive analysis has and will continue to be an important method for studying the body, but also represents the first of the three dilemmas in the theory and practice of body history, which are "bodies that are singularly discursive or abstract; bodies that are excessively material and undertheorized; and bodies that are not made visible at all."[37] Canning has argued that the discursive/signified/symbolic body can be susceptible to superficiality by being too "immaterial/dematerialized."[38] Moreover, discursive analysis and discourse have been a major stumbling block in the study of the subaltern and have proven to be problematic in body studies as well. They are a major stumbling block because while discursive study can access the subaltern or the body through textual remainders of the state, law, et cetera and configure a social, abstract body that is inscribed upon, it is more difficult for discursive study to offer insight into the subaltern or the body as a site of experience, memory, or subjectivity.[39]

A Materialist Reading of *Many Tender Ties*

Where discursive bodies are too abstract, then, the reverse is true of material bodies, which remain problematically undertheorized. Ruth Roach Pierson's assessment of *Many Tender Ties*, published in 1991, hits on this crucial dilemma of body studies: how to reconcile the discursive-material divide. Pierson's analysis comes the closest to viewing history *through* the body with her discussion of "experience." She argues that if we focus on the roles (positions occupied and tasks performed) of the Indigenous women of *Many Tender Ties*, then Van Kirk captured and explained the exterior dimensions of experience well. However, if experience is defined as the "interiority of human life" (consciousness and subjectivity), then Van Kirk exceeded the bounds of her source material.[40] To bridge the gap between the discursive body and the corporeal body, Canning proposes the concept of "embodiment" as a way to encapsulate the complex physiological and inscriptive environment through which the body exists and can be accessed. Bringing the disparate approaches of the body together, since Van Kirk first made the female body visible in fur trade studies and subsequent scholars have discussed the implications of the female social body first identified by Van Kirk, it is now time for a theorization of the material body. A materialist reading of *Many Tender Ties* can help to accentuate how to best theorize the body and put this theory into practice.

This materialist reading of *Many Tender Ties*, I argue, must begin with Van Kirk's methodology, which emphasized a cognition of the other that does not "dilute the material." Van Kirk mentioned the problem of sources early on in the book. She stated:

> In reconstructing the role of women in the fur trade, the paucity of sources, in particular those written by native women, presents a difficult challenge. One is forced to piece together snippets of information from the extensive collections of traders' journals, letters and wills which have survived. Although a substantial body of evidence can be amassed in this way, it is understandably coloured by the male perspective. As is often the case in the history of women, an analysis of this material reveals that there is a significant disparity between the traders' perception of the women's position and the reality of their actual lives.[41]

It is true that Van Kirk was able to locate women only through documentation usually written by and for men.[42] Her reading, however, reveals the somatic realities, material presence, and affective power of the women she sought to study.[43] These women were usually the partners, wives, or children of fur trade employees or factors. Whatever the relationship, Van Kirk read these sources carefully to point out that women were present and mattered greatly to partners, industries, and nations. Since these women left little or no written evidence behind, Van Kirk had to rely on the words and accounts of others to help inform her. We can view this as simply succumbing to the traps of textual archival work steeped in colonial sources. Alternatively, we can view the historian's role with and in the archive as more nuanced. For example, in discussing the preference of European traders for mixed or Métis wives, Van Kirk cites an unusually detailed description of an Indigenous woman by Englishman John McNab in 1816. Janette was the sixteen-year-old daughter of an "old French-Canadian freeman and his Indian wife": "She was neither bold, nor bashful, her behaviour was free, unconstrain'd and remarkably modest. – She was, with regard to her person, a handsome brunette, fine black expressive eyes, arch'd eye brows, high forehead, shaded with natural ringlets of black flowing hair, an aquiline nose, pretty mouth, teeth exquisitely beautiful, and the contour of her face of an oval form. – She was tall & slender, well proportion'd but very delicate."[44] Van Kirk quickly points out the "racial and colour prejudice" that frames the description and that was obvious in the text. However, the description also accentuates the centrality of the body for creating the relations and interactions of the historical people she studied. A useful metaphor by which to understand the significance of the body is to conceive of the body as the "motor of history."[45] In their marriages and relations, Indigenous women and European men were bodies interacting. It was correct to view McNab's description of Janette as a racial and sexist inscription on her body. It is also possible to read the passage as confirmation of Janette's bodily presence in a material sense and how crucial her body's relation was to other bodies. Janette was the product of a sexual relation between her white father and Indigenous mother; she was the sexual future of McNab; as an *engagé*'s daughter, she was the connection point to a vast familial and trade network; as a mixed woman, she was a repository of custom and cultural knowledge passed down for generations. It is not adequate to read the description of Janette as a simply discursive representation of her that requires saving by or from a "first-world feminist." She was an essential relation or nexus for larger social, political, and cultural happenings in the fur trade. Her body was simultaneously a site of entrenchment of racism and colonialism, the possibility of a next generation, and the assurance of economic success and survival of her family through her labour.

Returning to the significance of methodology, Van Kirk's historical subjects are stalked through the experience of others. Along with Van Kirk, we track her subject through her relations, through her industry, through her kin, through feelings of affection. This metaphor draws inspiration from Keith Basso's discussion on "Stalking with Stories" and how stories/history have somatic and psychological effects.[46] Indeed, the tracking emerges from the textual, but is grounded in the material. Moccasins are made, hides are treated, children are born and reared, relationships are entered into and endured. Through all this, though, we can recognize the material body – the labouring, productive body – of Van Kirk's methodology and text. We can understand Van Kirk's stalked subject as heterogeneous, as a retrospective self, made up of multiple intensities, of immanence and becoming. This hints at a different conceptualization of the subject as body, as body-without-organs, as organism and subjectivity.

We can look to the theorizing of Gilles Deleuze and Félix Guattari to understand the subject that Van Kirk was attempting to study – a subject made up of multiplicities. The Deleuzian subject is neither pre-existent nor stable, but always in the process of becoming. Rather than being a specific form, in this framework the body is more correctly described as uncontained matter or a collection of heterogeneous parts.[47] Therefore, when Van Kirk locates the subject within the archival record, she is not interacting with a coherent subject but a subject that is the "tensive arrangement of many larval subjects."[48] Applying Deleuzian thought to Van Kirk's method can be extended to show that it was not about representing the subaltern, in this case Indigenous women, but following their "rhizomatic" reach as they propagated themselves through their relations, labour, and presence. For Deleuze and Guattari, rhizomatic research permits the mapping of networked, relational, and transversal thought and relationships. "Rhizomatic" commonly refers to specialized root growth and the rampant, dense propagation of roots that characterizes plants such as mint or crabgrass.[49] Each rhizome may extend in its own singular direction and make its own connections, forming a dynamic composition of "interkingdoms and unnatural participations" that has no prescribed form or end.[50] Rhizomatic research, in Deleuze and Guattari's conception, contrasts with "arborescent thought," which is a metaphor for a tree-like mapping structure that orders epistemologies and forms of historical frames and homogeneous schemata. Arborescent thought is concerned with ordering the lineages of bodies and ideas in order to trace them back to an original and individual base – everything rhizomatic thought is not.[51]

These concepts challenge the philosophical concept of representation. Deleuze's concepts question thinking that distinguishes between "the original – the thing that most resembles itself, characterized by exemplary self-identity – and the copy, which is always deficient in relation to the original."[52] To go beyond representation, Deleuze argues, it is necessary to undermine the primacy of the original over the copy and to give precedence to the simulacrum, the copy for which there is no original.[53]

If we apply only representational thinking to Van Kirk's subject, then it becomes clear that when she represents the lone, individual Indigenous, mixed, or Métis woman, Van Kirk is representing an inferred inferior copy of some ideal progenitor that she was meant to represent, and that Van Kirk as historian truly does not know or understand. In so doing, the historian can fundamentally strip those they represent of their position as ontologically separate and real entities within the world. The representational model of thinking that underlies historical writing is not capable of expressing the difference-in-itself of any single thing. Applying Deleuzian rhizomatic thought to the understandings of the past fundamentally changes the representational nature of historical writing. I suggest that we should instead embrace a rhizomatic approach, with its emphasis on propagation and repetition, to challenge representational thinking: Instead of representing something in an author's work as an inferior copy of a past original, it repeats that original through the subject's, the author's, and the reader's bodies' affective exchanges. For example, the figure of Janette in McNab's journal and Van Kirk's history is not an artificial copy created by others, but an extension of Janette through her interactions with others.

All of this discussion about subject and representation invokes, as I've already stated, Spivak's most considered question: Can the subaltern speak? *Many Tender Ties* epitomizes this debate. Historian Lata Mani argues that Spivak's question disappoints by foreclosing too quickly a set of complex issues about voice and agency. As Mani explains, Spivak's insistence that the "female subaltern cannot speak" needs to be read in the context of Spivak's examination and interrogation of the multiple determinations of archival sources, as well as her rejection of any simplistic desire to counter discourses of domination by simply "letting the native speak." Mani determines that as a general conclusion about colonial discourse, Spivak's position raises as many questions as it answers. For example, does the question mean "cannot" as in "does not know how to" or "cannot" in the sense of "is unable to under the circumstances"? To Mani, there must be a distinction between these two understandings of "cannot." This does not negate how important it is to heed Spivak's methodological concerns if we are to avoid the dangers she describes (such as the risk of objectifying the subaltern and eventually controlling them through knowledge as the subaltern is narrated and created in discourse).[54] In seeking to answer her own question, Mani suggests that it may not be about whether the subaltern can speak so much as whether she can be heard to be speaking in a given set of materials and what has been made of her voice by colonial and postcolonial historiography. Mani's rephrasing of Spivak's question is meant to enable us to remain vigilant about the positioning of the subaltern woman in colonial discourse without conceding to colonial discourse the erasure of women as subaltern.[55]

Mani's warning to remain vigilant about how we position the subaltern is an essential aspect of a materialist reading of *Many Tender Ties*. I am suggesting that we rethink not only the multiplicity of the subject, but also our relation to the subject to better facilitate whether "she can be heard to be speaking" in the material. An example of how the subaltern can be differently positioned through a materialist lens in *Many Tender Ties* is the case study of Thanadelthur. In arguing for the economic influence that Indigenous women exercised in trade relations, Van Kirk recounts the interaction of a "Chipewyan" (Dene) woman, whom Governor James Knight refers to as "the Slave Woman" and whom Van Kirk identifies as Thanadelthur. Van Kirk describes Thanadelthur's capture by the Cree, her escape to York Factory, and her indispensable role to Governor Knight as interpreter and diplomatic agent.[56] Others have criticized Van Kirk's portrayal of Thanadelthur for downplaying the colonial violence perpetuated against her by Knight's exploitation. I argue, however, that Thanaldelthur should be understood, using Deleuzian concepts, through her body's power to affect and be affected.

For Deleuze, the body is the most basic organ of life. It is a social organ whose structure and limits change in relationship with other bodies. The body desires to connect to other bodies (organic and inorganic) to form assemblages, which are themselves also bodies.[57] Put another way, an assemblage can be understood as a constellation of bodies. This harkens back to the idea, discussed above, that bodies are multiplicities. Deleuze asserts, in conversation with Michel Foucault, that "desire [not power as Foucault argued] makes the social field function."[58] In this sense, desire should be understood not as a lack that needs to be fulfilled, but as a productive force that can be viewed through the body's desire to connect with other bodies to form assemblages through territorialization. Territorialization (deterritorialization/reterritorialization) is indicative of the creative potential of assemblages to free up relations of the body to create new organizations.[59] These theoretical insights can be useful to historians because becomings and assemblage formations can be studied and scrutinized historically.

In the spring of 1713, Thanadelthur stumbled upon some goose hunters on Ten Shilling Creek after fleeing her Cree captor. She was brought to Governor Knight, who immediately believed Thanadelthur would be useful to brokering peace between the Cree and Dene, thus expanding the company's trade and fur networks. Between 1714 and 1717, Knight sent Thanadelthur on several diplomatic missions to entice her people into relations with the Hudson's Bay Company and to establish peace with the Cree. In his journals, he referred to her only as "the Slave Woman" and wrote that she would "be of great Service" to his intentions. In an entry after her death, Knight wrote that her passing was enough to break his heart and that she was of "great Courage & forecast," unlike anyone he had ever encountered.[60]

It is completely acceptable to read these events as Knight's exploitation of Thanadelthur by inscribing her as his slave and using her as a tool in his colonization. However, we might also think of Thanadelthur as a bound-Dene-woman-water tributary assemblage, who deterritorialized by fleeing her Cree captor and becoming through desire (desire to be reunited with her people, survive the upcoming winter, effect peace) an intermediary-Dene-woman-York Factory assemblage. By incorporating Thanadelthur into his mission to expand the trade around York Factory, Knight (a company-man-colonizer assemblage) blocked the Thanaldelthur desiring assemblage and reterritorialized it by rerouting her passage to her home and people, forming another assemblage. These two readings are not simply restating the same thing in different words. In the first, exploitive, reading of the body of Thandelthur, systems of power and resistance to these systems make the body. In the second, affective, reading, it is the body/assemblage desire that drives becoming and systems of power that bind and block this becoming.[61] The second reading attempts to view history through the body. Since the "interiority of human life" of Thanadelthur was not present in Van Kirk's sources, and we can read only the perspective of Knight, it is therefore necessary to rethink how to understand and portray an active agent and to access the subaltern from the given materials. This requires of the historian to view history through the body, not just about the body. This is done by recognizing the multiplicity of the subject body, the body's desire to connect to other bodies, the formation of assemblages, and the body's affective relations. These are recognizable aspects of the material world that can be tracked and analysed historically.

Reorienting the Historian and the Reader

In recognizing *Many Tender Ties* as a history of the body through a materialist reading, I am reorienting how the historian and reader relate to the subject of study. To avoid the "dilution of the material," historians can begin with a reassessment of their own discursive interactions as affective exchanges. I return to my original contention that the material (and the body) must be central to discussions of relationships and must guide understanding of how we as bodies – bodies of uncontained multiplicities – perceive and cognate. The underlying assumptions about materialism in the history of the body have far-reaching ramifications. Van Kirk makes it clear that her subject is not the writer of the sources, but the women at the heart of the affective exchanges that prompted the writing of the sources. The bodies of women are what moves Van

Kirk's story and analysis forward. Her focus in this was unwavering; in each of her chapters the central focus is an aspect of the body's affective exchanges. For example, chapter 1, "Enter the White Man," is about the possibility of new bodily connections; chapter 2 informs how bodies interact legally and culturally; chapter 3, "Your Honors Servants," is about the labouring body. Chapter 4, "Women in Between," best epitomizes the affective exchanges happening throughout the book.[62] The chapter title alone invokes the language of becoming, desire, and assemblage formation I discuss above. Once again, Van Kirk tracks the history of the fur trade through the affective exchanges of Indigenous women as they in their reterritorialization with European men form and maintain the trade. The affective exchanges are carried on to the historian and then on to the reader, through the simple act of reading Van Kirk's narrative – yet another assemblage formation.

This chain of events (historical bodies => historian => reader) represents an affective exchange between autopoietic systems. Biologist Humberto Maturana coined the term "autopoiesis" to explain the self-creating and self-referential state of living systems, and I believe it provides a useful way to think about a materialist reading of *Many Tender Ties*.[63] Autopoietic systems can be understood through the metaphor of houseplants, as Maureen Leyland explains:

> If one compares a living houseplant with an artificial houseplant – in the living plant, the overall maintenance of the identity of the plant is based on the continuous overall process of maintaining the relationships between all its components as they interact with each other in a constant series of chain reactions. By maintaining these relationships, the plant operates as a self-regenerating and self-referring entity. Alternatively, the artificial houseplant exists only in the context of its components having been placed together by its "maker," who determined its very organization, and which remains static. It does not dehydrate or respond to sunshine, whereas the former does based on its internal self-referring messages.[64]

In this metaphor, Van Kirk and historians, as well as historical actors and readers, are living houseplants, in so far as they are distinct entities that are not dependent on one another but may exist together. I use this metaphor to discuss the relation of entities or bodies within a discursive field like history writing and research. Autopoiesis accounts for assemblage formations, but also allows for the separateness of those multiple bodies within those assemblages. This is to guard against the subsuming of the subaltern into colonial identity, but to also avoid turning the subaltern into the signified opposite.

I suggest that we must think of Van Kirk – and all historians – as a material being and an interacting autopoietic system that is structurally coupled, autonomous yet disturbed by stimuli, and ultimately unable to denotatively communicate. In his conceptualization of autopoiesis, Maturana posits that communication is not reciprocal in a denotative fashion. Instead, it is connotative, and two autopoietic beings cannot determine one another's response. To Maturana, since language as communication is connotative and its function is to "orient the orientee" within her own cognitive domain, there is no transmission of information through language.[65] Maturana's theory should be used in a materialist reading of Van Kirk's work on two levels: First, that Indigenous, mixed, and Métis women are no longer actors trapped within a narrative of colonial dependency, where they are understood and determined by Western paradigms of intent and action. Second, it provides a way to think about our relation to historical subjects – especially the subaltern – where the historian, in this case Van Kirk, is the interacting autopoietic system described above. Fundamentally, historians in the written, colonial archive cannot denotatively communicate with the historical subject. It is not a reciprocal relationship.

Through this argument, I wish to provoke a different way of thinking about historical sources and our interaction with the archive. If we understand ourselves as autopoietic beings, then the disturbance we receive from the subaltern within the archive (and all subjects and objects) that we record is one built not on discursive exchange, but on somatic interaction. Somatic interactions are the simple act of reading the archive, the psychological effect we experience from the stories, or the emotive remains we consume. These somatic interactions help to contextualize and trace the affective exchanges underway within and through the sources. Therefore, the interaction or representation is not about whether the subaltern can speak as an artificial original, but about how, through a complex system of affective rhizomatic relations, the subaltern, who is located through her (corporeal, labouring, affective) body, comes to disrupt the autopoietic being's reality.

Van Kirk's title, *Many Tender Ties*, suggests how to locate this somatic reality in the reading of her work. Discussing Chief Factor James Douglas's feelings about family, she quotes him that life "would be perfectly insufferable, while habit makes it familiar to us, softened as it is by the many tender ties, which find a way to the heart."[66] With this quote, we are to recognize the important and necessary relation between Douglas and his wife, Amelia Connolly Douglas. It is their relation that is significant and that produces the important historical insights. There are many ways to understand or interpret this relation, but a materialist reading that focuses on the body recognizes Amelia's affective capacity.

To recognize Amelia's affective capacity, her capacity to act and be acted upon, is also to recognize the affective capacity Amelia acts upon Van Kirk and the reader. Amelia is not a historical subject accessed through the colonial archive but is a body with the capacity to act – first upon Douglas, next the historian, and then on the reader. A materialist reading of Van Kirk's work considers these parallel relations. Here, Amelia as subaltern does not speak to be heard, but affectively expands through somatic possibility. A materialist reading recognizes not only Amelia's body in relation but understands that the somatic translation upon which the somatic interaction is possible happens through the historian's body, brought about by an affective exchange. A materialist reading of Van Kirk's work not only focuses on the corporeal, labouring body of Amelia, but admits the physical reality and body of the historian and reader in relation to her as well.

I argue that concerns about representing the subaltern are not solely about discourse, but about somatic realities and affective exchanges. This is not to reinforce Spivak's suggestion that the subaltern will remain an "inaccessible blackness."[67] Rather, it demonstrates that our histories are not a simple relationship between speaker and receiver, but a complex relationship where our perception of the other is autopoietic and is experienced along parallel materialist lines. The subaltern of the archive's capacity to affect is a very real somatic experience for the historian. The subaltern can speak and be heard, if we consider these actions from a material standpoint that is enacted on our bodies, in an autopoietic sense. These are powerful forces of disruption experienced by the historian. This is all to say that *history is of the body.*

NOTES

1 Sylvia Van Kirk, *Many Tender Ties: Women in Fur-Trade Society, 1670–1870* (Winnipeg: Watson & Dwyer, 1980); Robin Jarvis Brownlie and Valerie J. Korinek, eds., *Finding a Way to the Heart: Feminist Writings on Aboriginal and Women's History in Canada* (Winnipeg: University of Manitoba Press, 2012).
2 Some anthologies that cover this turn include Stacey Alaimo and Susan J. Hekman, eds., *Material Feminisms* (Bloomington: Indiana University Press, 2008); Tony Bennett and Patrick Joyce, eds., *Material Powers: Cultural Studies, History and the Material Turn* (New York: Routledge, 2010); and Diana Coole and Samantha Frost, eds., *New Materialisms: Ontology, Agency, and Politics* (Durham, NC: Duke University Press, 2010).

3 Susan Yi Sencindiver, "New Materialism," in *Oxford Bibliographies: Literary and Critical Theory*, ed. Eugene O'Brien (Oxford: Oxford University Press, 2017), https://www.oxfordbibliographies.com/view/document/obo-9780190221911/obo-9780190221911-0016.xml.
4 Zoe Todd, "An Indigenous Feminist's Take on the Ontological Turn: 'Ontology' Is Just Another Word for Colonialism," *Journal of Historical Sociology* 29, no. 1 (2016): 4–5; Zoe Todd, "An Indigenous Feminist's Take on the Ontological Turn: 'Ontology' Is Just Another Word for Colonialism," *speculative fish-ctions* (blog), 24 October 2014, https://zoestodd.com/2014/10/24/an-indigenous-feminists-take-on-the-ontological-turn-ontology-is-just-another-word-for-colonialism/.
5 Todd, "An Indigenous Feminist's Take on the Ontological Turn" (2016), 7.
6 Paolo Heywood, "Anthropology and What There Is: Reflections on 'Ontology,'" *Cambridge Anthropology* 30, no. 1 (2012): 143.
7 Other significant shifts include the rise of ethnography and the articulation of the formalist-substantivist debate, which moved away from traditional economic/rational terms, as discussed in Jacqueline Peterson and John Afinson, "The Indian and the Fur Trade: A Review of Recent Literature," *Manitoba History* 10 (Autumn 1985): 10.
8 Adele Perry, "Historiography That Breaks Your Heart: Van Kirk and the Writing of Feminist History," in *Finding a Way to the Heart: Feminist Writings on Aboriginal and Women's History in Canada*, ed. Robin Jarvis Brownlie and Valerie J. Korinek (Winnipeg: University of Manitoba Press, 2012), 83.
9 Robin Jarvis Brownlie and Valerie J. Korinek, "Introduction," in *Finding a Way to the Heart: Feminist Writings on Aboriginal and Women's History in Canada*, ed. Robin Jarvis Brownlie and Valerie J. Korinek (Winnipeg: University of Manitoba Press, 2012), 3.
10 Jennifer S.H. Brown, *Strangers in Blood: Fur Trade Company Families in Indian Country* (Vancouver: UBC Press, 1980).
11 Van Kirk, *Many Tender Ties*, 1.
12 For a thoughtful discussion about differences of Métis identity within Indigeneity, see âpihtawilosisân, "Who Are the Métis?," *Law. Language. Culture* (blog), 10 May 2016, https://apihtawikosisan.com/2016/05/who-are-the-metis/; Adam Gaudry, "Communing with the Dead: The 'New Métis,' Métis Identity Appropriation, and the Displacement of Living Métis Culture," *American Indian Quarterly* 42, no. 2 (2018): 162–90.
13 Brownlie and Korinek, "Introduction," 3.
14 Peter C. Newman, *Company of Adventurers*, 3 vols. (Markham: Viking, 1985).
15 Daniel Francis and Toby Morantz, *Partners in Furs: A History of the Fur Trade in Eastern James Bay, 1600–1870* (Montreal and Kingston: McGill-Queen's University Press, 1983); Gray Whaley, "'Complete Liberty'?

Gender, Sexuality, Race, and Social Change on the Lower Columbian River, 1805–1838," *Ethnohistory* 54, no. 4 (2007): 669–95.
16 Van Kirk, *Many Tender Ties*, 56–64.
17 Van Kirk, *Many Tender Ties*, 64–5.
18 Jennifer S. H. Brown, "'All These Stories about Women': 'Many Tender Ties' and a New Fur Trade History," in *Finding a Way to the Heart: Feminist Writings on Aboriginal and Women's History in Canada*, ed. Robin Jarvis Brownlie and Valerie J. Korinek (Winnipeg: University of Manitoba Press, 2012), 27.
19 Van Kirk, *Many Tender Ties*, 5–7.
20 Susan Sleeper-Smith, *Rethinking the Fur Trade: Cultures of Exchange in an Atlantic World* (Lincoln: University of Nebraska Press, 2009); Carolyn Podruchny and Laura Peers, eds., *Gathering Places: Aboriginal and Fur Trade Histories* (Vancouver: UBC Press, 2010); Anne F. Hyde, *Empires, Nations, and Families: A History of the North American West, 1800–1860* (Lincoln: University of Nebraska Press, 2011); Jean Barman, *French Canadians, Furs, and Indigenous Women: The Making of the Pacific Northwest* (Vancouver: UBC Press, 2014); George Colpitts, *Pemmican Empire: Food, Trade, and the Last Bison Hunts in the North American Palins, 1780–1882* (Cambridge: Cambridge University Press, 2018).
21 Joan Sangster, "Making a Fur Coat: Women, the Labouring Body, and Working Class History," *International Review of Social History* 52, no. 2 (2007): 249, 249n39; Lisa Helps, "Body, Power, Desire: Mapping Canadian Body History," *Journal of Canadian Studies* 41, no. 1 (2007): 127.
22 Jane Nicholas and Patrizia Gentile, eds., *Contesting Bodies in Canadian History* (Toronto: University of Toronto Press, 2013), 9; Helps, "Body, Power, Desire," 127–8.
23 Wendy Mitchinson, *The Nature of Their Bodies: Women and Their Doctors in Victorian Canada* (Toronto: University of Toronto Press, 1991); James Opp, *The Lord for the Body: Religion, Medicine, and Protestant Faith Healing in Canada, 1880–1930* (Montreal and Kingston: McGill-Queen's University Press, 2005); Mona Gleason, "Embodied Negotiations: Children's Bodies and Historical Change in Canada, 1930–1960," *Journal of Canadian Studies* 34, no. 1 (1999): 112–38. For a longer list, refer to page 127 in Helps, "Body, Power, Desire."
24 Sangster, "Making a Fur Coat," 244–5.
25 Sangster, "Making a Fur Coat," 246.
26 Kathleen Canning, *Gender History in Practice: Historical Perspectives on Bodies, Class, and Citizenship* (Ithaca and London: Cornell University Press, 2006), 171.
27 Peterson and Afinson, "The Indian and the Fur Trade: A Review of Recent Literature," 12.

28 Perry, "Historiography That Breaks Your Heart," 83.
29 Perry, "Historiography That Breaks Your Heart," 85.
30 Julia Emberley, "'A Gift for Languages': Native Women and the Textual Economy of the Colonial Archive," *Cultural Critique* 17 (1990–1991): 21–50.
31 Thanadelthur appears in chapter 4 of *Many Tender Ties* ("Your Honors Servants") and in Van Kirk's 1974 *Beaver* article entitled "Thanadelthur" (Sylvia Van Kirk, "Thanadelthur," *Beaver* [Spring 1974]: 40–5). Emberley refers to these two sources interchangeably and also critiques *Many Tender Ties* through a textual analysis on writing found only in the latter. Emberley does not differentiate or contextualize the two works, viewing them as a cohesive whole. There are many ways to define the term "subaltern," and some have criticized that it is often employed far too vaguely to denote "oppression" or "otherness," as Jill Didur and Teresa Heffernan have pointed out in "Revisiting the Subaltern in the New Empire," *Cultural Studies* 17 (2003): 2. The category of the subaltern was taken from the Italian Marxist Antonio Gramsci's *Prison Notebooks* (Antonio Gramsci, *Prison Notebooks*, ed. Joseph Buttigieg [New York: Columbia University Press, 1991]). For my purposes, I follow the definition given by Ranajit Guha, and followed by Lata Mani, who use the term to refer to people of inferior rank, thereby drawing attention to questions of disempowerment and hierarchy rather than to the sociological and stratifying concept of class. Guha defines as subaltern all those who do not constitute the elite, whether foreign or Indigenous (Ranajit Guha, "On Some Aspects of the Historiography of Colonial India," *Subaltern Studies 1* [Delhi: Oxford University Press, 1982], 8; referred to in Rochona Majumdar, *Writing Postcolonial History* [London and New York: Bloomsbury Academic, 2010], 26; Lata Mani, *Contentious Traditions: The Debate of Sati in Colonial India* [Berkeley: University of California Press, 1998], 212n7).
32 Emberley, "A Gift for Languages," 22, 23.
33 Emberley, "A Gift for Languages," 22. Emberley uses Dominick La Capra's notion of transference, described in *History and Criticism* (Ithaca: Cornell University Press, 1985), 72ff, and *Soundings in Critical Theory* (Ithaca: Cornell University Press, 1989), 37ff.
34 Emberley, "A Gift for Languages," 23.
35 Gayatri Chakravorty Spivak, "Can the Subaltern Speak?," in *Colonial Discourse and Post-colonial Theory: A Reader*, ed. Patrick Williams and Laura Chrisman (Hemel Hempstead: Harvester, 1993), 93.
36 Emberley, "A Gift for Languages," 32.
37 Canning, *Gender History in Practice*, 178.
38 Canning, *Gender History in Practice*, 173.
39 Important to this discussion, Caroline Bynum has argued that the absence of a clear definition or conceptualization of the body, because it is based

on totally diverse assumptions across different disciplines, has rendered discussions of the body within and across disciplines incommensurate and mutually incomprehensible. "Why All the Fuss about the Body? A Medievalist's Perspective," *Critical Inquiry* 22 (Autumn 1995): 5.

40 Ruth Roach Pierson, "Experience, Difference, Dominance and Voice in the Writing of Canadian Women's History," in *Writing Women's History: International Perspectives*, ed. Karen Offen, Ruth Roach Pierson, and Jane Rendall (London: Macmillan, 1991), 82, 94.

41 Van Kirk, *Many Tender Ties*, 6.

42 Van Kirk, *Many Tender Ties*, 32, 104n28, 118.

43 Brian Massumi notes that there are two words for power within the French language, *puissance* and *pouvoir*. They are associated with very different concepts in Deleuze's (and Guattari's) work. Here power refers to *puissance*, which means a range of potential. Massumi, "Notes on Translation and Acknowledgments," in Gilles Deleuze and Félix Guattari, *A Thousand Plateaus: Capitalism and Schizophrenia*, trans. Brian Massumi (Minneapolis: University of Minnesota Press, 1987), xvii.

44 Van Kirk, *Many Tender Ties*, 113–14.

45 Helps, "Body, Power, Desire," 130.

46 Keith Basso, *Wisdom Sits in Places* (Albuquerque: University of New Mexico Press, 1996), 58–60.

47 Kylie Message, "Body without Organs," in *The Deleuze Dictionary*, ed. Adrian Parr (Edinburgh: Edinburgh University Press, 2005), 34.

48 Constantin V. Boundas, "Subjectivity," in *The Deleuze Dictionary*, ed. Adrian Parr (Edinburgh: Edinburgh University Press, 2005), 269.

49 Patty Sotirin, "Becoming-woman," in *Gilles Deleuze: Key Concepts*, ed. Charles J. Stivale (Montreal and Kingston: McGill-Queen's University Press, 2005), 100.

50 Deleuze and Guattari, *A Thousand Plateaus: Capitalism and Schizophrenia*, 242.

51 Eugene W. Holland, "Desire," in *Gilles Deleuze: Key Concepts*, ed. Charles J. Stivale (Montreal and Kingston: McGill-Queen's University Press, 2005), 50.

52 John Marks, "Representation," in *The Deleuze Dictionary*, ed. Adrian Parr (Edinburgh: Edinburgh University Press, 2005), 229.

53 Marks, "Representation," 269; Gilles Deleuze, *Difference and Repetition*, trans. Paul Patton (New York: Columbia University Press, 1994), 52–3.

54 Mani, *Contentious Traditions*, 159–60.

55 Mani, *Contentious Traditions*, 190.

56 Van Kirk, *Many Tender Ties*, 66–71.

57 Gilles Deleuze, *Nietzsche and Philosophy*, trans. Hugh Tomlinson (London: Athlone, 1983), 62.

58 Helps, "Body, Power, Desire," 130.

59 Adrian Parr, "Deterritorialisation/Reterritorialisation," in *The Deleuze Dictionary*, ed. Adrian Parr (Edinburgh: Edinburgh University Press, 2005), 67.
60 Van Kirk, *Many Tender Ties*, 66–71.
61 Helps uses this form of reading through the body; see Helps, "Body, Power, Desire," 129–30.
62 There is no simple definition for affect, but it has been recognized as that which arises in the in-between-ness and as the capacities to act and be acted upon. Affect has been described as "an impingement or extrusion of a momentary or sometimes more sustained state of relation as well as the passage (and the duration of passage) of forces or intensities." Melissa Gregg and Gregory J. Seigworth, eds., *The Affect Theory Reader* (Durham and London: Duke University Press, 2010), 1.
63 Magnus Ramage and Karen Shipp, "Humberto Maturana," in *Systems Thinkers* (London: Springer, 2009), 201.
64 Humberto Maturana and Francisco Varela, *Autopoiesis and Cognition: The Realization of the Living* (London: Reidel, 1980), 78, 79. Maturana explains that "an autopoietic machine is a machine organized (defined as a unity) as a network of processes of production (transformation and destruction) of components which: (i) through their interactions and transformations continuously regenerate and realize the network of processes (relations) that produced them; and (ii) constitute it (the machine) as a concrete unity in space in which they (the components) exist by specifying the topological domain of its realization as such a network." Maureen L. Leyland, "An Introduction to Some of the Ideas of Humberto Maturana," *Journal of Family Therapy* 10 (1988): 358.
65 Maturana and Varela, *Autopoiesis and Cognition*, 32.
66 Van Kirk, *Many Tender Ties*, 36.
67 Bart Moore-Gilbert, *Postcolonial Theory: Contexts, Practices, Politics* (London: Verso, 1998), 89n18.

14 Gender, Migration, and the Temporalities of Late Capitalism: Social Reproduction in the Economies of Affect

WINNIE LEM[1]

This chapter focuses on the temporal exigencies that migrant women confront as they labour in the affective economies of contemporary capitalism.[2] By drawing on ethnographic fieldwork among women who have relocated from China to France and who undertake the work of social reproduction, it explores how transnational migrants navigate the challenges wrought by the liberalization of economies. In the social sciences, migration is conceptualized pre-eminently as a process that is situated on a spatial scale on which people move across different politically and geographically bounded territories. However, as several scholars of migration have noted, the scale of space cannot be extricated from the scale of time.[3] Social scientists, particularly from a materialist perspective, have especially emphasized that they exist in a relationship that is dialectical.[4] So the discontinuities that are provoked in people's lives by displacements over space are much entwined with the disruptions of time.[5] Moreover, when significant changes in regimes of accumulation under capitalism were initiated in the late twentieth century, migration became intensified, particularly in its feminized form.[6] So discontinuities and asynchronicities in the lives of migrants are especially acute. This chapter, then, is an ethnographic examination of how the disjunctures of time ramify socially and somatically in the lives of migrant women[7] as they confront shifts in regimes of accumulation under capitalism. Such shifts are characteristic of the radical remaking of economies and societies across the globe as ruling forces have relentlessly pursued programs of market liberalization. In China, this shift may be encapsulated as the transition from a regime of state socialism to one of state capitalism. The extensive restructuring has conditioned the transformation of vast segments of the population into migrants who have been relocating to variegated sites of accumulation in national and international economies.[8] Here I focus on the everyday struggles of women who are engaged in the work of social reproduction[9] as transnational migrants who have relocated from China to Paris. They join a legion of migrant labourers who are inserted into an urban economy of a nation where political forces are also enagaged in economic restructuring. Reflecting the hegemony of the doctrines of the Chicago school of economic planning,[10] France has embarked on a program of refashioning its economic regime from one based on "state-managed capitalism" to one in which "financialized capitalism" has increasingly become salient.[11] To engage in this exploration of temporal implications of these shifts for transnational migrant women, I draw on the work of Henri Lefebvre and his methodology of rhythmanalysis.

Rhythmanalysis[12]

Lefebvre is of course mostly known for his work on the production of space, urbanism, and the effects of capitalist change on everyday life. But integral to his project of analysing the dynamics of capitalism is a concern with time and the effects of its rhythms on the lives of those who inhabit urban spaces. Lefebvre notes: "Everywhere there is an interaction between a place, a time and an expenditure of energy, there is a rhythm."[13] These concerns are addressed in his writings in *Rhythmanalysis*, in which he articulates a methodology for grappling with the temporalities of ordinary life under capitalist change. Key in this methodology is a concern with addressing the dialectical relationship that obtains between space and time. The complexities of his framework are of course not easy to encapsulate in these few pages. Nonetheless, I will briefly highlight elements of Lefebvre's insights that are particularly salutary in exploring how this dialectic ramifies in the everyday lives of Chinese migrant women.

Lefebvre advances a notion of temporality that distinguishes between the timescales that are subsumed by the rationalities of capitalism and those that are not. To Lefebvre, linear time is a feature of capitalism and is particularly rooted in industrial capitalism. Under industrial capitalism, time comes to be reckoned as linear as it is segmented into a succession of quantified, interchangeable moments. These moments measure the exchange value of labour-power.[14] Cyclical time, on the other hand, is rooted in the biophysical world and nature. That is to say, for people, the temporal round of birth, life, and death is embedded in nature and the physiological rhythms of the human body. So, everyday life is inflected by elements of repetition, the cyclical process of birth, growth, peak, then decline. Such cycles and rhythms are also inflected by the ruptures due to what Lefebvre calls the "interferences of linear processes."[15] So, he is particularly concerned with how cyclical time in human life comes to be subordinated to the linear time of capitalist development. He argues that postwar capitalism and its linear trajectory of development will colonize all times and spaces of human existence. In this process of colonization, rhythmic temporality is subjected to fractures, disruptions, and flattening as capitalism becomes more embedded in spaces of civil society and human existence. These elements of Lefebvre's insights on temporalities shed light on how characteristics of contemporary capitalism and the insistent demands of production and accumulation both disrupt the rhythms of human life and subordinate them to the imperative of generating a profit. Everyday life, then, for ordinary people involves struggles against such subordinations and temporal ruptures. The concerns over ruptures mapped out in Lefebvre's work extend beyond labour and work to include leisure, family, private life, and sexuality, as well as the unconscious, the imagination, and the body.

The inclusion of the body in this framework is especially apposite to my efforts to highlight the asynchronies that prevail between the somatic and the social for spatially displaced women as they are manifested in two biophysical rhythms of the human body. One is the epigenetic rhythm, which refers to the biological clock of human life. The second is the circadian rhythm, which refers to the body clock and to the twenty-four-hour cycle of the states of being awake and asleep. While both the epigenetic and circadian rhythms refer to the biophysical characteristics of human bodies, they are also linked to social rhythms or social time. The epigenetic rhythm is connected to age and associated with social definitions of periods of life. The circadian rhythm refers not only to the physical changes that respond to light and darkness but also to those that are mental and behavioural. As many anthropologists have noted, conceptualizations of social time vary across societies and cultures. In my discipline of anthropology, discussions of time tend to be the domain of the culturalist and phenomenological schools of thought, and while the emphasis is placed on cross-cultural experiences of diverse temporalities, these considerations tend to circulate in the realm of the ideological. So many prevailing conceptualizations of plural temporalities are often dematerialized and also ahistorical.[16] My efforts here are an attempt to move beyond such ideologocial framings of the temporal by engaging a materialist and dynamic perspective in reckoning with time. I do this by drawing on Lefebvre's concerns with the dialectics of the relationship between space and time under capitalism. Lefebvre's methodology also advocates moving beyond epistemologies of time that are merely chronological. By focusing on the processes of restructuring over time that have been implicated in the making of migrants in China and that continue to assert their influence over women in France, my efforts reflect Lefebvre's emphasis on the "interferences of linear processes" in the rhythms of everyday life. In these respects, my efforts here are also consistent with Joan Sangster's concern with delineating the structural and material realities that inform the lives of women over time, and I direct attention to how the processes of neoliberal restructuring have conditioned the experiences of migrants.[17]

Restructuring and the Making of Migrants

The transformation of significant segments of China's population into vast numbers of migrants is linked to the reform of an economy based on surplus redistribution in the Maoist era (1949–70) into one based on surplus accumulation. This transition of the national political economy from a regime of centrally planned state socialism to a regime of relative laissez-faire state capitalism was initiated in the late 1970s. It involved a series of massive restructurings that proceeded unevenly across space and time in the different rural and urban economies of reform-era China (1980–present).

In the first phase of reform, programs of restructuring focused largely on agrarian economies. In the late 1970s, agricultural reforms were initiated to dismantle collective forms of economic organization that had been established under state socialism and were replaced with mixed (private and public) forms of access to land, labour, and resources. State control over the production and sale of agricultural products was reduced. Private marketing was revived in the countryside, as was the commodification of labour-power. Moreover, resources that were once held collectively as the means of production were contracted to individuals in ways that came increasingly close to de facto ownership.[18] As these rural reforms were pursued, a series of legislative changes was made in the 1990s that added impetus to expand market-led growth. These changes allowed the appropriation of agricultural land for large-scale manufactures and real estate development as national programs shifted to emphasize industrialization and urbanization. So, China's economic growth came to be increasingly driven by heavy investment in infrastructural and real estate development, both of which required extensive amounts of land. Legislative changes followed that altered land use practices. This resulted in the loss of millions of hectares of arable land and enabled "land enclosure rushes" that took the form of speculation, industrial development, and rehousing.[19]

The dismantling of rural collectives, the development of private forms of cultivation, and the transfer of collective resources to individuals, as well as land rushes for infrastructure, real estate, and forms of massive industrial development, have fuelled the well-publicized meteoric rises in China's GDP and the transformation of peasants into millionaires.[20] However, for the vast majority of farmers, peasants, and inhabitants of rural places, these processes have meant the decimation of livelihoods and the creation of a huge population of "surplus labourers."[21] For rural cultivators, such processes have "freed" peasants from land and conditioned their transformation into a force of mobile contingent labour. Dispossessed of the means of making a living, they form a mobile proletariat, that provides the low-skilled labour for the massive industrial developments in China. Much of these proletarianized labourers have headed for China's southeastern provinces of Guangdong, Fujian, and Zhejiang, where special economic zones were developed in the early 1980s. These were new spaces of accumulation created by the state and its experiments with private enterprise as well as foreign investment as reform was pursued in tandem with opening China's economy to global capital.[22]

As the twenty-first century approached, further restructurings of the urban and industrial economy were pursued by the Chinese government. In the late 1980s and 1990s, reforms began to target state-run industries as the Chinese government aimed to radically and quickly reduce the involvement of the state in the economy. Such reforms were seen as creating a context favourable to foreign trade as China sought to meet the conditions of membership in the World Trade Organization (WTO). Reform and economic restructuring were particularly acute in the northeastern provinces of Heilongjiang, Liaoning, and Jilin. Formerly called Manchuria, this region was the industrial heartland of China, where state-run heavy industries formed the backbone of the socialist economy. Restructuring was accompanied by the dismantling of the "iron rice bowl" system, which was a system of job security and benefits introduced under state socialism for the industrial workforce.[23] Extensive privatizations in this region were accompanied by the privatization and contracting out of a range of social goods such as healthcare, education, and daycare. These services became increasingly commodified as items to be bought and sold on the market within a much-diminished state welfare system.

The spatial and temporal unevenness of the shift from state socialism to state capitalism is encapsulated by the emergence of what has been called a "sun belt" in China's southeast in the 1980s and a "rust belt" in the northeast in the 1990s.[24] This unevenness is also reflected in a series of divides that emerged socially, spatially, and economically. With the emphasis placed on industrialization in programs and policy, an economic divide emerged between rural and urban inhabitants. This converged with a spatial divide that emerged between the interior and the highly industrialized southeastern coast. These divides are complicated by divisions and polarizations that were emerging within regions. In Zhejiang, a coastal province located in the sun belt, for example, some towns such as Wenzhou have been favoured over others for industrial development and foreign investment. Industrialization in these regions and in the special economic zones has produced millionaires. Yet the majority of the population that lives outside the investment zones in villages in the coastal areas gains little from investment.[25] Growing class divisions mean that many inhabitants of towns and cities within the zones of high investment are underemployed and seek access to employment opportunities not available locally.[26] So, as the forces of class differentiation eject people from local socio-economies, segments of this population form a force of mobile proletariat propelled toward new spaces of intensified investment. In China, many of these mobile peoples swell the ranks of the abject "floating population," who hover around and migrate between the established and emerging spaces of capital accumulation.[27] Segments of this mobile proletariat also move through international borders to converge on key spaces of capital investment in North America, Europe, and beyond. Paris is one example of such a space, embodying the features of what Saskia Sassen has called the "global city."[28] These are places where, in the wake of industrial decline, a financial and service economy is burgeoning, along with a differentiated workforce composed on the one hand of executives and managers and on the other of increasing numbers of migrants, whose labour is deployed to sustain this complex. So, migrants from China and elsewhere constitute a significant segment of the labour force that occupies the lower rungs of the labour hierarchy in the growing economy of services of this globalized city.

Transnationalized Mobile Labour: Two Cohorts of Women

Two socially and demographically distinct cohorts of women who form part of the service proletariat in Paris have been generated by the spatial and temporal unevenness of neoliberal reform in China. One cohort of women arrived in France from China's southeastern sun belt in the 1980s. Another cohort of women arrived from China's northeastern rust belt in the 1990s. The sociodemographic characteristics of these cohorts of migrants are significant in thinking through how the scale of time ramified in the lives of women as they navigated the exigencies of mobility over space. Many women who came from the sun belt were largely young single unmarried women from small towns and rural areas whose families were unable to sustain a livelihood in the wake of the restructuring of the agricultural economy. A good number of the women in this cohort came from the prefecture of Wenzhou in Zhejiang province. While many Wenzhounese women undertook migration as individuals, others migrated with kin and family. In either case, such migration was not entirely autonomous as migration from Wenzhou to France had an extensive history dating from at least the nineteenth century.[29] This history enabled the establishment of transnational communities of kin, friends, and family that enabled further migration from Wenzhou. Recent migrants were incorporated into localized networks and quickly absorbed into the economy of Paris by finding work in restaurants and retail businesses established by kin and friends or secured employment in industries. In Paris, many met and married their spouses and established families.

By contrast, the second cohort of women, who arrived in Paris from China's northeast in the 1990s, tended to consist of women who were middle-aged, already married, or divorced, with children of varying ages who remained in China. A distinction also prevailed in terms of class: Migrant women from China's northeast were largely urban inhabitants and relatively well educated. They often formed part of the managerial class and were employed in state industries, enterprises, and organizations, but they lost their means of making a living as state enterprises were shut down and privatized. The migration of people from China's northeastern rust belt to France was relatively new, having few precedents before the 1990s. So, migrants from the provinces of Heilongjiang, Liaoning, and Jilin had few pre-existing networks that enabled their easy insertion into the economy and community in Paris.

The difficulties experienced by many recent migrants to France, from the different regions in China and elsewhere, were exacerbated by the programs of restructuring that were being implemented in France itself. Women from China's sun belt and rust belt both arrived in Paris at a time when France was also itself undergoing a series of neoliberal economic reforms. The reform programs were initiated in the 1970s and fostered a shift from a regime of state managed-capitalism to one in which financialized capitalism had become increasingly salient as a dynamic of accumulation. The spread of neoliberalism as a set of economic policies proceeded slowly within what has been called France's "pragmatic" approach and focused initially on price controls and limited privatizations. In the 1980s, privatizations became a central platform in economic policies, and the restructuring of industry and state enterprises was pursued extensively, along with efforts to reduce social spending. As the twenty-first century approached, successive governments implemented programs that were more akin to the aggressive Anglo-American approach to liberalizing the economy and restructuring the welfare state. Deep cuts were made to taxes, extensive reforms of pensions and healthcare were undertaken, industries were deregulated or shut down, and privatizations proliferated.[30] In effect, an economy that was once premised on surplus accumulation through industry and agricultural production moved toward one in which surplus accumulation was increasingly coming to be based on an economy of services.

The consequences of this shift are reflected in the work histories of migrants and their struggles to sustain their livelihoods. Many migrants from China's southeast, particularly from Wenzhou in Zhejiang province, earned their livelihoods through wage work in industry when they first arrived in Paris. As the process of deindustrialization unfolded with production lines moving offshore, factory closures, and downsizing, many were made redundant. Many migrant men and women then shifted to making a living by activating long-established social networks of kinship, community, and friendship to locate work. Some managed to secure work as wage earners in the economy as members of the service proletariat, working for long periods in small restaurants and retail operations located in Paris's Chinatowns and also beyond. Others were able to establish small businesses by activating social ties to help finance their transition to becoming members of the "entrepreneuriat." Many entrepreneurs who operated restaurant and retail businesses in Paris often employed new arrivals from China. In the 1990s, migrants from the northeast were often hired to work behind shop counters or in back kitchens of restaurants run by southern Chinese. Many women from China's northeast also very often secured work as nannies and housekeepers for southern Chinese families who ran businesses. Mei Li, Gin Jie, and Xiao Li,[31] who migrated to France from northeastern China, were engaged in the work of reproduction in Paris. Such work refers to the labours of the hand, brain, and heart that require people to use their affects, knowledges, capacities for cooperation, and skills in communication to create and renew humans as social and sentient beings in the everyday world.[32]

Migrant Women's Struggles: Time, Space, and Social Reproduction

Mei Li, Gin Jie, and Xiao Li arrived in Paris in the mid-1990s from Heilongjiang, a province in China's rust belt. Sharing very similar backgrounds, all three had been employed in state enterprises that were shut down in the early 1990s. They are also married to men who were employees in state enterprises and who, after having been made redundant, migrated to different parts of southern China. The men headed toward different locations to seek work in the industries and service economies in such neo-industrial cities as Shenzhen and megacities like Guangzhou in Guangdong province. Each recounted to me how their husbands became part of the "floating population," a force of contingent mobile labour in China, emphasizing that their experiences of employment tended to alternate with long periods of unemployment. They each emphasized how such economic uncertainties contributed to their own decision to follow a livelihood strategy that involved considerable socio-economic and physical risks associated with international migration. Gin Jie, Mei Li, and Xiao Li also shared a history similar to that of undocumented migrants. Each arrived in France on a tourist visa and stayed after her visa had expired. As visa overstayers, they entered into the semi-clandestine world of *les sans papiers*, undocumented migrants who work in the informal economy.

Gin Jie

Gin Jie worked as a live-out nanny for a Wenzhounese family, helping the stay-at-home wife of a state employee care for a family of six. As a care worker, Gin Jie considered her work taking care of children to be valuable and not too much out of line with the kinds of employment associated with her class background. She thought of herself as an educator. Gin Jie was given strict instructions to speak to the children only in Mandarin and to help with the homework of the older children, who attended Mandarin classes on the weekend. The parents were much committed to the sinification of their children born in France, a common practice among many Wenzhounese. Gin Jie enjoyed thinking that her labour was dedicated to "mental" tasks and not merely to the menial "manual" labour that focused on the temporal round of caring, cleaning, and cooking for the children. She stressed that this was more valuable than the work done as a labourer in a factory – much less repetitive and monotonous, so she claimed, and less subject to the pressures of time to "work faster to produce more and make more profit for someone else."

The work of reproduction undertaken by Gin Jie in the home was nonetheless deeply entangled with the temporal demands of contemporary capitalism. As many scholars have noted, one of the striking characteristics of contemporary capitalism is that the demands of its cycles of production and accumulation not only inform but also disrupt the rhythms of human life while subordinating them to the imperative generating a profit.[33] Labourers who are devoted to sustaining life are also of course attached to the non-commodified work of care as a parent. Gin Jie, Mei Li, and Xiao Li are also parents of children in China, and the care that they as transnational mothers can commit to the daily needs of their children is attenuated by separations of space and time. So, a "care deficit" prevails in families for children left behind. These deficits are partially filled by grandparents, usually grandmothers. The work of raising children is often transferred to such women, who find that the duties involved are out of sync with a time in their lives when retirement and post-parenting are the norm. Indeed, for such women, the expectation is to be care receivers rather than caregivers. In China, caring for aging parents is also largely the work of middle-aged children.

For transnational mothers, these discrepant temporalities are manifested as disruptions in the tempos, cadences, and paces of the epigenetic rhythm. For women in China (and elsewhere), the middle years are a period in the life cycle when labourers tend to be devoted to raising offspring. Such transnational mothers, then, are an absence in the phases of a child's life when mother work is normally done and most needed both by their children and ageing parents. Gin Jie, for example, arrived in Paris at the age of forty, and her experience of contingency and precarity was very new and arrived at a time of life when she, as a mature woman, was carrying much responsibility for tending to the needs of her family. For Gin Jie, fears about her ability to provide for the well-being of her family in China were magnified as social goods such as education and healthcare became increasingly privatized and fees for school and hospital visits strained family resources and intensified household debt. Those fears transformed into panic as household debt accumulated. These debts were exacerbated by having to pay the costs of healthcare for her husband, who was injured in a factory fire while working as a labourer in Shenzhen in Guangdong province. Her husband had no residency rights and therefore no rights to healthcare and was forced to borrow money to pay for treatments with an unregistered private health clinic and an unlicensed doctor in the city.

These are the elements that inform what Raymond Williams[34] has called the structure of feelings in the world inhabited by migrant mothers, who navigate the pulls of mothering and the demands of mitigating the crises of sustaining families through migration. This world is saturated with anxiety, distress, sadness, and worry over fractured families and the alienation of children. This distress is often exacerbated by the irony of engaging in the commodified work of care for the children of others, as such women are employed to mitigate the care crises that have emerged in advanced capitalist countries. In such countries, programs of austerity have been applied to cut social programs, including public daycare, and families are increasingly impelled to buy the services of migrant women such as Gin Jie and Mei Li to raise children, clean, care, and cook.[35] For migrant women engaged in the mental, manual, and emotional work that is dedicated to the production of people, the daily, weekly, and yearly rhythms of labours of the hand, brain, and heart are persistently ruptured. For women who have relocated in space and for whom the relations of kinship and the affective ties of family extend across borders, the work of mothering is transnationalized and beset by asynchrony and temporal tyrannies in the social time of life and work. Temporal tyrannies are much built into the conditions of work for live-in care workers such as Mei Li.

Mei Li

Mei Li works as a live-in nanny for the Wenzhounese owner-operators of a restaurant and provides care for two preschool-aged children. The daily routine of Mei Li's work tends to extend across the twenty-four-hour daily cycle and across the weekly cycle of six days. She is meant to get up early in the morning to prepare breakfast for both parents and children, while also using part of her day to maintain the cleanliness of the home, shop, and prepare meals for the children during the day. Her duties as a live-in caregiver extend into the night, and she is on call to tend to the needs of the children, who wake frequently, particularly when they are ill. It was made clear to her that when the children awake at night, they are her responsibility. Mei Li's employers let it be known that they had to have their sleep as without it they would not be able to do their work and therefore not be able to pay her. As the restaurant was a family-run enterprise, both parents are on the shop floor for at least nine hours a day, six days a week.

Mei Li claims to have seldom had an uninterrupted period of sleep before having to wake early for the next round of daily duties. Night work and constant disruption to her body's circadian cycle mean days of extended fatigue. Her fatigue hearkens to an insight made by Jonathan Crary,[36] who notes that capitalism requires the despoliation of sleep in the interest of maximizing the individual's potential as a producer in order to generate a profit. The night work of nannies and the conditions of perpetual circadian disruption align these migrant women with the mass of nocturnal workers who sustain Paris as a city, its people, and the economies of capitalism. Such nocturnal workers consist largely of immigrants who in a segmented labour market are channelled toward the notorious 3D jobs – the dirty, dangerous, and demeaning jobs – street cleaners, office cleaners, garbage collectors, shift workers in factories. Indeed, one of the most demeaned jobs in nocturnal economies is the work of sex workers.

Xiao Li

Like the women whose stories Joan Sangster[37] found in the Canadian archives, many women from China's northeast turned in desperation to sex work as a means of securing a livelihood after working in precarious, insecure, and often exploitive jobs. Xiao Li, for example, makes a living as a sex worker. After being fired from her job as a nanny to a southern Chinese family "for being difficult," Xiao Li turned to sex work as a short-term solution to making a living while she looked for another job as a nanny. Because, so she claims, word spread very quickly about her being an uncooperative person, Xiao Li was not able to find another position as a nanny. Meanwhile, her personal economic situation became more fragile. She had borrowed money from her roommate, Gin Jie, for her rent and groceries and was not able to remit funds to her two children, who were living with their grandparents and attending school in the town where she once lived in Heilongjiang province. With rising household debt owed to many people in their personal networks combined with the increasing demands to support her children and ageing parents, Xiao Li found it difficult to turn her back on work that was relatively more lucrative than nannying.

Xiao Li services a clientele that consists largely of middle-aged immigrant men who are not Chinese. Xiao Li refuses Chinese clients to minimize any discussion and explanations of why she has taken up such work and the gossip that would target her and her work activities. The labour market in sex is not exempt from the forces of racialization, class, and age segmentation. Younger women and white European sex workers service a bourgeois clientele in the prosperous areas of the city.[38] Xiao Li's clientele tends to be working-class men whose desire for recreation is serviced by women in the dark corners of Paris's mean streets and shady hotel rooms after working hours. Despite the shame associated with what she sees as the "dirty" work of selling her body, she feels some measure of pride that she has been able to make a living and sustain her family. Yet Xiao Li's present is very much framed by the nightmare of being unnable to extricate herself from this economy of affect at some point. So for her, the short term has become the long term, and her present is very much shaped by enduring the arrhythmias manifested in the subversions of the diurnal and nocturnal cycles of activities of work and rest. Here it becomes apparent how labours devoted to capitalist reproduction are inextricable from the labour dedicated to the production of people. The labour of nocturnal workers is deployed in the economies of need and of desire that support the reproduction of the people as workers, whose own labours are dedicated to the reproduction of capitalism. These needs and desires are met in the market through the commodification of the labour of care in the service economy.

Contemporary, or late, capitalism is, as Crary suggests, in these respects a post-circadian order in which the diurnal and nocturnal cycles of work and repose are disrupted, collapsed, and subverted. The social time of family life also prevails in intervals between the times of work, school, and sleep. For migrant women and transnational mothers such as Mei Li, Gin Jie, and Xiao Li, social time is despoiled not only by the spatial separations that prevail in transnational families but also by the discrepancies imposed by the temporal demands of their work in the service economy of capitalism. Late capitalism might also be called a post-epigenetic order, in which the rhythms of the social activities of the social reproduction of the families of migrant women are also disrupted. The epigenetic rhythms of elderly parents and children that migrant women leave behind are simultaneously unsettled. On the one hand, grandparents in their geriatric years are called upon to parent young children, and their daily round involves rising early to get them ready for the day, supervising homework when they return from school, preparing meals, and also tending to the ill, often in the late hours of the night. On the other hand, children are called upon to carry the burdens of responsibility that befall older children in caring for younger siblings and elderly family members in the absence of their parents. Xiao Li's elderly parents looked forward to lives of repose following a long period of pursuing a livelihood and sustaining a family. But this time of life seems out of reach for them as Xiao Li continues to pursue a livelihood away from home in the semi-clandestine world of the night in centres of capital accumulation.

The night has of course always been the time for daylight's dispossessed and marginalized.[39] Xiao Li works along with the legions of migrant workers who toil at the service of capital, cleaning streets, office buildings, factories, and retail shops to support its rhythms of ceaseless production. Those who participate in these nocturnal economies travel the streets in semi-darkness. According to Matthew Beaumont,[40] for these internal exiles of the city, travelling at night is travailing at night.

They work when most people are sleeping to prepare for the next day's labour. So, in the economy of capitalism, where time is money, the night is when money circulates as work, production, and service are incessant in fuelling the processes of accumulation.

Conclusion

My focus in this chapter has been to ask what the temporal ramifications are of the daily reproduction of people whose social and economic activities extend across the space of borders and territories. I conclude by considering some issues that arise from this exploration. First, I reflect on the nature of the politics that might emerge from a political economy in which migrants' lives and livelihoods are aligned with, while subordinated to, the spatio-temporalities of capitalist transformation. To do this, I draw on Bryan Palmer's[41] observation that the night is also the time for the deviant and the dissident. This observation suggests that the people who work in and inhabit the time of the night are filled with the politics of possibility and possibilities for subversion. Much scholarship has focused on the nature of sex work and the subversions attached to the idea of women who are engaged in the commodification of sex: for example, that it subverts moralities as well as normative spatio-temporal orders.[42] Workers in such economies of the night tend to subvert the relations between the state and the economy, as they labour in a semi-clandestine world. As undocumented migrants, sex workers like Xiao Li participate in the underground and informal economy, which is a space or domain that is out of the reach of the state and its regulatory apparatus. Yet there are persistent attempts made by the state to capture this space, particularly by rendering this source of livelihood criminal. In 2015, the French Senate, dominated by the opposition conservatives, attempted to change existing legislation from penalizing clients to penalizing sex workers. In March 2015, a group of sex workers, including many women from northeastern China, mobilized to bring down this legislation. Whether this form of militant particularism translates into other forms of solidarity that subverts prevailing structures of domination and exploitation in capitalism may be linked to the question of time. But it is inescapably linked to challenges of organization and the power of human agency. It is, nonetheless, a question that opens up another avenue for inquiry into the politics of scale, space, the economy of temporalities, and migration. Questions centre on whether mobilizations of the spatially displaced may be informed by or aligned with struggles of citizenship, gender, and also class.

In this chapter, I have tried to highlight how transformations in the dynamics of capitalist reproduction over time have configured distinctive labour regimes and forms of human mobility over space. I have stressed the ways in which shifts in regimes of accumulation have provoked crises of social reproduction for ordinary people, who have transformed into migrants who provide the labour to support these regimes. By doing this, I have attempted to shed light on the dialectic between the scales of time and space by examining the effects of what might be called a post-circadian or post-epigenetic capitalism for spatially displaced women and men in their efforts to reproduce themselves through labouring in an economy of affect.

Questions of spatiality and temporality also provoke us to engage in other projects of thinking and rethinking. In the current regimes of financialized capital that are spatialized in the phenomenon of global cities, migrants constitute the labour force in the production not only of material products but also of the immaterial products required in the maintenance of the infrastructure of buildings, roads, offices, machinery, hotels, schools, shops, and entertainment complexes. They also dedicate their labour to the reproduction of the families of managers, CEOs, engineers, teachers, accountants, clerks, entrepreneurs, and construction workers. These are people whose own labours are directly inserted in the processes through which capital is reproduced. As materialist feminist scholars, like Joan Sangster, continually stress, any confrontation with the problematic of capitalist reproduction must contend with the entanglements of labour dedicated to the production of people through mental, manual, and emotional work. The experiences of Gin Jie, Mei Li, and Xiao Li underscore not only how the lives of subaltern women are subordinated to the temporal and spatial dynamics of capitalism. They also amplify the case for confronting how the work of social reproduction is multiply entwined with the reproduction of capitalism. The insistence that the labour that attends to the needs and desires of people must enter the calculus of surplus-value creation and accumulation can only enhance our understandings of how capitalism is reproduced.

NOTES

1 The fieldwork upon which this chapter is based has been generously supported by the Social Sciences and Humanities Research Council of Canada, the Wenner-Gren Foundation for Anthropological Research and Trent University. This is a much-revised version of an essay that appears

in Donald M. Nonini and Ida Susser, eds., *The Tumultuous Politics of Scale: Unsettled States, Migrants, Movements in Flux* (New York: Routledge, 2020).
2 Such work refers to the labours of not only the hand and brain but also the heart, and so it is also referred to as a form of affective labour. See Kathi Weeks, "Life within and against Work: Affective Labor, Feminist Critique, and Post-Fordist Politics," *Ephemera: Theory and Politics in Organization* 7, no. 1 (2007): 233–49. See also Arlie Russell Hochschild, *The Managed Heart: Commercialization of Human Feeling* (Berkeley: University of California Press, 2012), 47–54.
3 For a discussion of issues of time and migration, see Saulo B. Cwerner, "The Times of Migration," *Journal of Ethnic and Migration Studies* 27, no. 1 (2001): 7–36. See also Ruben Andersson, "Time and the Migrant Other: European Border Controls and the Temporal Economics of Illegality," *American Anthropologist* 116, no. 4 (2014): 795–809.
4 See David Harvey, *A Brief History of Neoliberalism* (Oxford: Oxford University Press, 2007). See also Robert Hassan, "Globalization and the 'Temporal Turn': Recent Trends and Issues in Time Studies," *Korean Journal of Policy Studies* 25 (2010): 83–102.
5 For a discussion of these entanglements, see Pauline Gardiner Barber and Winnie Lem, *Migration, Temporality, and Capitalism* (Basingstoke: Palgrave Macmillan, 2018). See also Ayse Çağlar, "Still 'Migrants' after All Those Years: Foundational Mobilities, Temporal Frames and Emplacement of Migrants," *Journal of Ethnic and Migration Studies* 42, no. 6 (2016): 952–69.
6 The feminization of migration refers not only to a rise in the number of women who are migrating, but also to the fact that many women are undertaking to migrate autonomously as individuals.
7 These cases are drawn from my ongoing research on economic restructuring, transnational migration, and the livelihoods of Chinese migrants in urban France.
8 See Niv Horesh and Kean Fan Lim, "China: An East Asian Alternative to Neoliberalism?," *Pacific Review* 30, no. 4 (2017): 425–42.
9 In much feminist literature, the work of reproduction refers to the labour dedicated to the care and maintenance of people. For discussions from a materialist perspective, see Lise Vogel, "Domestic Labor Revisited," *Science & Society* (2000): 151–70; Cinzia Arruzza, "Functionalist, Determinist, Reductionist: Social Reproduction Feminism and Its Critics," *Science & Society* 80, no. 1 (2016): 9–30; Tithi Bhattacharya, ed., *Social Reproduction Theory: Remapping Class, Recentering Oppression* (London: Pluto, 2017); and Olivia Harris and Kate Young, "Engendered Structures: Some Problems in the Analysis of Reproduction," in *The Anthropology of Pre-capitalist Societies* (London: Palgrave, 1981), 109–47.

10 For a discussion of how neoliberalism achieved this hegemony, see Timothy Mitchell, "The Work of Economics: How a Discipline Makes Its World," *European Journal of Sociology/Archives Européennes de Sociologie* 46, no. 2 (2005): 297–320. Mitchell traces the links between the organizations, actors, intellectuals, and think tanks that transformed neoliberalism from a fringe right-wing intellectual current to the most powerful political orthodoxy and political tool. Among the many organizations involved in what he calls a neoliberal movement to extend the free market across the globe were the Mount Pelerin Society, the Chicago school of economics, and the American Enterprise Institute.
11 See Nancy Fraser, "Enrichment: The New Form of Capitalism? A Reply to Boltanski and Esquerre," *Teoria politica* 6 (2016): 307–14.
12 See Henri Lefebvre, *Rhythmanalysis: Space, Time and Everyday Life* (London: A&C Black, 2004).
13 See Lefebvre, *Rhythmanalysis*, 5.
14 See also Edward P. Thompson, "Time, Work-Discipline, and Industrial Capitalism," *Past & Present* 38 (1967): 56–97. Thompson argues that this temporal "work-discipline" is linked to the rise of capitalism, as increasingly precise units of clock time became the basis of quantifiable value in a manner that was imposed on the workforce. See also Ryan M. Moore, "The Beat of the City: Lefebvre and Rhythmanalysis," *Situations: Project of the Radical Imagination* 5, no. 1 (2013).
15 See Lefebvre, *Rhythmanalysis*, 9–15.
16 See Helga Nowotny, "Time and Social Theory: Towards a Social Theory of Time," *Time & Society* 1, no. 3 (1992): 421–54; Nancy D. Munn, "The Cultural Anthropology of Time: A Critical Essay," *Annual Review of Anthropology* 21, no. 1 (1992): 93–123.
17 See Ted McCoy, "Joan Sangster's Socialist-Feminist History," in this volume.
18 See Mei Zhang, *China's Poor Regions: Rural-Urban Migration, Poverty, Economic Reform and Urbanisation* (London: Routledge, 2004); Ellen R. Judd, *Gender and Power in Rural North China* (Redwood City: Stanford University Press, 1994); and Rachel Murphy, *How Migrant Labor Is Changing Rural China* (Cambridge: Cambridge University Press, 2002).
19 For a discussion of land rushes, see B.R. Deepak, "China's Rural Land Grabs: Endangering Social Stability – Analysis," *Eurasia Review*, 6 April 2011, https://www.eurasiareview.com/06042011-chinas-rural-land-grabs-endangering-social-stability-analysis/; and also Greg Guldin, *What's a Peasant to Do? Village Becoming Town in Southern China* (London: Routledge, 2018).
20 See Swapna Banerjee-Guha, "Status of Rural Migrant Workers in Chinese Cities," *Economic and Political Weekly* (2011): 33–7.

21 See Rachel Murphy, *How Migrant Labor Is Changing Rural China* (Cambridge: Cambridge University Press, 2002).
22 See Barry J. Naughton, *The Chinese Economy: Transitions and Growth* (Boston: MIT Press, 2006).
23 This is a system developed under the Maoist period in China, which guaranteed job security as well as benefits to employees in state-run enterprises as well as to military and civil servants.
24 See Ching Kwan Lee, *Against the Law: Labor Protests in China's Rustbelt and Sunbelt* (Berkeley: University of California Press, 2007).
25 See Frank N. Pieke, *Transnational Chinese: Fujianese Migrants in Europe* (Redwood City: Stanford University Press, 2004). See also Yehua Dennis Wei and Xinyue Ye, "Regional Inequality in China: A Case Study of Zhejiang Province," *Tijdschrift voor economische en sociale geografie* 95, no. 1 (2004): 44–60.
26 For a fuller discussion of the unevenness of these development trajectories, see Winnie Lem, "The Dialectics of Uneven Spatial-Temporal Development: Migrants and Reproduction in Late Capitalism," in Pauline G. Barber and Winnie Lem, *Migration, Temporality, and Capitalism* (London: Palgrave Macmillan, 2018), 185–206.
27 The "floating population" refers to people who have not migrated officially and have no residency or *hukou* rights. *Hukou* refers to the system of household registration in which rights to residence, jobs, and welfare benefits are tied to place of birth. See Li Zhang, *Strangers in the City: Reconfigurations of Space, Power, and Social Networks within China's Floating Population* (Redwood City: Stanford University Press, 2001). See also Dorothy J. Solinger, *Contesting Citizenship in Urban China: Peasant Migrants, the State, and the Logic of the Market* (Berkeley: University of California Press, 1999).
28 Saskia Sassen, *The Global City* (Princeton, NJ: Princeton University Press, 1991). See also Saskia Sassen, "Locating Cities on Global Circuits," *Environment and Urbanization* 14, no. 1 (2002): 13–30.
29 See Carine Guerassimoff, "Gender and Migration Networks: New Approaches to Research on Chinese Migration to France and Europe," *Journal of Chinese Overseas* 20, no. 1 (2006): 134–45; Carine Pina-Guerassimoff, *La Chine et sa nouvelle diaspora. La mobilité au service de la puissance* (Paris: Ellipses Marketing, 2012).
30 See Monica Prasad, "Why Is France So French? Culture, Institutions, and Neoliberalism, 1974–1981," *American Journal of Sociology* 111, no. 2 (2005): 357–407; Timothy B. Smith, *France in Crisis: Welfare, Inequality, and Globalization since 1980* (Cambridge: Cambridge University Press, 2004).
31 These are pseudonyms.
32 See, e.g., Kathi Weeks, "Life within and against Work: Affective Labor, Feminist Critique, and Post-Fordist Politics," *Ephemera: Theory and Politics in Organization* 7, no. 1 (2007): 233-49.

33 See Jonathan Crary, *24/7: Late Capitalism and the Ends of Sleep* (London: Verso Books, 2013).
34 Raymond Williams, *Marxism and Literature*, vol. 392 (Oxford: Oxford Paperbacks, 1977).
35 See Nancy Fraser, "Contradictions of Capital and Care," *New Left Review* 100, no. 99 (2016): 117.
36 See Crary, *24/7: Late Capitalism and the Ends of Sleep*.
37 See Joan Sangster, *Regulating Girls and Women: Sexuality, Family, and the Law in Ontario, 1920–1960* (Toronto: University of Toronto Press, 2001). See also McCoy, this volume.
38 This is a competitive economy in which migrants from many other parts of China take up sex work as soon as they arrive, having few options to make a living in France. Competition also comes from younger Chinese women, who have legal status and who are able to seek a wealthier clientele. Like many white European sex workers, they work in wealthier areas of Paris. See Florence Levy, "Les femmes du Nord, une migration au profil atypique," *Hommes & migrations* 1254, no. 1 (2005): 45–57.
39 See Bryan D. Palmer, *Cultures of Darkness: Night Travels in the Histories of Transgression* (New York: Monthly Review Press, 2000), 16–17.
40 Matthew Beaumont, *Nightwalking: A Nocturnal History of London* (London: Verso Books, 2015).
41 Palmer, *Cultures of Darkness*.
42 See Arlie Russell Hochschild, "Love and Gold," in *Global Woman: Nannies, Maids, and Sex Workers in the New Economy*, ed. Arlie Russell Hochschild and Barbara Ehrenreich (New York: Metropolitan Books, 2003), 34–46; and also Sangster, *Regulating Girls and Women*.

15 Joan Sangster's Socialist-Feminist History

TED McCOY

Writing on women's history in Canada is deeply connected to movements for social change. A political project for women's liberation has animated the work of feminist historians for more than forty years and produced an expanding field of historical knowledge about women's lives. Historian Joan Sangster occupies a central and intriguing position in this field. She emerged alongside Canada's New Left on the vanguard of women's history by combining feminism with historical materialism. Part of a small cohort of socialist-feminist historians, Sangster's early work illustrated the importance of a class-conscious women's history in Canada. In time, this view, and Sangster's interpretation of history, was challenged by the rising influence of gender history and postmodernism. In both polemical debate and her expanding research interests, Sangster insisted that women's history could coexist alongside gender history and rejected the postmodern argument that class consciousness was no longer a useful goal of historical study. However, in an intriguing way, even as Sangster defended the principles of historical materialism, her own work slowly evolved to incorporate some of the methodologies of postmodernism – wedding them to her ongoing commitment to older historical materialist perspectives – and to address questions of race, ethnicity, and representation in women's history. Ultimately, Sangster has illustrated the elasticity of the socialist-feminist project and the ways its goals of understanding social history can continue to develop and expand. In the process of this development, Sangster has created a body of work that illustrates the ongoing strengths of a socialist-feminist view of history that combines class and gender analysis. Looking at this longer perspective on Sangster's career reveals a body of work that illustrates the powerful possibilities of a commitment to the politics and praxis of socialist-feminist history.

Joan Sangster's work began in the 1970s at the confluence of working-class and women's history, both undergoing a renaissance driven by the rise of the New Left. But they did not emerge together. Although both disciplines had common concerns and methodologies, there was a central divide. Women's history was assumed to be linked to gender theory, while labour history proceeded from class analysis. For a new cohort of historians that included Sangster, the desire was to bring these worlds together and make their seemingly separate politics a common ground. This was captured in a 1974 collection called *Women at Work, 1850–1930*. The introduction by Linda Kealey positions the collection like this: "Working within a Marxist framework, the authors have attempted to demonstrate the interrelations between economic and social factors in the secondary position of the female worker."[1] These were very early days for the movement, but the job at hand for socialist-feminist history in the 1970s came into view. It was a new project to grasp at capitalism as a totality and understand women's experience within it. Even though her first published works appeared slightly later than the 1975 collection, we could place Sangster in this cohort of socialist feminists who were at the forefront of writing working-class women's history in a way that placed politics at the foreground of the choices made about topics, theory, and methodology.[2]

We can broaden this perspective to consider the early days of socialist feminism itself in a somewhat larger context than the world of academic history. Socialist feminism emerged alongside radical feminism at the end of the 1960s in groups based in Chicago, Boston, and New York, as well as Toronto and Vancouver. The early radical groups sought to differentiate themselves from both peace movements and the New Left in their insistence upon not subordinating women's issues to other causes. But the politics were not exclusionary, and those who espoused them were not unwilling to debate other forms of liberation. Instead, socialist feminism emerged with many of the same goals as other areas of the Left but with the insistence that ending male supremacy was essential for all causes of social justice.[3] In 1976, Barbara Ehrenreich addressed the new label "socialist feminism" and provided some clarity around the fledgling movement. She argued that "socialist" on its own seemed inadequate and narrow and that feminist theory could not properly address class concerns. Imperfect as the term was, Ehrenreich admitted that "socialist feminism" would have to stand in for what the movement truly represented: "socialist internationalist anti-racist, anti-heterosexist feminism."[4] These are critical ways of looking at the world, according to Ehrenreich, and they bring us to a way of understanding society in terms of its antagonisms.[5] Looking back in 1990, Elizabeth

Fox-Genovese noted that attempts at defining socialist feminism faced the difficulty of distinguishing it from both radical feminism and Marxism.[6] It shares elements of both; it resists the biologism of radical feminism and simultaneously enlarges the Marxist project to understand alienation to include women's subordination as a structural feature of capitalist society.[7] Writing in 2003 on the legacy of the "second wave," Linda Gordon characterized the early movement as a part of the broad New Left, arguing that socialist feminists saw their work as part of a larger campaign against injustice. She wrote, "They believe that sex/gender inequality contributed to class, race, sexual, militarist and environment injustices, soon adding in disability, and various forms of sex and gender queerness."[8]

If we are to understand the emergence of women's history as a central and important concern, we also need to see it in relationship to the rise of the new labour history. The two fields were mutually beneficial to each other, particularly in their relationship to social history. In some ways, women's history had a steeper hill to climb. Canadian labour historians in the early 1970s could draw on an emerging field of new labour history in the UK and the United States that included Herbert Gutman, Eugene Genovese, and E.P. Thompson. The new labour historians also fell into more masculinist studies of work and labour that, without care, could exclude the experiences of women without raising much objection within the field. In contrast, women's history on the left was being written against the backdrop of an older tradition of liberal middle-class women's history that did not typically address working people or tended to emphasize biographies of prominent women.[9] It is easy to see why early socialist-feminist historians looked to the new labour historians as compatriots in a common project. Another mutual point of interest between them was the cultural approach associated with the new labour history, which was keenly interested in the different ways that class mattered in Canadian history *outside* of union halls and shop floors. The lived experiences of working people were a place to start and could be found in churches, community halls, pubs, and importantly, the home. The lives of men *and* women were to be found in this methodological approach and counted as one cornerstone in the early construction of a working-class history that included women. This methodology connected back to striving to understand the totality of capitalist society. While the new labour historians in Canada were attuned to gender in a way that previous generations of labour historians were not, there was still much to be done to bring these perspectives together. In her career-spanning retrospective collection published in 2011, Sangster discusses her own relationship to New Left scholars and the different directions that feminist historians embarked upon in the early days of women's history. She writes:

> Some historians put more emphasis on gender oppression, seeing this as a means of "changing the past and the present," while others drew on E.P. Thompson's Marxist-humanist vision of history and feminist socialist debates about the relationships between capitalism and patriarchy. My socialization was shaped particularly by the latter two currents: Thompson's emphasis on class formation as both a material and cultural phenomenon, on experience as a dialectical process, and on the importance of human agency seemed to offer a vision of the past that opened up rather than closed down the possibilities of a feminist and socialist analysis.[10]

Sangster's first book made important connections between politics and praxis in several interesting ways. *Dreams of Equality*, published in 1989 but drawing on Sangster's dissertation research from the late 1970s, explores the history of women on the Canadian left between 1920 and 1950. Sangster researched women on the Canadian left at a time when socialist-feminist thought was blossoming. But she realized that the movement also suffered from a type of amnesia about the contributions of a previous generation of women on the left. Here was a moment where socialist feminism felt brand new and exciting, but the history of feminist organizing was often forgotten. A fascinating interplay between historian and subject is at work in Sangster's early research on the left. She was revealing the historical links between women's experiences of class and gender oppression as a way of understanding the developing tradition of feminist socialism. She was also answering larger questions about the real material conditions women were fighting for in their search for equality. In his piece in this volume, Alvin Finkel addresses similar questions about how leftist regimes have delivered greater equality and opportunity for women, illustrating that such goals could be more than just dreams.

In this early research, we find the seeds of Sangster's own development as a historian and the early connections she must have made between politics and praxis as a researcher. Where to place her focus? What was important about women's lives? The choices she made in this early work shaped much of what came after because she had discovered, and built upon, a socialist-feminist tradition from the early twentieth century that had already made important conclusions about gender and class. There is no doubt that Sangster's politics and approach to socialist-feminist history itself were shaped by her research on the political world of the Communist Party of Canada (CPC) and the Co-operative Commonwealth Federation (CCF).

As much as Sangster's first book was about the politics of socialist feminists, it was also intended to understand the lives of the women who made up the movement and to chronicle their experiences fighting for a utopian future. The lives and experiences of women are a unifying theme in the entire first decade of her work, illustrating the wedding of Sangster's Thompsonian perspective to feminist politics. We could learn something of this connection by tracing Sangster's history of women on the left and following the thread forward to her second monograph, *Earning Respect*. This progression hints at Sangster's efforts to understand not just left politics but the greater totality of women's lives. Between her first two books, Sangster chronicled the important ways that women's economic lives and family roles intersected with politics. This model of totality gave her early work the ability to see structure and experience as mutually constitutive of women's history. The resulting research was not always explicitly political. For example, in a 1978 *Labour/Le Travailleur* piece on the 1907 Bell Telephone strike, Sangster writes about a failed strike that was rooted in demands for women's wages and working conditions at the Bell switchboards. She notes that the women were not radicals; they were pragmatists who were protesting conditions at work, which Sangster then connected to the material conditions of their lives at home.[11] The work lives of these women were different from those of the political CCF and CPC party members, but they shared many of the same goals connected to combating exploitation and making a stand against the damage that capitalism could wreak on women's home and family lives. There are also important continuities linking the earliest decades of the twentieth century with the 1960s, as is noted in Mason Godden's chapter in this volume on the Dare Foods strike of 1972–3. Withholding their labour would always be a marker of women's agency and political potential, and this commitment deepened in the 1960s as women found their place in the New Left and working-class struggles for equality.[12] Andrea Samoil's chapter in this volume on the 1995 Calgary laundry workers' strike presents additional parallels of these themes but in a very different era of neoliberal industrial conflict and legality.

Earning Respect

True to the roots of her early influences, Sangster's projects after *Dreams of Equality* moved to more fully integrate women's history with labour history as she examined topics ranging from the gendered nature of employer paternalism to feminist methodologies in the pursuit of working-class histories. Sangster's *Earning Respect* includes a clearer distillation of how socialist feminism informs the theoretical framework and methodology of her research. *Earning Respect* is a much wider investigation, looking at the experience of women in the workplace in a small Ontario city. But the book is constructed in a way that illustrates Sangster grappling with the scope of women's history. She argues that gender and class must be brought together, building upon Joan Kelly's feminist theory of doubled vision.[13] Discussing the need for a dual view, Sangster writes, "The assumption that there are two distinct social systems of oppression can, however, lead to a fragmented understanding of what is actually experienced as unified social life; or it can lead to an inherent privileging of either class or sex oppression, or to the assumption that patriarchal oppression is located in the family, and class oppression in the workplace."[14] *Earning Respect* illustrates the ways that we can move beyond this dichotomous view of women's lives. Socialist feminism reaches for an interpretation that is a unified theory of capitalist patriarchy in which class and gender are interdependent and inseparable.[15] *Earning Respect* is about one small town but reaches for a transcendent totality that has moved our understanding of how women lived and worked in twentieth-century capitalism. This has entailed understanding the multiple manifestations of patriarchy in women's lives, and at the same time, understanding the materialist roots of patriarchy itself. Sangster writes, "The social, familial, and psychic structures that shape male dominance need to be analysed in the historical context of class relations."[16] This is among the strongest statements Sangster makes in her body of work about the value of socialist-feminist history, staking a claim for what it can accomplish and also suggesting what it is *not*. Sangster gestures toward a debate that would come to overtake women's history in the 1990s. Describing *Earning Respect*, Sangster notes that her writing is influenced by the socialist-feminist tradition and is distinct from the "antihumanism, and pessimism about human agency that is ingrained in so much poststructuralist writing."[17] Here Sangster marks a sharp divide between a Marxist-humanist position and the growing influence of postmodernism and a turn toward discursive gender analysis as the primary analytical lens of women's history.

At the same time that *Earning Respect* was published, Sangster engaged in a written exchange about the trajectory of women's history and the influence of postmodernism in shaping the field. "Beyond Dichotomies," published in *Left History*, assesses the field and responds to the irony of some writers of women's history being portrayed as out of touch and out of date with the advances of postmodernism and the insights of the new gender history. In just two decades, the emerging field of women's history was already in the rear view as a new generation rode toward a more complete understanding of history defined by gender. This was the disruptive tendency of the postmodern turn at work – creating a false dichotomy between the structural and the poststructural and casting aside what women's history had created. The new practitioners even sought to reclaim feminism from the world of women's history; true feminists, it was suggested, would be concerned with gender, not merely women.[18]

It isn't difficult to see why Sangster chose to write polemically on the topic at this particular moment in the 1990s. The debate that Sangster describes was also about a deeper divide in the field of women's history in which the positions of socialist feminism were challenged. More than challenged, really, as the newer insights into gender and poststructuralism effectively flattened the theoretical and methodological contributions of the entire field of women's history – particularly socialist-feminist history. Sangster's *Left History* piece insists on the larger project that socialist feminism initiated in the 1970s and clarifies some of its enduring contributions. First among these is the need to continue to recognize the ongoing marginalization and oppression of women – indeed, that there was still a "woman question" that required attention. Sangster connects this to the real politics of academic spaces, in which women were forced to fight politically just to find the space, resources, and support necessary to engage in this work.[19] The second key contribution Sangster returns to is the centrality of class to the socialist-feminist project and the inherent problems of moving past it to focus instead on questions of identity. This position is a reminder of the value of women's history that is really an attempt at a more encompassing social history of women, understanding them in relationship to the many structural and material realities that make up their experience. This is lost, Sangster suggests, in the rush toward understanding gender as a constructed identity. Sangster is arguing that long before gender historians insisted on incorporating concepts like masculinity into our understanding of gender, there was a concerted effort to reveal the totality of women's experiences throughout Canadian history.[20] Moreover, the project is not finished. This project is a return to the notion of the Thompsonian approach to women's history – a socialist feminism that seeks to understand women's experiences in a more complete way.

Sangster's polemic prompted a number of responses, some more agreeable than others. The point of pausing on this debate is not to relitigate the controversy in Sangster's favour. Rather, it is to highlight an interesting moment in the development of Sangster's socialist feminism (and the movement in general) where scholars engaged in a deep consideration about what the women's history project in Canada had become and could accomplish in the future.

Franca Iacovetta and Linda Kealey wrote a response in *Left History* that was collegial but challenging. They drew attention to recent works of feminist history that bridged that gap between women's history and gender history emphasized by Sangster.[21] A more confrontational response was written by Karen Dubinsky and Lynne Marks. They portrayed Sangster as narrow and rigid, suggesting that the dichotomies described in her piece were of her own creation.[22] Dubinsky and Marks argued for the need to see a relationship rather than a succession: "Gender history, as we see it, is closely linked to women's history – it neither supersedes it nor renders it obsolete."[23] Dubinsky and Marks also challenged what they saw as Sangster's privileging of the socialist-feminist perspective and criticized Sangster's insistence on an experiential history using the Marxist-humanist model. This critique contains hints of an older debate that had unfolded within Canadian labour history as a new generation of labour historians like Wayne Roberts, Bryan D. Palmer, and Gregory Kealey advanced interpretations of history that emphasized working-class culture.[24] The older debate revolved around how historians should understand and privilege the process of class formation. In Sangster's interpretation of this debate, her *Left History* piece juxtaposed experience with identity as a shorthand for talking about the poststructuralist movement away from understanding class and class formation that would align with a socialist-feminist interpretation of history. Dubinsky and Marks made a similar point, but their repeated refusals belied the exact shift in direction that Sangster was commenting upon in her original piece. In their response, the field of women's history was being subordinated to gender history by the suggestion that gender history addressed the inadequacies of the older approaches. In a final response to Dubinsky and Marks, Sangster objected to this privileging and the suggestion that gender history was methodologically and theoretically superior to existing feminist history. There was no resolution in the debate, just a serious dissention by Sangster that reiterated the importance of the original socialist-feminist project and the continued insight that it could bring to both women's history and gender history.[25]

Expanding the Story

Sangster continued to write historiographically about feminism and working-class history. An essay published at the turn of the twenty-first century in *Labour/Le Travail* looks back at thirty years of feminist and working-class history to assess accomplishments, evolutions, and missed opportunities.[26] This historiographical essay from 2000 strikes a pessimistic note about the state of leftist organizing, resistance to capitalism, and the direction of the historical profession. At the root of this pessimism is a thought that contrasts the present day with the possibilities of alternatives that once existed and were not chosen. (One wonders what an updated version of the essay for 2024 might conclude about our current trajectory!) Things remain particularly inauspicious, Sangster notes, for the state of the socialist-feminist project inside and outside the academy. Sangster addresses the feminist project begun in the 1970s and finds that its attention to class is in a state of decline, if not crisis. Sangster writes, "In the broader historical profession, changes in social theory engendered an aversion to the very notion of structure in history, to the grounding of texts in historical contexts, to 'modernist empiricist' strategies of recovery, and certainly to Marxist 'interventions of dissent' lodged against mainstream history."[27] This moment is contrasted with a reminder that the first decade of women's history, in concert with historians of the new labour movement, was a decade of genuine optimism and possibility that was characterized by a common emancipatory politics that animated both working-class history and women's history.

At a moment when few voices came to the defence of a socialist-feminist approach, Sangster continued to defend her position. She writes, "It seems inescapable that core post-structuralist ideas will pull the rug out from many of the traditional concepts underpinning working-class history. By rejecting class as a taken-for-granted 'foundational' category and deriding 'grand theory,' they question a basic starting point for past analysis." Sangster also makes a stand against the poststructuralist deconstruction of experience, the subject, and agency.[28] This is a return to a long-held position that roots her understanding of history in the Thompsonian model, identifying the centrality of class consciousness. This position emerges, Sangster states again in her 2000 piece, "from the interplay of human agency with social, cultural, and economic foundations and ideologies."[29] The same questions emerge that animated both socialist feminists and the new labour historians: Can we know the history of experience? As it was twenty years ago, it now seems essential to continue to struggle toward this goal, particularly if we are to continue an interest in understanding histories that connect human agency with the possibilities of resilience and resistance. Sangster concludes this sweeping essay by returning to a simple question: whether the story of class formation has become thoroughly gendered.[30] She attempts to remember the praxis of historical research, reminding us that we are not bystanders to our political context. What is the purpose of history if not to make radical connections to the present? Starting this overview of thirty years of feminist history, Sangster includes a warning about the direction of capitalism. She returns to this note at the conclusion of the essay and adds the reminder that the praxis of labour history is to counter these trends. She writes, "Surely, as globalized capitalism and the deconstruction of the welfare state become menacing forces, even a 'totalizing logic' for working peoples, some of the traditional topics of labour history, including wage work, the sexual division of labour, consumer organizing, and socialist politics, should seem more, not less prescient."[31] This point from the year 2000 is more powerful still in the year 2024, as every trend Sangster identified is accelerated and exacerbated by our troubling political trajectory.

A decade after Sangster's study of socialist feminists in the Communist Party and the CCF, she was moving beyond the study of work and toward a consideration of women and the law. In her millennium *Labour/Le Travail* historiography, she gestures toward this shift somewhat apologetically, grouping herself together with other feminists who were moving beyond or away from the study of women and work. Sangster needed no apology for this direction. There is a clear connection between these two distinct eras of her career. The link is forged in how the different studies apply similar research and methodological questions about women in different social, political, and domestic settings.

Sangster's departure into legal history was not an abandonment of socialist-feminist history, but an expansion of her original projects. It was critical for socialist-feminist writers to begin applying the insights of women's history and labour history to questions about the law, particularly in response to concurrent investigations by other historians that assumed a far more postmodernist approach to the law.[32] Sangster's approach to the law, applying socialist-feminist and radical perspectives, illustrated a way forward and a method by which future historians could adopt the insights of historical materialism and feminism, and in the process, providing a toolkit to respond to the inherently conservative impulses of older approaches to legal history.

Sangster is part of a socialist-feminist tradition that includes writers like Pat Carlen, who advanced a radical critique of punishment and the law and did this in part by applying a new perspective to shift our understanding.[33] For example, Carlen writes about "breaking the legal bond" by disconnecting crime from punishment and refuses to see imprisonment as the natural consequence of the ways that a patriarchal society defines the lives of criminalized women.[34] This helps us to answer simple questions differently – questions such as, why do some women end up in prison? Why do we treat the incarcerated in particular ways? What are the types of oppressive structures that incarceration reproduces?

This research appears primarily in two books, *Regulating Girls and Women* and *Girl Trouble*. Echoing Carlen's work, in *Girl Trouble* Sangster suggests that girls and women were not in conflict with the law, they were in conflict with society. This seemingly simple distinction is revolutionary to the study of law from a radical perspective. We can see punishment, regulation, and oppression on their own terms and understand the materiality of how women come to be the target of different types of regulation and imprisonment. It allows us to see imprisonment not just as the sentence, in terms of months and years, but also as what happens within the penitentiary and what imprisoned women endure. Rather than stories about legal conviction, these women's lives are stories about poverty, class division, and patriarchal relations.

Sangster's two monographs on women and the law also reveal a historian deeply engaged in academic debates and influenced by them. In *Regulating Girls and Women*, she acknowledges the influence of the shifting academic tides toward questions of deconstruction and subjectivity, finding that they have pushed her toward a different way of looking at particular evidence.[35] In looking at the history of girls and the law, Sangster confronts a topic that demands engagement with the history of representation and discourse. Case files, court records, and the testimony of parents and social workers frequently depict the lives of girls and affected the outcomes of their entanglements with the law, but they do not tell the entire story. P.E. Bryden's chapter in this volume on the silences of the historical record reflects Sangster's approach to reading these sources for the deeper stories that bring to light how women experienced regulation and the law.

Moral regulation is a complex historical phenomenon to untangle, and to do so without consideration of Foucauldian notions of power leaves the historian without a powerful tool for understanding the ways in which discourses gained ascendancy. But as Sangster notes in *Through Feminist Eyes*, "Foucault helped me understand the 'how' of criminalization, but not entirely the 'why.'"[36] In looking back at her own engagement with Foucault and postmodernism, Sangster reaffirms her commitment to socialist feminism: "Without understanding the relations of production and social reproduction that framed these girls' lives (including patriarchal familial relations), and without understanding the legacies of colonialism, we could not completely understand how many girls became designated as delinquents by the experts, the state, and by their own families."[37] Even though Sangster was moving into areas outside the world of labour and the workplace, it is clear that she continued to work with the methodologies of working-class history. Like the best social historians, Sangster was reaching for totality in her view. Doubtlessly driven by an organic curiosity about uncharted areas of the archive such as court records and family case files, her view remained firmly rooted in trying to understand working-class experiences and in expanding the world of women's history.

One of the criticisms of the first generation of Canadian women's history that predominated in the 1980s was the charge that it had paid insufficient attention to race and ethnicity. Women's history expanded so significantly in the 1980s and early 1990s that numerous studies of working-class history began to more fully address questions of race and ethnicity and integrate these perspectives into histories of work.[38] One of the enduring values of a socialist-feminist perspective is that it does not preclude thinking about the ways that racialization and colonialism have contributed to the oppressive structures of the law. Looking at the history of girls' incarceration, Sangster confronts the undeniable reality that racialized girls and women faced moral and legal regulation disproportionately compared to those who were white and middle class.

Sangster's writing on Indigenous topics demonstrates the scope of what feminist scholarship in Canada might accomplish. This she does by bringing Indigenous women inside the world of labour history, working to see their labour and contributions, but also by expanding the toolkit of how labour historians see Indigenous people. Sangster continued to push the margins of socialist-feminist history to understand colonialism in new ways. Focusing on Indigenous women's labour, she recovers the history of a group of workers who were once invisible to the political economy of Canadian fur due to the absence of a feminist lens, or who were abstracted by postmodern analysis into bodies that helped facilitate desire, commodity, and consumerism. Instead, Sangster returns to some of the "old-fashioned" (her words in 2007) questions that have animated socialist feminism and continue to resonate. How did women experience their economic relationships? Focusing on Indigenous women as labouring bodies, she asks, "If bodies are recognized only within an abstract circle of discourse, will we not lose our connection to a politics of social transformation that understands that the oppression, maiming, and utilization of bodies is facilitated by a particular set of social relations, economic structures, and forms of injustice?"[39] This writes Indigenous women back into labour history, illustrating that they are not on the margins or invisible unless historians consciously choose not to see them. Here too representation matters, illustrating again that Sangster successfully incorporates cultural analysis into her understanding of labour history. For she argues that if we see only the colonialist image of labouring Indigenous women, we contribute to the "erasure of their labouring bodies."[40] Though the incorporation of discourse analysis is new, this is an old idea, or rather, a consistently important idea since the days of Sangster's first steps in women's history. Sangster would expand on her analysis of colonialism, representation, and women in 2016's *The Iconic North: Cultural Constructions of Aboriginal Life in Postwar Canada*. The questions raised in *The Iconic North* around cultural discourses about the North emerged from Sangster's work on Indigenous women and paid labour and an insistence that the underlying principles of socialist feminism can illuminate questions about culture. She writes, "Cultural constructions of the North must be framed within the changing political economy and history of postwar Canada. A focus on culture need not generate a *culturalist* discursive determinism or assume a rejection a historical materialism, feminism, or traditional empirical methods of historical research, all of which assume there is a reality out there to be grasped – perhaps not definitively known, but grasped."[41] Sangster's expansive discussion of cultural construction in and about the North illustrates another iteration of the elasticity of the socialist-feminist project. This more expansive view was particularly true as it matured into the twenty-first century and writers moved in and out of topics traditionally associated with political economy or women's history. The expanding range of Sangster's historical interests was no doubt facilitated by the multiple ways her founding methodology could illuminate new topics.

Back to Work

Much like Sangster's earliest history of women on the left, when she returned wholly to labour history in 2010's *Transforming Labour*, she found the past rushing to meet the present. Starting in the immediate postwar period, *Transforming Labour* tracks the experience of women in the workplace into the early 1970s. This places her subjects in the same era as the one that gave rise to her own political sensibilities at the moment of the rise of the new labour movement. Full circle indeed.

Transforming Labour is notable among Sangster's work for its nuanced discussion of socialist feminism. Sangster seeks to work within the tradition of feminist political economy to address questions of class and gender, both analytical categories informed by an understanding of the centrality of capitalist accumulation, colonialism, and state initiatives. These projects raise questions about the effect of ideology, culture, and human agency on class, gender, and race relationships.[42] Here Sangster gestures toward the necessity of understanding these questions through an intersectional analysis. But she cautions that this should not lead to the deconstruction of certain categories, particularly class relations. Pointing toward feminist political economy to add insight, Sangster writes, "[Feminist political economy] has built on political economy's assumption that material conditions are a 'starting point' for social analysis, but rather than accepting class as the (over)determining category of analysis, it insists that other hierarchies and oppressions, both within and across class relations, be addressed as well ... Class formation is always mediated by gender and race relations, and while theoretically distinct, these categories are actually inseparable."[43] Sangster connects the macro-structures provided by political economy to her feminist historical materialism, adding the crucial elements of the accumulated evidence about women's lives and searching for a more nuanced and complete view of class formation. This combination brings together material structure and human agency, social formations and lived experience.[44] There is also an ongoing tension in these positions with the postmodern response that Sangster has debated throughout her career. *Transforming Labour* is a confident response to two decades of postmodernist writing that steps around concepts of structure and agency as unimportant to a more discursive interpretation. As part of the same ongoing debate, Sangster also offers a robust defence of the idea of Thompsonian experience: "'Experience' remains useful to the writing of women's labour history if we explore it as a layered process that is both lived and construed; as both a point of origin and as discursively constructed: as a dialectic of both 'first and third person' perspectives. If viewed with the reflective scepticism that is central to all historical research, it need not be 'put on a pedestal, reified, or taken as self-evident.'"[45] What is the inherent power of this approach? Sangster makes a simple argument, that there is a political judgment at work in the willingness to see the experience of oppression and exploitation in her subjects' history. This is a judgement that Sangster has made throughout her career as she has expanded and deepened her understanding of working people. In *Transforming Labour*, she concludes, "If we dismiss the complaints, voices, and actions of workers in the past as little more than rhetorical devices, discursive possibilities, or one of many contending perspectives of the time, the concepts of exploitation, oppression, and justice become rather meaningless."[46] Using these insights, Sangster has continued to expand her view of history both within and beyond working-class and labour history. Her choices in the past decade illustrate the essential strengths and elasticity of the methodologies of socialist-feminist history. In 2019, Sangster published *One Hundred Years of Struggle*, which examines the push for women's suffrage in Canada.[47] Here she circles back to a historical topic that traditionally spotlighted middle-class suffragists in Canada like Nellie McClung. By reordering the chronology of suffragism in Canada, Sangster recovers the forgotten voices of radical feminists like Margret Benedictsson and Mary Ann Shadd Cary. In bringing together both prominent and forgotten voices, Sangster finds the enduring lessons in struggling against patriarchy and toward women's emancipation.

Conclusion

The years since the start of the COVID-19 pandemic have laid out a brutal and unforgiving political landscape, and the way forward for historians can sometimes feel uncertain. We are coming to grips with the rise (and fall) of Black Lives Matter protests calling for police and prison abolition, related decolonial movements in Canada, and a growing interest among a new generation in leftist ideals. Among the calls for legal revolution are ongoing struggles toward socialism and gender equality, both characterized by the brief surge (and ultimate retreat) of the Bernie Sanders campaign for the American presidency. The times are difficult, but they always were. And if we want to chart a path in which history can speak to possibilities and the future, there are examples that can help. Socialist-feminist historical scholarship has long served as an example. If we look back at the recent past, there some encouraging examples of where feminist history highlighted alternatives and possibilities that can move us beyond this moment in time and into the future. One clear example of scholarship that can do this is work attuned to the political and analytical concerns illustrated throughout Joan Sangster's socialist-feminist history. Things are perhaps not as dire as Sangster imagined twenty years ago. The left in Canada, if not resurgent, has at least been awakened by wave after wave of crisis and the absolute absence of realistic solutions offered by liberal politics. Sangster has contributed to the historical field through the volume and breadth of her writing and thirty years of teaching at Trent University. The compounding effect of this lifetime of research and teaching is immeasurable and gives credence to the depth of conviction of Sangster's socialist-feminist politics. Always reaching for the elusive totality that will bring the past to light, she has shown an example of how we might still join praxis and politics in a way that is radical and emancipatory.

NOTES

1 Janice Acton and Bonnie Shepard, *Women at Work: Ontario, 1850–1930* (Toronto: Canadian Women's Educational Press, 1974).
2 In Canada, this included Janice Acton, Bonnie Shepard, Linda Kealey, Wayne Roberts, Alice Klein, and Joan Sangster.
3 Elizabeth Lapovsky Kennedy, "Socialist Feminism: What Difference Did It Make to the History of Women's Studies?," *Feminist Studies* 34, no. 3 (2008): 499–500. On this era, see also Ruth Rosen, *The World Split Open: How the Modern Women's Movement Changed America* (New York: Viking, 2000); Sarah M. Evans, *Tidal Wave: How Women Changed America at Century's End* (New York: Free Press, 2003).
4 Barbara Ehrenreich, "What Is Socialist Feminism," *Marxists Internet Archive*, accessed 12 August 2014, https://www.marxists.org/subject/women/authors/ehrenreich-barbara/socialist-feminism.htm.
5 Ehrenreich, "What Is Socialist Feminism."
6 Elizabeth Fox-Genovese, "Socialist-Feminist American Women's History," *Journal of Women's History* 1, no. 3 (1990): 181.
7 Fox-Genovese, "Socialist-Feminist American Women's History," 182.
8 Linda Gordon, "Socialist Feminism: The Legacy of the 'Second Wave,'" *New Labor Forum* 22, no. 3 (2013): 20–8.
9 An excellent overview of the development of Canadian women's history in the 1970s appears in Margaret Conrad, "The Re-birth of Canada's Past: A Decade of Women's History," *Acadiensis* 12, no. 2 (1983): 140–62.
10 Joan Sangster, *Through Feminist Eyes: Essays on Canadian Women's History* (Edmonton: Athabasca University Press, 2011), 12.
11 Joan Sangster, "The 1907 Bell Telephone Strike: Organizing Women Workers," in *Through Feminist Eyes*, 119.
12 Joan Sangster, "Radical Ruptures: Feminism, Labor, and the Left in the Long Sixties in Canada," *American Review of Canadian Studies* 40, no. 1 (2010): 1–21.
13 Joan Kelly, "The Doubled Vision of Feminist Theory: A Postscript to the 'Women and Power' Conference," *Feminist Studies* 5, no. 1 (1979): 216–27.

See also Judith R. Walkowitz, Judith L. Newton, and Mary P. Ryan, eds., *Sex and Class in Women's History*, Routledge Library Editions: Women's History (London: Taylor and Francis, 2013).
14 Joan Sangster, *Earning Respect: The Lives of Working Women in Small-Town Ontario, 1920–1960* (Toronto: University of Toronto Press, 1995), 6, 7.
15 Sangster, *Earning Respect*, 6, 7.
16 Sangster, *Earning Respect*, 7.
17 Sangster, *Earning Respect*, 35.
18 Sangster's *Left History* article includes this quote from Valverde: "Feminist history is more important than women's history ... [for] feminist history is about gender, not women." Joan Sangster, "Beyond Dichotomies: Re-assessing Gender History and Women's History in Canada," *Left History* 3, no. 1 (Spring/Summer 1995): 110, quoting Mariana Valverde, *The Age of Light, Soap, and Water: Moral Reform in English Canada, 1865–1925* (Toronto: University of Toronto Press, 1991), 12.
19 Joan Sangster, "Beyond Dichotomies," 113.
20 Sangster also acknowledges that this perspective is connected to an older idea of feminist history that incorporates the totality of men's and women's histories. She cites Alison Prentice and Ruth Roach Pierson, "Feminism and the Writing and Teaching of History," *Atlantis* 7, no. 2 (Spring 1982): 37–46.
21 Examples of such works include Suzanne Morton, *Ideal Surroundings: Domestic Life in a Working-Class Suburb in the 1920s* (Toronto: University of Toronto Press, 1995); Mark Rosenfeld, "'It Was a Hard Life': Class and Gender in the Work and Family Rhythms of a Railway Town, 1920–1950," *Historical Papers* 23, no. 1 (1988): 237–79; Janet Guildford and Suzanne Morton, eds., *Separate Spheres: Women's Worlds in the 19th-Century Maritimes* (Fredericton: Acadiensis Press, 1994).
22 Karen Dubinsky and Lynne Marks, "Beyond Purity: A Response to Sangster," *Left History* 4, no. 1 (1996): 207.
23 Dubinsky and Marks, "Beyond Purity," 207.
24 For a good discussion of the debate around working-class culture, see Chad Pearson, "On Polemics and Provocations: Bryan D. Palmer v. the Liberal Anti-Marxists," in *Dissenting Traditions: Essays on Bryan D. Palmer, Marxism, and History*, ed. Sean Carleton, Ted McCoy, and Julia Smith (Edmonton: Athabasca University Press, 2021), 127–67.
25 Joan Sangster, "Reconsidering Dichotomies," *Left History* 4, no. 1 (1996): 239.
26 Joan Sangster, "Gender, Family & Sex: Feminism and the Making of Canadian Working-Class History: Exploring the Past, Present and Future," *Labour/Le Travail*, no. 46 (2000): 127–65.
27 Sangster, "Gender, Family & Sex," 154–5.

28 In particular, Sangster cites the work of Marianna Valverde, in which these questions are raised. See Valverde, "Post Structuralist Gender Historians: Are We Those Names?," *Labour/Le Travail* 25 (1990): 227–36; "Deconstructive Marxism," *Labour/Le Travail* 36 (Fall 1995): 329–40.
29 Sangster, "Gender, Family & Sex," 158.
30 Sangster, "Gender, Family & Sex," 162.
31 Sangster, "Gender, Family & Sex," 164.
32 See Mariana Valverde, *The Age of Light, Soap, and Water*; Mona Gleason, *Lost Kids: Vulnerable Children and Youth in Twentieth-Century Canada and the United States* (Vancouver: UBC Press, 2010); and Kelly Hannah-Moffat, *Punishment in Disguise: Penal Governance and Federal Imprisonment of Women in Canada* (Toronto: University of Toronto Press, 2001).
33 Pat Carlen, "Radical Criminology, Penal Politics, and the Rule of Law," in *Radical Issues in Criminology*, ed. Pat Carlen and Mike Collison (Totowa, NJ: Rowman & Littlefield, 1980), 7–25. See also Carol Smart, *Women, Crime, and Criminology* (London: Routledge, 1976).
34 Pat Carlen, "Radical Criminology, Penal Politics, and the Rule of Law," 15.
35 Joan Sangster, *Regulating Girls and Women: Sexuality, Family, and the Law in Ontario, 1920–1960* (Toronto: Oxford University Press, 2001), 2.
36 Joan Sangster, *Through Feminist Eyes*, 245.
37 Joan Sangster, *Through Feminist Eyes*, 245.
38 For a very selected list, see key works such as Ruth Frager, *Sweatshop Strife: Class, Ethnicity, and Gender in the Jewish Labour Movement of Toronto, 1900–39* (Toronto: University of Toronto Press, 1992); Dionne Brand, *No Burden to Carry: The Lives of Black Working Women in Ontario, 1920s to 1950s* (Toronto: Women's Press, 1991); and Franca Iacovetta, *Such Hardworking People: Italian Immigrants in Postwar Toronto* (Montreal: McGill-Queen's University Press, 1992).
39 Joan Sangster, "Making a Fur Coat: Women, the Labouring Body, and Working-Class History," *International Review of Social History* 52, no. 2 (2007): 246.
40 Joan Sangster, "Making a Fur Coat," 268.
41 Italics in original. Joan Sangster, *The Iconic North: Cultural Constructions of Aboriginal Life in Postwar Canada* (Vancouver: UBC Press, 2016), 5.
42 Joan Sangster, *Transforming Labour: Women and Work in Post-war Canada* (Toronto: University of Toronto Press, 2010), 11.
43 Sangster, *Transforming Labour*, 12.
44 Sangster, *Transforming Labour*, 12.
45 Sangster, *Transforming Labour*, 14.
46 Sangster, *Transforming Labour*, 14.
47 Joan Sangster, *One Hundred Years of Struggle: The History of Women and the Vote in Canada* (Vancouver: UBC Press, 2018).

Contributors

Sean Antaya is an independent researcher and library worker based in Windsor, Ontario. His research focuses mainly on North American labour history. He is also interested in music history and runs an ongoing event series promoting traditional blues and folk music at the Windsor Public Library.

P.E. Bryden is a professor of history at the University of Victoria and the author or editor of numerous volumes on Canadian history and politics, including *Canada: A Political Biography* (Don Mills, ON: Oxford University Press, 2016). She has recently served as the president of the Canadian Historical Association and as co-editor of the *Canadian Historical Review*. Her current project is a study of political scandal in Canada since Confederation.

Gabriela Castillo is a PhD candidate in the socio-economic history of the Americas. Her current work focuses on Canada-Chile relations and navigates the intricate intersections of gender, race, and labour from a decolonial perspective while challenging the multifaceted dynamics of power and oppression.

Lori Chambers has published books on the history of adoption law, marital property, single parenthood, and gender-based violence. She is a professor in the Department of Gender and Women's Studies at Lakehead University, Thunder Bay, where she teaches courses in feminist legal history, feminist theory, gender-based violence, and queer studies. She is also actively engaged in community-based reform and shares her scholarly insights widely with the public. In 2021, she was inducted into the Royal Society of Canada.

Alvin Finkel is professor emeritus of history at Athabasca University. He is author, co-author, editor, or co-editor of fourteen books, including *Social Policy and Practice in Canada: A History* (Waterloo, ON: Wilfrid Laurier University Press, 2006); *Compassion: A Global History of Social Policy* (London: Red Globe Press, 2019); *The Social Credit Phenomenon in Alberta* (Toronto: University of Toronto Press, 1989); *Working People in Alberta: A History* (Edmonton: Athabasca University Press, 2012); *Our Lives: Canada since 1945* (Toronto: J. Lorimer, 1997); and the two-volume *History of the Canadian Peoples* (Toronto: Pearson, 2021), currently in its seventh edition.

Barbara M. Freeman is a media historian and an adjunct research professor in the School of Journalism and Communication, Carleton University. Her current project examines Canada's female broadcasters, 1945–2000, within the context of the women's movements of those decades. She is the author of three books about women, feminism, and the news media: *Kit's Kingdom: The Journalism of Kathleen Blake Coleman* (Ottawa: Carleton University Press, 1989); *The Satellite Sex: The Media and Women's Issues in English Canada, 1966–1971* (Waterloo: Wilfrid Laurier University Press, 2001); and *Beyond Bylines: Media Workers and Women's Rights in Canada* (Waterloo: Wilfrid Laurier University Press, 2011).

Judy Fudge is the LIUNA Enrico Henry Mancinelli Chair of Global Labour Issues at McMaster University and a fellow of the Royal Society of Canada. She takes a socio-legal approach to studying work and labour and has published extensively on employment and labour law from a range of critical perspectives.

Mason Godden is a PhD candidate in the School of Labour Studies at McMaster University. His research focuses on the Canadian labour movement post-1945, with an emphasis on the relationship between labour unions, the left, and the women's movement. His dissertation explores the impact of left-nationalist politics on the Canadian labour movement through a case study of the Confederation of Canadian Unions (CCU).

June Hannam is professor emerita of modern British history at the University of the West of England, Bristol. She has published widely on socialism and feminism in Britain from the 1880s to the 1930s, including *Isabella Ford* (Oxford, UK: Basil Blackwell, 1989), *Socialist Women: Britain, 1880s to 1920s* (London and New York: Routledge, 2002), with Karen Hunt, and *Feminism* (Harlow, England: Longman, 2012). She is co-chair of the West of England and South Wales Women's Network. Her current research is on women and politics in Bath and Bristol in the 1920s.

Linda Kealey taught history at Memorial University of Newfoundland and later at the University of New Brunswick, where she is professor emerita. Her work on women's and gender history has primarily focused on Canada in the late nineteenth and twentieth centuries. Her most recent work centres on the history of healthcare in Newfoundland and Labrador and labour organizing among nurses in New Brunswick.

Ragnheiður Kristjánsdóttir is professor of history at the University of Iceland. She has published works on nationalism, democracy, the politics of the left, and gender. She is editor of the *Scandinavian Journal of History*, and her most recent book is *Konur sem kjósa. Aldarsaga (A Century of Women Voters)* (Reykjavík: Sögufélag, 2020), a co-authored work about the history of women voters in Iceland.

Winnie Lem is an anthropologist and is professor emeritus of international development studies at Trent University. Her research focuses on migration, the political economy of transnational livelihoods, urbanization, agrarian change, regional nationalism, gender, social reproduction, class formation, family enterprise, popular protest, and citizenship and the politics of exclusion. She has authored and co-edited several books that include *Migration, Temporality, and Capitalism: Entangled Mobilities across Global Spaces* (London: Palgrave Macmillan, 2018); *Migration in the 21st Century: Political Economy and Ethnography* (New York: Routledge, 2012); *Confronting Capital: Anthropology, Critique, Praxis* (New York: Routledge, 2012); *Cultivating Dissent: Work, Identity, and Praxis in Rural Languedoc* (Albany: State University of New York Press, 1999).

Ted McCoy is an associate professor of law and society at the University of Calgary and a historian of incarceration and punishment. His books include *Hard Time: Reforming the Penitentiary in Nineteenth-Century Canada* (Edmonton: Athabasca University Press, 2012) and *Four Unruly Women: Stories of Incarceration and Resistance from Canada's Most Notorious Prison* (Vancouver: UBC Press, 2019).

Katie-Marie McNeill recently defended her dissertation in the Department of History at Queen's University. Her dissertation examines the history of prisoner aid societies in the mid-twentieth century across Canada, Australia, New Zealand, and the United States.

Silke Neunsinger (PhD 2001) is an associate professor of economic history and director of research at the Swedish Labour Movement Archives and Library. She is affiliated with the Department of Economic History at Uppsala University in Sweden. She is the editor of the Swedish labour history journal *Arbetarhistoria*. Her research is concerned with feminist and global labour history and methodology. She has worked on the history of funding women's organizations and the global history of equal remuneration, and currently, she is working on the history of minimum wages in India. Her recent publications include the edited volumes *Towards a Global History of Domestic and Caregiving Workers* (together with Dirk Hoerder and Elise van Nederveen Meerkerk) (Leiden: Brill, 2015), *A Global History of Consumer Co-operation since 1850: Movement and Businesses* (together with Mary Hilson and Greg Patmore) (Leiden and Boston: Brill, 2017), *Labour, Unions and Politics under the North Star: The Nordic Countries 1700–2000* (together with Mary Hilson and Iben Vyff) (New York: Berghahn Books, 2017), and *Home-Based Work and Home-Based Workers (1800–2021)* (together with Malin Nilsson and Indrani Mazumdar) (Leiden and Boston: Brill, 2022).

Lisa Pasolli is an associate professor in the Department of History at Queen's University. She researches and teaches the history of women, gender, and social policy in twentieth-century Canada. Her publications include articles on the history of childcare politics, as well as the book *Working Mothers and the Child Care Dilemma: A History of British Columbia's Social Policy* (Vancouver: UBC Press, 2015).

Andrea Samoil is a PhD student at Simon Fraser University studying modern Alberta labour history. Her thesis focuses on the working-class response to neoliberalism in the 1980s and 1990s.

Julia Smith is an assistant professor in the Labour Studies Program at the University of Manitoba. She studies the history and politics of women's labour activism in Canada. Julia has published articles on feminist union organizing and labour relations in the airline and banking industries. She is also a member of the Graphic History Collective and a co-author of *1919: A Graphic History of the Winnipeg General Strike* (Toronto: Between the Lines, 2019).

D.Y. Turner is a doctoral candidate at Queen's University. Her current research centres upon Canadian publishing history and seeks to interrogate the semblances of national history as they are portrayed over time and across multiple authors through the Canadian Centenary Series. Her interests also include historiography and historical theory.

Nadia Verrelli, PhD, is an associate director (part time) at the Institute of Intergovernmental Relations, Queen's University. Her research interests focus on federalism, secession, and Canadian institutions. She has published articles and chapters on Canadian institutions, the Constitution, and federalism in various journals and edited books. Currently, she is writing a book on the Quebec Secession Reference. The book will provide a detailed analysis of the events leading up to the secession reference, the reference, and media reaction to the case. She is also interested in violence against women and children. She continues to research court, government, and media responses to domestic violence. Her recent publication includes *No Legal Way Out: R v. Ryan, Domestic Abuse, and the Defence of Duress* (co-authored with Lori Chambers (Vancouver: UBC Press, 2021). In 2021, she was the federal NDP candidate for the riding of Sudbury.

www.ingramcontent.com/pod-product-compliance
Lightning Source LLC
Chambersburg PA
CBHW020352080526
44584CB00014B/989